Production, Trade, in Pre-Roman Italy

This book explores the complex relationship between production, trade, and connectivity in pre-Roman Italy, confronting established ideas about the connections between people, objects, and ideas, and highlighting how social change and community formation are rooted in individual interactions.

The volume engages with, and builds upon, recent paradigm shifts in the archaeology and history of the ancient Mediterranean which have centred the social and economic processes that produce communities. It utilises a series of case studies, encompassing the production, trade, and movement of objects and people, to explore new models for how production is organised and the recursive relationship which exists between the cultural and economic spheres of human society. The contributions address issues of agency and production at multiple scales of analysis, from larger theoretical discussions of trade and identity across different regions to context-specific explorations of production techniques and the distribution of material culture across the Italian peninsula.

Production, Trade, and Connectivity in Pre-Roman Italy is intended for students and scholars interested in the archaeology and history of pre-Roman and early Republican Italy, but especially production, trade, community formation, and identity. Those interested in issues of cultural interaction and material change in the ancient Mediterranean world will find useful comparative examples and methodological approaches throughout.

Jeremy Armstrong is Associate Professor of Classics & Ancient History at the University of Auckland, NZ.

Sheira Cohen is a PhD candidate in the Interdepartmental Program in Classical Art and Archaeology (IPCAA) at the University of Michigan-Ann Arbor, USA.

Routledge Monographs in Classical Studies

Recent titles include:

Ancient History from Below
Subaltern Experiences and Actions in Context
Edited by Cyril Courrier and Julio Cesar Magalhães de Oliveira

Ideal Themes in the Greek and Roman Novel
Jean Alvares

Thornton Wilder, Classical Reception, and American Literature
Stephen J. Rojcewicz, Jr.

Married Life in Greco-Roman Antiquity
Edited by Claude-Emmanuelle Centlivres Challet

Future Thinking in Roman Culture
New Approaches to History, Memory, and Cognition
Edited by Maggie L. Popkin and Diana Y. Ng

Aristotle and the Animals
The Logos of Life Itself
Claudia Zatta

The *Aeneid* and the Modern World
Interdisciplinary Perspectives on Vergil's Epic in the 20th and 21st Centuries
Edited by J.R. O'Neill and Adam Rigoni

The Province of Achaea in the 2nd Century CE
The Past Present
Edited by Anna Kouremenos

Making and Unmaking Ancient Memory
Edited by Martine De Marre and Rajiv Bhola

Production, Trade, and Connectivity in Pre-Roman Italy
Edited by Jeremy Armstrong and Sheira Cohen

For more information on this series, visit: www.routledge.com/Routledge-Monographs-in-Classical-Studies/book-series/RMCS

Production, Trade, and Connectivity in Pre-Roman Italy

Edited by
Jeremy Armstrong and Sheira Cohen

Routledge
Taylor & Francis Group
LONDON AND NEW YORK

First published 2022
by Routledge
4 Park Square, Milton Park, Abingdon, Oxon OX14 4RN

and by Routledge
605 Third Avenue, New York, NY 10158

Routledge is an imprint of the Taylor & Francis Group, an informa business

© 2022 selection and editorial matter, Jeremy Armstrong and Sheira Cohen; individual chapters, the contributors

The right of Jeremy Armstrong and Sheira Cohen to be identified as the authors of the editorial material, and of the authors for their individual chapters, has been asserted in accordance with sections 77 and 78 of the Copyright, Designs and Patents Act 1988.

All rights reserved. No part of this book may be reprinted or reproduced or utilised in any form or by any electronic, mechanical, or other means, now known or hereafter invented, including photocopying and recording, or in any information storage or retrieval system, without permission in writing from the publishers.

Trademark notice: Product or corporate names may be trademarks or registered trademarks, and are used only for identification and explanation without intent to infringe.

British Library Cataloguing-in-Publication Data
A catalogue record for this book is available from the British Library

Library of Congress Cataloging-in-Publication Data
A catalog record for this book has been requested

ISBN: 978-0-367-63793-4 (hbk)
ISBN: 978-0-367-63172-7 (pbk)
ISBN: 978-1-003-12072-8 (ebk)

DOI: 10.4324/9781003120728

Typeset in Sabon
by Apex CoVantage, LLC

Contents

List of contributors	vii
List of maps, figures, and tables	x
List of abbreviations	xiv
Acknowledgements	xv
Maps	xvii

1 Communities and connectivities in pre-Roman Italy 1
SHEIRA COHEN AND JEREMY ARMSTRONG

2 Enchanted trade: technicians and the city 15
CHRISTOPHER SMITH

3 Metallurgy and connectivity in northern Etruria 33
SETH BERNARD

4 Hephaestus' workshop: craftspeople, elites, and bronze armour in pre-Roman Italy 53
JEREMY ARMSTRONG

5 Potters and mobility in southern Italy (500–300 BCE) 82
E.G.D. (TED) ROBINSON

6 'The potter is by nature a social animal': a producer-centred approach to regionalisation in the South Italian matt-painted tradition 99
LEAH BERNARDO-CIDDIO

7 Bronzesmiths and the construction of material identity in central Italy (1000–700 BCE) 129
CRISTIANO IAIA

8 The 'Bradano District' revisited: tombs, trade, and identity
   in interior Peucetia   152
   BICE PERUZZI

9 Etruscan trading spaces and the tools for regulating
   Etruscan markets   170
   HILARY BECKER

10 A mobile model of cultural transfer in pre-Roman
   southern Italy   204
   CHRISTIAN HEITZ

11 Mechanisms of community formation in pre-Roman Italy:
   a latticework of connectivity and interaction   226
   SHEIRA COHEN

   Epilogue: writing of connectivity at a time of isolation   244
   ELENA ISAYEV

   Bibliography   252
   Index   306

Contributors

Jeremy Armstrong is Associate Professor in Ancient History at the University of Auckland, New Zealand. He received his BA from the University of New Mexico and his MLitt and PhD from the University of St Andrews. He works primarily on archaic central Italy and most specifically on early Roman warfare. He is the author of *War and Society in Early Rome: From Warlords to Generals* (CUP, 2016) and the editor/co-editor of a number of volumes, including *Rituals of Triumph* (Brill, 2013), *Circum Mare: Themes in Ancient Warfare* (Brill, 2016), and *Romans at War: Soldiers, Citizens, and Society in the Roman Republic* (Routledge, 2020).

Hilary Becker is Assistant Professor of Classics at Binghamton University. She earned her AB at Bryn Mawr College and her MA and PhD at the University of North Carolina at Chapel Hill. She has published widely within the field of Etruscan and Roman archaeology, especially on the Etruscan and Roman economies and ancient pigments. She also co-edited the volume *Votives, Places and Rituals in Etruscan Religion* (Brill, 2009).

Seth Bernard is Associate Professor of Roman History at the University of Toronto. His work focuses on aspects of ancient social and economic history, and his publications have explored themes such as urbanisation, trade, and labour history in Republican Rome and Italy, employing a wide range of archaeological and historical methodologies. Since 2018 he has been co-directing excavations on the acropolis of Populonia in collaboration with colleagues from the Università di Siena and the Soprintendenza Archeologia, Belle Arti e Paesaggio per le province di Pisa e Livorno.

Leah Bernardo-Ciddio is a PhD candidate in the Interdepartmental Program in Classical Art and Archaeology (IPCAA) at the University of Michigan–Ann Arbor and holds an MPhil in Classical Archaeology from the University of Oxford. Her dissertation ('Ceramics, Craft Communities, and Cultural Interactions in the First Millennium Adriatic: Production and Trade of Apulian Matt-Painted Pottery') uses ceramic evidence in Iron Age Apulia to explore communication and relations across the Adriatic in prehistory. She has participated in fieldwork projects throughout Italy, at Ossaia, the Basentello Valley, Roccagloriosa, Gabii, and Melendugno.

Sheira Cohen is a PhD candidate in the Interdepartmental Program in Classical Art and Archaeology (IPCAA) at the University of Michigan–Ann Arbor. She holds an MA in Classics and Ancient History from the University of Sydney and a BA (Honours) in Ancient History and Anthropology from the University of Auckland. Her dissertation explores the intersection of community formation and mobility, especially seasonal pastoralism, in western central Italy during the first millennium BCE, drawing on stable isotope analysis of human and animal remains, as well as archaeological and historical evidence. She is a staff member at the Gabii Project, and her recent publications include a catalogue and analysis of the Iron Age infant burials from Gabii and a discussion of their sociopolitical significance in urbanisation processes.

Christian Heitz is Senior Lecturer in the Department of Archaeologies at the University of Innsbruck. He received his MPhil from the Department of Archaeology and Anthropology at the University of Cambridge and his PhD from the Department of Classical Archaeology at the University of Heidelberg. He has conducted research across a wide area, from the Aegean Bronze Age to Roman Art. He is currently working on pre-Roman southern Italian contexts and is excavation director at Ascoli Satriano (prov. Foggia/Apulia). His recent publications, including the detailed presentation and analysis of the finds from the necropolis of Ripacandida (northern Basilicata), deal with cross-cultural comparisons of cultural contact, the role of textiles and pastoralism, as well as social developments in Archaic-Classical southern Italy.

Cristiano Iaia is a tenure-track Assistant Professor in Prehistory and Protohistory at the University of Turin in Italy. He trained as an archaeologist at Sapienza University in Rome, where earned his PhD. He has taught European prehistory and protohistory courses in the Modena and Viterbo universities (2008–2012). Between 2015 and 2017, he was a Marie Skłodowska-Curie Fellow at Newcastle University (UK). Cristiano's main area of interest is the later prehistory of Italy, particularly the technology of metal artefacts and its interlinkage with social practices. Protohistoric central Italy is the main focus of his research activities. He is the author of two monographs and several academic papers on topics ranging from ideology in funerary rites, classification and analysis of metalwork, and the relationships between material culture and identity issues.

Elena Isayev is a historian and archaeologist whose work focuses on questions of migration, movement, belonging, displacement, and encounter, as well as the politics of exception and constructions of place. Drawing on the ancient Mediterranean, she explores these subjects in her writings *Migration Mobility and Place in Ancient Italy* (CUP, 2017) and

Inside Ancient Lucania: Dialogues in History and Archaeology (BICS, 2007), for the Red Cross, and in co-editing *Displacement and the Humanities*. Her research also draws on practice with colleagues of *Campus in Camps* and *Decolonising Architecture*, and as co-founder of *AlMaisha*, to understand and move beyond the cracks in the nation-state regime. She is a member of the United Nations Office for Disaster Risk Reduction and the International Centre for the Study of the Preservation and Restoration of Cultural Property's (UNDRR/ICCROM) expert panel on traditional knowledge systems in disaster risk reduction. Currently leading *Imagining Futures through Un/Archived Pasts* (an AHRC, GCRF Network+), she is Professor of Ancient History and Place at the University of Exeter, UK.

Bice Peruzzi is Assistant Professor in the Department of Classics at Rutgers University in New Jersey (USA). She holds a PhD from the University of Cincinnati (OH) and Master degrees from the Universities of Padova and Perugia. She has published on Apulian and Etruscan tombs, pedagogy, and Corinthian pottery. Her current research projects are a monograph-length social biography of the inhabitants of central Apulia and a re-examination of the pottery production debriefs from the Archaic Potters' Quarter at Corinth. She uses material culture, primarily ceramics, to investigate ancient behaviours and practices, especially of those individuals who would be otherwise mute as they have left no written accounts and are only tangentially described in Greek and Roman sources.

E.G.D. (Ted) Robinson is Senior Lecturer in the Department of Archaeology at the University of Sydney. His current fieldwork focuses on the excavation of a rural site at Chiaramonte di Tolve, where occupation spans both the Lucanian period and the early years of Roman domination. He has an ongoing programme for the chemical analysis of South Italian ceramics (PIXE-PIGE analysis and ICP-MS) and is also interested in exploring the colonial relationships in southern Italy through iconographic sources. His recent publications include the 2014 volume *The Italic People of Ancient Apulia: New Evidence from Pottery for Workshops, Markets, and Customs*.

Christopher Smith is Professor of Ancient History at the University of St Andrews. He was Director of the British School at Rome from 2009 to 2017. From 2017 to 2020 he held a Leverhulme Trust Major Research Fellowship on 'The Roman Kings: A Study in Power' and held visiting positions in Erfurt, Princeton, Otago, Pavia, Milan, Siena, Aarhus, and Paris Panthéon-Sorbonne. Professor Smith's research explores constitutionalism and state formation with a particular emphasis on the development of Rome as a political and social community, and how this was represented in ancient historical writing and subsequent political thought. He is currently Executive Chair of the Arts and Humanities Research Council.

Maps, Figures, and Tables

Maps

Map 1	Northern Italy	xvii
Map 2	Southern Italy	xviii
Map 3	South-eastern Italy and Albania	xix

Figures

4.1	Basic *chaîne opératoire* for producing bronze armour	59
4.2	Making a Corinthian-style helmet, from cast form to final product	63
4.3	Corinthian-style helmet (early fifth century BCE). Metropolitan Museum of Art	64
4.4	Repoussé girdle with faces and a suspended pectoral, possibly a single-disc. Reggio Calabria, Museo Nazionale	65
4.5	*Chaîne opératoire* for bronze armour with 'nodes' of control	69
4.6	Bronze armourer working on a helmet (late eighth to early seventh century BCE). Metropolitan Museum of Art	73
4.7a–d	Experimental archaeology in the construction of a Negau helmet. (a) Melting bronze in a temporary furnace; (b) Shaping the Negau helmet; (c) Hammers used to shape the Negau helmet; and (d) use of a pneumatic power hammer to stretch the initial bronze sheet to c. 1.5 mm	78
5.1	Proposed movements of ceramic artisans in southern Italy and Sicily in the second half of the fifth century BCE	92
6.1	Example of a matt-painted vessel, from the Borgo Nuovo deposit. Museo Archeologico Nazionale di Taranto	102
6.2a–d	(a) Bag-shaped jug from the Borgo Nuovo deposit. Museo Archeologico Nazionale di Taranto; (b) bag-shaped jug from the Borgo Nuovo deposit. Museo Archeologico Nazionale di Taranto; (c) two-handled vessel from the Borgo Nuovo deposit. Museo Archeologico Nazionale di Taranto; (d) new motifs in SMG pottery – pendent rays (solid and hatched) and hanging ladders	103

Maps, Figures, and Tables xi

6.3a–d	(a) Matt-painted, two-handled vessel with pendant ray motif. National Archaeological Museum of Korçë; (b) matt-painted, two-handled vessel with pendant ray motif. National Archaeological Museum of Korçë; (c) matt-painted, one-handled vessels. National Archaeological Museum of Korçë; (d) selected motifs typical of Devollian Iron Age pottery in the Barç tumulus	105
6.4a–d	(a) (Coefficients of Variation CV) for height (to rim) of one-handled vessels; (b) CV for rim diameter of one-handled vessels; (c) CV for height (to rim) of two-handled vessels; (d) CV for rim diameter of two-handled vessels	119
7.1	Pratica di Mare (ancient Lavinium), tomb 21. Cremation burial with set of miniaturised weapons	131
7.2	Tarquinia, tomb Poggio Selciatello 75, Early Iron Age phase 1A, c.900–850 BCE	133
7.3	Cinerary Urns (1) Tarquinia, Arcatelle necropolis, bronze bell helmet with knob; (2) Tarquinia, Villa Bruschi Falgari, pottery helmet lid with roof-shaped apex; (3) Veii, Quattro Fontanili, pottery helmet lid with roof-shaped apex; (4) Tarquinia, Arcatelle necropolis, pottery hut urn; (5) Tarquinia, Villa Bruschi Falgari, stone receptacle of a cremation burial with roof-shaped lid	133
7.4	Tarquinia, Arcatelle necropolis, tomb Monterozzi 3, Early Iron Age 1B, c. 850 BCE	135
7.5	Tarquinia, Poggio Impiccato tomb I, Early Iron Age 2A, c. 830–800 BCE	136
7.6	Tarquinia, pottery crested helmets used as lids for ossuaries, Early Iron Age 1B-2A, c. 850–780 BCE. The helmet on the left features bronze bosses to imitate the repoussé decoration on bronze prototypes	137
7.7	The iconography of a warrior wearing a crested helmet on bronze artefacts, north-central Italy: (1) Ornament detail on a crested helmet of unknown provenance (possibly Vulci), Musée du Louvre; (2) Reggio Emilia; (3) Lozzo Atestino (Padova); (4) Tarquinia, Monterozzi	138
7.8	Map showing the distribution of bronze crested helmets of the Villanovan type	141
7.9	Zavadintsy (Kamenets-Podolsky, Ukraine), bronze-crested helmet found in the nineteenth century CE, formerly preserved at the Musée Massena, Nice	142
7.10	Bronze lozenge belt from Veii, tomb Quattro Fontanili OP 4–5, early eighth century BCE	147
7.11	Latium Vetus and southern Etruria, main examples of ornament sets including bronze suspension rings, eighth to early seventh century BCE	148

8.1	Map of Peucetia	155
8.2	Distribution of pottery classes at the four sites (525–350 BCE)	160
8.3a–b:	Pottery assemblages from 5/1957 at Monte Sannace (Archivio fotografico – Museo Archeologico Nazionale di Gioia del Colle) and 17/1976 at Rutigliano	163
8.4	Distribution of pottery by function at the four sites (525–350 BCE)	164
8.5	Map of road system in Apulia	166
9.1	Product ranges for different categories of products	179
9.2	Lotto 14, late archaic house at Gonfienti (Prato), plan following the 2002 season (scale 1000:1).	183
9.3	Inscribed weight from Caere (fourth to early third centuries BCE)	186
9.4	Bronze weight from Caere (second half of sixth century BCE)	186
9.5	Weight from the farm of Pian d'Alma (second half of the sixth to the middle of the fifth century BCE). Museo Archeologico Nazionale di Firenze	188
9.6	Stone weight from Marzabotto, inscribed with tally marks reading '4' and '10'	190
9.7	Inscribed *aes rude* from Suana. Museo Archeologico Nazionale di Firenze	195
10.1	Map with sites mentioned in the text and area of the modern *statonica*-system	211
10.2	Typical vessels of the bichrome local pottery production at Ripacandida. From left to right: *olla* with triple zig-zag motif on the shoulder; jug with 'spherical' lines and inscribed stars on the lower part of the vessel; jug with alternating horizontal bands and small zone with lozenge decoration at the widest point; squatted *askos* with vertical spout and bull's head protome (not to scale)	212
10.3	Schematic plan of the Ripacandida necropolis with indication of burial clusters	213
10.4	Image of a Latin shepherd family, taken on May 19, 1935 at Carpineto close to the dam of Rio Sermoneta.	215
10.5	*Askos* of the local Ripacandida ware and zoomorphic bronze pendants (not to scale)	216
10.6	Plans and friezes of the buildings of Braida di Vaglio (a, left) and Torre di Satriano (b, right)	219

Tables

6.1	Types of specialisation and proposed corresponding levels of standardisation	116

6.2	Coefficients of Variation associated with varying scales of production	116
6.3	Comparison of Coefficients of Variation for bag-shaped jugs from Italian sites and one-handled vessels from Albanian sites. This includes versions with articulated neck and without articulated neck	118
6.4	Coefficients of Variation for two-handled vessels from Italian and Albanian sites	118
6.5	Salentine matt-painted fabric groups, as identified in Brigger (2007) 20–3	122
8.1	Comparison of the pottery assemblages from tombs 5/1957 at Monte Sannace and 17/1976 at Rutigliano, divided by function	164
9.1	Weights on the Etruscan 'light pound'	185
9.2	Weights set to the Vetulonian weight standard, dating from the late sixth to early fifth centuries BCE	187

Maps 1–3 and Figures 4.1 and 8.5 produced by Joshua Emmitt using EMODnet Bathymetry Consortium (2020): EMODnet Digital Bathymetry (DTM) [https://doi.org/10.12770/bb6a87dd-e579-4036-abe1-e649cea9881a] and data from the Ancient World Mapping Centre [http://awmc.unc.edu/wordpress/map-files/].

Abbreviations

Unless otherwise noted, all ancient Greek and Latin texts and all translations are taken from the *Loeb Classical Library* series. Ancient abbreviations generally follow those in the *Oxford Classical Dictionary*, 4th edition. Modern bibliography abbreviations follow those in *l'Année philologique*.

AE = (1888-) *L'Annee Epigraphique.*
BNP = Cancik, H., and H. Schneider (eds) (2010), *Brill's New Pauly: Encyclopedia of the Ancient World. Volumes 1–22.* Leiden.
CIL = (1893-) *Corpus Inscriptionum Latinarum.* Berlin.
CVA = (1925-) *Corpus Vasorum Antiquorum.*
FGrH = Jacoby, F. (1923), *Fragmente der griechischen Historiker.* Berlin.
RVAp = Trendall, A.D., and A. Cambitoglou (1978–1984), *The Red-Figured Vases of Apulia. Volumes 1–2.* Oxford.

Acknowledgements

The volume emerged out of the conference 'Exchanging Ideas: Trade, Technology, and Connectivity in Pre-Roman Italy', held at the University of Auckland, New Zealand, 3–6 February 2020. The conversation across those four days was incredibly lively and stimulating, and we would therefore like to thank all who were involved – our co-organiser Aaron Rhodes-Schroder, those represented in this volume, those who contributed to its sister volume (Armstrong, J. and A. Rhodes-Schroder (eds), *Adoption, Adaption, and Innovation in Pre-Roman Italy: Paradigms for Cultural Change*), and everyone else who presented and participated. The present volume would not have been possible without you.

We would also like to thank the Royal Society of New Zealand Te Apārangi Marsden Fund, who supported the overall project ('Blood and Money: The 'Military Industrial Complex' in Archaic Central Italy', 17-UOA-136, awarded to Jeremy Armstrong), of which this was a part. Thanks must also go to the many individuals who gave input and advice on both the various chapters and the overall volume. This includes our nine peer reviewers, who must remain anonymous, as well as colleagues and friends, whom we can thankfully name – Joshua Emmitt, Joseph Frankl, Gala Morris, Sally Mubarak, Matthew Naglak, Rebecca Phillipps, J. Troy Samuels, and Nicola Terrenato. Many thanks to you all for your help and feedback.

Most importantly, we would like to thank our contributors. As the conference was finishing, and indeed before it began (although unbeknownst to us at the time), the world was thrown into the maelstrom of the COVID-19 pandemic. As a result, this volume gestated and was born almost entirely in that context, full of illness, grief, stress, lockdowns, limited resources, and countless other issues. Through it all, our fearless contributors worked tirelessly and kept amazingly to schedule. We are tremendously grateful for all of their hard work, particularly given the trying circumstances. This volume is a testament to their effort.

Finally, thanks must go to our families and immediate support networks, who sustained us throughout this process – Ashle, William, Theo, Etta, Michael, Jonathan, Dafna, Tali, Emily, Leah, Lauren, Troy, Joey, Kevin, Joelle. You all had a far more personal relationship with this volume than you likely wanted or deserved, putting up with awkwardly timed video calls, an inability to talk about anything else, and far too much 'working from home'. Thank you all, as always, for your love, support, and patience.

Jeremy Armstrong
Auckland, New Zealand
&
Sheira Cohen
Ann Arbor, Michigan, USA

Maps

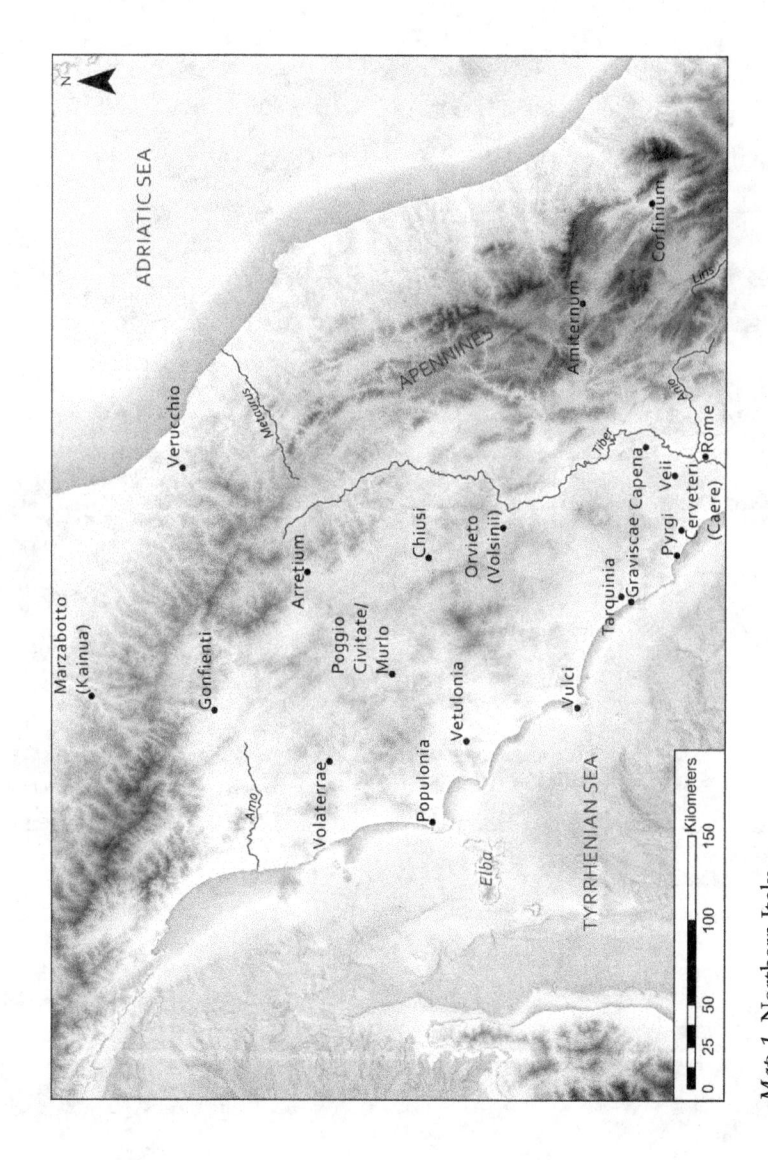

Map 1 Northern Italy.
Source: Map produced by Joshua Emmitt.

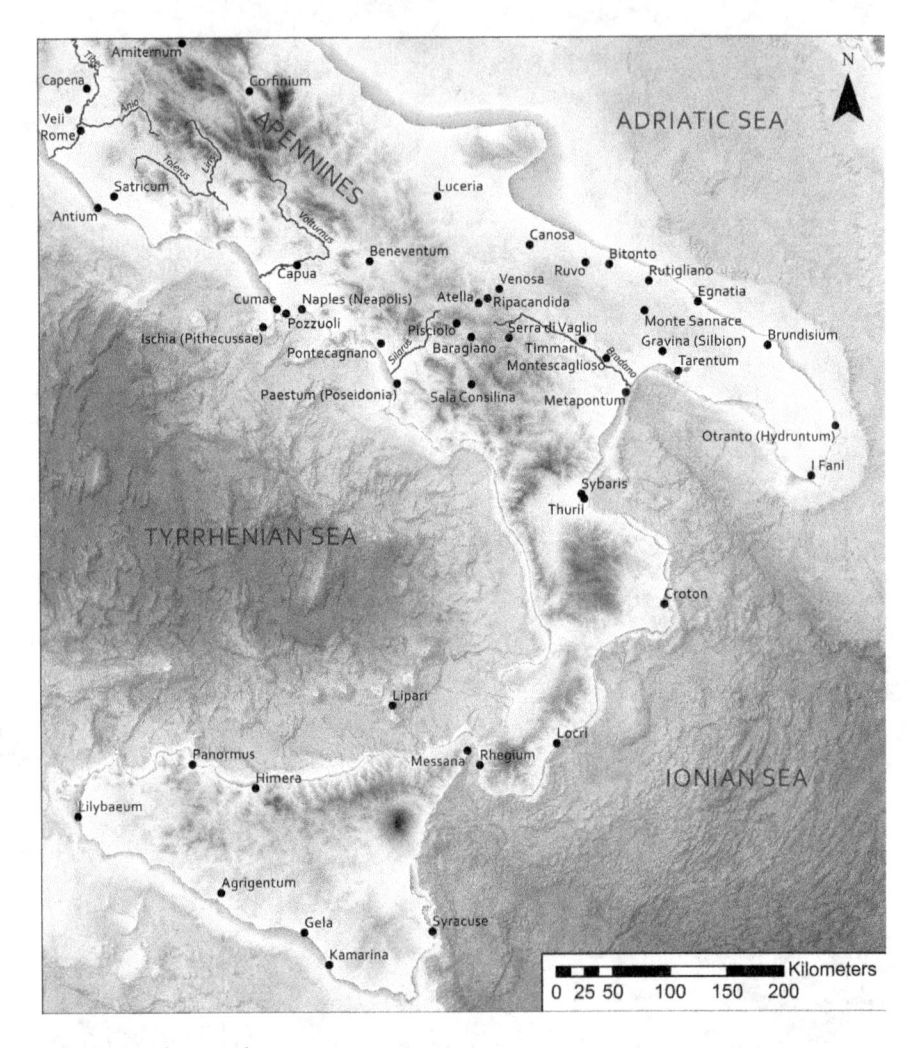

Map 2 Southern Italy.
Source: Map produced by Joshua Emmitt.

Map 3 South-eastern Italy and Albania.
Source: Map produced by Joshua Emmitt.

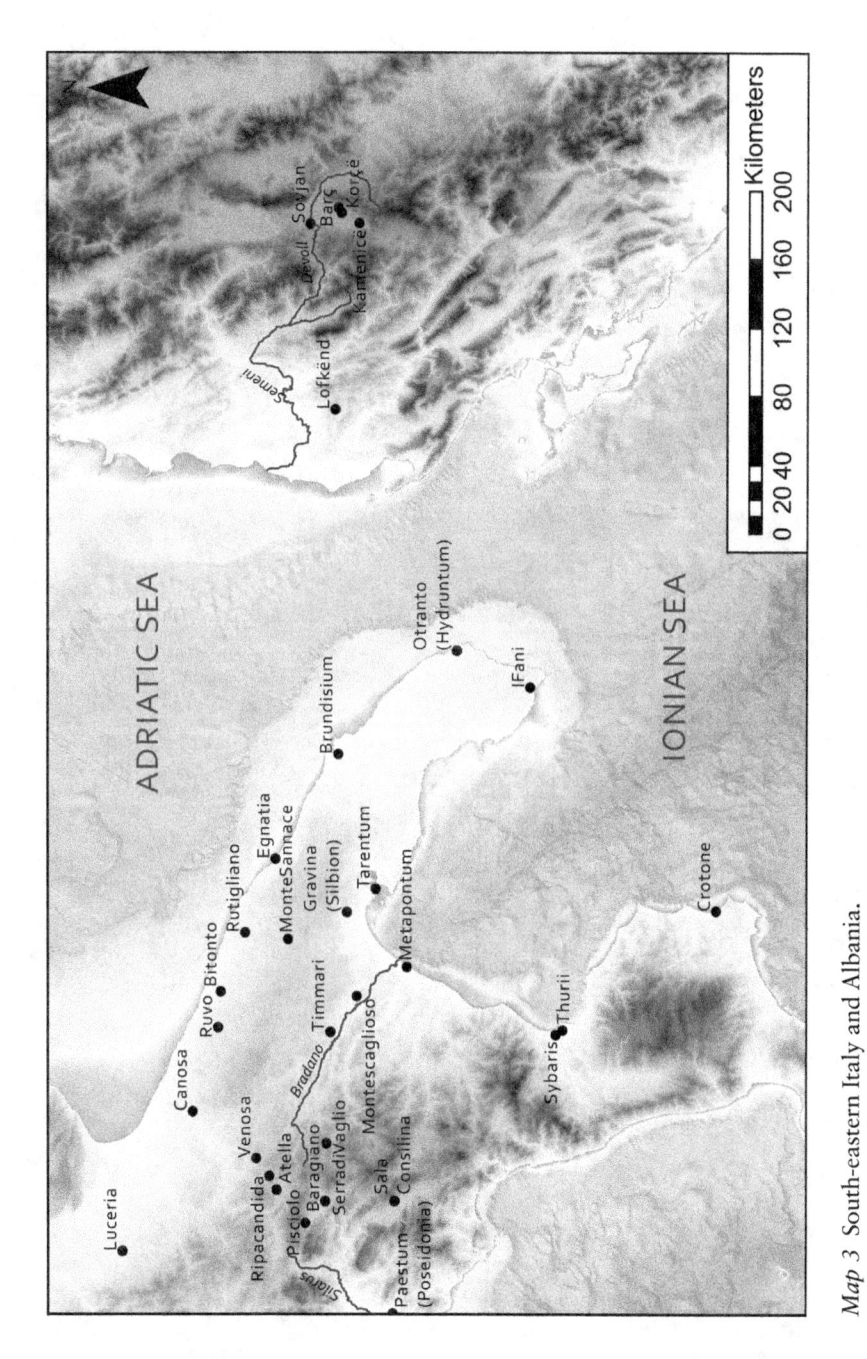

1 Communities and connectivities in pre-Roman Italy

Sheira Cohen and Jeremy Armstrong

In a 2009 chapter on ancient Lucania, Elena Isayev questioned the value of 'regionalism', or defining populations by regional cultures, as a useful framework for analysis in early Italy. As part of this argument, Isayev cited, among other things, the problematic nature of the literature-based ethnic labels typically used as well as the overlapping footprints of different material culture practices.[1] In challenging these pre-existing ethnic labels and paradigms, and particularly in contrasting them with the emerging archaeological picture, Isayev was certainly not alone.[2] The past half-century of archaeological and historical enquiry, rather than clarifying our understanding of both communal and individual identity in antiquity, has in many ways done the reverse. Modern scholarship, particularly in the aftermath of postmodernism, has proven very adept at deconstructing and problematising long-accepted models of ancient culture, demonstrating how once seemingly unshakable concepts (e.g., 'Roman' or 'Greek') often fall apart when explored in detail.[3] Additionally, the increase in archaeological evidence and the development of new interpretative methodologies have given us far more data, and far greater specificity, upon which to base our understanding of life in the ancient Mediterranean. We are much more aware of both the complexity and diversity of ancient society at all levels, particularly as evidenced in material culture. Consequently, scholars, working with both the literature and archaeology, have increasingly sought to replace the old 'grand narratives' – the idealised stories of stable and

---

* Many thanks must go to Elena Isayev, Troy Samuels, Joshua Emmitt, Rebecca Phillipps, Nicola Terrenato, Gala Morris, Sally Mubarak, and many others who read and commented on various drafts of this chapter. All errors and omissions, of course, remain our own.
1 Isayev (2009).
2 See, for instance, Bradley (1997), (2000a) for earlier suggestions along the same lines.
3 These issues were popularised with the 'cultural turn' of the 1980s and brought to the forefront of ancient world studies by works like Woolf (1998). Mattingly (2009) offers an appropriate contextualisation. For some recent work on this issue, see, for instance, Clackson *et al.* (2020) and Gruen (2020), amongst many others, grappling with this issue.

DOI: 10.4324/9781003120728-1

homogeneous cultures which previously defined the discipline – with local histories and detailed case studies.[4]

It is clear, however, that this shift in focus has not solved the fundamental issue. The overlapping footprints of different material cultures have disrupted regional models that relied solely on archaeological classification while simultaneously challenging the applicability of literary-derived labels to material culture. We have yet to find a way to replace the regional labels and, without the structure provided by these regional entities and systems, even if only heuristic in nature, we have struggled to knit detailed local histories (i.e., studies of specific sites, assemblages, or communities) together into broader social and cultural narratives of identity and society.[5] In turn, this has limited both the scope of our interpretations and, perhaps most importantly, our ability to tell engaging stories about ancient peoples and their lives.[6]

At the core of our dilemma lies a fundamental disconnect in how our two primary forms of evidence for the ancient Mediterranean – archaeological material and written sources – encode and preserve notions of identity.[7] In the ancient literature, identity is generally conceived of socially, politically, or ethnically, and often in idealised terms. It is an intellectual or perceptive identification, an immaterial idea. These 'cognitive communities', although nominally defining groups and often deployed at a regional level, are expressed and filtered individually by discrete authors and, in many cases, reflect an etic perspective. Although some of these biases have been increasingly counterbalanced by *New Historicism* and similar approaches, adding an extra layer of context to the interpretation, we cannot escape the fact that the nature of the original identity expressed in this material is profoundly ephemeral and myopic.[8] It is an individual's view, expressed at a specific point in time and in a specific context, which is also part of a much wider,

---

4 Gosner and Hayne's forthcoming edited volume on local experiences of mobility and connectivity is an excellent recent example of such an approach. See also Hodos (2008).
5 Isayev (2009) 224.
6 While there has been some notable theoretical discourse in recent decades to address this issue – such as on the principles of hybridity and connectivity (a principle, as the title of the chapter indicates, we will be returning to), as well as the attempted rehabilitation of terms like 'Romanisation' – the field has struggled to shape new narratives out of the ruins left by our deconstruction. See, for example, the pieces in *Archaeological Dialogues*, Volume 21, and particularly those by Versluys (2014); Stek (2014); van Dommelen (2014), and Woolf (2014). On hybridity, see, for example, van Dommelen (2005).
7 Each of these broad types of evidence contains a tremendous amount of diversity as well – and there are certain areas of overlap. For instance, a written text is also a material object, featuring its own object biography and materiality. Conversely, artefacts can also be read in symbolic ways more common in the study of literature. For the purposes of this discussion, this (overly) strict dichotomy does allow us to capture the different concepts to identity that still guide approaches to the evidence in the modern academic field.
8 Gallagher and Greenblatt (2000). On the expression of identity in literature, see Gruen's oeuvre (esp. Gruen 2020). See also Balot's (2021) useful epilogue in the special issue of *Polis*, entitled 'Discourses of Identity in the Ancient World'.

and typically theoretical or idealised, whole. In archaeology, by contrast, identity has traditionally been difficult to access directly. It has instead been defined circuitously through analysis of form, style, and function within the material record, often building on Childe's problematic model of archaeological cultures and grouping together assemblages based on shared characteristics.[9] These 'material communities' are defined by modern scholars along somewhat arbitrary lines drawn around sets of unique items and, despite their origin as a typological heuristic, are at times assumed to represent real and distinct groups or identities present within ancient populations. Although the 'material turn' in archaeology has appropriately shifted attention towards the dynamic relationality between objects at multiple scales of analysis, the artificial grouping of material culture, now on the basis of consumption or depositional patterns, remains.[10] We are therefore left with two systems. On the one hand, the ancient literature offers a limited set of idealised and absolute labels, but ones which seem to reflect how (at least some) ancient individuals seem to have understood and expressed various identities and relationships. On the other hand, the archaeology works from an exponentially growing corpus of evidence with virtually infinite options for categorisation and analysis, albeit always through a modern lens.[11] It is the conflation of these distinctive approaches to ancient identity, each built on different bases of evidence and answering different questions, which often lies at the heart of scholarly disagreements about the ancient past.

In the same 2009 study, Isayev suggested that one way to combine these two forms of evidence, and their conceptions of community and identity, might be through 'imagined communities', critically drawing on Benedict Anderson's model, and particularly the dynamic and multifaceted use of material culture for the performative construction of identities.[12] This approach to identity, common across many postcolonial theoretical movements, represents one of the more fruitful approaches which has been applied in recent years. Indeed, cognitive and material communities have been profitably linked through concepts of performativity and social signalling – a view which sees material culture differences as the physical manifestation of conceptual and subjective experiences of identity.[13] However, while there is an undeniable relationship between one's cognitive identity and one's use of

---

9 Trigger (2006), 232–313, on Childe's models and culture-historical archaeology throughout the twentieth century.
10 Pitts (2019) and van Oyen (2016) offer recent examples from the Roman period.
11 Statistical methodologies, particularly multivariate techniques (such as correspondence analysis), are powerful tools for analysing 'big data' in archaeology. See Pitts (2019) and Murray (2020) for a recent use of these techniques.
12 Isayev (2009) 224; Anderson (1983).
13 See, for example, Hall (1997); Botchkovar et al. (2009); Riva (2009); papers in Knapp and van Dommelen (2010). On senses of 'place' as practiced space, see Lefebvre (1974/1991), amongst others.

material culture, this can be highly individual; the relationship is often not generalisable at the group level and correlates poorly with textually attested identities in the ancient world. Further, the approach increasingly falls apart in areas and periods like pre-Roman Italy, where the relevant literature (and its labels and cultural constructs) is largely late, anachronistic, and often coming from a different cultural perspective.[14]

Connective communities

The present volume, and its varied contributions, offers (albeit often indirectly) an alternative solution to this seemingly intractable issue, moving away from the traditional concept of 'identity' completely, in either a geographically local or ethnic sense, towards a more connective view of community. In this model, communities can be understood and described by the nature, frequency, durability, and directness of the various connections identifiable between people.[15] In this, we draw inspiration from network analysis to explicate the overlapping layers of connectivity that emerge across the different domains of ancient life.[16] In brief, we would suggest that one of the reasons why modern scholarship has struggled with the issue of identity, and particularly how to approach it through different forms of evidence, is because we are asking the wrong questions of our evidence. In societies and cultures without contemporary literary evidence for cognitive communities, we cannot, and should not attempt to, develop the same types of identity frameworks using the archaeology. In this volume, we explore another possible approach by emphasising and exploring connections and relationships as a different way to conceive of communities and groups, whether local, regional, or inter-regional. We do not seek to determine the personal significance of specific objects or labels for creating an individual sense of identity.[17] Rather, we seek to investigate the actions preserved in the evidence and trace the connections and associations they reveal. Thus, we suggest that groups, at least in contexts like pre-Roman Italy, are perhaps more productively

---

14 Armstrong and Richardson (2017) 1–20. While contemporary inscriptions are a useful body of evidence, they also have limitations – see following discussion.
15 This approach owes much to Blake (2014), who advocated for an interactionist view of ethnicity and identity, with the aim of explaining ethnogenesis during the Italian Iron Age on the basis of pre-existing social networks from the Bronze Age. Drawing on principles of path dependence, Blake argued that past interactions can predict future identities. Her view of interaction as fundamental to understanding community formation is thus applied here, but as a paradigm of community in its own right rather than a predictor of later cognitive communities.
16 Marsden (2005); Graham (2009); Brughmans (2010); etc.
17 A comparison to relational identity/identification within social network analysis is instructive as it highlights the importance of direct and indirect connections between individuals, rather than a sense of common membership. Yet the focus of the analysis on identity – an innate sense of belonging and self-recognition about one's place in relationship to others – is not taken up here. See Peeples (2018), chapter 2, for discussion.

defined not as collections of individuals but as overlapping, and potentially non-coterminous, collections of connections; they are defined by their relationships rather than their self-perception or performance.

The study of material culture and economic behaviours – namely the production, trade, and use of objects – provides a crucial source of evidence for the social networks and connectivities that existed in prehistoric societies and therefore for connective communities. In particular, vertical social integration and relationships – between elite and non-elite – as well as horizontal connections – between individuals in ostensibly different communities – can be captured through this largely economic lens.[18] A focus on technology also provides access to the contact points between these different connectivities, as we follow the biography of different objects from initial resource extraction, through refinement, initial production, decoration, trade, primary use, and secondary deposition. At each stage we can see how the objects contain clues about the different communities that interacted with it, formed it, used it – each step an insight into different connections – sometimes overlapping and sometimes distinct. By exploring the multiple layers of connectivities visible in the productive networks, without subordinating material culture to the performance of some regional identity, it may be possible to provide a meaningful and workable replacement to the unitary and stable groups presented in the literature.

Focusing on connections and relationships is obviously not a new approach within the ancient Mediterranean. Indeed, if anything, 'connectivity' currently reigns supreme at the macro level in ancient Mediterranean studies. As an explanatory paradigm, it first gained mainstream acceptance with Horden and Purcell's *The Corrupting Sea* and was expanded with Broodbank's *The Making of the Middle Sea*.[19] Connectivity provided a counter-narrative to then-prevailing models of the Mediterranean which saw movement as exceptional and, when it did occur, as being connected with the mass movement of ethnic groups – the Dorian invasion, Greek colonisation, 'Orientalising' movements, and Roman imperialism. These colonialist models had a simultaneously localising approach to trade and a diffusionist approach to cultural change.[20] Post-colonialism shifted our understanding of these narratives, bringing out connectivity as a powerful driver of cultural change. Where cultural contact had initially been framed in hierarchical terms, with roots in modern European colonialism, scholars now explore the complex and bi-directional cultural exchanges that occur at these distinct points of contact – exchanges which produce unique 'hybrid' or 'creolised' cultural forms.[21] Although this

---

18 Bioarchaeological data – especially stable isotope analysis – provides another possible vector for study, although it is not dealt with in this volume and so will not be discussed here. See, among others, Trentacoste *et al.* (2020); Killgrove and Montgomery (2016).
19 Horden and Purcell (2000); Broodbank (2013).
20 Finley (1973); Boardman (1964).
21 Bhabha (1994); Gosden (2004); Malkin (2011); Knapp and Van Dommelen (2010); Versluys (2014), among many others.

is certainly a movement in the right direction, these models have continued to be frustrated by the complexities of the situation in the ancient Mediterranean.[22] One aspect of this may be that many of these interpretative paradigms emerged from post-colonial revisions of modern European colonial encounters and therefore assumed a lack of previous connectivity in the interaction between two previously distinct, homogeneous, and stable cultural groups.[23] This model, obviously, does not reflect the situation in the ancient Mediterranean, where long-standing connections existed between communities across the region from the Bronze Age onwards.

This image of a churning background connectivity across the Mediterranean allows us to account for the movement of objects and ideas between areas. That being said, we still have not moved very far beyond the basic premise that the peoples of the ancient Mediterranean were simply 'connected'. Each new study on the subject highlights new evidence for connectivity, and our understanding of the depth and breadth of the networks in the region has expanded immensely as a result. But our models for them remain frustratingly unsophisticated and ad hoc. Various types of connection (economic, religious, artistic, legal, military, etc.) are thrown together into the same 'connectivity' matrix without being fully understood as proxies of human behaviour and interaction, or understood within a larger socio-economic framework. Additionally, although connectivity has been profitably applied at the Mediterranean scale, analysis of the Italian peninsula itself often stops at the coast, privileging coastal cities and their interactions, and struggles to penetrate the dense connective networks within the peninsula itself.[24] The broad 'connectivity' approach thus either treats the peninsula as a monolith or simply fits in-between and binds together the existing identities and groups found in the literary evidence. It has yet to permeate or breakdown those groups themselves. Indeed, the regional approach has arguably flattened analysis of local and regional trends in these areas of high-intensity and long-standing connectivity and frames them in terms of hybridity, middle-ground, or third-space – concepts designed to describe distinctive points/zones of contact between distinct cultural groups. In the historical period, this same trend continues with a discussion of Romanisation and Hellenisation. The Italian peninsula, however, with its interlocking cultural spheres, 'fuzzy' material communities, and long history of interaction struggles to accommodate such models.

We would suggest that we are currently only scratching the surface of the potential of the concept of connectivity in ancient world studies as it can be far more than simply descriptive. Connectivity can provide a viable interpretative framework for understanding communities – and one which is particularly useful in periods and areas like pre-Roman Italy, where other approaches seem to struggle. Rather than focusing on how people perceived their relationship to

---

22 See particularly the discussion in *Archaeological Dialogues*, Volume 21 (1994).
23 Isayev (2017) 129.
24 Nowlin (forthcoming) highlights this phenomenon.

the wider group or how they may have manifested identity through material culture, we can focus simply on the various ways in which these individuals were connected to each other. These connections – whether consciously sought, actively resisted, or structured by numerous factors (economic, technological, geographic) – are transformative and meaningful in their own right. It is these connections that drive social, political, economic, and cultural change at all levels. By understanding the structure of these connections we can discover multiple interlocking and overlapping connective communities and provide a way to move from particularism to regionalism once again.

Approaching the evidence: material culture and production

Although connective communities are a viable organising principle in contexts where we have both contemporary emic literature and archaeological evidence, they are perhaps most important in situations where such texts are lacking or limited. That material culture provides an uncertain and fundamentally unreliable proxy for social groups – that 'pots are not people' – is, by now, axiomatic in archaeological literature. As with our disclaimers on the applicability of later, historical, ethnic groups to the archaic period, scholarship often asserts that we should employ archaeological cultures as purely heuristic categories that are distinct from the individuals that create them. Yet the typologies, forced upon us by a need to categorise and organise the enormous quantity of material culture we uncover, are deceptively difficult to shake off. The long history of connoisseurship and curation of objects for display in museums creates a self-perpetuating practice of identification and comparison with past typologies which are themselves tied into historical labels. Categorisation is undoubtedly an important part of the analysis as it allows us to accurately describe and compare objects as more or less alike and forms the basis of our chronological frameworks. While it does often capture the different stylistic influences and resonances of an object, this traditional descriptive process privileges the object as a single, fixed data point, a finished product. At most, two data points might be acknowledged – creation and deposition.[25] Objects, however, are dynamic; they are created through multiple stages of production, they age, they break, they are repaired and repurposed, they are used and discarded, they move, they are co-located (with other objects where meaning is created relationally). While debates still rage over exactly *how* dynamic they are, it is clear they are more complex than the traditional approach allows.[26] In order to allow a more dynamic understanding of the

---

25 This duality is particularly visible in discussions of Greek vases found in Etruscan tombs. See, recently, Bundrick (2019) for a discussion of the limitations of this approach and how it should be expanded to include production, merchants, consumers, repairs, deposition, etc.
26 The agency of objects has sparked considerable theoretical debate across multiple disciplines, see, among many others, Appadurai (1986); Latour (1996); Gell (1998); Brown (2001); Hodder (2012). For some recent application, see Pitts (2019) and van Oyen (2016).

links which objects illustrate and facilitate in the ancient Mediterranean, we need a more dynamic understanding of the objects themselves.

Archaeology as a discipline presupposes some relationship between, as Dietler and Herbich put it, the 'material and non-material', and, as such, we cannot escape the impact that our typologies have on the analyses we are able to do.[27] Some slippage is inevitable. Given this, archaeologists have sought to shift the mode of enquiry from typology of whole forms, often reliant on style and form as the defining motifs, to a more comprehensive exploration of an object's biography, following it through the different stages of production to consumption behaviours and, ultimately, depositional practice.[28] This volume seeks to partially mirror that lifecycle. Through a focus on specific aspects of an object's life, we are able to more directly access the relationship between the material world and the immaterial behaviours that it preserves. The area of interest is not the object, per se, nor do we make any claims to the 'specialness' of any particular objects as cultural markers or even attempt to use material culture to understand social groups. Rather, our focus is the physical techniques and processes that are, in turn, the result of countless choices of which the material is the only remaining witness. The relevant variable that is extracted is thus human action. In this volume, we argue that this approach, which eschews the goal of identifying groups in favour of identifying layers of connectivities, provides a fruitful perspective from which we can access social and cultural change.

To study production (and commissioning) is obviously not a novel concept either and has arguably formed the basis of much of the study of ancient vases and vase painting. Indeed, many facets of an object's creation are already incapsulated in the categorisation of style and form. However, it may be possible to push this focus a bit further. As Dietler and Herbich have argued:

> Material style can serve as a useful concept for archaeologists attempting to investigate the social role and meaning of material culture only if it is seen as the objectified result of techniques (rather than as straightforward objectified information); and more specifically it must be seen as the result of characteristic ranges of responses to interlinked technical, formal, and decorative choices made at all stages of a chaîne opératoire of production. . . . Understanding material culture as a social phenomenon, including the processes of stability and innovation within their historical trajectories, then becomes a matter of understanding the factors that condition these choices, their interrelations, and the reciprocal effects stemming from new choices made at various stages of the chaîne opératoire. This approach requires that we understand craftspeople as social actors (rather than simply as products/bearers of culture or as

---

27 Dietler and Herbich (1998) 233.
28 Kopytoff (1986).

acultural adaptive engineers) and that we understand the production and use of objects as social activity.²⁹

Although an object can certainly be viewed and categorised based on its final form, many of the more important connections to its generative society relate to the active processes involved in its creation. As such, Dietler and Herbich advocate for an approach to objects which defines them in terms of technique and *habitus*.³⁰ Things are the product of, and can also be defined by, the processes which created them. This is a useful construct in approaching the analysis of ancient artefacts as it also results in removing objects from the rigid confines of their final state and context and creates additional nexus points through which an object can be understood.

The alternative set of approaches presented within this volume therefore shifts our focus to the specific actions that, we argue, underlie connectivity across the Italian peninsula and thus provide access to different communities. This approach allows us to move beyond the proliferation of categories for dividing individuals and artefacts which, regardless of their contingent and porous nature, constrain our models with static concepts. Instead, we choose to analyse a wide range of possible connective networks by breaking down broad labels, such as production, trade, and use, to their component phenomena. In doing so, we are able to build up a picture that assesses the entire system of connectivity at multiple scales and levels of social analysis. This redirection of enquiry towards action gives greater access to the edges that lie between the nodes in network analysis and allows for the vast array of actions that form society but are often lost in our search for the perfect node, typological category, or system.

Pre-Roman Italy

As should now be clear from the preceding arguments, pre-Roman Italy represents both an important and timely arena to explore concepts of production, trade, and connectivity in the ancient Mediterranean. Despite concerted moves to shake off the tendrils of past debates, pre-Roman studies are often still wedded to ideas of political, ethnic, or geographically defined groupings and the intellectual and academic silos they create. On the one hand, this is entirely natural, as the foundations of some of these silos were arguably constructed by the ancient Italians themselves. We have extensive works on origin myths and the retrojection of later sociopolitical identities to help explain how these ideas came to hold such sway.³¹ However, the continued prominence of these labels and constructs, and both their impermeability and

---

29 Dietler and Herbich (1998) 246.
30 Bourdieu (1977).
31 See, for example, Wiseman (1974); Farney (2007); Dench (2005); etc.

timelessness, is arguably holding back the discipline through unnecessary regionalisation. Indeed, several recent books demonstrate this explicit tension between the history of scholarship on specific ethnic groups and regional studies on the one hand with a desire to show the importance of inter-regional connections on the other.[32] Either through the juxtaposition of individual chapters on ethnic groups and those on pan-Italic themes or the explicit pairing of archaeological and literary-historical treatments of ethnic groups, the very structure of our scholarship highlights the difficulty of extricating our debate from that of decades past. Scholars have long recognised the limited utility of ethnicity or politics as an explanatory and conceptual category for the period, as evidenced in the frequent placement of cultural labels into scare-quotes to indicate their sole heuristic value and 'fuzzy' boundaries. If our cultural typologies must be so loose in order to be accurate, to what extent is it worthwhile to continue employing them?

Pre-Roman Italy is also experiencing a rather radical decentring. The study of urban areas and the organisation of space around urban communities and their hinterlands are other prominent factors that have left their mark on scholarly debate in pre-Roman Italy. While Thiessen polygons are by now largely abandoned as a strict explanatory framework and rural field surveys proliferate, Weberian models of the city–country interaction still make their mark on analyses that track settlement expansion.[33] Pre-Roman Italy, and indeed Roman Italy, is still generally conceived of in fundamentally urban terms. This has been slowly changing, with work on rural sanctuaries, Hellenistic farmsteads the mid-Republican 'rural infill', the increasing placement of powerful *gentes* in the hinterland instead of within urban centres, and a new awareness of the relationship between different ecological zones (most notably mountains and coastal plains).[34] It must be noted, though, that the temporal focus for rural landscape analysis is still primarily in the Middle Republic and onwards, as ceramic chronologies become more visible. Debates around the Roman 'expansion' across Italy often recall the narrative of contact between distinctive cultures that is common in colonisation debates. For earlier periods, the difficulty of locating rural sites or dating survey pottery has limited our ability to make meaningful conclusions that are not focused on urban landscapes.[35] The historical framework, additionally, is fundamentally teleological and urban in its outlook as it places the nexus of Roman and other identities within their urban (or other nucleated) settlements. The Roman historical tendency to project their own organisational constructs onto their neighbours has likewise led to an urban mindset proliferating across the peninsula.

---

32 Farney and Bradley (2018); Aberson *et al.* (2014); Bradley *et al.* (2007).
33 Fulminante (2014).
34 Stek (2009), (2018a), (2018b); Armstrong (2016a); Bradley (2020); Smith (2006).
35 Tol (forthcoming); Bowes (2021).

In our focus on production and trade as actions that shape community and connectivity, we also differ from approaches already popular in studies of pre-Roman Italy which have focused, often through necessity, on the most visible aspects of these ancient societies. Both the archaeological and textual evidence have, for differing reasons, largely focused on the output of elite individuals and specific political arenas. Legal sources have preserved evidence of voting regimes which sought to differentiate groups, but these provide a limited window – excluding women, slaves, and foreigners – and pick up as a useful category of analysis only later in the period under study here. Additionally, for exploring pre-conquest areas of Italy beyond Latium, voting limits our inquiry to how individuals integrated with Roman-specific legal systems rather than their own methods of self-categorisation and organisation.[36] Writing has also been an area of continued inquiry. Indeed, as recent studies have shown, a re-evaluation of traditional approaches has been profitable in exploring written language as an arena in which different ideological statements and manipulations could be made.[37] The window provided by writing practices is, however, also narrow and skews later in this period in terms of uptake. That being said, and while epigraphy and other aspects of writing and language are not explored in this volume, we affirm the importance of these recent nuanced approaches to writing as performance in providing another facet of ancient society. The third main area in which human action has gained sustained attention for this period is religion and the various ritual networks across the peninsula that are evident in shared practice, use of syncretic or related deities, and the grafting of Greek and other imported deities onto what may have been pre-existing ritual networks.[38] These ritual connections have claimed a central place in cultural definitions for this period, particularly through their association with ethnicity as a structuring principle and the abundant archaeological, artistic, and literary evidence from which these networks can be constructed. The minimal focus placed on ritual throughout this volume is not intended to minimise the importance of such networks but rather to highlight other critical areas – namely, areas of trade and technology. While ritual played a central role in these ancient societies, it was socially and economically embedded (see Becker and Cohen in this volume), and as such an exploration of other aspects of connection can further develop the aspect of the picture presented through a study of ritual.

All of this work has shaped the current models for production, trade, and connectivity in the Italian peninsula during the period from c. 900 to c. 400 BCE. The present volume merely scratches the surface but does, we

---

36 Roselaar (2019).
37 Clackson *et al.* (2020). See also Feeney (2016) and the work of Katherine McDonald (e.g., McDonald [2019] on the dedications to the goddess Reitia).
38 Torelli (2018); Potts (2015); Bradley (2005).

hope, offer a roughly indicative spectrum in its range of studies – moving from sourcing raw materials to production, trade, and ultimately deposition. Following Isayev's lead, many of the chapters in this volume seek to place cyclical background mobility at the centre of discussions of cultural interaction within the Italian peninsula.[39] While large-scale migrations have always been present in historical and archaeological discourse on the ancient Mediterranean,[40] the picture of ancient society outside these migrations has struggled with how to understand different scales of mobility and therefore account for the impact this mobility would have had on social, political, and economic activities.[41] Tracking the movements of individuals is still difficult at present, as the biochemical and bioarchaeological analyses required are only beginning to find funding in the last decade.[42] Assessing the different mechanisms and arenas in which mobility occurs provides some insight. In this volume, Heitz and Cohen explore pastoral mobility as one aspect of this cyclical mobility which connected communities, thus shifting our focus away from fully static communities to ones that allow for co-existence of varying levels of mobility and sedentism. While the degree of this mobility and the scale of transhumant pastoralism are still debated, it remains an underexplored aspect of cultural interaction throughout the peninsula. Similarly, market spaces are another arena for interaction and cultural contact and act as nodes (both transient and more fixed) within the larger trade network. As Becker demonstrates, these defy simple typologies or correlations with political and economic systems. In fact, the intertwined and embedded nature of social, political, and economic facets forms the core of many contributions (see, particularly, Smith), engaging in an active discourse with rational economic modelling, specifically New Institutional Economics (NIE). The contributions instead highlight the importance of socially embedded understandings of trade and shift our attention towards social and cultural production in early communities.

The various contributors to this volume also address techniques and processes of production, particularly for ceramics and metals, and the relationship between producers and consumers. While objects themselves, and the behaviours associated with their use, are often seen as important mechanisms for connecting different groups, the producers of these objects and the connections formed through the production process, from initial extraction (see Bernard) to final decoration (see Robinson), have received considerably less attention. In this volume, attention is paid to the predictable constraints imposed upon

---

39 Isayev (2017).
40 This stands in stark contrast to the rejection of diffusionism in other spheres of archaeological enquiry, see Trigger (2006).
41 Although see Bradley (2020); Isayev (2017) for recent important works attempting to do this.
42 Recent projects have largely focused on stable isotope analysis and aDNA, e.g., Trentacoste (2020); Killgrove and Montgomery (2016); Cavazzutti *et al.* (2019); Emery *et al.* (2018); Prowse *et al.* (2007); Stark *et al.* (2020).

production by the location of natural resources and the requirements of different production stages (see Armstrong and Bernard), although an emphasis on the social aspects of production organisation (see Bernardo-Ciddio) pushes against previous environmentally deterministic interpretations. Likewise, in current scholarship, the relationship between producer and consumer is not always well explicated in isolating the locus of cultural decision-making. The degree of mobility among non-merchant groups is often held to be much lower, even as the movement and trade of objects is considered substantial. In this volume, mobility is therefore also explored in relation to the movement of producers at all stages of the production process (see Bernardo-Ciddio, Robinson, Armstrong, and Iaia). As agents of cultural change in their own right, we argue that producers deserve greater attention in the discussion of cultural exchange and connectivity more broadly. These overlapping connective networks continue through the trade and consumption phases of an object's life, particularly when the use and function of an object in context are considered, rather than just its stylistic qualities (see Peruzzi).[43]

Conclusions

In sum, the present volume represents an attempt to use connectivity as a lens to reshape how we discuss and approach community and identity in pre-Roman Italy (and hopefully other contexts). While ancient world studies have rightly thrown off the chains of the traditional labels, we are in many ways still bound by their memory as we find new labels to replace the old without fundamentally rethinking the types of categories they describe and the evidence needed for them. Additionally, as Gruen recently noted, we are also bound by our own modern view of identity – and particularly ethnicity, on which he suggested 'the topic of ethnicity speaks more to our concerns than to [the ancient]'.[44]

As a way of moving the conversation forward, Gruen suggested "that ancients expressed the collective identities of their societies less in terms of ancestry, genealogy, and inherent character than in a conglomerate of traditions, practices, and shared convictions. In other words, cultural commonality counted for more than shared lineage."[45] There is clearly some truth to this, and the connective character shares many resonances with the approach we propose in this volume. However, a focus on shared traditions and convictions – on 'cognitive communities' – is, as we have argued, already

---

43 Due to constraints of time and space, we were not able to address all aspects of an object's biography in detail, most notably, the role of merchants in trade, repair, and reuse of objects in new contexts, and use and deposition outside the funerary context. Many of these areas have been addressed in recent work on pre-Roman Italy (for a recent example, see Potts [2015]), while others, especially repair and reuse would benefit from more detailed study.
44 Gruen (2020) 6.
45 *Ibid.*

difficult to apply to historic contexts and arguably impossible when we lack substantial contemporary emic texts. For these contexts, we would suggest that the increase of archaeological data, which, virtually by definition, contains details of production, opens the door for another approach. An emphasis on connectivity – especially trade, production, and consumption – may offer a different set of tools. As noted earlier, this approach seeks to define communities not as collections of individuals but as collections of connections and networks. In doing so, we can not only cross the chasm between the literature and the archaeology but perhaps also bridge the divide between local and regional.

This book's alternative approach to connectivity and community is rooted in specific actions and takes a pluralistic and multivariate approach that seeks to understand the economic activities and interactions with the physical world which, we argue, are fundamental to the formation of communities, societies, and identities. By tracing the productive processes, connecting them to transmission, trade, and ultimately deposition, we can reveal networks of interaction at different scales and resolutions. Each of these provides a new layer of understanding to the sociocultural processes at play in pre-Roman Italy. Rather than a story of two cultures, which meet and negotiate their interaction and are marked and defined by an artefact in a specific context, the narrative of pre-Roman Italy is one of deep, profound, and typically swirling and recursive connections where communities develop together in multiple overlapping and interconnected networks. We seek to explicate multiple connectivities rather than a singular connectivity that has often been a catch-all explanation for all types of cultural change or interaction. In this respect, a collaborative volume with multiple approaches such as this is ideal both as metaphor and in scholarly reality. If our goal is to more deeply understand pre-Roman Italian society in all its permutations, and the connectivity that lies at the heart of that society, a multivariate approach is required. Each author in this volume presents only a particular aspect of these economic and social networks. In isolation, these will be by necessity incomplete pictures – whether, itinerant smiths and ceramicists, market administrators and merchants, transhumant pastoralists or sedentary consumers – but it is in the overlay and connections between these different pictures and associated communities that we can gain a deeper understanding of pre-Roman Italy.

2 Enchanted trade
Technicians and the city

Christopher Smith

The purpose of this chapter is to explore what new ground has been gained in theorising about the archaic economy in recent years and what insights might be gained in future work. It is, of course, possible to continue to gather evidence. This is a valuable and important task as theory without evidence is somewhere between philosophy and theoretical physics – it is certainly not history. But evidence without theory risks being little more than 'stamp collecting'. What progress is actually being made in understanding the cultures of the Mediterranean basin in the period between the eighth and fifth centuries BCE? What are the big questions, and how might they be resolved?

In order to see what ground has been gained I will begin by discussing how scholars have addressed the archaic economy, especially in Italy, over the last 30 years and how models deriving from Mauss' idea of reciprocity and Polanyi's embedded markets have developed. I will also assess the extent to which the evidence we have for the archaic period fits with New Institutional Economics (NIE), a contemporary model often employed for subsequent periods. I will then explore approaches which place the artisan and trader more centrally in our models and which, I argue, seem to offer a path forward. These approaches, much like others discussed in this volume, largely derive from a renewed emphasis on craft and production, with the 'producer' and 'trader' as vectors of change. In the end, I will argue that we risk radically underplaying community models in favour of 'elite' models, and I will suggest that assemblage theory offers a helpful paradigm for rethinking the material evidence we possess. Indeed, as illustrated by the chapters in the volume which follow, there is much that the non-elite community can offer to this discussion.[1]

---

* I am grateful to the editors, and anonymous reviewers, for wrestling with the text – they improved it greatly but the faults which remain are mine. I am also grateful to the Leverhulme Trust for a Major Research Fellowship during which the chapter was written.
1 The conference held in Auckland at the beginning of 2020 had as a core theme the exchange of ideas in archaic society; it was a remarkably fruitful instantiation of the exchange of ideas in contemporary intellectual society, but it was also at a strange inflection point in our own history. Just a few weeks later, our interconnected globalised world was frozen, certainties

The exchange and evolution of ideas

To begin, it is worth highlighting several areas where we have gained greater clarity over the last 30 years of scholarship and which are now firmly established.

First, we cannot get any further with Moses Finley's models.[2] *The Ancient Economy* has figured in enough literature reviews. The ancient economy was more sophisticated than Finley thought it was, and every literary prejudice he carefully replicated was precisely that, a prejudice rooted in the self-posturing of a later elite who behaved differently from the narrative they offered. At the same time, extraordinarily, we still have much to gain from engaging with Finley's predecessors, specifically Polanyi,[3] who was a critical influence on Finley (though Finley was able to see his flaws), and with the debates that led to Finley's own positions.[4]

Second, our patterns of connectivity are swirling, not unidirectional. The time spent debating over who did what first was not completely useless, in that arguments were sharpened and evidence analysed, and we are still to some extent trying to assess the points at which economies flare into greater life, abate, or intensify (to use the language of Horden and Purcell's *The Corrupting Sea*). But we now understand how deep Mediterranean history is, as Cyprian Broodbank's magnificent account shows,[5] and how rarely abatement is absolute. Knowledge transfer must be conceived differently. Rather than the *ex oriente lux*, we are tracing the repeated interactions of different symbolic and knowledge systems.[6]

Third, there was quite a lot of 'stuff' around the ancient Mediterranean when seen over the *longue durée*. Late Bronze Age and Early Iron Age people liked physical objects. They filled their houses, their graves, and their hoards

---

overturned, connections cut or moved to a new (typically online) medium. We have some distance to go in analysing what this means for our practical understanding of the future, but even more distance to go in understanding where this leaves the theoretical frameworks which have dominated disciplines such as politics and economics. The game of predictions is foolhardy, but the financial crash of 2008 has still not yet provoked the depth of rethinking at a theoretical level one might have expected for such a momentous event – we will have to wait a while (three critical contributions are Graeber [2011]; Tooze [2018]; Piketty [2014]). This paper was delivered with a half an eye on that previous crisis and has been revised in a time of pandemic. As well as being a reflection on the themes of the conference, I offer it as a very modest, distinctly non-definitive contribution to what I hope will be a more conscious engagement with the moral and political baggage of the theories which swirl around our academic discourse.

2 Finley (1972), (1973).
3 Polanyi (1944).
4 On Finley see Nafissi (2005), and now Jew *et al.* (2016).
5 Broodbank (2013).
6 On connectivity, abatement, and intensification, see Horden and Purcell (2000); Harris (2005). On mobility, see Isayev (2017). On the Etruscans, see Riva (2009). On the disappearing Dark Ages, the overwhelming case made by Lemos (2002) has only gotten stronger.

with it, and this only increased over time. And, as far as one can tell, they were unabashedly aspirational about this. What they did with all this 'stuff' is one of the critical questions.[7]

Fourth, 'things' do things to people. The naturalisation of complex network theories is one of the major advances of recent times; it makes us enrich our descriptive language. Latour's insistence that, rather than seeing history as a problem to be solved, we should see it as a set of patterns to be described is a welcome development.[8] Within this, the necessity of understanding the profundity of human engagement, or better, entanglement, with the material world is critical. It offers an enhanced notion of agency – not just individuals but also objects, nodes, and flows can be seen as active and shaping. Network theory pushes us beyond seeing connectivity as an artefact to seeing what connectivity does.[9]

Fifth, we are more scientifically literate and sophisticated. With this scientific expertise, such as on bones, chemistry, palaeobotany, aDNA, or climate change, come new possibilities and new questions. There seems to be no doubt now that one of the factors which is at stake in the development of Iron Age and archaic Italy is related to increased opportunities for resource extraction. This is becoming visible in multiple proxies – increased rainfall, increases in livestock size, cultivation of vines and olives earlier than previously assumed, and so forth. This is fast becoming a critical element for our discipline.[10]

Sixth, we are getting a bit better at being relaxed about settlement typology. It was not so unusual, in years past, to witness, or be caught in, thunderous rows about 'tribes' and 'states' or to sit through entirely circular arguments about rank-size. I hope we have seen enough diversity in the archaeological record to move beyond this. The consequence of deep histories, filled with meaningful networks and actants, is that individual sites can be understood, each in their own complexity. Indeed, one can step beyond the particularist sense of the individual site to see the wider environmental context. Even 'urbanisation' is (thankfully) beginning to appear in scare quotes.[11]

---

7 For the relative object richness of the Late Bronze Age and Early Iron Age, we lack a clear account or proper quantitative data, but it is arguably obvious in any museum collection. On the importance of things, and their accumulation and movement, see the classic account in Appadurai (1986).
8 Latour (2005).
9 On networks, see Latour (2005); Knappett (2011), (2013). On entanglement, see Hodder (2012).
10 On the science of the archaic period, see Manning (2018) for climate change. For an example of tracking long-term patterns see Roberts *et al.* (2019). For an illustrative case-study of the prospects of scientific work in Italy, see Trentacoste *et al.* (2020). The risks are also significant, especially when drawing out conclusions for relatively short periods; see Perkins (2009) on the unhappy application of DNA analysis to the origins of the Etruscans.
11 On urbanization, see Smith (2005a). For complexity, see Fernández-Götz et al. (2014). Woolf (2020) shows the power of the paradigm.

One simple illustration of the progress we have experienced is that we had very little, 30 years ago, that would have matched, in content and sophistication, a book which will inform this discussion and, I argue, our future work: Joseph Manning's *The Open Sea*, which offers a detailed and environmentally informed picture of Mediterranean commerce and exchange.[12] The very idea of writing about the economic life of the Mediterranean before the Roman Empire would have seemed optimistic 30 years ago, and, for that reason, we tended to look to Braudel and others and infer similarities.[13]

We should not, however, be too triumphalist. In 1990, at the fourth Conference of Italian Archaeology, John Wilkes noted:

> One major problem with the way in which we as archaeologists and ancient historians go about our reconstruction, especially in the pre-urban period, is that we take what we assume to have been human beings like ourselves, individuals with everyday lives, ideas and aspirations inter-relating with other human beings, and we put them together into anonymous clumps which we call periods, phases, peoples, trends, developments etc.[14]

He goes on to argue for the importance of 'idea networks' of which 'urban-type societies' are one, and that is very much the crux of the modern debate around archaic Greece and Italy. Indeed, it is sobering to note how much of the modern conversation would have not been out of place in 1990, although the focus is now tighter.

The archaic economy: from gift to market

Karl Polanyi offered a compelling vision of the relationship between society and economy that continues to be relevant for modern scholarship. This vision was also highly influential on Finley; Manning notes how Finley was responding to a long story in economic history, and Polanyi was Finley's clue as to why the ancient economy was not a modern economy.[15]

Polanyi was a fascinating individual – a Hungarian Jewish émigré who learnt his craft in Vienna in the 1920s and embraced Christian socialism in the UK in the 1930s. Like so many who sought to explain the disasters of the late nineteenth and early twentieth century, Polanyi's question was about modernism. Polanyi's notion of the disembedding of the market from social relations is in many ways the same question that Marx was trying to address in his account of capital, or Weber in his notion of disenchantment,

---

12 Manning (2018).
13 Braudel (1972), (1981–4). This was, in fact, the optimistic (and firmly rejected) subject of my original doctoral proposal.
14 Wilkins (1992) 227.
15 Manning (2018) 9–12.

or E. P. Thompson in his account of the working classes, as Tim Rogan has recently shown.[16] The obsession of the time was to understand the fracture that seemed to have taken place in contemporary society. The more committed were anxious to heal that fracture, and Polanyi's argument was that 'social life must include more than the contractual relationships of barter and exchange'.[17] In other words, *The Great Transformation*, his seminal book, was about how we had got the theory and practice of the economy wrong.[18]

Finley was not blind to the moral force of Polanyi's argument and made strong interventions himself on the relevance of the past. But *The Ancient Economy* is perhaps a less significant work for our purposes than *The World of Odysseus*, since there Finley made a less problematic case for the significance of anthropological theory.[19] Alongside Polanyi, the other key figure in Finley's thought was Marcel Mauss. It is Mauss' theory of 'the gift' which, for Finley, explains how the ancient economy functioned as an economy embedded in social relations – it is the link between Mauss and Polanyi which underpins Finley's key methodological position: 'I deliberately select anthropology, not sociology, as the mentor. Ideally, we should create a third discipline, the comparative study of literate, post-primitive (if I may), pre-industrial, historical societies.'[20]

In his recent work *The Open Sea*, Manning is a strong proponent of NIE. This is a label for a loose association of ideas which Manning defines as follows:

> Transaction costs, property rights, methodological individualism and (bounded or perfect) 'rational choice', and the cost of information are the core concepts of NIE analysis. The aim has been to establish in historical time the connection between institutions and performance.[21]

NIE analysis is not unaware of social anthropology. Indeed, Douglass North, a key proponent, also engaged with Mauss' arguments. But North's view was that an economic understanding fully explained reciprocity and transactional modes, and indeed Mauss himself saw the gift as an economic activity, as well as a social one.[22] These delivery systems and mechanisms are what North calls 'substitutes for the market', that is, the market that was to come and which is a key stage in human development and requires the constraint of institutions to lower transaction costs and improve efficiency. NIE is, in this

---

16 Rogan (2017).
17 Rogan (2017) 91.
18 Polanyi (1944); see also Cangiani and Thomasberger (2018). On Polanyi and the critique of capitalism, see Rogan (2017).
19 Finley (1972); Finley (1973).
20 Mauss (2016); Finley (1972) 118–9.
21 Manning (2018) 28.
22 Cedrini *et al.* (2019).

sense, profoundly evolutionary, and it is ironic that Manning recommends adding some more evolutionary theory to make it work even better.[23]

One of North's interests is in the relationship between informal and formal mechanisms. How, why, and how well did they work? The answer was that they worked surprisingly well, but with serious limitations in comparison with the modern world. This led him, and colleagues, to the notion of limited access orders where an elite, based on rent extraction, suppressed violence by monopolising economics and politics. A key passage serves to illustrate this model:

> Human history has known just three types of social orders. The first was the *foraging order*: small social groups characteristic of hunter-gatherer societies. Our concern is with the two social orders that arose over the last ten millennia. The *limited-access* order (or *natural state*) emerged between five and ten thousand years ago, and was associated with the increasing scale of human societies. Increasing scale is accomplished through a hierarchy of personal relationships among powerful individuals. Personal relationships among the elite form the basis for political organization and constitute the grounds for individual interaction. A natural state is ruled by a dominant coalition; people outside the coalition have only limited access to organizations, privileges, and valuable resources and activities. *Open-access orders* emerged in the nineteenth century, and are associated with the beginnings of sustained economic and political development. Identity, which in natural states is inherently personal, becomes defined in open access orders by a set of impersonal characteristics. The development of impersonal categories of individuals, often called citizens, allowed people to interact over wide areas of social behavior where no one needed to know the individual identities of their partners. The ability to form organizations that the larger society supports is open to everyone who meets a set of minimal and impersonal criteria. Both limited- and open-access social orders have public and private organizations, but natural states limit access to those organizations. Open-access societies do not.[24]

Essentially, in economic terms, nothing changes between the agricultural revolution and the nineteenth century, when impersonal markets, disenchanted transactions, and open access burst forth. It is easy to see how the archaic economy gets left under-theorised in this vast frozen waste of elite-driven, personal connections. The gift is a personal, reciprocal exchange between relative equals, which is thus inefficient because it is outside organisational structure. It is highly dependent on individual relationships and

---

23 Manning (2018) 32–4.
24 North *et al.* (2009) 56.

only available to a few people. It works, because those limiting factors also permit a less violent society, but it is not very efficient.

Most ancient historians who work with NIE tend to pull bits of the 'evolved', institutional world back into the past. Their argument is that there may have been a transformation in the nineteenth century, but it was not as stark as previously suggested. They point to private property and to public and private law defending property rights. They also argue for quasi-rational choices leading to growth performance across numerous proxies. This is not to say that the ancient world is as rational or institutional as the modern, but it is possible to claim some connection to modernity.[25] As Mark Granovetter argued, we have probably overstated the embeddedness of early markets and understated the embeddedness of modern markets.[26] In other words, social relations always matter, as Polanyi said and as Finley insisted. This can help us include the archaic economy in a modified NIE world.

NIE was born to celebrate the social and economic changes which earlier theorists had regarded as anomalous and worrying, which is why it carries problematic risks. Recasting what Weber called 'disenchantment' as 'lower transaction costs' normalised neoliberal economics. But it has also focused on important questions. Along the way, a Granovetter-inflected NIE started to look, to some, like a positive way of doing ancient economic history – though its evolutionist 'wolf' shows through the pastoral landscape. Scheidel, Morris, and Saller's NIE-driven *Cambridge Economic History* focuses extensively on economic performance and transformations. For Ian Morris, however, the seventh, sixth, and fifth centuries BCE were something of an economic 'sweet spot' for Greece: 'a structural revolution pushed Greece into the "optimality band", in which the state is strong enough to provide security and guarantee property, but not strong enough to engage in destructive rent-seeking'.[27] So, one can recast the emergence of the *polis* within a predominantly economic model and set that economic progress into a fundamentally evolutionary framework. In seeking to explain what is, effectively, the teleological triumph of the *polis*, Manning also resorts to claims about knowledge transfer as an evolutionary process – 'the power of a good idea to catch on'.[28]

If one pursues this line of reasoning, then it is possible to arrive at 'urbanisation' as a successful meme, and it is interesting that North and others found Richard Dawkins a congenial fellow-traveller. Dawkins' notion that memes or carriers of cultural identity behaved in a quasi-evolutionary manner sustains the conceit that economic progress through lowering transaction costs and the notion of urbanisation are a self-replicating cultural package.[29]

25 The obvious place to look is in Scheidel *et al.* (2007).
26 Granovetter (1985).
27 Morris (2007) 241
28 Manning (2018) 34.
29 Dawkins (1976).

This has provoked the ire of commentators, from Marshall Sahlins through to Francesco Boldizzoni,[30] as exemplified in Sahlins' critique of Dawkins and Edward Wilson:

> In place of a social constitution of meanings, it offers a biological determination of human interactions with a source primarily in the general evolutionary propensity of individual genotypes to maximize their reproductive success. It is a new variety of sociological utilitarianism, but transposed now to a biological calculus of the utilities realized in social relations.[31]

John Wilkins took a rather different line when he wrote 'urbanisation represents not only a very dominant set of ideas presumably across the Mediterranean by the middle of the millennium, but its power is also greatly enhanced by the almost proselytising fervour of the newly urbanised'.[32] The idea alone was not enough; it had to be sufficiently advantageous to 'catch on'.

The recent revival of interest in Fustel de Coulanges offers a rickety bridge between the evolutionist urban paradigm and economic advantage.[33] Isolating Fustel's approach to the city as an ideological construct, a *mentalité*, Nicola Terrenato noted that families develop private property to bury their dead and then aggregate into wider groups. This process is transposed to the city, which is thus a form of organisation predominantly suited to elite behaviour and therefore a natural object of peer polity interaction. Elites, with sufficient resources and stability, emulated the successful evolutionary move. The city was one of the fittest social forms in the tangled hedgerow of Darwinian state formation. Moreover, it can be argued to have been a successful mechanism for the extraction of resources from others, thus reinforcing its attraction to elites. What Wilkins, with some degree of irony, called 'proselytising fervour' might have looked like conquest or the deliberate propagation of inequality to the unconverted.

Putting all of this together, one arrives at a rationalist, elite-driven interpretation of human history, and specifically the development of cities, as maximising economic advantage and institutionalising asymmetry. You can get to this model as easily from a position of brash neoliberal rationality as you can from one of concerned leftward empathy; many roads are converging. This is a fascinating outcome, in that there is a tendency to argue that the nineteenth century's 'great transformation' finds an early precursor, and it is not entirely surprising then that some of these accounts toy with the notion of the 'axial age' – Manning is an example. The 'axial age' was Karl

---

30 Boldizzoni (2007).
31 Sahlins (1976) x, cited at Boldizzoni (2007) 46.
32 Wilkins (1992) 227.
33 Yoffee and Terrenato (2015); Rüpke (2020) 30–46.

Jaspers' effort to explain what he saw as an early cultural revolution in the mid-first millennium BCE – the development of an 'age of faith' but also an 'age of expansion'.[34] Critically, Jaspers was again responding to this central issue of how and when we became 'modern', and why it went so wrong; the implication was that we needed a new axial age (not run by Heidegger) or to recover the old one. It is equally instructive to see how this conception of recurrence and similarity also allows scholars to use globalisation as a persistent process, not a specifically modern one. So, for instance, Justin Jennings argued that globalisation has happened repeatedly, and the development of cities is always part of the story.[35]

Between North's NIE, Granovetter's economic sociology, and the interest in globalisation, we see a trend towards what has been called 'global history'.[36] The combination of a concentration on economic drivers and the use of a quasi-biological framework is popular and attractive, but it is potentially reductive. A number of the critical elements of this pattern of argument can be flattened into ideal types – cities, trade, and elites – while there is a combination of 'natural state' and evolutionism which inevitably makes one worry that this is leading to the justification of 'inevitable' processes.

One way in which historians have reacted against this is by emphasising the local and the micro against the global and the macro. This idea, that microhistory can save global history, was the subject of a recent *Past and Present* Supplement.[37] Being attentive to what Ginzburg and Poni called the 'decisive importance of those traces, those clues, those details previously overlooked, which upset and throw into disarray the superficial aspect of the documentation',[38] Ghobrial suggests that 'microhistory could play a role in carrying us one step closer to a more rigorous, reflexive and critical form of global history'.[39]

It is particularly interesting for archaeologists, then, to think about the challenge of agglomeration, of what we do when we have 'collected all our stamps' (to use an earlier metaphor). If we take all the specific examples of knowledge transfer, which we have been working on for the past few decades, do we end up with a greater whole? Do our case studies simply mask the enormous gaps in our knowledge? Is there a smooth passage between case study and pattern? Does case study interfere with pattern? Are they fundamentally incompatible exercises? How does the study of particular actants, agents, and networks in their intense specificity put into question the broader outlines we have seen emerge from a global, and to a degree globalising,

---

34 Jaspers (1953); Joas and Bellah (2012).
35 Jennings (2010).
36 Hunt (2014); Conrad (2017).
37 Ghobrial (2019a).
38 Ginzburg and Poni (1991) 8.
39 Ghobrial (2019b) 22.

macrohistory? All these issues are associated with middle-range theory and the challenge of arriving at convincing frameworks of interpretation.

I want to pick two areas where, potentially, we might be able to disrupt the explanatory framework of economy and evolution, and to argue that we can find another, and I think more intriguing, way of understanding archaic economies. First, I will sketch out some problems with the emphasis on economic drivers by thinking about the role of religion, and second, I will focus on artisans and technicians.

On the edge of institutionalisation

The institutionalisation of economic activity can be readily located in religion. Temples and sanctuaries allow for the transformation of value, and the development of polytheism and of sacred spaces forms part of the development of denser settlements, intensification of space utilisation, and accelerated social interaction.[40] In this section I want to sketch out a model which sees the religious aspects of community as not only essential to the construction of community but also part of the process of defining communities. This is perhaps one of the critical forms of knowledge which characterise the 'long' Iron Age.

The traditional model of *polis* religion made elite domination of religion, and its functional use as an instrument of that domination, relatively straightforward. However, that model is now under significant stress. It allows little room for individual belief or localised action, and its functionalism is too blunt to be helpful in describing the relationship between community and the gods.[41] Nevertheless, for our purposes, the role of the temple as a meeting place, a marketplace of ideas, has significant value. Furthermore, there is no doubt that elites are inextricably connected with the development of what we call 'urban settlements'. If we then think about elites as fragile, potentially unstable groupings which require huge performative effort to sustain, then religion appears to play an important role in the definition of elites, and the hierarchical nature of polytheistic religion mirrors the construction of unequal social orders.[42]

The notion of the sanctuary as a marketplace of ideas does not need much illustration; it works well for the Panhellenic sanctuaries, and Charlotte Potts has used this notion well for central Italy.[43] Yet, in addition to its enabling force for connectivity, religion also played a constraining role. Religion serves to institutionalise the notion that princes and kings were not at the top of the hierarchy – the gods are above them. John Scheid has made some striking points about the ways in which developed notions of sacrifice instantiate

---

40 Govi (2017); Agusta-Boularot et al. (2017).
41 Kindt (2013); Smith (2019).
42 For this understanding of the elite see Fisher and van Wees (2015) or Cicero or V. Gordon Childe.
43 Potts (2015).

hierarchies – from vegetable to animal to human to god.[44] While Homer offers little challenge to an established elite ordering, that order is hedged round with obligation and expectation. The elite are under question and attack from their very first appearance in Greek literature; Hesiod's (*Op.* 38, 220, 263) complaint about gift-eating *basileis* is both an insight into inequality and a reminder that elite performance was judged and scrutinised.[45] Where did this idea come from? Jaspers would have said that it was part of the axial age ethical mentality. The NIE perspective might argue that a wider interrelationship between members of society was economically rational. I, instead, will argue for a 're-enchantment' of our notion of community, and of communal institutions, that is to say, a more determined emphasis on community as sanctioned by, and performed with reference to and in company with, the gods. In other words, we ought to take seriously the previously held notion that modernity had significantly lost some element of interpersonal relations and of relations between humans and the transcendent – a point strongly argued for in social anthropology.[46]

Scholars have argued that a critical feature in the development of archaic Greece and central Italy is the emergence of the city; we can also see a close relationship between cities and the institutions of religion, with temples being simply the most obvious. As a concept, the city has often been characterised as a 'rational' enterprise, to use Oswyn Murray's term.[47] Certainly, Mediterranean city-states are not like the theocracies known from the ancient Near East or Egypt. Yet it is also the case that one of the most obvious developments of the period in which we identify Mediterranean urbanisation is the articulation of myth, differentiated polytheism, and increasingly monumentalised arenas for religious performance.

The community of citizens was, at least to some extent, defined as a community of believers, and, while political elites monopolised religious office, effective religious performance was essential for political prominence. Religion and politics were coterminous, which opens up the idea that there was no politics that was not also the working out of the will of the gods.[48] Critically, the creation of poliadic deities, the 'nationalisation' of cult, the communal oversight of family *sacra*, the overlapping of local, regional, and international deities support an overall sense that ritualised communication did not belong in only one place or at one level of society. It is absolutely pervasive, at and across borders, for men and women, and it transforms value persistently through deposition and votive behaviour. From Perachora to Pyrgi, the gods are at work.

---

44 Scheid (2012).
45 For brilliant work in this area, see Duplouy (2006).
46 Strathern (2019) for the arguments.
47 Murray (1990), (1991).
48 Champion (2017) for a first attempt to do better for mid-Republican Rome; the field is transformed by Padilla Peralta (2020).

To give some chronological shape to this, it is striking how many other processes are coterminous with the beginning of spatial redefinition and/or the increase in settlement size across the long Iron Age. First is the differentiation of the gods into recognisable mythical figures. Second is the proliferation of religious spaces inside and outside borders. Third is the creation of foci of expenditure, such as temples, that are distinct from the personal or familial aggrandisement most visible in funerals. Fourth is the development of literacy for non-bureaucratic purposes. Fifth, and latest, is the emergence of codifications of law which enshrine notions of private property and behaviour vis-à-vis the sacred.[49] On this last point, it seems plausible that the emergence of a notion of private property entails, and arises from, an enhanced notion of community; in other words, that rather than thinking of the evolution of family, private property, and the state from the perspective of communal sharing, we should contemplate an inverse process whereby a notion of the commons emerges alongside the definition of private space.[50] The community is the essential intellectual and social space within which it becomes possible to imagine and sustain the notion of ownership, which then encourages the creation of groups to manage transmission and inheritance. Some groups may have been 'elite', but some possessions are the property of different social levels, and that may include specialised ritual knowledge.

Rather, therefore, than think about urban space as the critical category, it is perhaps more profitable to reckon on the formalisation of rituals, some of which are specifically about the construction of community, in terms of people and boundaries.[51] And this remarkably sophisticated notion of what it is to be a part of a community, and how to define communities within communities, might be the critical knowledge which is transferred in the early Iron Age.

Technicians of the city: forging community, weaving worlds

Who carried this knowledge about how to undertake formal rituals? Although religious expertise is often located at an elite level, this deserves some degree of challenge. Chalcas the seer is not a king. Tarchon, Romulus, and Numa are 'kings', but the notion of a king in Italy is not unitary or stable. Some Roman priests are shut out from other activity. Not all priests are patricians, and Attus Naevius, the augur from an apparently non-noble background who learnt his skill from the gods and stood up against a king, is a good example of a different genealogy of religious wisdom. Not all

---

49 See now Bell and Du Plessis (2020).
50 Mackil (2017) 63–90.
51 Gargola (2017) has reshaped our understanding of some of these rituals but see also the reissue in English of Rüpke's (2019) ground-breaking work, *Peace and War in Rome: A Religious Construction of Warfare*. I also want to flag here the focus of Humphreys (2004) on the intellectual work needed to confront unpredictable gods.

religious stories are told by elite players. Athenian vase painters were not part of the elite, nor, one suspects, were those who created central Italic terracotta friezes. What is the nature of artisanal agency in creating the city?[52]

Storytellers, myth makers, image carriers, seers, mystics, and strangers were all culture heroes of the archaic age (and some are retrojected into even earlier times). Regular and repeated acts of creativity characterised ancient societies. The rapidity of knowledge transfer and cultural transmission in what we (increasingly reluctantly) call 'the Orientalising period' was a symptom of a remarkable intellectual openness, which was likely the product of vigorous interpretative behaviour.[53] In other words, the cultural packages, which were in motion, were accompanied at the point of reception by a persistent and imaginative set of commentaries.

To simply state that artisans were at the service of the elite would understate the degree of innovation present in craft production. Moreover, it restricts the value of ideologically freighted material production to a single patron–client commissioning moment, therefore omitting any consideration of cultural expectations on the act of production by the viewers and the producers.[54] Rather, artisanal and craft activity constitutes, creates, and perpetually transforms the notion and reality of power.[55] What we see, and what we search for, are the attributes of power, which emerge from a dialogue, however asymmetrical, between those temporarily possessing these attributes and those who are prepared to allow them to be meaningful and read them.

To take this argument further, we can refer to Mary Helms' *Craft and the Kingly Ideal: Art, Trade and Power*, which is obliquely one of the best books ever written on what orientalisation was all about. It is first worth recalling that Helms' previous book, *Ulysses' Sail: An Ethnographic Odyssey of Power, Knowledge, and Geographical Distance*, made the case for the importance of distance in adding allure to objects and for differential knowledge of space and distance as being an aspect of power.[56] *Craft and the Kingly Ideal* adds to this by focusing on the production of movement. Taking a very broad account of craft as an act of transformation, Helms argues that trade itself is a craft:

> The capacity for successful travel may be seen not only as comparable to but also as a manifestation of a form of skilled crafting involving the creation or organization of an orderly, cultured, ritually sanctified social entity (for example, a caravan or ship's society) which can successfully mediate geographical space/time and can pass between permanent and

---

52 Brilliantly addressed in Osborne (2018).
53 See Snodgrass (1988) for an influential account.
54 See Bernardo-Ciddio in this volume for similar arguments.
55 Recent important attempts to focus on artisanal activity include: Biella *et al.* (2018); Gleba and Pasztokai-Szeöke (2013).
56 Helms (1988), (1993).

settled foci of human society and more distant domains of the outside world.[57]

The skilled artisan is often an outsider and highly mobile.[58] The specialised knowledge of the artisan is prized and feared, and the artisan may be represented not only as a flawed creator (for instance, physically disabled in some way) but also as essentially a human empowered to come close to the repetition of an original act of creation. This power, this aesthetic of transforming value, is akin to, and in Helms' account often controlled by, a king or elite.

Turning then to acquisition, Helms differentiates the reciprocity involved in exchange with nearer neighbours from acquisition from distant places: 'the locus of value of long-distance goods lies not in the reciprocity of exchange but in the inalienable qualities derived from association with a qualitatively defined but not necessarily accurately known distant place of origins'.[59] Giving in order to receive something in return should be differentiated from the more embedded versions of neighbourly exchange. This makes the market a particularly important place – a place of order in potential disorder in which the maintenance of peace has cosmological significance. It is unsurprising therefore that the market is often also a place where craft – production most likely but also religion, poetry, music, and dance – is also performed.[60]

The acquisition of naturally endowed and specially crafted goods underlies Helms' notion of political authority. Helms quotes Irving Goldman's characterisation of the Kwakiutl chiefs of British Columbia as 'the assemblers, the concentrators and the managers of supernatural powers'.[61] Acquisition, accumulation, and transformation underpin the legitimation of power; one draws authority from the display of connection with an outside world, which can only be imagined by most of the community, and precisely because it is imagined it can acquire extraordinary characteristics. The connection with 'centres-out-there' works both horizontally across space, but also symbolically as a connection with spiritually imbued realms, and as a reinforcement of aspirational power across time.

It is worth noting that Helms makes little reference to ancient Greece or Rome, but the general relevance of her argument is clear, particularly the way that craft operates, both in terms of local production and in long distance acquisition. This cleverly allows us to track analogous processes, even in less well-connected areas. Less robust, however, is Helms' slightly flat-footed approach to power and its operation in society. Although she quotes Benedict Anderson's idea, derived from his study of Javanese culture, that

---

57 Helms (1993) 43.
58 See Armstrong and Robinson's contributions in this volume for discussion of mobile craftspeople.
59 Helms (1993) 99.
60 See Becker in this volume.
61 Helms (1993) 168, citing Goldman (1975) 198–9.

'power exists, independent of its possible users', her description of society is dichotomous and without nuance.[62]

There may be a way forward by combining how Helms associates craft and acquisition with the notion of assemblage, which is hinted at by Goldman. More recently, Delanda has theorised the idea of assemblage as an extension to, and development of, network theory, derived from the theoretical work of Deleuze and Guattari.[63] On this account, assemblages have a fully contingent historical identity, and each of them is therefore an individual entity. They are always composed of heterogeneous components; Delanda gives the following example:

> persons, the material and symbolic artifacts that compose communities and organisations: the architecture of the buildings that house them; the myriad different tools and machines used in offices, factories, and kitchens; the various sources of food, water, and electricity; the many symbols and icons with which they express their identity.[64]

Assemblages can become component parts of larger assemblages, and while they 'emerge from the interactions between their parts . . . once an assemblage is in place it immediately starts acting as a source of limitations and opportunities for its components'.[65] Assemblage theory is complex but it is intended to link micro and macro scales because assemblages are active, combinatory, and define potential, as well as actual, opportunity. They are territorialised (they have a spatial component, however described) and they are, to varying degrees, coded – that is to say, subject to rules and norms which they perpetuate and are perpetually bringing into being.

Interestingly, Delanda turns regularly to Braudel's theories in *Civilization and Capitalism*, which likewise moves between the micro and macro scales. Braudel, of course, thought across long stretches of history.[66] One of his preoccupations was how markets turned into more consolidated economies, and his emphasis on fairs and bazaars was taken up by Delanda as an example of how to work with assemblages.[67] Their physical space, the objects traded, the people involved, and the knowledges transmitted are all part of the assemblage; the agglomeration and interaction of markets form a larger assemblage; the increased coding of the assemblages is part of the structuring of economic activity. The more coded, long term, and durable these assemblages, the closer we get to an economic system which supports,

---

62 Helms (1993) 9, citing Anderson (1972) 7.
63 Delanda (2006), (2016).
64 Delanda (2016) 20.
65 Delanda (2016) 21.
66 Braudel (1981–4).
67 See Becker in this volume.

and is supported by, asymmetrically solid social structures, that is, capitalism, which Braudel famously saw as 'potentially visible since the dawn of history'.[68]

Helms' arguments about crafting and trade fit easily into the Braudelian wheels of commerce. Each market moment is an assemblage, but each constructed store of resource is also an assemblage. At the market, we find objects that enact and encode their cultural capacity, whether they are from far away or are part of burgeoning artisanal production. These objects flow in and out of assemblages which (among other things) denote social status. And each assemblage is always being made and unmade, valued, revalued, and devalued by time, by the tension between the lure of innovation and the memory of tradition, and by entanglement with contingent political process.

Elsewhere, I have suggested that we might need to take more seriously theories such as Chayanov's peasant or domestic mode of production in shaping early intensification.[69] This argument points to two further themes. First, it would be pointless to fight against the clear significance of the elite capture of exchange networks, of elite motivation and mobilisation of resource, and of the relevance of exchange and acquisition to shoring up asymmetrical relations. However, it is certain that the assemblages we are discussing include – indeed require – a wider community and that in noting the significance of artisans and traders we are encouraged to look down the social order and across geographical boundaries. We need to include the 'real' technicians of the city, who forge community values in their smithies and weave worlds of meaning on their looms. These figures, and these acts, are coded symbolically as well as economically, and my focus on assemblages suggests that their symbolic code is being unduly overshadowed by current economic models. The conclusion I am gesturing at is that the symbolic coding we see in and around artisanal activity constrained behaviour in the direction of a broad notion of community, within which the power of the elite should be seen as transient, contingent, and performative. It takes time, and very complex processes of coding, to arrive at anything like a stable aristocracy. What we tend to see is repeated overlaying of social

---

68 Delanda (2006) 17, and for Braudel (1981–4) on capitalism: 'Throughout this book, I have argued that capitalism has been potentially visible since the dawn of history, and that it has developed and perpetuated itself down the ages. (III: 620). . . . The worst error of all is to suppose that capitalism is simply an 'economic system', whereas in fact it lives off the social order, standing almost on a footing with the state, whether as adversary or accomplice: it is and always has been a massive force, filling the horizon. Capitalism also benefits from all the support that culture provides for the solidity of the social edifice, for culture – though unequally distributed and shot through with contradictory currents – does in the end contribute the best of itself to propping up the existing order. And lastly capitalism can count on the dominant classes who, when they defend it, are defending themselves' (III: 623).
69 Chayanov (1966); Smith (2021).

structures – that is one of the key findings, for instance, of Sally Humphreys' account of Athenian kinship and religion.[70]

An entangled meshwork

What I have outlined here does not, by itself, invalidate the NIE evolutionist model of an ever-improving market. At some level, human history is about the steady intensification of symmetrical economic exploitation in a competitive world. But this picture excludes so much of the messy and contingent details, and occludes agency at different levels of society and in different kinds of actors. It calls to mind the fantastic Borgesian dictionary entry – animals that from a long way off look like flies.[71] If you are far enough away, everything looks the same and, as a definition or indeed a description of reality, the NIE evolutionist world can be so unhelpful as to be misleading. It is a flaw of big data, and of thinking solely at the macro-economic level. We have to include all the descriptive levels to come closer to reality; assemblage theory has been my way to illustrate this.

I have suggested that assemblage theory might help us scale back and forth, and might help us understand whether the agglomeration of instances of knowledge transmission gets us to an economy. I have argued that they perhaps get us to another imperfectly understood assemblage, a set of objects, individuals, and practices, at least some, and probably all, of which were deeply embedded in imperfectly articulated and never completely reproducible social relations and actor-networks. All these operate across the human landscape, but also in the vertical relationship between the world and the gods, as I have discussed earlier. It was an enchanted, not a disenchanted, world. This meshwork, to use Tim Ingold's phrase, has an extraordinary horizontal and territorial extension throughout the Iron Age, but it is also both the product of and one of the constitutive elements of persistently rearticulated vertical cosmologies.[72] The immensely complicated dance of structures, objects, and people, as it constantly reshapes, is also entangled in the understanding of ritualised and theologised cosmologies.[73] They are inextricable, one from another.

This chapter has argued that the notion of the assemblage allows us to create dense and sophisticated descriptions which go beyond, and animate, collections of data. It has also argued that these assemblages have to be understood cosmologically and that this coding offers a more nuanced, accurate, and enchanted picture of the ancient economy than other current

---

70 Humphreys (2018).
71 Borges (2000).
72 Ingold (2015).
73 Some of what I say here is influenced by neo-Spinozist approaches to materiality, for instance Bennett (2010).

theories. The most important knowledge that was exchanged in the archaic period was that value and power are constantly shifting and being reassessed across time and space and in relation to pervasive immanent forces.[74] It is precisely this fluidity that allowed archaic society to reimagine itself and rethink its values. Politics, religion, and economy were coded in the objects and processes of knowledge transmission and embedded in the broader economy of ideas, things, people, and gods.

74 On immanence, see Strathern (2019).

3 Metallurgy and connectivity in northern Etruria

Seth Bernard

As a case study of ancient connectivity, this chapter focuses on the iron trade emanating from northern Etruria and involving much of Tyrrhenian Italy. Iron production was among the most important features of the region's early economy, and this metal trade has featured prominently in research and publication, starting with two volumes on *L'Etruria mineraria* in the 1980s.[1] In this chapter, I return to the topic to analyse northern Etruria's metal trade as a form of connectivity, not analytically different from the phenomenon of movement carrying people, commodities, and technologies around the region. This optic allows us to expand the lens to take into account broader research on early iron technology and incorporate new evidence of seaborne commerce in ore. I suggest that a detailed examination of this trade is useful for thinking more broadly about connectivity's effects on Iron Age Italian society.

The idea that the population of the historical Mediterranean was generally and regularly mobile has become more or less axiomatic in scholarship. Ancient historians call the phenomenon 'connectivity', following the landmark work of Horden and Purcell; the concept may be compared to the 'connectedness' explored by recent global histories of the early modern period.[2] Arguments for the universality of movement in human history can even now turn to science for support: recent genetic work associates the presence of the DRD4 7R allele, the so-called 'wanderlust gene', with willingness to seek novelty and therefore to travel.[3] For historians, the obvious danger in

---

* I am grateful to the editors and anonymous readers for their guidance; Alex Moskowitz provided me with useful information about *tuyeres*, and Sarah Murray provided helpful comments on an earlier draft.
1 Aa.Vv. (1981); Camporeale (1985); among voluminous subsequent work, I highlight Corretti and Benvenuti (2001). For Populonia, see Cambi *et al.* (2009), esp. Acconcia and Milletti (2009). For Elba, Alderighi *et al.* (2013); Corretti *et al.* (2014) and other publications of the Aithalia project, esp. Pagliantini (2019); an excellent recent synthesis appears in Corretti (2017).
2 Horden and Purcell (2000); for 'connectedness' see Ghobrial (2014) 56.
3 Campbell and Barone (2012).

DOI: 10.4324/9781003120728-3

this trend is that, as connectivity becomes a constant feature of the human past, it also risks becoming a vague concept like 'influence' or 'interaction' were to previous generations of scholars; its ubiquity explains everything but nothing in particular. Some reviewers of Horden and Purcell's *Corrupting Sea* raised similar issues, complaining that the book offered a perspective of the Mediterranean past which replaced diversity with 'frightening featurelessness'.[4] This view underestimates the degree to which the authors' concept of microecology allows for the incorporation of diverse Mediterranean landscapes and resources through the integrative effects of human movement.[5] However, Horden and Purcell's equation is often held to grant greater variability in the human exploitation of landscapes while simultaneously holding movement itself as a sort of constant; the sea formed a perpetually available means of smoothing over the stochastic outcomes of regional ecologies. As a result, consequent scholarship often tends to view connectivity as inherently economically beneficial; ancient economic life was characterised by risk, while communication and exchange formed 'ineluctable imperatives' for those seeking ways beyond the limits of unpredictability.[6] This idea, that connectivity is conducive to economic success, has been used to great effect, especially by research informed by New Institutional Economics. By identifying, as New Institutional Economic theory does, the mitigation of transaction costs as the pathway to pre-modern economic growth, scholars have often privileged the role of long-distance trade within our wider understanding of long-term economic development in ancient Mediterranean history.[7]

Problematically, this deductive assertion of connectivity's beneficent economic role contains assumptions that do not always match what we find on the ground. Smith's chapter in this volume elegantly contends with the wider theory by reminding us that we are not dealing, in archaic Italy, with a world of atomised rational actors. Social relations mattered in decision-making processes then as they do now, and embeddedness need not imply a return to old views of economic primitivism. Regarding the particular link between connectivity and economic growth, we might respond by posing one of the oldest questions about Mediterranean trade: why were commodities, like olive oil and wine, which were seemingly producible everywhere, also the most frequently exchanged and often over long distances? In this world, it would appear that the simple availability of, or demand for, resources cannot

---

4 Squatriti (2002) 277; see also Algazi (2005).
5 Horden and Purcell (2005) 366–7 respond directly to this critique, noting their Mediterranean is one in which 'differences . . . resemble each other,' citing Horden and Purcell (2000) 52, quoting Lévi-Strauss.
6 Horden and Purcell (2000) 178; see now Isayev (2017) 17: 'Movement was the prerogative of all levels of ancient society, which depended on it for survival and growth.'
7 Terpstra (2019); see also Roselaar (2019); Smith in this volume. Long distance trade has likewise been used to explain the origins of iron in Greek antiquity, although see Morris (1989) for a critique of this theory.

fully explain commercial movement, and this encourages us to look more closely at the complex of concerns which must have informed decisions to exchange and connect at the local level.

To this end, we can turn to a growing body of recent historical scholarship on the early modern world, which asserts that movement itself is highly contingent and therefore deserves study in its own right. The work of Ghobrial and others promotes the concept of 'global microhistory', emphasising the value in detailing individual experiences moving within globalising worlds as a way to counteract the impulse towards simplification or generalisation.[8] The approach holds clear applicability to antiquity, where there has been long-standing discomfort with ideas of a uniformly 'Roman' or 'Hellenised' Mediterranean, even as there is the need to acknowledge the period's globalising trends.[9] I suggest one way forward is to speak of 'connectivities', rather than the singular connectivity, attending in detail not only to microregions but also to the modes or agents of their interaction.[10] Of course, plural connectivities will imply plural outcomes, and this shift therefore challenges models of connection as a predictable pathway to economic advancement. Within this framework, this chapter offers a microhistory of the connectivities linking North Etruria with wider Tyrrhenian Italy based upon the exploitation of iron. Analysed in this way, the movement of iron reveals the complex and particular interaction of local and 'global' factors, while its long-run effects were not always positive.

The nature of North Etruria's Iron trade between text and archaeology

In tracing the development of North Etruria's iron economy in time and space, a common starting point is a chapter from the universal history of Diodorus Siculus. The lengthy excursus represents one of the most detailed ancient accounts of Tyrrhenian economic connectivity:

> Off the city of Tyrrhenia known as Poplonium there is an island which men call Aithalia. It is about one hundred stades distant from the coast and received the name it bears from the smoke (*aithalos*) which lies so thick about it. For the island possesses a great amount of iron ore, which they quarry in order to melt and obtain iron, and they possess a great abundance of this ore. Those engaged in working this ore crush the rock and burn the broken lumps in certain ingenious furnaces. And in these they smelt the lumps by means of a great fire and form them into pieces

---

8 Ghobrial (2014), (2019a); see further Andrade (2010) and Trivellato (2011).
9 For globalizing antiquity, see Pitts and Versluys (2014).
10 See Cohen and Armstrong in this volume for further discussion; the papers in this volume offer a useful set of case studies.

of moderate size which are in their appearance like large sponges. These are purchased by merchants in exchange either for money or goods and are then taken to Dicaearchia or the other *emporia*, where there are men who purchase such cargoes and who, with the aid of a multitude of artisans in metal whom they have collected, work it further and manufacture iron objects of every description.[11]

Diodorus here shows intimate familiarity with the ancient production of iron and its stages, from the extraction of ferruginous ore to the roasting or beneficiating of that ore at very high temperatures into blooms or sponge iron – a semi-worked, but still raw, material. This smelting process produces enormous quantities of waste material or slag, often called *scoria* in Italian, whose regular appearance in the archaeological record we will discuss shortly. This sponge iron then needed further treatment, with high heat and hammering, to refine its metallic content, remove impurities, and be worked into iron implements – steps we refer to as the smithing process. In this passage, Diodorus portrays the process as a remarkable chain of productive relationships between those who mined ore on the island of Elba, those who refined ore into 'sponges' (probably working on the mainland where timber for fuel was more abundant as Strabo's account informs us), and Campanian merchants and artisans who purchased and further processed this material into finished implements. Each link in the chain differed both geographically and technologically, forming a horizontally diffuse production sequence along Italy's coastline.

As Diodorus wrote in the mid-first century BCE, the question is how far back in time we may trace this articulated network of metal production. Diodorus' account shows a general fascination with the long distances over which metal trading connected ancient communities, elsewhere turning to Hellenistic authors like the Massiliote Pytheas to describe the trade in tin from Cornwall to the Rhone Valley (5.37–8).[12] The source of information for Elba's iron distribution is less clear but also likely early. Corretti notes that, among the list of donations given by Etruscan cities to Scipio's expeditionary fleet to Africa in 205 BCE, Populonia gave *ferrum*, while Arezzo gave arms and armour, suggestive already of dislocated production.[13] Moving further back in time, reference to Pozzuoli by its Greek name Dicearchia suggests a possible *terminus post quem* of that colony's foundation by Cumae around 530 BCE.[14] Another noteworthy aspect is Diodorus' use of Elba's nickname *Aithalia* ('Sooty') in reference to smoke from metal production. The name appears first in a fragment of the sixth-century BCE writer Hecataeus and

---

11 Diod. Sic. 5.13.1–2, translation modified from Loeb edition.
12 Cunliffe (2003).
13 Corretti (2009).
14 On the foundation of Pozzuoli, see Adinolfi (1987).

is prominent in Hellenistic sources.[15] While these authors recognise Elba's involvement in iron production, none mentions the southward shipment of ore or any relationship with Campania as found in Diodorus. Aithalia appears in a fragment of the fourth century BCE writer Philistus' work on Dionysius I of Syracuse, the monarch whose imperial ambitions extended to Etruscan Italy and Corsica, and perhaps also Elba and Populonia. Syracusan interest is sometimes connected to a story in Aristotle's *Politics* (1259a) about a Sicilian merchant retailing iron ore at high price. Perhaps this was bloomed Elban iron, but Aristotle does not specify.

Considering this state of uncertainty with regard to the literary sources, we may turn instead to the archaeological record. One significant discovery is that of some fragments of Elban iron in a semi-refined state from an eighth-century BCE context at Pithecussae, the Euboean Greek colony on Ischia which also housed an industrial complex with metalworking workshops. For Ridgway, this material not only proved the early existence of something resembling Diodorus' commercial network linking Campania to Etruria but also explained its origins: as Phoenician presence shut off Sardinia and Corsica from Euboean Greeks in the ninth and eighth centuries, they instead sought colonial territory far to the south, in the Bay of Naples, from where they formed links with Etruscan mines to the north.[16] This grand idea of protectionary trading spheres claimed by territorial states in the Early Iron Age western Mediterranean seems anachronistic, while the archaeological record of a very early phase of Elban iron distribution is ambiguous. Although finds of bloomed Elban iron from Pisa or Tarquinia have been claimed for the eighth century, few examples have been subjected to scientific analysis to confirm provenance, and none furnishes a firm date.[17] Some recently published evidence of metalworking from Cumae, both bronze and iron, may offer further validation but awaits fuller analysis.[18] The Pithecussae material itself is not unassailable, as iron slag found in the site's metal workshops belongs to dumps dated by the excavators to the early seventh century BCE, while tuyeres resemble Greek examples of the sixth century BCE.[19] While the industrial site speaks to metal craftwork at Pithecussae, it cannot, on its own, confirm large-scale ironworking in the eighth century.

More importantly, there is no significant evidence for iron mining or processing on Elba or the adjacent Etruscan shoreline until the sixth century

---

15 See the catalogue of sources in Pagliantini (2019).
16 Ridgway (1992) 100.
17 Corretti and Benvenuti (2001) 142–3; Ligurian territory around Genoa is also sometimes included in this list, but see Cucini (2013), who affirms that much of that material is later and probably locally sourced.
18 D'Acunto (2018) 301.
19 Ridgway (1992) 91; cf. Corretti and Benvenuti (2001) 143; see also Nijboer (1998) 166–7; Alex Moskowitz's presentation on tuyeres at the 'Exchanging Ideas' conference in Auckland, New Zealand from which this chapter derives identifies the Pithecussae example as a *lasana* type with parallels from Greece and Massilia.

BCE. While this absence should not preclude the possibility of exploitation at some level, it casts doubt on the idea of surplus production or a stable export trade in iron at an early date.[20] The lowest layers of ironworking waste material on Populonia's Baratti beach also contained bronze working slag dated to the mid-eighth century BCE, drawing from mixed sulphide copper deposits inland in the Colline Metallifere.[21] However, such production appears limited by comparison to the later iron industry.

Etruscan ironworking underwent a radical shift in scale and organisation in the early sixth century BCE. Evidence of this shift comes from the coastal site of Rondelli, in the gulf of Follonica, where excavation of an industrial area, relating to a small settlement of the early sixth century, revealed 21 smelting furnaces of the sort used for roasting raw ore, consisting of circular depressions lined with clay and vegetal material. These received loads of ore and charcoal of heather and holm oak, while high temperatures, achieved by forced air, bloomed raw ore into the iron sponges described by Diodorus. The Rondelli installation is the best explored of a series of similar sites with reduction furnaces along the coast.[22] Around the same time, an industrial quarter was built near the beach at Populonia. Signs of ironworking appear at the site by the early sixth century BCE, while in the last part of the same century two buildings were constructed with rooms hosting an articulated process of metal production. Hematite dust in one room suggests the workshop received ore in completely raw form, while basins and hydraulic architecture in another room pertain to mineral-washing installations comparable with those from the Attic silver mines of Thoricus.[23]

The furnaces of Rondelli went out of use by the late fifth century, while the Populonia installation was long-lived, continuing into the mid-third century. The surrounding area at Populonia remained an active site of ironworking for centuries, and thick strata of ironworking slag and debris from used furnaces blanketed the beach. Camilli identified three main layers of accumulated material. The first dates to the seventh and sixth centuries, reasonably associable with the metalworking activity to which the industrial quarter also relates, while the thickest of the three layers of slag dates to the third and second centuries BCE.[24]

---

20 Note that early iron mining was done by non-sedentary groups in the Levant; see, e.g., Ben-Yosef (2016). I would not exclude the idea of very early iron mining on Elba because of a lack of settlement in the island's eastern iron-rich areas; however, in terms of what the archaeological evidence can tell us, the sixth century represented a significant turning point in the region's iron economy.
21 Chiarantini *et al.* (2009); Zifferero (2009).
22 Aranguren *et al.* (2009); Ciampoltrini (2018) 150 suggests the furnaces' construction matches Diodorus' account, but this is an overoptimistic reading of the vague *philotechnoi* applied to *kaminoi*. Another possible metalworking site is located at Scarlino, see Cambi (2002) 11–12.
23 Bonamici (2015) 412, 422.
24 Camilli (2016), (2018).

In sum, the initially small-scale metallurgy of northern Etruria, perhaps concentrated on inland ore sources, expanded quickly in the decades following 600 BCE as Elban iron ore was brought to coastal smelting sites and refined in ever greater quantities. This activity first occurred at a number of centres in the region but increasingly concentrated at Populonia, which was well-equipped to process raw ore into beneficiated sponges. The urban focus of the industry at Populonia may have given it a durability not displayed by smaller centres tied to non-urban settlements in the sixth century.[25]

Turning to the distribution of bloomed iron, sixth-century production immediately linked into a wide network of consumers. The list of sites where bloomed Elban iron appears includes many in southern Italy but is not limited in that regard. Northern Etruria itself is rich in finds, with Elban iron known from the area of Lucca, the territory of Pisa, and possibly several sites around Genoa.[26] Blacksmithing evidence frequently appears in the Albegna Valley at Doganella, Fonteblanda, and Ghiaccioforte.[27] Further south, Elban iron is identified at Caere and its port at Pyrgi.[28] While no testing has been done on material from the large forges at Gravisca, one suspects an Elban source, as may also have been the case for Rome, where archaic ironworking installations have been found beside the Capitolium and beneath the Forum of Caesar.[29] Iron made from Elban ore was also moving into the Po Valley, to Marzabotto and Bologna, and all the way to Spina by the fourth century BCE.[30] Along with this list of urban sites, we can cite rural contexts such as evidence of blacksmithing at the recently discovered farmhouse at Spolverino in the Ombrone Valley.[31] Iron emanating from northern Etruria appears almost ubiquitously along the Tyrrhenian coastline.

We turn now to an important piece of this puzzle, which has not yet featured in this discussion. The first known Iron Age shipwreck carrying fragments of bloomed Elban iron has been identified: the *Grand Ribaud F*, which sank off

---

25 Cambi (2002) 11–3 reconstructs a situation in which Vetulonia controlled Rondelli's ironworking operations until the rise of industry at Populonia reflected its rising domination over the region. There is little evidence to support this assertion other than an assumption about these communities' territorial interests, which may be anachronistic for the period. The appearance of smelting at Populonia, its decline of Rondelli, and the decline of Vetulonia's Archaic settlement are not sufficiently related in time to be conclusive to this point.
26 For further bibliography, see Bonamici (2015) 414–5; for Genoa, an archaeometric study by Cucini (2013) 91–7 raises the possibility of a more local source.
27 Doganella: Perkins and Walker (1990) 49–50; Fonteblanda: Ciampoltrini (2018); Ghiaccioforte: Firmati (2017).
28 Alderighi (2013) 173.
29 Gravisca: Fiorini and Torelli (2007); Rome: Giardino and Lugli (2001) for the Capitolium; De Santis *et al.* (2010) for the Forum of Caesar.
30 Cf. Bonamici (2015) 415.
31 Sebastiani (2012).

Hyères in the first quarter of the fifth century BCE.[32] This was an exceptionally large ship, with an unusually homogeneous cargo of nearly a thousand wine amphorae, the majority of which are Py4a containers from Caere. While the *Grand Ribaud F* was loaded for its last journey in southern Etruria, its geographical coverage was wider. One amphora from the wreck bears graffiti in two languages, an Etruscan inscription naming *MANIIES* on its neck and the Roman numeral *CCCCCCCCII* (902) in Latin on its shoulder. The name is assimilable with a personal name of Campanian origin known in Latium and Rome (Manilius), while the number may be a bill of lading as it seems close to the count of amphorae in the ship's hold. We have no way of determining this Maniies' involvement in the ship's journey – whether he was a captain, landowner, or merchant, for example. However, his name as well as the two languages on this amphora suggest a highly fluid and mobile orientation. This ship was part of ongoing connectivity between the Italian seaboard and the Rhone Valley.

Beneath the layer of amphorae on the seafloor were discovered approximately 30 fragments of bloomed iron sponges. There are no signs of the containers in which the iron was carried, but the original quantity in the hold was likely larger than that.[33] Excavators identify this material's source as northern Etruria. While this assertion should be secured through future scientific analysis, both the spongiform nature of the iron and its stratigraphic position beneath the cargo of amphorae (and thus from an earlier voyage) support this provenance. The identification also gains plausibility from scientific confirmation of Elban hematite from Pyrgi, Caere's port.[34] We can therefore reconstruct this ship's probable route, travelling first south from Populonia to southern Etruria with iron, unloading that cargo near Caere, perhaps even exchanging metal for wine, before taking its final cargo north to France. Iron retained in the hold may have served as ballast.[35] The *Grand Ribaud F* provides the missing merchant ship to complete Diodorus' picture of the southward movement of bloomed iron from Elban mines, in this case in the early fifth century BCE. At the same time, the wreck importantly recontextualises iron's movement within the larger Tyrrhenian distribution of wine and other commodities. The interconnectedness of these movements of goods seems logical but often gets lost in discussions of a discrete metal trade emanating from northern Etruria.

Other evidence confirms that Etruscan connectivities in metal and agricultural produce overlapped. At Fonteblanda, the port of Talamone, in the

---

32 Long *et al.* (2006); the wreck is often overlooked with respect to these finds; see, e.g., Poehler *et al.* (2019), 257, who state flatly that no such maritime evidence exists of trade in slag.
33 Metal ore and ingots seem regularly to have been transported in containers or wrapped in hay or other protective material; I thank Sarah Murray for drawing my attention the fact that bronze ingots in the Uluburun wreck showed signs of hay or other organic material and in the Cape Gelidonya wreck appear to have been transported in baskets; see Bernard (2014) 182 on epigraphic attestation of ore shipped in *skeuai*.
34 Alderighi *et al.* (2013) 173.
35 Cf. Bernard (2014).

context of an articulated settlement, excavation revealed a significant blacksmithing installation relying on Elban iron, while survey of the settlement turned up a consistent scatter of Py3a wine amphorae. The site is interpreted as an *emporium* for the trade of wine and metal. It is even possible wine from the Albegna Valley was exchanged for incoming Elban iron. In any case, these different commodities were all part of overlapping and interacting maritime exchange networks.[36]

Returning to Diodorus' account of a geographically extended chain of iron production linking Elba to Campania, archaeology reveals some parts are accurate and others misleading. It is less apparent that a specific economic relationship ever existed between Elban mines and Campania. Compared to the abundant appearance of bloomed ore at sites along the Italian coastline further north, evidence for Elban iron in the pre-Roman Bay of Naples is not particularly rich. The recently discovered Cumaean evidence for Early Iron Age metalworking has already been noted, and more work is needed to determine the source of metal.[37] Certainly, Campania received its share of Etruscan iron ore, as confirmed by recent excavation of late Republican furnaces at Velia containing spongiform iron fragments identified as Elban.[38] However, these findings do not contradict the broader point that Campania was by no means a special destination for Etruscan iron, and there does not appear to have been a direct vector of metal trade linking the two regions.

How to reconcile the wider distribution of Elban ore with Diodorus' more particular trade network? First of all, it should be emphasised that Diodorus speaks of iron shipments to Pozzuoli 'or other *emporia*', not limiting receipt of iron sponges to the Campanian port city. Pozzuoli may have been singled out because of its fame, or because it was the most important *emporium* at the end of the coastal route south from Etruria, with few other commercial ports in Tyrrhenian Italy further south. Whatever the case, we should emphasise what we know to be accurate, that Elban ore was beneficiated before shipping and smithing this raw material was not undertaken at its place of origin. Instead, northern Etruria, by an early point and possibly already in the sixth century, specialised in a sort of factor market for partially refined iron ore, which was traded widely in its bloomed spongiform state.

Deciding to connect

In an important and still influential paper published 20 years ago, Corretti and Benvenuti reached this same conclusion: that iron from Pithecussae was

---

36 Ciampoltrini (2018).
37 It is worth highlighting the metal work in the urban quarter at Cumae starting from 720 BCE, discussed in preliminary form by D'Acunto (2018). Further work will prove valuable considering the proximity to Pithecussae's metal workshops as well the fact that Cumae colonised Dicearchia.
38 D'Angiolillo and Gasner (2017) 11.

not sufficient to support the hypothesis of an articulated metal trade linking Etruria to Campania already in the seventh century BCE and that the real turn in the region's association with iron production came instead in the sixth century BCE. As we have seen, their hypothesis continues to find support from more recent archaeological discoveries. They also argue that the scenario makes little economic sense. The Euboean Greeks reaching Pithecussae, they point out, could have found iron resources in their immediate vicinity. Why establish far-flung trade networks with Etruscans in the first place?[39]

Iron is one of the more common metals in the earth's crust, far more common than copper and its alloying metals, and it is true that communities south of the Tiber could access iron ore from local sources.[40] High levels of manganese in iron objects from Iron Age Satricum, for example, may suggest the use of bog iron in Latium.[41] Producing usable iron from these local resources was perhaps more labour-intensive, as Elban ore was of high quality and had comparatively high iron content. However, the idea that local resources diminished the impulse to exchange over longer distances fundamentally misunderstands the nature of ancient connectivities. As I have noted already, because many of the commodities moving around the Mediterranean were widely produced, we cannot assume that commercial movement was always the straightforward result of the availability of local resources. The large-scale movement of wine and oil run counter to the principles of a modern economy. The cargo of the *Grand Ribaud F* wreck, as it confirms that metal was a part of this larger commercial movement, suggests that we should also not expect principles of supply and demand to fully explain iron distribution.[42]

In keeping with recent discussions of ancient metal use, I contend that social and political contingencies should be favoured in explaining the development of northern Etruria's iron industry.[43] Of course, the availability of local resources was crucial for the region. This includes both the rich iron mines on eastern Elba and abundant timber for charcoal on the mainland.[44] However, it is also important to recognise that northern Etruria's

---

39 Corretti and Benvenuti (2001) 136.
40 Erb-Satullo (2019) 580.
41 Nijboer (1998) 179.
42 Indeed, one can note that Euboea itself was the area of some of Greece's best local iron mines, and Bakhuizen (1976) 65–9 therefore suggested that early Euboean explorers came to Italy not in search of ore but to trade metal craftwork.
43 Discussions of the Eastern Mediterranean Iron Age have also moved away from trade-based explanations, see Morris (1989); Erb-Satullo (2019).
44 The comment of Strabo 5.2.6 that ore was unable to be brought up to sufficient temperatures for smelting on Elba and was therefore brought to Populonia is usually taken in relation to the necessary supply of timber for charcoal. When Elba's limited timber supplies first necessitated the bringing of ore to the mainland is hard to say for certain, but the fact that raw ore was brought to Baratti by the sixth century BCE may suggest an early date.

elite predated its significant involvement in iron production. That is, the region hosted a complex, stratified society with a wealthy elite before it became a prominent source of iron. Moreover, while Cristofani supposed that the discovery of abundant iron resources helped transform northern Etruscan aristocracies from Villanovan warrior elites into commercial elites whose wealth was based on trading iron – the reality seems less binary.[45]

Elite burials on Elba are attested prior to the sixth century BCE, with some locations showing continuity from the Final Bronze Age. Populonia's first chamber tombs date to the ninth century BCE.[46] In addition, a large elite structure, a hut of the ninth century dubbed by excavators the *casa del Re*, has been found at the summit of Populonia's acropolis, confirming that society was focused on that hill from an early date.[47] Warfare remained an important aspect of northern Etruria's society into the archaic period and beyond, while the dominant classes of northern Etruria, leaders of the so-called *società gentilizia* of Early Iron Age Italy, participated in the exchanges characteristic of Italian elites of the period.[48] Connectivity and commerce were also vital to sociopolitical success in this prestige economy, as is evident from the material culture. Grave goods from Early Iron Age tombs at Populonia included numerous objects produced on Corsica or Sardinia, as well as locally made imitations of such objects, perhaps suggesting that craftspeople were also moving.[49] One particularly rich hoard of metal objects from the site of Falda della Guardiola, perhaps relating to early fortifications around Populonia's hill, contained an eighth-century bronze ship model, well-known from Sardinia and sites along the Italian coast from Croton to Pontecagnano, Portus, Vulci, and Vetulonia.[50] Burials from the Early Iron Age necropolis at Piano and Poggio delle Granate at Populonia include objects with parallels in Latium and further abroad, including a bronze fibula of possible Anatolian origin.[51]

It is likely, in the context of the elite exchange and mobility supporting the consumption of these prestige goods, that Elba and Populonia were brought into closer contact. There has been much discussion over when Populonia gained control over the island, or at least reliable access to its mineral resources.[52] The relationship between the two areas extended back to the Final Bronze Age, when objects of likely Populonian manufacture appear on Elba. The aforementioned Early Iron Age hut on the acropolis of Populonia was sited with a privileged view from its location towards the

---

45 Cristofani (1969); see Bartoloni (2015) 345.
46 For Elba, see Pagliantini (2019) 151–3; for Populonia, see Bartoloni (2005).
47 Acconcia and Bartoloni (2007).
48 For *società gentilizia*, see Di Fazio and Paltineri (2019).
49 Bartoloni (2015).
50 Lo Schiavo and Milletti (2011).
51 Bartoloni (2005).
52 Summary in Corretti (2017) 449–51.

strait of water between Elba and the mainland, suggesting the importance to elite authority of the surveillance of maritime movement along that route.[53] It is clear that Populonia's Early Iron Age elites were engaging in the production of bronze, drawing on inland resources, as evidenced by the aforementioned slag from Baratti beach as well as some evidence for local craftwork. However, this small-scale production was not intended for significant export, and the region's elite groups were as much consumers of metal objects as they were connected with their production, as demonstrated by prestige objects from Sardinian and elsewhere in Early Iron Age tombs. In this early period, the scarce iron objects found are mostly prestige goods, like ornaments or spits which are well associated with elite burials across the Mediterranean, rather than utilitarian instruments.[54]

What then was behind the dramatic increase in iron exploitation and processing in the early sixth century BCE? Research on *Etruria mineraria* has rarely engaged with the question of motives and has generally been content to describe, rather than explain, the emergence of Etruscan ironworking. In discussing the origins of *Etruria mineraria*, scholarship sometimes employs the language of discovery and exploration, with prospectors ranging increasingly widely for novel sources of ore. While there was novelty in the scale of early sixth century BCE ironworking, this chapter's discussion also emphasises continuity in terms of the social networks and seaborne connectivity upon which production depended. Importantly, sixth-century economic changes did not entirely efface the structures of the *società gentilizia*. Bonamici's analysis of the industrial quarter along the beach at Populonia emphasises similarity of architecture and finds with palatial complexes such as Murlo or Acquarossa, where there is also evidence of metal craftworking.[55]

The observation of sociopolitical continuity down to the point of the metal trade's emergence presents the question of why a stable social and technological system transformed when it did. Drawing from work on the rise of iron in post-Bronze Age societies of the Greek Aegean and Near East, we may emphasise the particular role which metal played in state formation processes, and especially the advantages gained by iron over bronze in terms of increased malleability and hardness. As smiths grew increasingly sophisticated at hardening iron, these aspects became important to the production of edged weaponry.[56] Snodgrass identifies a transition in Greece from iron's use

---

53 Pagliantini (2019) 148–9.
54 For iron finds from Piano and Poggio delle Granate, see Bartoloni (2005); for spits, see Kohler and Naso (1991); on their general relation to elite status, see Murray (2017) 269–71.
55 Bonamici (2015) 411–2.
56 Representative of a larger body of scholarship are Waldbaum (1980); Muhly *et al.* (1985); for the Western Mediterranean, see now Nijboer (2018). Relying on archaeometallurgical data, Erb-Satullo (2019) 576–80 questions whether the earliest Near Eastern smiths working with bloomery iron yielded noticeable advantages of hardness over bronze until they mastered carburization and quenching, but it is relevant that Tyrrhenian Italy's ironworking

for ornaments and elite-status goods to tools and, significantly, weapons. A similar pattern takes hold in northern Etruria as well, if at a somewhat later date, whereby iron was devalued from a luxury metal to a base metal prized for its hardness and utility.[57] From the seventh century BCE onwards, spears and swords in central Italy were predominantly made of iron.[58] In ninth and eighth century BCE tombs from Populonia, swords and spear tips (albeit of bronze) appear inconsistently, while at other Villanovan necropoleis from the region, such as that at via Marche at Pisa, weaponry is conspicuously absent among grave goods, and iron is limited to prestige ornaments.[59] In the so-called *tombe a cassone* of the sixth and fifth centuries BCE at Populonia, iron lance points and blades start to appear with more frequency.[60]

Contrary to the idea that the discovery of iron transformed Early Iron Age warrior elites into commercialists, it may have been that involvement in war drove initial demand for good iron. Warfare was changing in scale and scope in the same period that iron production began to expand. The Battle of Alalia, the large naval conflict between Phocaeans, Phoenicians, and Etruscans around 540 BCE, is the earliest encounter of its size known in the region and seems emblematic of a trend of increasingly organised violence. Following the lead of ancient accounts by Herodotus and others, scholarship tends to see the battle as a conflict between territorial states competing over resources and routes. Things may have been trending in that direction and possibly reached that point by the fifth century when the Kingdom of Syracuse sent a fleet to Elba and a series of hilltop fortresses appeared on the island and mainland. However, it is possible that later Greek sources retrojected notions of territorial empire back to a time when, as Bonamici's analysis of Populonia's industrial quarter indicates, elite groups still controlled the exploitation of resources.[61] The earlier situation was fluid, but we might think that iron weaponry increasingly provided means for political groups to

---

developed hundred years after the period to which he refers, by which time hardening techniques were well established in Greece and the Near East. Hardness testing of iron blades from Satricum confirms that their edges were worked to a hardness above or at the upper limits of what was then characteristic for bronze artifacts, although they were not as hard as quenched steel; see Nijboer (1998) 171; Abbingh and Nijboer (2014).

57 Snodgrass (1980) 336–7, noting the comparatively late transition in Italy, although some of his views have been overturned by more recent discoveries in Latium. A similar transition is identified in South Etruria by Hartmann (1985) 285–9. See also Nijboer (2018), extrapolating largely from the appearance of iron knives in Italy a somewhat earlier transition in Latium and Calabria of iron from luxury good to base metal than the one proposed here for Etruria.
58 Egg (2017).
59 For Early Iron Age weapons in tombs from Piano and Poggio delle Granate at Populonia, see Biagi and Milletti (2017).
60 Alderighi (2015).
61 For this process see Terrenato (2019); for the transition of warfare and its relation to state formation and warfare in Rome in this period, see Armstrong (2016a).

gain advantage in the violent conflicts through which territorial control was established and maintained. In short, sixth-century Etruria saw parallel trends of state formation, urbanisation, and the organisation of collective violence, with iron bestowing important advantages in this context.

The rising sociopolitical significance of iron weaponry may explain why elite groups on Elba and the Italian shoreline in the sixth century started to invest in exploiting native iron ores. We still must explain the decision to focus on blooming iron and producing sponges, rather than capture the entire market by producing and exporting finished iron weapons and other implements. The primary motivations in this case are likely ecological and technological. The geographical dislocation of the stages of iron production eased the tremendous demand for timber for charcoal-making, as only charcoal could achieve high temperatures necessary for beneficiating iron. Considering the quantity of metal processed in northern Etruria, the decision to limit production to blooming ore made a major difference in fuel when extrapolated over the long run at such a large scale. One attempt at quantification suggests Populonia's smelting industry at its peak required 77,000 tons of charcoal per year, equivalent to some 270,000 tons of wood, to operate.[62]

There is also the fact that technologies and techniques for smelting ore and for refining and shaping the resulting material (smithing) were sufficiently different such that the former was more readily monopolised while the latter was more diffuse.[63] Calling ancient smelting operations 'industrial' is somewhat misleading, as ethnographic research suggests that blooming iron could be done by teams of four men per furnace, so there is no reason to think that smelting operations extended beyond the capacity of the elite household economies to which Bonamici refers.[64] Nonetheless, smelting was more capital- and technology-intensive than smithing. The high temperatures for smelting were achieved with tall shaft furnaces and forced air through specialised tuyeres. Furnaces lasted a single bloom and then needed to be rebuilt. Because various impurities or overheating could have detrimental effects on the quality of resulting iron, smelters attended closely to the firing process, often lasting several days, manipulating it to change the quality of the bloomed sponges. By contrast, refinement of iron sponges was less resource-intensive, achieved by heating in less controlled fires in open hearths and then repeated hammering. The process as a whole required less labour, although much more skill – and indeed would have required dedicated artisans and craftspeople.[65] Smithing hearths or forges could be simple

---

62 Saredo Parodi (2013) 42–4.
63 For the following, see Nijboer (1998) 150–8. See also Armstrong in this volume.
64 Moesta (1983) 159.
65 See Armstrong in this volume.

constructions, although more complex examples including some with tuyeres are known.

The confluence of specialisations and resources required by the smelting process meant that the circulation of related technological knowledge was more easily controlled. This fact, in combination with the considerable capital cost, may have contributed to a more circumscribed geographical spread as opposed to smithing technology, which is nearly ubiquitous in peninsular Italy and likely circulated along with the craftspeople who engaged in it. It is also important to highlight potential affinities between the ore-processing facility at Populonia and those of Attica. It would not be surprising if the process of smelting created longer chains of technological transfer, with highly specialised artisans connected with it moving along the same exchange networks bringing prestige goods, like Attic pottery, to Etruria.

What we may emphasise is that this entire system worked because of existing connectivities. Not only was technology and knowledge imported into the region via elite exchange, but elites making major investments in smelting equipment could operate under the assumption that bloomed iron ore would find consumers everywhere who possessed the more basic technological knowledge and infrastructure for smithing. The stability of elite society up till the early sixth century was important, as it provided the social networks that made all of this possible. Without the ability to connect, it is hard to understand the initial decision to invest in smelting technology and infrastructure.

Connectivity and social transformations

While this chapter has so far emphasised the continuity of elite groups down to the starting date of northern Etruria's iron industry, by contrast, social transformations accelerate considerably in the subsequent period. The region's metal economy developed during a period of dramatic sociopolitical change across Etruria in the late sixth century; such changes did not spell the end of the elite nature of these societies but rather tended to transform their basis.[66] Evidence from northern Etruria supports the idea that the shift was a radical one in the region. Starting at the macro level of settlement patterns, Elba, by the early fifth century, saw cessation of burial in the island's west and central areas and the rising importance of burial sites towards the island's eastern side, closer to the iron mines, where some of the earliest archaeological signs of iron processing now appear.[67] At Populonia, the Iron Age hut discussed previously, the *casa del re* on the hilltop, was ritually destroyed in the seventh century BCE, while the whole hilltop was

---

66 Synthesis in Pallottino (1984); for the particular effects of this trend on connectivity, see Dietler (2010) 102–3.
67 Pagliantini (2019) 164.

completely abandoned by the mid-sixth century, as the settlement's focal point moved elsewhere.[68] Around the same time, the appearance of a new form of tomb architecture at Populonia, the *tombe a cassone*, has supported discussions of the rise of a 'middle class' of commercial aristocrats involved in trading iron.[69] These *tombe a cassone*, also mentioned earlier for the inclusion among their burial assemblages of iron lance points, were slab-built in rectangular form as self-standing sarcophagi intended for single burials. From the early sixth century through the late fifth century BCE, they appear in the same burial area as monumental *tombe ad edicole*, multi-burial tombs which continued the tradition of the grand tumuli of the earlier period. We should be cautious in interpreting individuals buried in *tombe a cassone* as a sort of 'sub-elite', as is sometimes done, as various sociocultural concerns shaped burial practices, and tomb size, contents, or monumentality cannot be taken as straightforward indices of wealth. Yet, whatever the standing of individuals buried in them, these tombs of strikingly different form, but similar date and spatial arrangement, to earlier burials confirm the growing complexity of the city's social hierarchy.

Around the same time as we see these changes in funerary architecture, we can also detect clear economic interests in the external world. While the epigraphic record is sparse for this period, it furnishes examples of mobile individuals with Greek or other non-Etruscan names.[70] In the fifth, or perhaps even sixth, century BCE, Populonia, Vetulonia, and possibly also Lucca began to strike precious metal coinage on Greek weight standards, far earlier than silver and gold coinages appear elsewhere in Etruria.[71] The extension of exchange networks, on both commercial and social terms, is also legible in the ceramic record. In the mid-seventh century, a group of bucchero high-handled cups of Caeretan manufacture appears at several coastal sites in northern Etruria. Examples from the region, as well as from Caere itself, carry inscriptions with the Etruscan personal name *paiθina*, probably attesting to a Caeretan aristocratic family whose network extended to the mining districts of northern Etruria.[72] By the sixth century, while Etrurian pottery continued to reach the area, its arrival was now paralleled by rising quantities of imports from further afield, particularly with the appearance of Attic pots in large numbers at Pisa and Populonia from c. 540 BCE onwards.[73]

In light of all of this evidence, Cambi justly speaks of a 'Populonian miracle' brought on by the exportation of iron, as the capillary extension of exchange networks for ore returned transformative wealth to the region's

---

68 Bartoloni *et al.* (2015); settlement does not return to the hilltop until the later fourth century BCE.
69 Romualdi (1993) 105.
70 Maras (2015) 57–8; cf. Maggiani (2004), (2006).
71 Vecchi (2012).
72 Cappuccini (2007).
73 Bruni (2004) 244; Maras (2015) 57.

elite.⁷⁴ As we have seen, this efflorescence appears at a time of great social upheaval. What I would like to point out is that it also failed to produce a stable or long-lasting elite. Rather than any particular social group or family emerging from the turbulent changes of the sixth and fifth centuries BCE, it is sociopolitical instability itself that continues to characterise the region for centuries afterwards.

An important ingredient to consider in the failure of any stable social order to consolidate from the changes observed in the material culture of the fifth and fourth centuries BCE is the onset of Roman imperialism. Rome becomes a factor in northern Etruria by the last decade of the fourth century BCE, and the Romans' expansionist ambitions accelerate after the capture of Roselle in 294 BCE.⁷⁵ The effects of this imperial process on the landscape and local populations of northern Etruria were inconsistent. A series of fortresses on Elba and the mainland, built in the fifth and fourth centuries, go out of use, some violently destroyed, in the early third century in the context of expanding Roman military activity. By contrast, the hilltop of Populonia itself re-emerges as an urban site slightly before the arrival of Rome and never seems to have been sacked or destroyed.⁷⁶ No extant source describes Populonia's capture by Roman armies, or any change of the settlement's status into a Roman colony as happened at Roselle. Instead, the recent discovery of a monumental Etruscan inscription from the area of the city's temples confirms an Etruscan-speaking elite continued to inhabit the site into the second century BCE.⁷⁷

It is possible that the continuity visible at Populonia through this period reflects Roman interests in maintaining the region's specialised technological knowledge of iron smelting. While other areas of Etruria saw dramatic change, with the implantation of colonies and villas, the economic basis of northern Etruria remained the same through this period. Indeed, the scale of iron exploitation expanded, likely in response to the considerable new, and Roman-dominated, market for iron. As noted, Camilli's study dates the thickest slag deposit at Populonia to the third and second centuries BCE, while an installation for ironworking was built on the shoreline around 300 BCE and survived down to the late first century BCE.⁷⁸ Archaeologically datable deposits of waste material from iron processing on Elba also point to intensive exploitation during the Republican period. The second century BCE forms a peak for ironworking installations on Elba with sites even located on the island's west side, opposite the iron mines.⁷⁹

---

74 Cambi (2002) 12.
75 For historical narrative, see Harris (1971).
76 For the relevant archaeology, see Acconcia and Nizzo (2009) 61; the acropolis walls may date either before or after the Roman conquest.
77 Benelli (2015).
78 Camilli (2016); Acconcia and Cambi (2009).
79 Pagliantini (2019) 183–4.

Despite this evidence for energetic metalworking, it remains hard to pinpoint elites responsible for this activity. Epigraphy confirms this is not simply a case of the imperial Republican state exercising distant control and removing the local aristocracy, but Etruscan elites seem to have been incorporated into the region's post-conquest society, as we sometimes find elsewhere.[80] The majority of onomastic epigraphy from Populonia in the period remains Etruscan, while names indicate the continued influx of non-local groups.[81] Still, there is little sense that any single family used their new position as an intermediary between the local community and the Roman state to achieve durable sociopolitical success. The region's Etruscan texts reveal few families appearing for more than a generation, and binomial and patronymics are scarce, suggesting a generally lower social background of known individuals, many of whom come from servile backgrounds.[82]

The region's limited Latin epigraphy similarly attests to few individuals with political power on a supraregional, or even regional, level.[83] North Etruria produced no Republican or early Imperial senators. Inscriptions do reveal connections to metalworking, but among individuals of lower status. Two rare instances of the family name Ferrarius (blacksmith), normally an occupational title, appear at Pisa and Populonia.[84] The latter individual, Aulus Ferrarius Salvius, was a freedman whose funerary inscription records his wife or daughter Vettia Nicenus, also a freed slave. Her name suggests a possible connection with an Aulus Vettius inscribed on a third-century BCE black gloss bowl from Elba, found in connection with an active metalworking site on the island. This Vettius is identified as a Roman merchant active in the iron industry. If true, these two individuals provide the only long-term onomastic connection related to the region's metal economy. In general, like this Vettia Nicenus, the region's early imperial epigraphy shows the dominance of freedmen and subaltern classes.[85]

---

80 The foremost study of this phenomenon is now Terrenato (2019).
81 E.g., from the Hellenistic necropolis at Buca delle Fate, a lintel inscribed with the Etruscan name *Craik*[, perhaps *Graecus*; Arbeid (2009).
82 Maggiani (1992) 184.
83 *AE* 1995.500 (Populonia): L. Vesonius IIIIvir, on whom see Ciampoltrini (1994–5); *AE* 1985.388 (Pisa): L. Septimius S.l. IIvir; *CIL* 11.1440: Q. Severus Q.f. VIvir. From later periods, after the iron industry had largely ended, there are a few more individuals of rank: *CIL* 11.7248: P. Acilius Attianus *praef. pr.*, Hadrianic,; *CIL* 11.1432–3 attest to L. Venuleius L.f., a senator from Pisa of the Antonine period; along with these, few members of the *augustales* are attested from Vetulonia (*AE* 1980.429, unnamed) and Pisa (*CIL* 11.1443–4), as are some members of Pisa's *ordo* of decurions (*CIL* 11.1421, 1439, 1440, 1447; *Insc. It.* VII.1.22). For a *princeps coloniae* from Pisa of equestrian rank, see *CIL* 11.1428.
84 *CIL* 11.1471 P. Ferrarius Hermes; *CIL* 11.2605 A. Ferrarius A.l. Salvius. It is hard to find another clear example.
85 Ciampoltrini (2003) 320–1.

Conclusions

While the initial formation of an iron industry in northern Etruria supported, or even perhaps facilitated, changes to the existing social order, over time this iron-producing society was marked by continuous turnover and ultimately failed to produce wider geopolitical power, something revealed not only by new burial patterns, but also by the epigraphic record. A crucial question here is the role of Rome as a limiting factor on the region's social and economic capacity. However, we have seen that iron productivity increases under early Roman hegemony, when there are indications of the continued presence of Etruscan elites. This militates against the idea that Rome was directly responsible for either ending northern Etruria's economic livelihood or altering the possibility for local control and benefit.

In seeking to explain the fate of the region's metal-producing elite, we might focus instead on the initial decision to smelt iron from Elban ore on a large scale. As we have seen, this step was justifiable in light of technological and ecological parameters inherent to metallurgy, and it found a ready consumer base among new, iron-using elites across Tyrrhenian Italy. Thus, the local abundance of good quality iron formed a way for communities in northern Etruria to join into an existing background of maritime movement, at the same time reshaping this connectivity around the export of bloomed iron sponges. However, this particular connectivity may have also carried a certain fragility. The decision to focus on a factor market for only partially processed iron, rather than produce iron weapons and implements, left the region susceptible to alternative sources of ore. By the second century BCE, just as slag deposits suggest exploitation reached a peak on Elba, the region was also beginning to encounter competition. Spain, newly incorporated into the Roman Empire, is widely known for precious metal mines but was also an important source of iron.[86] By the late first century BCE, following the conquest of Gaul, wrecks in the Rhone delta are found carrying iron ingots, and the number of iron sources multiplies into the Empire.[87]

By the late Republic, the iron industry of northern Etruria was in serious decline. Cities in the region were sacked in the aftermath of war between Marius and Sulla, but there was little attempt to rebuild afterwards, and this suggests problems were deeply rooted. Sources report the increasing abandonment of the area by the early Empire. The iron workshop along Baratti beach at Populonia goes out of use, and Elba's iron economy also largely disappears. Archaeology on Populonia's hilltop suggests progressive abandonment in keeping with Strabo's report (5.2.6) that in his time the acropolis was mostly abandoned except for its temples, and only the port showed signs

---

86 Spain's importance as a source of iron is emphasised by Cato in the second century BCE: Gell. *NA* 2.22.28–9 = Cat. *Orig. FRH* M. Porcius Cato F116.
87 Pagès *et al.* (2008).

of occupation. These urban trends may be reflected in the absence of political elites from the region's early Imperial epigraphic corpus.

Later imperial sources report that northern Etruria's landscape of urban settlements, crucial to the production of iron, was transformed into one of agricultural estates.[88] Land on Elba and the opposite coastline was given over increasingly to villas specialising in viticulture or salted fish products.[89] The rise of this villa landscape reflects the replacement of a particular connectivity tied to metal with the more familiar Roman Mediterranean transmarine movement of surplus agricultural produce grown on slave estates.

In sum, metal offered the societies of northern Etruria a way of opting into seaborne connectivities that linked together the communities and economies of Tyrrhenian Italy. However, the particular way in which those links formed posed its own risks. For the wider network of people and goods, the source of beneficiated iron used for smithing operations in Italy did not matter, as the chain of production could continue independent of any particular link. In this situation, connectivity offered possibilities for the iron-producing societies of northern Etruria, while at the same time making those possibilities ephemeral. One central tenant of microhistory is the ability of seemingly idiosyncratic or exceptional examples to reveal broader trends.[90] The aim of this chapter's history of a particular form of Italian connectivity dependent on locally specific resources has not been to suggest that all connectivity was detrimental or produced fragile gains but rather the situation as a whole was less predictable. Just like the metal trade of northern Etruria, we should expect other connectivities in Iron Age Italy to be contingent upon complex concerns with equally complex results.

---

88 Rutilius Namatianus *De reditu suo* 1.224: *nunc villae grandes, oppida parva prius*; this shift was not absolute, however, as confirmed by a new study by Pagès *et al.* (2020) identifying Elba as the source of unworked iron found at several Imperial-period sites in the Rhone delta. Because of inland iron sources in Gaul, the authors suggest this Elban iron was for non-metallurgical, that is cosmetic or medicinal, purposes, but to my mind this evidence reveals the same issues in the later period with understanding distribution as strictly based on market forces.
89 For discussion focusing on villas on Elba, see Pagliantini (2019) 196–206; Genovesi and Megale (2016) publish a coastal fortress at Poggio del Molino north of Populonia transformed in the first century BCE into a productive villa with fish salting vats.
90 Ghobrial (2014) 58.

4 Hephaestus' workshop
Craftspeople, elites, and bronze armour in pre-Roman Italy

Jeremy Armstrong

So saying,
he left her there, and went back to where his bellows were,
turned them to face the fire, gave them their working orders;
and the bellows, twenty all told, blew through their nozzles,
sending out blasts of air from every angle –
at times to support Hephaestus' quick actions, or again
to do whatever he needed to make his work complete.
Into the fire he now cast solid bronze and tin,
silver and precious gold; next he set a large anvil
to stand on its anvil block, and then grasped in one hand
a weighty hammer, in the other his forging tongs.
First he fashioned a shield, both huge and sturdy, adorned
intricately all over, and around it set a bright rim,
three-layered and glinting, complete with silver baldric.
Hom. Il. 18.468–480 (trans. Green)

Made from materials which seem to have held intrinsic value (even in their raw forms), requiring skill, knowledge, and resources to fashion, and representing a physical embodiment of military power (along with, perhaps, social status), the basic characteristics of ancient bronze armour[1] seem to

---

* I would particularly like to thank the Royal Society of New Zealand Te Apārangi Marsden Fund for supporting this work and the invaluable feedback from the two anonymous peer reviewers, and from my co-editor Sheira Cohen. Thanks as well to Seth Bernard, Josh Emmitt, Sally Mubarak, and Gala Morris for reading and commenting on drafts. All errors and omissions remain my own.
1 It is worth noting at the outset that, due to the fundamentally different nature of ironworking and its associated industry/*chaîne opératoire*, this chapter will only focus on bronze equipment and bronze working. While some broad principles may be applicable to both industries, exploring these (and the differences) are beyond the scope of this work. For discussion of the ironworking industry, see Bernard in this volume.

DOI: 10.4324/9781003120728-4

encapsulate much of what we think about when considering ancient 'elites'.[2] The literary evidence suggests that in Regal and Republican Rome, as in classical Greece, bronze armour was effectively synonymous with citizenship and political power, with citizens categorised politically by the types of military equipment they owned.[3] Like the imported pottery often deposited alongside it in archaeological contexts, bronze armour found in Italy typically carried foreign associations. These range from the use of styles and forms which first appeared outside the peninsula,[4] to hybrid designs and decoration with subtle artistic nods to other cultures,[5] to the use of imported technologies and materials.[6] Indeed, almost every facet of bronze armour seems to have emphasised some sort of connection with the wider world – itself a common feature of 'elite' identity across the Mediterranean basin since the Bronze Age.[7]

Despite being both influenced by, and part of, wider networks and interactions, these pieces of armour were not wholly foreign though, nor could they be. As much of this equipment (or something similar to it) was likely used on the battlefield and in combat situations,[8] it presumably needed to

---

2 'Elite' status is a difficult term to unpick in any period, but particularly in the early periods of Italian prehistory before we have solid evidence for stable and embedded hierarchies. Given the absence of evidence, it is arguably impossible to identify elites via the usual methods in this period and place, and thus put them into the categories typically deployed for historical societies (reputational, decisional, or positional). However, the broad definition of a group 'defined by their influence on strategic (political) decisions that shape the living conditions in a society' (Hoffmann-Lange [2007]) is arguably still applicable – at least at the local level. In addition, it may be useful to adopt a more archaeologically sensitive definition, like that offered by Earle and Kristiansen (2010), whereby elites are seen as those who are able to express status and wealth through the ownership of objects deemed valuable by a society. Finally, we can consider elite status as functioning in connection with, and in support of, wider elite networks, where status was partially determined and modulated by principles of hospitality, gift-giving, and reciprocity.
3 For Greece, e.g Ar. *Ach*. 57, 278; Plut. *Mor*. 241; Xen. *Lac. Pol*. 11.3.4; Plut. *Pel*. 1. For Rome, famously, Livy 1.43 and Dion. Hal. *Ant. Rom*. 4.18.
4 This includes the crested bronze helmets which seem to have origins in continental Europe (see Iaia in this volume for discussion).
5 See particularly the various Italic derivatives of helmet designs which seem to have originated in Greece – most notably the Apulo-Corinthian varieties. See Paddock (1993) 78–81 for discussion.
6 This will be discussed in more depth below, but, given the geographically bounded sources for copper and tin in Italy, for most pieces of bronze armour, the raw materials required for their construction would have needed to be sourced far from their end-users.
7 See, most notably, Broodbank (2013).
8 It must be noted that there is a longstanding debate over the practicality of some pieces of equipment (see Egg [2017] for discussion), and particularly the bronze crested helmets of the Late Bronze Age/Early Iron Age. Some of these pieces of equipment, for instance the eighth century BCE helmet from Tomb 871, Casal del Fosso necropolis, Veii (now on display in the Museo Nazionale Etrusco di Villa Giulia in Rome), would never have been worn in battle due to its crest of over half a meter. However, many other crested helmets could have been functional and it is likely that they at least resembled equipment worn in battle in order to keep their martial overtones.

be something which worked for local people on a practical level.[9] While scholars might allow archaic Italian elites to possess imported pottery simply to demonstrate their connections and status (a dubious proposition which has increasingly been challenged),[10] military equipment arguably requires a deeper and more functional place and role within a local culture.[11] It was worn to physically protect its user in a specific context and thus it needed to align with local military norms and practices.

Ancient bronze armour can therefore be found at the nexus point of at least two distinct elite networks – a wider social and economic Mediterranean network, full of symbolism and regional interaction, and a local framework which emphasised more political, practical, and often violent expressions of power.[12] Because bronze armour is found across the Mediterranean basin, the comparison of equipment types and styles can offer vital information about the position of the end-user within the complex set of relationships which bound together the ancient Mediterranean world.[13] A 'Greek style' helmet found in Italy may hint at links with the eastern Mediterranean, while the deposition of more 'Italic' forms of armour (e.g., the triple-disc cuirass) may emphasise more local connections. But even without these more subtle associations, bronze armour has become an easy and useful identifier for 'elite' status – if an individual is found buried or otherwise associated with bronze armour in the ancient Mediterranean, they are automatically considered part of the local elite.

I would suggest, however, that this picture of the elite associations of bronze armour is still incomplete. To date, most interpretations of ancient bronze armour have focused on their end-user(s): the elites who used, deposited, or were buried with it. Increasingly, however, it is clear that this may only be scratching the surface of the networks and contexts within which these items reside.[14] On the other side of the equation there exists another set of networks, which had both regional and local aspects, focused on producers – although it has not often been explored in this context. There is, in both the evidence and scholarship, a bias towards the final product and its consumer/user. This is due to a range of factors, including an assumption (within both the ancient literary evidence, and modern receptions of it) that industry is somehow naturally 'non-elite', at least in productive

---

9 Famously, on the connection between military technology and society, see Keegan (1993).
10 See particularly Armstrong and Rhodes-Schroder (forthcoming).
11 Bishop and Coulston (2006) vii; Echeverría (2011).
12 This sort of nexus point between local and Mediterranean-wide elite networks is obviously not limited to bronze military equipment.
13 This is particularly important in the context of the more unified and connected Mediterranean world, and Mediterranean elite, which has become common since Horden and Purcell (2000) and Broodbank (2013).
14 See Hirth (1996) for general discussion. More recently, and on the ancient Mediterranean, see Manning (2018).

terms. Elites were obviously allowed to (and indeed expected to) control the industry, but they are not thought to physically produce goods themselves.[15] This subtle denigration of production is also a result of the relatively light archaeological footprint left by most ancient industries, as many could be classified as household or cottage industries.[16] Additionally, there has long been an archaeological bias towards sites and contexts which contain finished items, and indeed towards recording and preserving finished items, rather than exploring production contexts. After all, a finished pot looks much nicer in a collection than the remains of a kiln. Thus, our current models and interpretations prioritise the consumers and end-users along with the role which the finished items played in expressions of their identities. However, it is increasingly clear that the finished product and its consumer(s) is only half the story.

Beyond simply representing symbols of elite status as finished artefacts, I would suggest that the very act of producing bronze armour may have also represented an expression of elite power. Bronze armour required metal to make, itself a form of wealth, and many stages of its *chaîne opératoire* were resource-intensive, requiring the mobilisation of significant amounts of wood (for charcoal) and labour. Additionally, and of at least equal importance, it required specific knowledge and expertise. The ability to mix bronze of a suitable composition for the piece being created,[17] cast it into an appropriate blank or sheet, and then work that by hand into its final shape required immense skill – even for what might be considered rather simple pieces.[18] The ability to do this work would have been incredibly valuable, particularly given the evident social and practical importance of the final objects. The skills involved would have also carried a strong interregional flavour, likely embedding the craftsperson within a wider network, as they were applicable across a wide area and often utilised forms, styles, and technologies from a range of regions and cultures. The production of bronze armour is therefore firmly entangled within a number of elite networks of varying size and reach, which included knowledge networks (of styles, productive techniques, and technologies), resources (most notably furnaces and charcoal), and likely even norms/agreements of movement and hospitality.[19]

15　McDonald and Clackson (2020) 75 note: '. . . individual artists . . . are much harder to track and, unlike the careers of elite men or soldiers, craftsmen's lives are rarely memorialised in literature or outlined on gravestones'. Cf. Kuijpers (2013) 140; Molloy and Mödlinger (2020) 177.
16　Molloy and Mödlinger (2020) 193–8.
17　Admittedly, by the Early Iron Age this phase may not have been a particularly difficult process, as many objects seem to have been relatively simple Cu-Sn alloys with Sn in the range of 7.5–12.5 wt.%. Further, this process would have been simplified by recycling bronze.
18　Doonan and Dungwort (2013).
19　Isayev (2017) 101–3; McDonald and Clackson (2020) 75–97. See also Robinson and Bernardo-Ciddio in this volume.

Exploring the production of bronze armour may therefore give some insight into a new, often invisible, 'productive' category of elites. This is not to say that early Italian elites, as traditionally considered, are never credited with creating things, as famously many of early Italy's temples and other public works are often seen as local elite productions.[20] However, the vast majority of elites who commissioned structures did not dirty their hands with the actual construction. For this, they relied on invited artisans and craftspeople, with established reputations and networks, to complete various projects. A notable example is the Etruscan artist Vulca, who famously made the cult statue for Rome's great temple to Jupiter Optimus Maximus (Pliny *NH* 35.157). These were not simply transactional hires, which occurred in a purely economic system. The Greek artist Phidias, although not descended from the traditional aristocracy, was seemingly able to cultivate a relationship with Pericles by virtue of his reputation and skill (Plut. *Per.* 13.10). I would suggest that exceptional artists like Vulca and Phidias represent merely the tip of a vast iceberg of 'productive elites' who were able to exist and operate in the Mediterranean's elite networks. These individuals' claim to power and status was perhaps closest to merchants, or even religious specialists, as it was channelled through their specific knowledge and connections.[21] They are therefore part of the wider discourse on 'travellers as agents of change' – practitioners of knowledge who acted as instigators of technological diffusion and cultural change.[22]

Investigating these productive elites and their networks should have a significant impact on how we understand military equipment functioning within ancient societies. This, in turn, can reveal much about the nature of elite networks more generally as the two connect and likely overlap. Most notably, while the consumers of the items remain a vitally important part of the equation, a fuller understanding of the productive networks which helped to create them may alleviate some of the burden which elite consumers carry in current models, particularly as the primary drivers for change and innovation.[23] While it is probable that consumers had significant input into the production of items, at the very least through selecting and commissioning pieces which suited their needs, they were also confined by the nature of the industry and the productive elites which created them. The power dynamic was not entirely one-sided.

The full exploration of the productive processes for ancient bronze armour is far beyond the scope or ability of this chapter. However, the discussion which

---

20 Smith (1996).
21 Interestingly, as Molloy and Mödlinger (2020) 208 argue, there seems to be a strong connection between ancient metallurgy, religion, and festivals. Indeed, as Haack (2017) 1002 noted, various aspects of metalworking in ancient Italy (during the archaic and early Roman periods) may have taken place in, or were otherwise associated with, shrines and religious spaces.
22 Aslaksen (2015) 12. See also Iaia in this volume.
23 See Bernardo-Ciddio, in this volume, for a discussion in relation to ceramic production.

follows will sketch out the basic principles by which they can be understood in this period. In this, it will focus on the nature of control and interaction within the various systems, resources, and networks involved in the production of bronze armour in pre-Roman Italy and the way in which this control was focused at particular nodes of production. These networks and nodes can further expose the wider productive systems and so-called 'communities of practice' which existed in various industries – and indeed are discussed elsewhere in this volume by Bernardo-Ciddio. In this model, the networks are composed of both the various entities and resources as well as the relationships which linked them together. In a basic sense, this can be understood as part of the *chaînes opératoires* and involves the procuring and movement of resources, both the basic materials needed for alloying bronze and the labour required to work it, as well as access to the knowledge required to use those resources to produce different items. The present chapter will highlight the relationships and networks of elite individuals that underpinned the production process. These networks seem to have come together at particular nodes of production where activity seems to have been focused and where we might be most likely to find productive elites in place to dominate the industry – either financially or through their control of specialised knowledge. These nodes include the initial mining and smelting operations as well as the craftspeople who carried the knowledge required to create these objects and the workshops where they worked. Understanding the basic nature of these networks and nodes, some of which existed outside of, or at least independent from, urban zones, may help to shed some light on the productive side of the elite equation.

Chaîne opératoire

The full *chaîne opératoire* for making bronze military equipment is complex and not always linear (Figure 4.1). However, it is worth running through the basic systems in order to understand the various types of control, and where that control might be focused, in the networks and nodes.

First, the raw materials for an item had to be sourced, most notably copper. Discussions of ancient Italian metalworking virtually always begin, and arguably quite naturally, with mining for the raw metals needed for bronze. Italy offers a range of metallic ores needed for the production of bronze, particularly in the Colline Metallifere, Elba, and Latium (Monti della Tolfa).[24] Indeed, the area between the Cecina and Bruna Rivers is so rich in these ores that it is often called the *Etruria mineraria*.[25] These deposits have

---

24 Zifferero (2017) 425. As Molloy and Mödlinger (2020) 201 note, scholarship has seen the 'pendulum swing away from analyses of crafting objects and towards the extractive metallurgy side of craft, along with research into the trade of metals. The technological and geo-graphical origins of copper have been at the forefront of archaeometallurgy since the early 1990s.'
25 See Corretti and Benvenuti (2001) for discussion. Ore deposits do not generally appear south of Latium, or indeed east of the Apennines (see Dolfini [2019]).

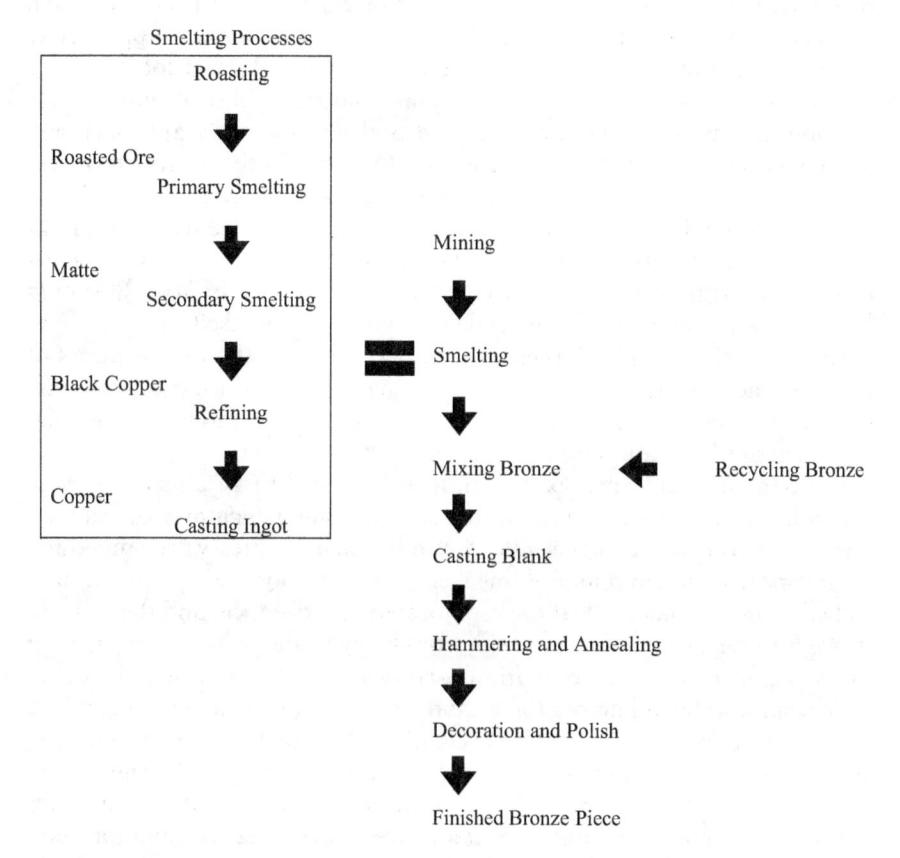

```
Smelting Processes
        Roasting
           ↓
Roasted Ore
        Primary Smelting
           ↓
Matte
        Secondary Smelting            Mining
           ↓                             ↓
Black Copper            ═══          Smelting
        Refining                        ↓
           ↓
Copper                              Mixing Bronze  ←  Recycling Bronze
        Casting Ingot                   ↓
                                    Casting Blank
                                        ↓
                                 Hammering and Annealing
                                        ↓
                                 Decoration and Polish
                                        ↓
                                 Finished Bronze Piece
```

Figure 4.1 Basic *chaîne opératoire* for producing bronze armour.

been exploited since at least the Chalcolithic period but were extensively mined during the Iron Age and would have formed one of the primary sources for raw materials supplying the metalworking industry in Italy.[26] Countless publications have been devoted to describing these mines and their exploitation, so this will be discussed only briefly here.[27] The process began with identifying a viable vein of ore. The easiest way to do this was to find one which was already being exploited. This occurred in the Renaissance (and indeed in modern times) when many ancient mining sites were reopened and likely occurred in antiquity as well. However, new veins were also exploited, which could be identified by seeking signs of sulphide deposits

26 Northern Italy, and particularly Liguria, should not be discounted; Dolfini *et al.* (2020).
27 E.g., Mascaro *et al.* (1991); Mascaro and Cuteri (1995); Giardino (1995) etc. See Zifferero (2017) for relevant summary.

or mineral-rich waters near karst caves. Once a vein had been identified, one needed to control the physical location and mobilise an appropriate labour force, both of which presumably required at least a local base of power. One should not overstate the point though. Although mining was a labour-intensive process and required both an organised approach and specific knowledge, the physical work itself was evidently not the most specialised.[28] Excavations in pre-Roman Italy were often entirely manual,[29] and there is little evidence that the work was particularly skilled – as pick marks are usually haphazard and uneven.[30] Given the size of the mines, with shafts of less than 1 m in diameter (although with galleries of up to c. 800 m in length), the number of people needed to work a mine itself may not have been large either.[31] Indeed, there is evidence that only the richest pieces of ores were actually taken out of the mine, suggesting a concern to maximise the quality, as opposed to quantity, of the output. It is entirely possible that a mine might be a family-run operation.

Once the ore had been extracted, it would need to be crushed, sorted, ground, washed, and transported to a smelting site, which may or may not have been connected to the mine.[32] While smelting sites were sometimes located near mines, and indeed this seems to be the norm, they did not have to be.[33] Indeed, sometimes they were located at a distance, and there is evidence for ores of various types (esp. iron) being traded and transported out of the region as well – not only from locations like Elba to the mainland, but also around Italy and across the Mediterranean.[34] Efficient smelting, which seems to have been the norm by the eighth century BCE (as the residual slag shows that the vast majority of copper was extracted), required a high degree of technical skill in controlling the furnace temperature and ore amounts. It was also a complex, multi-phased process involving roasting, primary smelting, secondary smelting, and refining, before the copper ingots could be produced.[35] More importantly, however, the smelting process required substantial amounts of fuel to be concentrated in a single place at a specific

---

28 Primas (2008) 135.
29 There is evidence of fire-setting from Bronze Age Liguria to loosen to the ore. See Dolfini (2019). However, by the Iron Age, most mining in Italy appears to have been manual.
30 Zifferero (2017) 430.
31 Ibid.
32 Nijboer (1998) 144.
33 Nijboer (1998) 31.
34 Nijboer (1998) 165. See Bernard, in this volume, for more discussion of iron ores. In addition to those noted by Bernard, iron ore was also found on the Les Sorres IV shipwreck near Barcelona dating to the second half of the first millennium BCE. For examples of other types of ore being shipped, over 1 ton of lead ore was found in the Bajo de la Campana A wreck (c. 600 BCE), lead ore was also found on the Rochelongue shipwreck (550 BCE) off the coast of France, and some evidence for it was also found on the Ma'agan Mikhael shipwreck near Haifa Israel – see Brown (2011) appendix for a more complete listing.
35 See Muhly and Kassianidou (2012) for discussion.

time. Ore must be heated to between 1100 and 1200°C to release the copper, although even then it may be difficult to recover and a flux is often needed.[36] This temperature cannot be easily achieved with an open fire but is possible with a simple furnace with good air supply.[37] The process also requires a large amount of fuel.[38] The charcoal-to-copper ratio for smelted oxide ores seems to range from a minimum of 20:1 to as high as 40:1.[39] Furthermore, even the most generous wood-to-charcoal ratios suggest that one would require at least three times as much wood (by weight) for the needed charcoal 'charge'. Thus, for 40 kg of charcoal, one would need 120 kg of wood.[40] In order to smelt a single 25 kg ingot of copper (the average size for an oxhide ingot), a smelter would need, conservatively, between 1,500 and 3,000 kg of wood – and that is without considering the additional requirements of high-efficiency smelting.[41] Given these issues, it makes sense to centralise this sort of process, and there is evidence for smelting occurring on a large scale in a single location, particularly when it comes to iron.[42] The same rules should generally hold true for copper as well, at least during the Italian Iron Age. Once the copper had been smelted, it could be (and evidently was) transported widely, as seen in the presence of copper ingots in ship cargo from the Middle Bronze Age onwards – most famously as part of the *Uluburun* shipwreck (c. 1300 BCE).[43]

36 The high efficiency copper smelting of the Italian Iron Age evidently required even higher temperatures, perhaps up to 1400°C. This allowed smelters to extract more of the copper from the ore, and to make use of poorer ore, although it also resulted in higher iron content (up to 40% in some cases) which had to be removed before the copper (or resultant bronze) could be worked by hand. See Merkel (1982), (1983), (1985); Craddock and Meeks (1987).
37 Coghlan (1975) 26–37; Tylecote (1987) 106–33, 179–83.
38 Cristofani (1986) 123; Craddock (1984) 216; Cucini (1992).
39 Horne (1982) 12; Craddock (2000).
40 *Ibid.*
41 Forbes (1966) suggests a figure of 90 kg of wood to 1 kg copper, resulting in a total of 2,250 kg of wood for a 25 kg ingot.
42 See Bernard in this volume. Smelting iron is generally a more intensive process, in virtually every respect, compared to smelting copper. Smelting iron benefits from an atmosphere which is low in oxygen, and so virtually necessitates the use of charcoal. The higher temperatures (at least 1535°C, likely closer to 1600°C) would have necessitated more fuel. The initial smelt also did not produce a finished ingot, but rather a 'bloom' ('a viscous, spongy mass of iron, slag, and charcoal' Horne [1982] 8) which must be further hammered, using heat of up to between 1250 and 1400°C (depending on carbon content), to create useable iron. After this, the working temperature of the iron is usually c. 800°C, which is achievable in a far more basic setup. The first phase of iron smelting would have required roughly comparable amounts of charcoal/wood to copper smelting (20–40 kg of charcoal per kg of copper, or 60–120 kg of wood), with the addition of another 20 kg of charcoal (60 kg of wood) for the second phase of working the bloom. It should also be noted that many early blooms seem to have been much larger in size, c. 50 kg, than copper ingots (Smil [2013] 137). All of this would have also, likely, required a specialist furnace needed to reach those temperatures consistently.
43 Hauptmann et al. (2002).

The next stage in the *chaîne opératoire* was alloying the copper into bronze and casting it into a shape suitable for working. Although these processes were often connected, it is worth considering them separately for reasons to be discussed later. First, there is the alloying process. The smelted copper is re-melted at between 1100 and 1200°C. However, this process is arguably much simpler than the smelting process due to its smaller scale. Instead of requiring a large furnace, suitable for holding many kilograms of ore, metalworkers only needed to heat up a small crucible usually holding 3 kg or less of material.[44] While this process still required a reasonable amount of fuel, it did not require a custom furnace, and the process could arguably function alongside other industries, most notably pottery production, which required comparable temperatures. Once molten, alloying agents would be added – including tin, lead, and possibly arsenic[45] – to create the required bronze. There is good evidence to suggest that metalworkers carefully manipulated the alloying elements in order to create a specific type of bronze which suited their needs – for instance, with a higher lead content to improve ductility and lower viscosity if they were going to cast a statue or bust.[46]

This brings us to the second part of this phase: casting the 'blank' or 'sheet'. Once the bronze was molten and of the right composition, it was cast into the shape which would then be worked/finished by hand. Weapons made from bronze (including swords and axes), more typical of the second and third millennium BCE, would have been cast into something roughly resembling their final form and then finished by hand with cold hammering and annealing.[47] However, these had been generally replaced with iron weapons by the first millennium BCE, and the vast majority of bronze equipment of this period consists of relatively thin armour (typically under 1mm thick) and shows little evidence of an initial cast shape. To create these, craftspeople cast the bronze into flat forms (typically 6–8 mm thick, as above that the metal is difficult to work) which were then shaped by hammering.[48] This system is uniquely visible in the Corinthian-style helmet, which typically features a

---

44 Gardner's (2018) work on crucibles in Roman Britain has shown this appears to be optimum size and it corresponds well with the typical weight of extant pieces of bronze military equipment, which are uniformly under this weight.
45 It must be noted that we are still uncertain how arsenical bronze was produced, although adding 'pure' arsenic (As) to the copper (Cu) is unlikely, as there is no evidence that As had been identified as a discrete element in this period. It is possible that the As was simply naturally occurring in some copper ores, or that it was added through the use of 'fahlore' or mixing different ores. This is in contrast to the use of tin or lead, which were certainly added as metal, given their lower melting and sublimation points.
46 There is evidence for this across Europe and the Mediterranean from the early Bronze Age. Manipulating the alloy to create a material with the right hardness (ability to resist deformation), toughness (ability to absorb energy), and malleability (ability to deform without breaking), was vital (Molloy and Mödlinger [2020] 210).
47 Sapiro and Webler (2016).
48 Papadimitriou (2001); Nerantzis (2012); Mödlinger (2014).

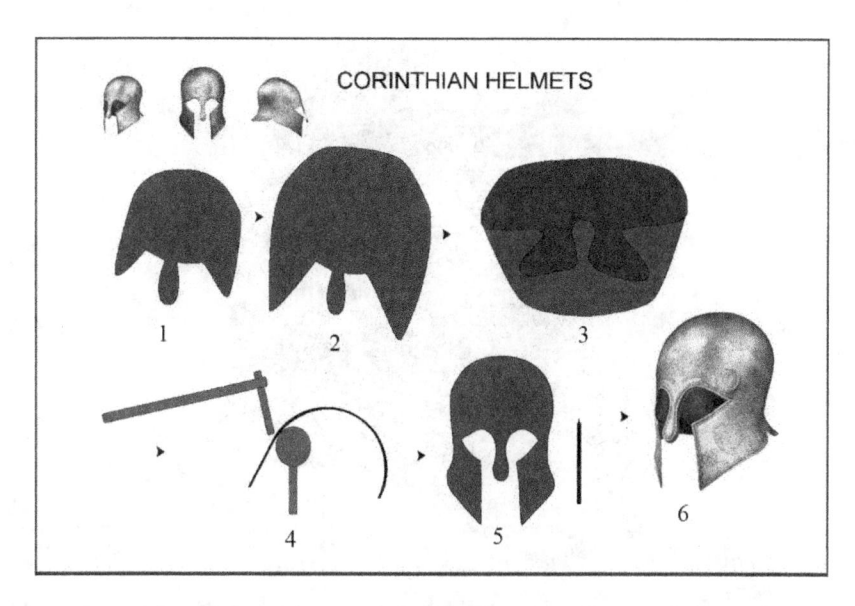

Figure 4.2 Making a Corinthian-style helmet, from cast form to final product.
Source: Courtesy of Nicholas Harrison, Redoubt Forge, NZ.

nose guard (and sometimes eye and rim features) that is cast into its final form (Figure 4.2), while the rest of the helmet is hammered into shape (see Figure 4.3).[49] This casting process for the Corinthian-style helmet is likely indicative of the degree of forethought used in casting shapes for all pieces, even when working from a sheet-metal base. While it is possible that craftspeople could work a simple, uniform sheet into any number of different armour types and shapes, it is probable that the dimensions of the cast sheet/form were planned with the finished product firmly in mind. Stretching a bronze form by hammering carries the risk of cracking the metal, which is difficult to repair without substantial reworking. Additionally, although the vast majority of individual pieces of Italian bronze armour weigh between 1 and 2 kg, and so could have been made using pours from comparable crucibles, it would have saved countless hours of hammering and annealing to cast the metal into something approximating the final dimensions of the desired piece.[50]

---

49 This productive process has been demonstrated by analyses done at the Royal Ontario Museum on their 'Nugent Marathon helmet' (ROM no.926.19.3), where the nose guard is an incredible 10mm thick, areas around the eyes thinned to between 2 and 3mm thick, while the crown and rear of the helmet has been hammered to less than 1mm thick. See Mason (2014) for images and discussion.
50 Treister (2001) 35–7.

Figure 4.3 Corinthian-style helmet (early fifth century BCE).
Source: Unknown provenance. Metropolitan Museum of Art (Accession Number: 2016.235a). Used with permission under OASC license.

There was only so much a craftsperson could do by casting though, at least when making armour and using the type of bronze which seemed to be favoured for this type of item down to c. 400 BCE.[51] The Cu-Sn alloy[52] used for military equipment typically resulted in a cast form which was both porous, due to dissolved gases, and brittle, due to the formation of the eutectoid.[53] In order to turn this cast alloy into a piece which could be useful as armour, it needed to go through an extensive hammering and annealing process. This process removed the porosity and increased its ductility and hardness, resulting in a thin piece of armour which was nevertheless effective when backed with organic elements (leather, felt, etc.). However, it meant that skilled hammering was always required for military equipment when using this type of bronze for this purpose. This is in contrast

---

51 Armstrong *et al.* (forthcoming).
52 Typically, c. 85% Cu, c. 10–12% Sn, and 3–5% trace elements. See Molloy and Mödlinger (2020) 202–6 for more general discussion of alloys in use broadly across Europe and the Mediterranean in this period. Molloy and Mödlinger (2020) 201 also note that smiths were 'unlikely to be working to the sub 1% margins of error that our [modern] scientific analyses reveal.'
53 Ancient bronzes were impure and imperfectly mixed, and so often display both dendritic structures and various types of segregation. See Scott (1991) 5–10 for discussion.

to the type of bronze working seen with statuary, which was generally cast, often using bronze with a higher lead content which improved the pour but resulted in a softer metal. Provided the surface was free from defects, it did not matter if the bronze of the statue was porous or brittle, as it usually did not need to withstand significant punishment. Consequently, the next stage of armour production involved extensive working of the cast item by hand – including annealing, hammering, polishing, punching holes, chasing or engraving decoration, adding attachments (often soldered on), and adding the final polish. The amount of work required at this stage would have varied significantly by item, period, and region – even within the relatively narrow confines of this study (Italy, c. 900–400 BCE) – but was always present. Finally, almost all bronze items were combined with organic elements of various types which functioned as liners, padding, harnesses, and straps/attachments.

Once completed, the items would then enter the 'marketplace', although what that means in practical terms is uncertain.[54] It is probable that many items were 'made to order' for specific individuals. While some types of equipment, for instance Negau-style helmets, often featured relatively uniform decorative elements, the elaborate decorations found on many others, from ornate crests to chased/repoussed designs (see Figure 4.4),[55] suggest at least

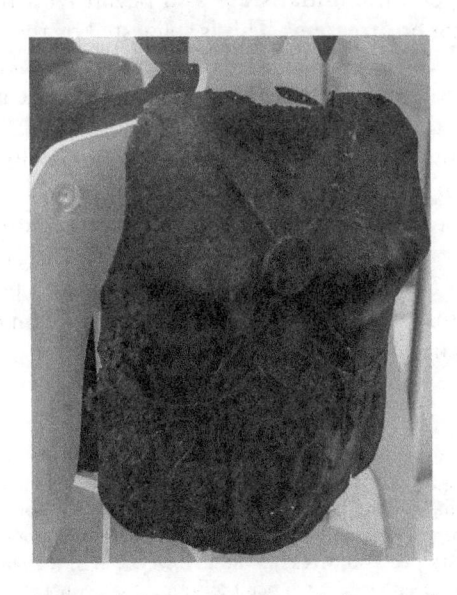

Figure 4.4 Repoussé girdle with faces and a suspended pectoral, possibly a single-disc.
Source: Reggio Calabria, Museo Nazionale, (Inv. 11803–11804). Photograph courtesy of Dan Diffendale.

---

54 See Becker in this volume for discussion of marketplaces.
55 See, for instance, the bronze cuirass shaped to mimic the anatomy of an Amazon from the Room Tomb, Marcellino, Fig. 4.4.

a degree of choice was involved. There is also some limited literary evidence for the commissioning of large orders, as with Dionysius I's order for 140,000 shields in the early fourth century BCE (Diod. Sic. 14.41–43). Alternatively, looking at fourth century BCE Athens, there do seem to have been stores and warehouses for these items as well (Dem. 45.85; Lysias 12.4–19). Although this aspect is beyond the limits of the present study, which is focused on productive processes, the control and distribution of completed objects is an important area which is deserving of further study.

Resource networks

In the *chaîne opératoire* given earlier, several different resource networks are required. First, those associated with the raw materials for bronze. The trade networks that were needed to acquire relatively rare elements, like tin, have long been a topic of research and hint at the wide-ranging nature of these productive networks from an early period.[56] At its most basic level, all bronze originates in this resource network. However, it is worth noting that metals could also be acquired through the use of recycled materials. Indeed, it is probable that the *chaîne opératoire* for the vast majority of bronze pieces of equipment skipped the initial steps and began with the re-melting and recycling of existing bronze items. This is suggested by the ease and efficiency with which bronze can be recycled (with a minimal loss of tin or other scarce elements),[57] the evidence for extensive recycling of bronze in Italy going back to the Bronze Age, the large hoards of bronze from the Early Iron Age found at sites like Bologna,[58] the limited nature of ore deposits compared to the wider metalworking industry, and the costly nature of smelting in terms of fuel. While access to local sources of new copper would have added to the available pool of material, control of mines and smelting operations did not give individuals or communities a monopoly on bronze production. Craftspeople, at least in this area and period, were not dependent on them as source of material for their work.

---

56 The source of tin for early Italian bronze is debated. Tin, in the form of cassiterite, can be found in Campiglia and it is often argued that this was exploited in antiquity (Warden [1984] 353; cf. Nijboer [1998] 164). Indeed, Craddock (1984) notes that bronze artefacts in Italy generally contain a slightly higher percentage of tin than those in Greece, hinting at increased availability. See also Meeks (1986). However, even if available within Italy, this element would have been far more difficult to source than copper and the recent discovery of tin ingots from a shipwreck at Hishuley Carmel off the coast of Haifa, originating in Britain and dating to the late Bronze Age (see Galili *et al.* [2013]), suggests that these networks could extend very far indeed. Pernika's (currently ongoing) ERC project exploring tin-isotopes may change this situation (see, for example, Berger *et al.* [2019]).
57 On the scarcity of tin see Pernicka (1998) and Vandkilde (2016). On the minimal loss of elements in recycling see Mödlinger *et al.* (2019).
58 For Bronze Age recycling see Iaia (2015), for the bronze hoards at Bologna see Sassatelli (1981).

A second resource network relates to fuel. Bronze working requires some degree of heat at almost every stage in the production. Whether it is the intense heat needed to smelt the raw minerals from the ore, to the more moderate heat needed to anneal a piece while working it with a hammer, the requirement for fuel for a fire was a virtual constant. However, the amount varies with different processes, as does the ability to utilise the same fuel/heat for different purposes. By far the most fuel intensive processes, and those which allow the least economy in terms of energy use, are those involved in smelting. As noted earlier, every 25 kg ingot of copper would have required, conservatively, between 500 and 1,000 kg of charcoal (which would in turn have required between 1,500 to 3,000 kg of wood). This fuel would have been packed into custom-made furnaces which would typically be destroyed after a single use. The re-melting and mixing of the copper with various elements to create the desired alloy (or, in the case of recycling, the melting of existing bronze pieces) was also fuel intensive. However, it was arguably more efficient and certainly more flexible. While the furnace still needed to reach roughly 1200°C,[59] it only needed to heat a crucible holding 3 kg or less of material and could therefore be achieved using a much simpler and more economical arrangement. It is possible that they could have used a pottery kiln or similar set up (although the different functions and the need to remove a crucible at 1200°C may have necessitated a slightly different design). Whether the crucible was heated in a pottery kiln or a custom furnace, kilns would have been ideally suited for both creating and preheating moulds. The ability to use the same space and resources for two industries would have lowered the effective fuel cost, and both would have used many of the same bellows and assorted infrastructure. Thus, the casting and working of bronze could have occurred anywhere with a functioning pottery industry. As many moulds are made from fired clay, the two industries likely functioned in tandem. Finally, the hammering of the bronze items would have required heat to regularly anneal the piece while working it. This could be achieved using an open flame, although a kiln would have been preferable.

A third resource network can be seen in the organisation of manual labour throughout the production process. The most labour-intensive processes were again those at the beginning – the extraction of large quantities of ore and the creation of copper ingots. This included mining the ore, removing it from the mine, transporting it to the smelting site, and then smelting it. However, the amount of labour needed should not be overstated, and the

---

59 Copper melts above 1083°C, but needs to reach a constant temperature of c. 1100°C to pool in the crucible. 1150°C would represent the operating range for alloying, and the temperature at which the tin usually be added; 1200°C would then be the optimum temperature for the alloy and crucible before removing it from the furnace, in order to keep it hot enough to stay fully molten for the pour.

way in which it was deployed was not uniform. Ethnographic parallels from iron smelting in Africa, which requires a higher melting point, suggest a furnace could be built and run by only four people.[60] The most significant labour would be in transporting the needed ore and fuel, which could take place over many weeks. Once the copper ingots were created, they were much more portable and could be transported along with other items of comparable size and weight. Labour would also be required in the re-melting and casting phase, similar to what would be needed to work a pottery kiln. The only other significant labour need would be the intensive hammering needed to produce sheets (perhaps no more than three people – one person to hold the metal, and one or two people to hammer it), as well as the hammering needed to complete the final item. However, for the latter at least, this required a highly skilled workforce.

Of all the resource networks in play in the production of bronze military equipment, however, the most important were the knowledge networks. All stages required knowledge of specific processes, although the amount of input needed varied. Mining required its own unique set of skills in terms of identifying sources of ore and planning the extraction layout. However, once a viable vein had been identified and developed, the work seems to have been largely a process of unskilled, manual labour. The same is true for the extraction of the ore and the transport of it, along with the fuel needed, to the smelting site. Smelting required knowledge of how to build and pack the furnaces as well as how to maintain sufficient heat to extract the copper. However, all of these systems could be managed using the input/knowledge of a single, well-placed individual coupled with large amounts of resources. Skilled knowledge became much more important at the next stage, which involved re-melting the copper and mixing the bronze. In every case, including where existing bronze was being recycled, the craftspeople needed to carefully select and mix the elements to create the right type of bronze for the desired product. For instance, too much iron would make the bronze brittle, although a small amount would result in a dense and ductile alloy. Higher lead content would create a very pourable bronze which was good for casting, but not particularly useful for armour. Thus, each individual crucible would have to be carefully prepared. Also in this stage, the craftspeople had to create the required mould and then cast the shape that would subsequently be worked by hand. In some cases, and particularly in later periods (c. 400 BCE), this cast shape required only minimal additional hammer work and polishing to complete. However, even with simpler casts, the process required skill and experience. A good knowledge of forms and styles was also important as the basic shape of items would be determined at

---

60 Moesta (1983) 159. See Nijboer (1998) 173 for discussion, who notes 'This figure includes the production of charcoal, the mining of ore and the building of a furnace which took about 2 days.'

this stage; the cast blank for a Corinthian helmet would have been entirely different from that needed for a Negau-style helmet or a Montefortino helmet. While quite a few items could be formed from a single sheet of bronze, including cuirasses and the bronze covers for aspides, even here the size and thickness mattered immensely. The difference of only 0.1 or 0.2 mm across an aspis would add a significant amount of weight and material.

The final stages of production – which involved hammering/annealing, engraving or stamping decoration, adding attachments, and polishing – were almost all highly skilled labour and would have required years of training and experience to master. While some aspects, for instance the flattening of sheets, could probably have been delegated to apprentices or assistants, even these would have required strict oversight in order to ensure that the metal was not being overly thinned or becoming too brittle and cracking – a duty presumably performed by the individual actually handling the metal, as it is typically done by feel.

Nodes of production, nodes of control

There are three distinct places where the various resource networks involved in the *chaîne opératoire* of bronze military equipment came together into what we might call 'nodes of control': the mine, the smelting site, and the workshop (Figure 4.5). These are places where the resources and knowledge needed within the industry were relatively centralised and localised in a single, physical space and thus where they could be easily controlled. They

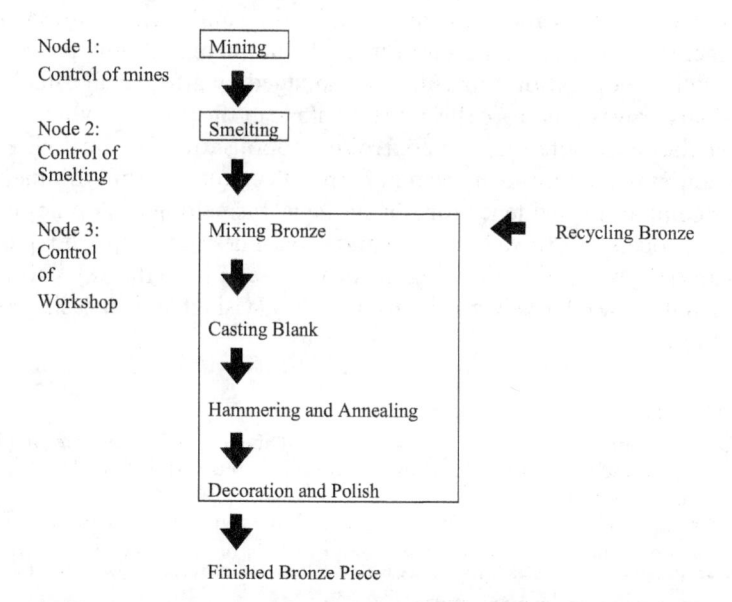

Figure 4.5 Chaîne opératoire for bronze armour with 'nodes' of control.

represent vital choke points within this industry, and it was only by controlling these nodes that one could control the production and spread of items.

The copper mines represent the first of these nodes.[61] In one respect, these were relatively easy to control as they were fixed locations, but they required labour to work them. As noted, there was probably significant labour costs involved in removing the ore and transporting it to the smelting site, although it is uncertain whether the transportation of the ore should be considered as part of mining, smelting, or an entirely different transport process. There seemed to be minimal skill involved in this aspect of the process, apart from identifying viable sites for mines. Although mining would have benefited from economies of scale, with the average yield of copper to ore being 1% or less, there is no reason to think that mines had to be large or 'elite' operations necessarily – although the control of land may have necessitated some degree of local power.[62]

Smelting sites were another key node of control. These sites would have required and contained huge amounts of resources, including literal tons of both ore and fuel as well as people able to work the furnaces. It is not clear how consistent or long-term such smelting work was, and it may have been seasonal.[63] The ability to mobilise, organise, and protect this collection of resources – almost all of which needed to be locally acquired – hints that at least this node should be associated with local elites and/or local communities (it is possible that this was achieved through a less hierarchical organisational model). It is therefore, perhaps, not surprising that recent excavations have found smelting sites associated with sanctuary sites in archaic Italy.[64] This process also involved significant skill and knowledge in terms of constructing the furnaces and managing their loading and temperatures in order to extract the maximum amount of metal from the ore, although even for a relatively large operation this could be managed by a relatively small set of individuals. It was therefore this node, or stage in the process, which seemed to offer the most potential for control/monopolisation by local elites and communities – and indeed, as seen in Bernard's chapter in this volume, there may be comparable evidence for this in the iron smelting at Populonia. The smelting process prioritised location and economies of scale with regards to raw materials, while also allowing the producers to keep the key knowledge in the hands of a relatively small group if they wished and to easily control the output.

---

61 It is worth noting that we do not know a great deal about tin mines and ore, and how it was produced, so tin steps into the network here only at the workshop level.
62 Ellingsen et al. (2015).
63 Molloy and Mödlinger (2020) 208 have suggested that certain parts of the *chaîne opératoire*, and particularly those associated with fire, may have been attached to festivals and other annual cycles. This would make some sense, given the need to stockpile charcoal in advance of major smelting operations.
64 Haack (2017) 1002.

Once this copper was smelted and put into circulation, however, the control of the product and production seems to have devolved.⁶⁵ This is a widely visible pattern and there are many ethnographic parallels illustrating that the groups who exploit the metal ore are often not the same as those who work it.⁶⁶ Once smelted, copper (and bronze) could be recycled almost endlessly, allowing craftspeople and consumers to circumvent the first two nodes of control.⁶⁷ Indeed, as noted earlier, bronze recycling was likely widespread in Italy from the start of the Bronze Age.⁶⁸ Not all pieces of bronze would have been as easy to recycle as others, most notably, the high iron content in the bronze often used for 'ramo secco' bars, *aes signatum*, and *aes rude* may have complicated matters as separating iron from copper alloys is problematic even in modern industry.⁶⁹ However, the vast majority of bronze found in archaeological contexts from 900–400 BCE in Italy could be recycled as part of new items. Craftspeople would need to be careful about the relative amounts of various elements, most notably tin and lead, as they crafted their new alloys. But, with the notable exception of iron (where even small quantities can make a significant difference to its properties),⁷⁰ bronze seems to have been a relatively forgiving medium which was conducive to recycling from multiple sources. In this way, bronze working was fundamentally different from many other industries, like pottery and textile production, as it did not necessarily require a connection to new, raw resources (clay, wool, etc.). The industry could sustain itself indefinitely by recycling older and broken pieces of bronze, which seem to have been relatively widely available.⁷¹ One should not push this too far, as it is likely that local warrior elites pursued and attempted to control bronze in whatever form it took from at least the Bronze Age.⁷² Indeed, as previously noted, bronze seems to have been a form of currency from the beginning of the first millennium BCE in Italy and there

---

65 As Georgakopoulou (2016) 47 suggested, these two activities represented part of the 'metal production' phase, which is separate from the 'metal working' phase, and seem to feature an entirely different set of choices and processes.
66 Rowlands (1971) 210–24, esp. 212.
67 Georgakopoulou (2016) 46–67.
68 See Zimmermann (2007) and Iaia (2017) 742. Cf. Bartoloni (1989) 32–3; Maras (2017) 281–2. There is comparable evidence from elsewhere in the Mediterranean as well, for instance there is evidence from Cyprus that this was widespread in the Eastern Mediterranean by the thirteenth century BCE (Pickles and Peltenburg [1998]).
69 This is one of the key functions of 'roasting' the ore, which is the first step in the smelting process. The copper ore is heated to c. 590°C, which removes some more volatile impurities (arsenic, mercury, etc.), as well as some iron through oxidation. However, Tylecote and Boydell (1978) suggested that one could drop the levels of iron down to 0.5% with relative ease – simply by sprinkling clean sand on the top of the molten bronze and skimming off the residue. The remaining amount still had a significant impact on the metal, however, and it is clear that craftspeople worked hard to purify things even further. See Craddock and Meeks (1987).
70 See Nerantzis (2015) for discussion based on experimental data.
71 Nijboer (1998) 146.
72 Earle and Kristiansen (2010) 227.

is a long tradition of capturing bronze armour from defeated warriors, visible from Homer onwards, which may have not only represented a trophy but also a way to control the raw material.[73] However, it is clear that the materials needed for the bronze industry were not controlled by the owners of mines and smelting sites, thus placing a greater emphasis on the final node of control, workshops, where this material was actually transformed into high-status items.

Workshops seem to have been one of the most important nodes of control, and yet also one of the more flexible. It must be noted that while, for the purposes of this study, we are considering that mixing/casting, hammering/finishing, and even the addition of organic elements all occurred at the same workshop, this was not necessarily the case. In the case of bronze Etruscan mirrors, the existence of blanks suggests that the final stages of work could occur much later and possibly in a different location – as the work which occurred after casting required very little in the way of infrastructure or fuel.[74] However, it is entirely possible (and indeed plausible) that they did occur in a single workshop and, even if they were spread across several different workshops, each of these dispersed spaces would have functioned along similar lines. We must also consider that these workshops were possibly multi-craft sites and thus metalworking may have only occurred for a portion of the time, or even infrequently, at such sites.

Perhaps the more accurate way to think about this node then is not as a 'workshop', at least in the sense of a physical space, but as a skilled craftsperson and their social circle.[75] Although work may have happened in dedicated workshops, as we can see in the late Bronze Age workshops at Frattesina[76] or various sites in Sardinia,[77] the industry was ultimately structured around a series of highly skilled craftspeople (and their associates/dependents) who carried the required knowledge and skill with them (Figure 4.6).[78] This con-

---

73 Armstrong (2016a) 100.
74 Swaddling *et al.* (2000) 117–40; Caccioli (2009) 39. Although it must be noted that it is entirely possible that they were never meant to be inscribed.
75 See Nørgaard (2018) esp. 307–8 for a discussion of a comparable situation in the Nordic Bronze Age. See also Levy *et al.* (2007) for a modern ethnographic example from southern India as well.
76 See Salzani (1989), (2000).
77 Lo Schiavo (2012).
78 It may be worth differentiating the various levels of 'craftspeople'. At the most basic level, this term could include anyone with the specialist knowledge which allowed them to control production beyond that of a novice. Within this, though, there would have been significant variation. Following Kuijpers' (2018b) 550 classification of four levels of metalworking ('the amateur, showing basic knowledge but little refinement; the craftsperson, producing well-made practical objects; the master, striving for perfection and setting the norm; and the virtuoso, taking risks in creating original and unique products.') there were undoubtedly various levels of expertise present amongst Italian metalworkers, each one presumably corresponding to a level of elite status, both within the industry and amongst other types of elites.

Figure 4.6 Bronze armourer working on a helmet (late eighth to early seventh century BCE).

Source: Unknown provenance. Metropolitan Museum of Art (Accession Number: 42.11.42). Used with permission under OASC license.

cept fits broadly with the literary evidence. The trope of an itinerant smith is a familiar one in the ancient Mediterranean and has been a regular theme in the study of ancient bronze working going back to Childe in the 1930s.[79] Although their level of embeddedness and role as fulltime craftspeople are still hotly debated,[80] it seems clear that these figures were both common and hugely important. They were capable of carrying with them all the most important aspects of the metalworker's trade in the form of their knowledge and skill, and only required readily sourced materials (a kiln/furnace with fuel, a small store of bronze to recycle, and perhaps extra tin or lead to include) to create bronze military equipment.[81] The specialist tools required by a bronze worker were minimal, including hammers, tongs, small crucibles, moulds for casting, chisels, and various types of small, stake

---

79 Childe (1930). See Iaia in this volume.
80 E.g., Rowlands (1971); Neipert (2006); Nørgaard (2014).
81 As Georgakopoulou (2016) 49 noted, since the Late Bronze Age, bronze working was an inherently mobile industry.

anvils. All of this could be easily packed onto the back of a donkey and carried from site to site.[82] Provided the next location has a functioning pottery industry with a kiln and access to fuel (arguably even at the household level), craftspeople could easily use existing infrastructure to work. Indeed, similar models may have also been at play in other industries, like the production of rooftiles, where epigraphic evidence hints at a highly mobile set of artisans and workers despite the industry's reliance on materials which were difficult to transport across long distances.[83] It is likely that the local community provided the infrastructure and raw materials, while the craftspeople supplied the expert knowledge to create a specific commission before moving on. This is not to say that this is how these individuals always functioned or that the most extreme position – of the smith as a 'nomadic outsider' – was the norm. Bronze working, and particularly military equipment production, seemed to function alongside other industries in the community, most notably pottery (which shared similar fuel requirements) but also textile and leather industries (for padding and organic elements), and eventually iron.[84] Additionally, given the elite associations with military equipment, smiths may have attached themselves to other elites or elite groups for protection, to facilitate travel, and perhaps even for a steady market/demand for their items.[85] However, this attached or embedded status should not necessarily diminish either their potential mobility or their status within the community, as there is comparable evidence for elites becoming 'attached' in archaic Italy – albeit in a social, military, and religious context (for instance as patron–client or, on more equal terms, as *suodales*).[86] The central point is that these craftspeople likely had transportable and transferable value, by virtue of their skill and ability, which they may have been able parlay into social and cultural status.[87]

This situation also allowed for a fluid and dynamic movement of style and technology. Rather than being tied to particular and geographically fixed 'productive centres' during the first half of the first millennium BCE, as is often supposed, bronze working was potentially as mobile as the craftspeople who practiced it. This allowed new techniques and styles to travel quickly across the Mediterranean, as indeed we see in the archaeological

---

82 Indeed, the presence of items associated with the production of bronze items (esp. moulds) in graves from Bronze Age Europe hints at both their strong association with specific individuals and their portable character. See Overbeck (2018) for catalogue and discussion.
83 Bernard (2017); Bonghi Jovino (1990) 49–54.
84 See Molloy and Mödlinger (2020) for more general discussion.
85 For examples from the Near East, see Zaccagnini (1983).
86 Armstrong (2016a) 142–4.
87 Alternatively, as Nørgaard (2014) 40 provocatively argued relating to the Nordic Bronze Age, the ability of craftspeople to embody value may have led to a slightly different types of exchanges amongst elites – as she suggests 'what if not the *goods* but the *craftsmen* able to produce such high quality work were exchanged?'

record. It also allowed for a dynamic, responsive, and direct relationship between producer and consumer which may have helped facilitate the range of regional styles we see across Italy during this period.[88] However, despite all of this dynamism, it may have also promoted a degree of conservatism in the fundamental nature of the craft. Key to the status of the craftspeople was their monopoly on the skills and knowledge needed to mix the bronze, cast the base shape, and work each individual item by hand. Thus, although styles varied, the basic nature of production – hammering Cu-Sn bronze alloys by hand into relatively thin pieces of armour – did not change for hundreds of years and indeed can be tracked back into the Middle Bronze Age.[89]

There are indications that this situation began to change from the fifth century BCE onwards with a rise in the use of casting for specific pieces of bronze armour. Beginning in the late fifth century, there is increasing evidence for items which were cast into a form very close to their final shape, as opposed to being cast into a rough blank or a sheet and then hammered into shape. Although there is nothing to stop an individual craftsperson from casting an individual item in this way, this technique is conducive to mass production and the shift coincides with what has been called a wider 'democratisation' of military equipment in Italy with simpler designs and placement in graves associated with a wider cross-section of the socio-economic spectrum.[90] Coinciding with this development, there is also an increase in the use of iron as part of bronze armour, particularly as hinges and attachments. The working temperature for iron (723–c. 900°C) is actually lower than that required for casting bronze and roughly the same as that needed for annealing bronze. Thus, this work could have occurred in the same workshop and using the same infrastructure, although the metals behave very differently and the skills required to work them (hammering iron and casting bronze) were increasingly diverging and possibly becoming more specialised in this period. This combination of factors suggests that the physical space and infrastructure of the workshop, in contrast to the individual craftspeople, was becoming more important in this later period. In this situation, a single workshop could produce a large amount of bronze military equipment relatively quickly with a single 'master craftsperson'. Skilled hammer work would still be required for the iron, although this was an industry which seems to have been far more widely spread and non-elite in nature, attested by the ubiquity of iron tools and implements which seem to have been produced in small farms and hamlets.[91]

Once items left the workshop, they were functionally complete and would have then gone to the marketplace, or wherever these items were transferred

---

88 Paddock (1993).
89 Mödlinger (2018) 177–98.
90 Burns (2003) 74; Paddock (1993) 45.
91 Nijboer (1998) 158–62.

from craftspeople/workshop to consumers. For the purposes of this study, we have not included this as a node as it is not technically a part of production, although it would have certainly represented another control point.[92] However, our information on the market for these types of items is incredibly vague, and indeed it likely varied based on region and context. As noted previously, speeches from Lysias offer evidence for stores selling armour and weapons in Athens and we have several references to states or leaders commissioning craftspeople to create equipment for armies. We have very little evidence for how individual warriors acquired their arms and armour and whether there were social and cultural controls on its acquisition, in addition to the obvious economic cost.

Evidence from craftspeople, ancient and modern

The tremendous importance, flexibility, and potential mobility of individual craftspeople in the production of bronze armour, suggested by the *chaîne opératoire* and nodes above, is also supported by the (admittedly limited) ancient textual evidence, as well as by modern experimental archaeology. Beginning with the ancient textual evidence, perhaps the best evidence for the military equipment industry in the western Mediterranean is given by Diodorus Siculus in his discussion of Dionysius I's preparations for war c. 400 BCE. He notes:

> At once, therefore, [Dionysius I] gathered skilled workmen, commandeering them from the cities under his control and attracting them by high wages from Italy and Greece as well as Carthaginian territory.... After collecting many skilled workmen, he divided them into groups in accordance with their skills, and appointed over them the most conspicuous citizens, offering great bounties to any who created a supply of arms. As for the armour, he distributed among them models of each kind, because he had gathered his mercenaries from many nations; for he was eager to have every one of his soldiers armed with the weapons of his people, conceiving that by such armour his army would, for this very reason, cause great consternation, and that in battle all of his soldiers would fight to best effect in armour to which they were accustomed. And since the Syracusans enthusiastically supported the policy of Dionysius, it came to pass that rivalry rose high to manufacture the arms. For not only was every space, such as the porticoes and back rooms of the temples as well as the gymnasia and colonnades of the marketplace, crowded with workers, but the making of great quantities of arms went on, apart from such public places, in the most distinguished homes.
>
> Diod. Sic. 14.41.3–6 (trans. Oldfather)

---

92 See Becker in this volume.

Although one should obviously take this account, written centuries after the fact, with a healthy dose of scepticism, the picture it paints is instructive and aligns well with the models presented earlier. We see that Dionysius I was able to recruit a large number of evidently mobile craftspeople from across the region who are able to produce equipment in a range of different styles with minimal infrastructure (e.g., in temples and gymnasia). In this account, it seems clear that the key component in the productive system was the mobile craftsperson and not a stable workshop or pre-existing industry.

Turning our attention towards Rome, although we do not have any direct evidence for the production of armour comparable to the passage in Diodorus, there are hints that Rome also existed within a similar system – acting as a hub for mobile metalworkers and craftspeople in this period. For instance, there is the reference to the Gallic craftsman Helico, who Pliny suggests may have contributed to the Gallic invasion of 390 BCE.

> It is related that the Gauls, separated from us as they were by the Alps, which then formed an almost insurmountable bulwark, had, as their chief motive for invading Italy, its dried figs, its grapes, its oil, and its wine, samples of which had been brought back to them by Helico, a citizen of the Helvetii, who had been staying at Rome, to practise there as an artisan (*fabrilem ob artem*). We may offer some excuse, then, for them, when we know that they came in quest of these various productions, though at the price even of war.
>
> Pliny *NH* 12.2 (trans. Bostock)

Although it is uncertain what sort of industry Helico was involved in, metalworking is arguably one of the more likely options given the long-standing associations between this industry and Cisalpine Gaul. Either way, we have some anecdotal evidence for a Gallic craftsman of some type moving from northern Italy to Rome, and back again, in the period c. 400 BCE,[93] and evidently one with enough wealth to purchase and transport dried figs, grapes, oil, and wine to take with him.

The ability of relatively mobile craftsmen to produce bronze military equipment is also supported by recent experimental data. Researchers from the University of Auckland, working in collaboration with Redoubt Forge

---

93 As has been hinted at previously, the situation after 400 BCE seems to change in Italy, and this is particularly relevant with the working of iron. Some of this might be evidenced by the fascinating discovery of the San Vittore sword (a La Tène sword found in San Vittore del Lazio) dating to the second half of the fourth century BCE which bears the inscription: TR POMPONIOS C (F.?) (M)E FECET ROMA(I). 'Tr[ebonius] Pomponius, (son of) Gaius, made (m)e in Rome' (see Taylor [2020] for discussion). The reference to the location where the sword was made, as well as the craftsman, is instructive. This is also the period within which we begin to get makers marks on some (Montefortino) helmets, albeit stamped and not inscribed (Paddock [1993]).

Figures 4.7a–d Experimental archaeology in the construction of a Negau helmet. (a) Melting bronze in a temporary furnace; (b) Shaping the Negau helmet; (c) Hammers used to shape the Negau helmet; and (d) use of a pneumatic power hammer to stretch the initial bronze sheet to c. 1.5 mm.

Source: Photographs courtesy of Nicholas Harrison, Redoubt Forge, NZ.

of Hamilton, New Zealand, have been working to recreate ancient Italian bronze armour since 2018, and the results have been instructive.[94] Much of the work is still ongoing and will therefore be discussed in detail in future publications, but an initial conclusion is that the work is incredibly portable. The c. 2 kg of bronze needed to create virtually any individual piece of bronze armour can be melted using a small furnace which can be constructed in a weekend (Figure 4.7a). The initial casting of the blank or sheet of bronze is a somewhat fraught process, in terms of achieving the right shape as well as issues with large grains, dendritic structures, and porosity,[95] although it turns out bronze itself is a very forgiving medium if it is going to be hammered. With annealing, which can happen in an open flame, the crystalline structure of the metal can be 'reset' and all gases and defects in the initial cast form can be worked out by hand with limited tools (see Figures 4.7b–d).

94 This work was supported by the Royal Society of New Zealand Te Apārangi Marsden Fund project 'Blood and Money: The 'Military Industrial Complex' of Archaic Central Italy' (17-UOA-136).
95 See Scott (1991) esp. 5–6.

The largest takeaway from this experimental work so far has been the central importance of the skilled craftsperson wielding the hammer. Indeed, almost all the work was completed by a single individual, although some phases would have benefited from the addition of assistants. For instance, the furnace would have been fed by bellows which needed to be worked by hand. The initial stretching phase, working the cast form down to a workable thickness of c. 1.5mm, would have likely involved the use of two 'hammer men' (one with tongs and one with a hammer) – this was replicated with the use of a pneumatic power hammer. Overall, however, this was not a large operation.

Conclusions

It seems clear from this brief exploration of the topic that the basic nature of bronze military equipment production in Italy has been misjudged. Typically, scholarship has focused on the end-users and, when production has been discussed, has highlighted the obvious connections between mining, smelting, and metalworking to connect Etruria – and particularly sites like Vulci or Arezzo – with important and supposedly established metalworking workshops. The industry has generally been envisaged as a fixed and stable one, under the control of communities and/or local elites,[96] and simply feeding the elite desire for metal items.[97] However, while the production of the raw materials needed for bronze working at these key sites is important and may have led to higher levels in circulation locally, this model places too much emphasis on a linear, and 'from scratch' *chaîne opératoire* and largely ignores the availability and implications of recycled bronze.[98] A significant percentage, and indeed likely the vast majority, of bronze equipment was made from recycled material and so could have circumvented these nodes of control. Instead, and of far greater importance to the industry, is the workshop level of production and, within that, individual craftspeople. These individuals held the knowledge needed to create the appropriate types of bronze, to cast it into the appropriate shape/sheet, and then to finish the work with a hammer and various surface treatments (grinding, polishing, decoration, etc.) before finally adding any organic elements (padding, etc.). The minimal infrastructure they required could be either carried with them

---

96 See, for instance, Paddock's (1993) regular references to hypothesised workshops associated with particular communities (e.g., Vulci workshop A, or Vulci workshop B).
97 As Molloy and Mödlinger (2020) argue, metalworking is often seen as supporting local elites, and not as an independent set of processes.
98 This is not to say that new material was never needed. While craftspeople could recycle bronze easily, and check the composition visually (similar to the medieval use of touchstones), at a certain point, or in certain situations, they would have needed new material (Cu and Sn) to achieve the desired alloys. However, I would emphasise that this was likely more the exception than the rule.

or sourced locally within any community which had a functional pottery industry. While significant casting operations, for instance those associated with large statues or later types of military equipment (from c. 400 BCE), may have somewhat prioritised the physical workshop over the individual craftsperson, it is likely that the master craftsperson still maintained a position of personal prominence.

A key aspect of this productive landscape therefore seems to have been its fluid, seemingly devolved, and dispersed nature.[99] The networks, through which the resources and knowledge seemed to flow, were in many ways fluid by definition. But, perhaps surprisingly (given our usual fixation on urban zones and communities), while some nodes were geographically stable, the most important ones may have been mobile and transitory. Physical workshops may have provided stable centres for production, but their importance for a single industry may have waxed and waned. It is likely that many workshops were multi-craft zones, and bronze working occurred alongside both pottery production and leather/textile working at many sites. Indeed, given the importance of fit for armour (a point emphasised by Xenophon),[100] and the use of padding and other organic elements to achieve it, significant cooperation between industries was almost certainly required along with some direct contact with the client. More importantly, craftspeople, the holders and curators of the specialist knowledge and skill required to make this equipment, seem to have been highly mobile and were able to travel across the Italian peninsula (and the wider Mediterranean) with an ease normally associated with elites. Indeed, as suggested at the outset, it may be useful to think about these craftspeople as representing part of a different type of 'elite' network based on their knowledge and skill and not, or at least not directly, due to any military or political power.[101]

Within this context, it is probable that these craftspeople were often attached to either other elites, traditional elite groups, or elite networks which may have facilitated their travel or accommodated their stay in various locations. Such connections were necessary at a basic level for craftspeople to know where their skills were required; how would Dionysius I have been able to summon enough craftspeople to produce his 140,000 shields without a network to communicate through? We should also not assume that, simply due to their knowledge and evident mobility, *all* metalworkers

---

99 The same is arguably true for iron working, and for good reason. As Corretti (2017) 456 notes, 'this system distributed the environmental and economic problems connected with charcoal production to a wider area, since every step of the ironworking process (from smelting to refining to forging and shaping) was located in a different place.'
100 Xen. *Eq. mag.* 13.1.3; Xen. *Mem.* 3.10.9–15.
101 Following here the view of 'elites' offered by Earle and Kristiansen (2010), who suggested that elites were those who were able to express status through the ownership of objects deemed valuable by a society. See also Helms (1993), who pursues a similar argument regarding the elite nature of productive transformations.

were independent elites or itinerants of the Childe model.[102] It is entirely possible that many individuals involved in this industry were enslaved people. In Nørgaard's analysis of craftspeople in the Nordic Bronze Age, she suggested that craftspeople were exchanged among the elite, effectively as a type of prestige good, in the same way the items they produced were.[103] Something similar may have happened in early Italy, reminiscent of the trade and exchange of Greek intellectuals as slaves in the later Republic.[104] However, as Bernard's analysis of workers' signatures on roof tiles and other architectural elements from Hellenistic Italy (300–50 BCE) has revealed, while skilled artisans were sometimes enslaved they could also be found across the socio-economic spectrum up to elite masters.[105] We should therefore be careful not automatically relegate all metalworkers to followers or enslaved people or vice versa. Taking the parallel of artists and coroplasts, it is clear that there were also men like Vulca or Damophilus who seem to have functioned within the same social, economic, and hospitality networks as the elite consumers who acquired their wares. Whether they were masters or slaves (or located somewhere in-between), it seems evident that craftspeople existed as part of an elite productive network which seems to have been distinct, albeit connected, to the more traditional elite networks developing around Italy's urban centres.

Like Hephaestus crafting armour for Thetis and Achilles offered in the passage at the beginning of this chapter, those who controlled the production of ancient bronze armour likely held power and prestige through their ability to create the tools needed by other elites to express their martial ability. Also, like Hephaestus, we should not always assume a strict economic relationship. The divine smith did not create armour for everyone, and indeed did not charge an economic fee for his labour – although, in this instance, it was in response to a personal debt (Hom. *Il.* 407). Armour was often gifted or formed part of the social and cultural relationships which bound elites together. We should consider the possibility that mobile craftspeople were an important part of the complex elite networks which existed across the ancient Mediterranean, not as humble servants, but as elites themselves. Or, at the very least, we must recognise that they were not quite as dependent on early Italy's burgeoning urban zones and traditional elite structures as we often suppose.

---

102 It is clear that the situation is more complex, see Rowland (1971) and Nørgaard (2014).
103 Nørgaard (2014).
104 Hunt (2018) 92.
105 Bernard (2017).

5 Potters and mobility in southern Italy (500–300 BCE)

E.G.D. (Ted) Robinson

We have become accustomed in these last few decades to understanding that mobility and migration were the norm in the ancient Mediterranean, rather than the exception. Already a decade ago, Moiatti was able to claim that 'The importance of mobility in early societies now no longer needs demonstration.'[1] She was mainly interested in the early Principate but Isayev's study, concentrating on Italy in the mid-late Republic, clearly shows that similar conditions existed earlier.[2] In southern Italy, though, conditions had changed dramatically in the third century BCE. Roman control had led to the disappearance of many towns and sanctuaries as well as large-scale population movements in and out of the region. Yntema characterised the major trends from the mid-third century as 'detribalization, peasantization, urbanization and Mediterraneanization'.[3] In the fifth and fourth centuries BCE, southern Italy gives the appearance of having settled into a series of polities with stable social and cultural institutions. The Greek cities on the coasts were large, urbanised centres with constitutional governments and clearly defined territories. Beyond those territories, in the zones controlled by Italic peoples, there was a wider variety of social, political, and territorial organisation. Strong levels of cultural diversity in the region was a persistent phenomenon over several centuries and, despite the appearance of various Greek objects, practices, and technologies in the Italic settlements (the phenomenon previously known as 'Hellenisation'), an argument could be made that an Italic settlement and a Greek 'colony' were *less* similar in 400 BCE than they had been in 700 BCE. How is this to be explained?

There has not been an explicit discussion of cultural diversity in South Italian archaeology. Since interpersonal encounters are generally seen to

---

1 Moatti (2013) 77.
2 Isayev (2017). I take the evidence of the comedies of Plautus to be highly significant, since they show us the assumptions of the audience. These were that mobility was ubiquitous and that people from elsewhere were commonplace, yet xenophobic ethic labels and caricatures are more or less absent in the plays (rather unlike Greek 'New Comedy').
3 Yntema (2013) 268.

be strong vectors of cultural assimilation,[4] the (largely unspoken) explanation for persistent cultural diversity in southern Italy is a presumed low level of interpersonal encounters. Greek and Italic communities are still seen as largely closed to each other. There was some trade, of course, but binary opposition and military hostility between the two groups are generally stressed.[5] This chapter seeks to reassess evidence for the mobility of individuals in 'classical-period' (c. 500–300 BCE) southern Italy from outside the region, between Greek cities, and between Greek cities and Italic centres.[6] It will argue that, in the fifth and fourth centuries BCE, painted pottery gives us by far the best evidence for personal mobility. It will ask whether the high level of mobility seen among ceramicists has implications for wider questions of trans-cultural mobility. That is, does the movement of artisans, that we can trace archaeologically, have any implications for our understanding of the larger number of people whose movements are more difficult to follow?

Stepping back into the immediately preceding period, the sixth century BCE in southern Italy was one of significant identity creation among the Greek cities as large cities and territories emerged; it was the period in which the *origo* myths, which offered a single, unifying origin story for each Greek city, were plausibly created.[7] Identities solidified, although we are perhaps too seduced by our knowledge of the strict citizenship laws of Periclean Athens since most scholars imagine that it was relatively difficult to move from one Greek city to another.[8] As for moving from an Italic centre to a Greek one, many seem to imagine a type of ethnic hostility which would have largely precluded it.[9] While it is true that there were major wars between Greek cities and their Italic neighbours, for which clear literary, epigraphic, and

---

4 Flache (2018).
5 Knapp and van Dommelen (2010) 1 argue that 'bounded cultures and well-defined populations with readily distinct identities may have been less common than usually assumed' and this was surely true in southern Italy.
6 I leave aside questions of mobility between Italic zones for which there is increasing archaeological evidence, such as the probable presence of Hirpinians, Oenotrians, and others at Pontecagnano (Della Fina [2013]; Pellegrino *et al.* [2017]; Petta and Russo [2017]; Desiderio [2018]), potential Etruscans at Ruvo and elsewhere in Peucetia (Montanaro [2010]), and 'Samnite' burials in south-eastern Italy, e.g., at Lavello (Bottini [1985]). Transhumant pastoralism is probably underestimated as a vector for the mobility of people, ideas, and technologies: see Heitz (2015b), and his contribution to this volume.
7 Yntema (2011).
8 Lomas (2002) 173. We do not have a clear idea, for this period in southern Italy, about the categories that might have existed between 'citizen' and 'foreigner'.
9 Tom Carpenter (2009) 28, in his celebrated article on Apulian red-figure, has many interesting and useful things to say, but he perpetrates the idea of hostility when he comes to characterising the relationship between the Greek cities and the Italic centres: 'Relations between the Greeks of Taranto and the Italic people of Apulia were usually fraught.'

archaeological evidence has been found,[10] it should be noted that accounts of warfare between Greek cities are even more dramatic: Siris was destroyed by a coalition of her Greek neighbours around 560 BCE, and Sybaris was destroyed by Croton in 510 BCE. Two large, rich, Greek cities were wiped off the map by other Greeks.

Generally in the ancient Mediterranean, trade and other contact activities seem to be rather poorly correlated with military competition whenever evidence has been available.[11] For example, Athenian manufactured products, and even Athenian artisans, plays, playwrights, and actors were, at the time of the Peloponnesian War, going to places that would be unthinkable in a modern 'total war' scenario.[12] It is relatively unlikely that there were high levels of binary thinking in southern Italy but, even in this generation of Horden and Purcell's *The Corrupting Sea*, Ian Morris' 'Mediterraneanization', Irad Malkin's 'Greek Networks' and Elena Isayev's *Migration, Mobility and Place*, there is still a persistent view that there were low levels of contact, and even familiarity, among the various groups living in southern Italy.[13] This is certainly the case with discussions of representations of Greek theatre on South Italian pottery. The vast majority of these vases have been found in non-Greek centres, at sites like Ruvo. How would they have been understood by the people in whose graves they were found? Luca Giuliani argued that such was the level of cultural disconnection that, for the understanding of the pictures, the presence of Greek experts to explain the vases in the context of a funeral oration or performance would have been necessary.[14] Others have gone further, arguing that bilingual experts would have been needed because no one at Ruvo would have been familiar with Greek language or culture.[15]

Views like these spark a series of questions to do with physical and cultural mobility, which can be listed as follows: Could people from Greek cities easily move from one to another? Could people from Italic centres easily move to Greek cities? Could people from Greek cities easily move into Italic areas? To what extent could people be ethnically and culturally mobile – that is, in moving from one place to another could they change their habits and material culture in such a way that they would become indistinguishable as

---

10 Pausanias mentioned dedications at Delphi commemorating Tarentine victories over her neighbours in the early fifth century BCE, for which the inscribed statue-bases have been found: see Nenci (1976). The last of them corresponds perfectly with the date of the destruction and abandonment of several Messapian sites, such as Cavallino and I Fani: see D'Andria (2005); Descœudres and Robinson (1993).
11 On this, see Cohen in this volume.
12 MacDonald (1982) for Attic pottery exports in the late fifth century. The plays of Euripides, even those with explicitly Attic political content, seem to have been widely performed in Doric cities in southern Italy and Sicily in the late fifth century: see Allan (2001).
13 Horden and Purcell (2000); Morris (2003); Malkin (2011); Isayev (2017).
14 Giuliani (1995); he does, however, accept that some Italic people must have had a good knowledge of Greek. It was more the obscurity of the texts which required an explanation.
15 Todisco (2012). I have argued against this position in Robinson (2014a).

Assessing mobility in southern Italy

There are various types of evidence that can be used to study mobility and permeability in southern Italy: literary, epigraphic (especially onomastics), scientific (e.g., genetics, isotopes), archaeological, and stylistic/technological. I shall deal with each in turn, with the last category particularly relevant to ceramics and, in my opinion, the most revealing.

Literary evidence for mobility offers some clues, but is largely anecdotal and best-known from the biographies of celebrities, like the philosopher Pythagoras. He was from Samos, migrated to Croton, was eventually expelled from Croton, but was able to settle in Metapontum. There is no literary evidence, in southern Italy, of the large-scale demographic manipulations typical of the Sicilian tyrants and Republican Roman views of the laxity of citizenship practices in southern Italian cities are unlikely to be reliable.[16] There is, therefore, little hope that the literary sources are going to give us a reliable picture of what was happening on the ground and at a large scale in terms of the general openness of Greek cities to migration.

There is no record at all of individual Italians moving into Greek cities, and only the odd intriguing anecdote about moving from Greek cities to Italic ones. Herodotus (3.138) recounts the story of Gillos, said to have taken place around 515 BCE, not long before Herodotus himself migrated to the Athenian colony of Thurii. The story is of Persian ambassadors shipwrecked on the coast of southern Italy and taken prisoner. An exile from the Greek city of Tarentum named Gillos is said to have been living among the Messapians in Brindisium and he is mentioned because he was able to intercede and have the ambassadors sent back to the Persian court. So, in the late sixth century BCE, it was apparently plausible that a Greek could live happily in an Italic community in southern Italy, although we don't know if this was exceptional.

Epigraphic and onomastic evidence doesn't help a great deal either, mainly because southern Italy did not have an especially epigraphic culture. There are a few Italic names in inscriptions from Greek cities, most notably on the Heraclea Tablets. The inscriptions, of the fourth/third century BCE, deal with the lease of land to citizens by sanctuaries in the territory and in them we meet one Dazimos Pyrrhou.[17] The first part of the name is Italic; the second, a patronymic, is Greek. He was certainly a citizen of Heraclea and was one of

---

16 E.g., Cicero (*Pro Archia* V.10): Southern Italian '... Greek states often went out of their way to associate with themselves in their civic privileges undistinguished men, of unimportant attainments, or of no attainments at all.'
17 Uguzzoni and Ghinatti (1968) 125–45; Lo Porto (1988–1989) 402–3.

the *horistai* who undertook the division of lands belonging to the sanctuary of Dionysus. These rare cases are not straightforward to interpret. It could be, for example, that Dazimos Pyrrhou testifies to a type of mobility quite different from migration: *xenia*, formal guest-friendships between foreigners.[18] It was common to name a son after your *xenos*; Thucydides' father, for example, had a foreign, Thracian name (Oloros), presumably because his grandfather was *xenos* to a Thracian.[19] This could be the case with Dazimos Pyrrhou; certainly a magistrate of the city would have been at the social level in which *xenia* relationships were possible, even probable (and such a relationship would imply a high level of mobility, at least among the elite groups of the Greek and Italic centres). Overall, epigraphic evidence is not very compelling in southern Italy, especially when an Italic name does not necessarily signify an Italic person.[20] A number of objects found at Italic sites have inscriptions in Greek or bear apparently Greek names; some of them, like the famous pyxis from Gravina, were produced locally,[21] but often they do not speak to us unequivocally about the origins of the persons concerned.

Scientific evidence – genetic studies and isotope analysis – ought to help us in looking at the question but, so far, the results have been mixed. In 2017 a team from Tübingen did a study of genetics, via non-metric traits, on teeth from a number of sites in southern Italy.[22] The teeth came from two Italic cemeteries dated before Greek settlement, at Santa Maria d'Anglona and Incoronata, and then from another Italic site dated after Greek settlement, Passo di Giacobbe. Added to this were two populations from the Greek city of Metapontum, one from the city necropolis and another from an urban necropolis about 5 km away. The results showed that the Italic sites had populations with significant genetic similarity to each other, and less similarity to the populations of Metapontum. The main problem was that no two sets of samples were more genetically dissimilar than the urban and rural populations of the Greek city. The authors offer two possible explanations for this anomaly which, while both interesting and plausible, are more or less diametrically opposed: (1) that there was significant genetic diversity among

---

18 The *tesserae hospitales* from Rome and Carthage show that formalised elite guest-friendship was already well-known in central Italy by the sixth century BCE: Isayev (2017) 101–3.
19 Malkin (2004) 349.
20 Malkin (2014); another Italic name in Heraclea was found inscribed on a marble block in the western sector of the Collina del Castello at Heraclea: Makkos. Like Dazimos, it is an Apulian name, further complicating the issue: Giardino (2005) 397–8. Captives and slaves were probably more important elements of mobility and technological transfer than we think, but here too the exiguous epigraphic record for southern Italy prevents any useful speculation. Even in Attica, with its abundance of inscriptions, deducing ethnicity from slave-names is far from straightforward: Lewis (2017). See McDonald and Clackson (2020) 77–8 for discussion of the 'onomastic fallacy'.
21 Most recently: McDonald and Clackson (2020) 79–81, with other examples cited. Lombardo (2014) 47 discusses further cases.
22 Rathmann *et al.* (2017).

the first Greek migrants, who tended to be the land-owners still living in the territory, with new Greek migrants to the city being less genetically diverse, or (2) that the early settlers were genetically fairly similar (i.e., from one place) and later arrivals came from various places and were more genetically diverse.[23]

A follow-up study, two years later and using both non-metric and metric traits in teeth, produced quite different results.[24] The authors claim to see low levels of human mobility before the arrival of Greeks in southern Italy and high levels afterwards, both in the Greek and Italic centres. They further claim that, in the post-colonisation period, approximately 18% of those living in both the Greek cities and the Italic settlements were of Greek ancestry. While evidence for greater admixture of people in southern Italy than previously thought is welcome, this result seems astonishing. Carter has proposed that the depleted population of the *chora* of Metapontum was refreshed by enfranchised Lucanians in the fourth century BCE.[25] The argument is based both on the evidence of changing burials customs and on physical anthropology.[26] The most important evidence, though, remains unpublished.[27]

Isotope analyses are desperately needed in southern Italy to pursue questions of mobility; so far, the results of only one small study have been reported, finding that 10% (two out of 20) of the individuals studied from Siris and Metapontum were of non-local origin.[28] Since DNA preservation is poor in many southern Italian skeletons, no new perspectives are available from that direction.[29] There have been some studies of modern DNA, looking at the extent of the Greek genetic contribution to the modern populations of southern Italy and Sicily.[30] An interesting bias was found: a few thousand Greek men were identified, but only a few hundred Greek women were in the estimated number of early migrants to Sicily. But areas like southern Italy and Sicily, where there has been constant population-churn for millennia, seem very poorly suited to these kinds of studies and it is difficult to see how anything specific can be concluded about population movements in the first millennium BCE on their bases.[31]

---

23 It should be noted that Carter's surveys have shown that there was apparently very little settlement in the *chora* of Metapontum before about 550 BCE: Carter (2011a). The first farmhouses may have been in the river valleys and are now covered with alluvium and invisible to field survey.
24 Rathmann *et al.* (2019).
25 Carter (2011b) 842–3.
26 Carter (2006) 81–3, 219–23.
27 Henneberg (1998).
28 The study, using strontium isotopes, was carried out as part of a Master's thesis at Leiden: Vos (2018). Its results are reported by Rathmann *et al.* (2019).
29 Rathmann *et al.* (2019) 2.
30 Tofanelli *et al.* (2016).
31 The frankly ridiculous conclusions made about the 'origins of the Etruscans' based on modern population genetics are a cautionary tale for the use of modern populations as proxies

Archaeological evidence for mobility is also extremely difficult to find, beyond the clear influx of Greeks in the eighth and seventh centuries BCE. That evidence has now demonstrated clearly that places which went on to become Greek settlements generally had mixed populations (Greek/Italic) in the earliest period of Greek migration.[32] But if a resident of ancient Brindisium, in Messapia, moved to Tarentum in 400 BCE, how could their presence be detected in the archaeological record?[33] It may be possible through distinctive worshipping, cooking, or eating practices,[34] but the presence of some Messapian habits in Tarentum could have also arrived through cross-cultural interaction.[35] If an enclave of people using foreign practices within Tarentum could be identified, we might be on firmer ground, although the level of preservation and excavation of domestic contexts in southern Italy means that the evidence is relatively unlikely to be found, if it exists. In any case, beyond the well-documented cases of foreigners living in ancient *emporia*, it is far from clear that foreigners in Greek cities would have lived in enclaves and continued to have identified with their places of origin. Imperial Rome, filled to the brim with migrants, does not seem to have had 'quarters' like a modern city.[36]

It is notoriously difficult to find evidence in the archaeological record of people making clear statements about their ethnicity or origins. Burials might be one such arena and, indeed, in Brindisium there seems to have been a small enclave of Greeks living in the town in the seventh century BCE based on a group of burials at Tor Pisana with burial practices and material culture that was entirely foreign to the local habits.[37] In the Greek cities of southern Italy, there are rare examples of graves that are completely unlike other burials for the town, but very similar to what is found in the Italic zones. Crucinia Tomb 17 and Torre di Mare Tomb 18 at Metapontum are two such burials, filled with Italic armour, weapons, and tools that are otherwise unknown in graves from the Greek city.[38] The burials presume at least a small community

---

for ancestral source populations, particularly in areas where we know that there have been very high levels of population replacement: see, amongst others, Achilli *et al.* (2007); Perkins (2009), (2017).

32 Good examples are Siris, Francavilla Marittima, L'Amastuola and Incoronata (the latter not surviving beyond the seventh century BCE).

33 See also Bernardo-Ciddio in this volume for an exploration of some of these issues and tensions.

34 For cooking practices see Quercia (2015).

35 The use of *cippi* outside houses and graves within the city-walls at Taranto has sometimes been seen as Messapian influences, but Lombardo is sceptical: see Lombardo (1994b).

36 Greg Woolf (2017) has recently argued for this in public fora. Varro (*LL* 5.46, 51) makes a claim that there had once been ethnic quarters in Rome, e.g., Etruscans on the Caelian, but the phenomenon is situated firmly in the past: Farney (2014) 438. Carroll (2020) has recently demonstrated how migrants in Rome seem not to have alluded to their origins, at least in their dress on funeral monuments; see also Tacoma (2016) and Elder (2020).

37 Lombardo (1994a); Yntema (2016).

38 Crucinia Tomb 17: De Siena (1993b); Torre di Mare Tomb 18: De Siena (1993a). There are a couple of other examples of such tombs from the urban and rural necropoleis; otherwise,

of Italians in Metapontum who knew how to bury these bodies in a 'proper' fashion, but what was the fate of this community? Either they were only in the city temporarily, or subsequent burials of people from this group have changed to completely conform to local habits.[39] But even these apparent 'Italic' burials in Metapontum are not necessarily crystal clear in their meaning. Christiane Nowak has recently argued that such burials may represent residents of the Greek cities who were emulating the customs of elite Italians.[40] Her study focused especially on Campania, where the situation seems rather different to the other parts of southern Italy; mass-migration from Italic areas into Greek (and Etruscan) cities seems to occur in the late fifth century, after which time Oscan names frequently appear in the lists of magistrates in Neapolis and in public and private contexts in Paestum.[41]

So, we have glimpses of mobility from the literary, epigraphic, scientific, and archaeological sources for southern Italy; should they be regarded as symbolic of a much wider phenomenon, for which evidence so far mostly lacks? Where does the burden of proof lie? Given the evidence for high levels of mobility in Italy and the wider Mediterranean in this period, perhaps it is the existence of closed societies in southern Italy that needs to be proven, rather than the opposite. For Isayev, assuming a mobile rather than a stable society will change the way we interpret cultural interaction,[42] and it is hard to see how using this assumption as a starting-point would not make better sense of a number of the phenomena we see in southern Italy.

Mobility and artisan production

One is always a bit hesitant to accept articles of faith (although simply accepting that there were relatively static societies in southern Italy has tended to be an unspoken article of faith until now). Fortunately, artisan production gives us a good opportunity to observe solid evidence for patterns of mobility and

---

weapons are only present at Metaponto in the highly unusual early aristocratic burials in loc. Crucinia: Bottini *et al.* (2019).
39 Something like this appears to have happened in Paestum, where a late sixth century burial in the Gaudo necropolis has significant analogies with the habits of the Etrusco-Campanian area; the subsequent ten burials in the cluster, ranging down to 450 BCE, are similar to standard Paestan burials (apart from the fact that a high proportion of them have plastered walls, a number of which were also painted with coloured bands): Cipriani (2000) 198. Cipriani presents evidence for further Italic groups that appear to have migrated to the city before the mass-migration around 400 BCE.
40 Nowak (2016). The proposition might be valid for certain burials in Campania but I find it harder to accept for the Metaponto graves. The problem yet again exposes the difficulty of linking material culture with ethnic identity.
41 A process labelled 'decolonization' by Asheri (1999), and seen in a number of other Greek cities. For Naples: Lomas (2002) 177–8; for artisans with Oscan names decorating tombs in Paestum: McDonald and Clackson (2020) 81–2; Cipriani and Longo (1996) 203, no. 98 for the inscription of the Paestan meddix Staiis.
42 Isayev (2017) 5.

migration. In the eighth and seventh centuries BCE, the migration and settlement of Greeks at many coastal sites is well-attested. Potters and painters from many parts of the Greek world were among the migrants. The literary record often tells us who 'founded' the Greek cities of southern Italy. The origins of the early potters at these sites, however, correspond rather poorly with the putative origin of the first settlers and this evidence has been one of the major planks in the 'revisionist' views of early Greek colonisation.[43] This is not to say that there is no correspondence between ceramics and the literary tradition: the Euboean component in the earliest locally made ceramics at early Pithecusae and Rhegium are interesting reflections of the literary sources. But what characterises the ceramics of most of these early sites, including Pithecusae, is the diversity in the origins of artisan migrants, quite unlike the single origins promoted by the later literary accounts.[44]

The effect of the new ceramic technologies seems to have been minimal beyond the coastal areas where Greeks settled, which is remarkable given that most, perhaps all, of the early 'colonial' sites probably included residents of Italic origin. One Greek potter/painter certainly settled in Pontecagnano in the eighth century and produced painted wheel-made pottery but the Italic communities generally stuck with their traditional matt-painted and impasto wares, at least until the sixth century BCE.[45] There is some evidence for itinerant Greek potters and/or coroplasts in Italic settlements in the sixth century BCE, such as the famous pyramidal clay votive inscription with a dedication to Herakles in the late Archaic Achaean alphabet from San Mauro Forte on the upper reaches of the Cavone River, made by the *kerameus* Nikomachus.[46] Giammatteo has demonstrated through archaeometric analysis that the relief slabs which decorated the so-called *anaktoron* at Torre di Satriano, with inscriptions in the Laconian alphabet on the reverses, must have been produced locally.[47]

It is perhaps surprising that there is so little evidence for the migration of ceramicists from mainland Greece into the Greek cities of southern Italy in

---

43 Donnellan and Nizzo (2016).
44 The centres of the Ionian Gulf seem to have collected a particularly diverse set of migrant ceramicists, with origins in Corinth, the Cyclades, Asia Minor and elsewhere: Denoyelle and Iozzo (2009) 49–52; Denti and Villette (2013); Denti and Bellamy (2016); Denti (2018). There is some imported and locally-made pottery of Achaean type, which does little confirm the literary accounts of the foundation of e.g., 'Achaean' Metapontum or Sybaris: Papadopoulos (2001).
45 For Pontecagnano: Bailo Modesti and Gastaldi (1999); D'Agostino (2014); Naso (2014). Between the second half of the sixth and the early fourth centuries BCE, Italic communities largely shifted to predominantly wheel-thrown pottery, and such a move is unlikely to have occurred without some degree of personal mobility since, as Gosselain (2016a) 204–5 noted: 'Adoption of wheel-throwing would have implied a long period of learning only made possible through participation in a community of practice.'
46 Guarducci (1967) 556.
47 Giammatteo (2009); Baglivo (2013).

the sixth century BCE. A few Corinthian ceramicists appear to have migrated to Tarentum,[48] and an East Greek painter seems to have been working at Oria, in Messapia,[49] but no Attic black-figure vase-painters moved to southern Italy (Chalcidian black-figure is an isolated group).[50] Many more Greek potters and painters migrated to the Etruscan-speaking towns of central Italy than to the Greek-speaking towns of the south.

In the middle of the fifth century BCE, a new class of pottery began to be made, apparently by immigrant artisans: red-figure.[51] The complexity of the decoration and the vast size of the corpus of vases give us broader access to a category of analysis now often ignored in archaeology: style. We can plausibly attempt to distinguish the hand of an individual artisan and see how their career developed, how they related to other artisans, and whether they moved around. Red-figure pottery was, of course, widely traded but, by studying in combination style, shapes, iconography, and provenience, we can aspire to distinguish traded ceramics from those made on the spot. In southern Italy and Sicily, there was intense migration of ceramicists both into and within the region from the middle of the fifth century onwards. Athenian potters and painters went from Athens to Metapontum,[52] probably to Tarentum,[53] to Campania,[54] and to Sicily (but, strangely, not to the two places where Athens were involved in colonial foundations at this time: Thurii and Heraclea; see Figure 5.1).

---

48 Neeft (2018).
49 D'Andria and Semeraro (2000). Elsewhere in Messapia at a similar period, see D'Andria (1977); D'Andria (1988) for the possibility of itinerant craftsmen from Corcyra or Epidamnos producing capitals in local limestone at Cavallino, Vaste, and Ugento.
50 Iozzo (1994).
51 Silvestrelli (2018) makes a case that migrant ceramicists from Athens had already arrived in Metapontum in the first half of the fifth century BCE, since Attic black gloss forms are produced there which have never been discovered as imports to the site, speaking against simple emulation.
52 The Pisticci Painter was probably an Athenian (rather than a southern Italian metic vase-painter who came home): see Denoyelle (1997). Lippolis (2018) looked at a large corpus of epigraphic material in Greece between the fourth century and the Hellenistic period. At Delos alone, he found the names of 652 artisans between 314 and 166 BCE; they came to Delos to do specific jobs, before departing again. At Ephesus, Rhodes, and Eretria ceramicists seem to have come to make vessels of Panathenaic shape as prizes for local sporting contests. The Pisticci Painter may conceivably have come to Metapontum for the same reason, and stayed. One black-figured pseudo-Panathenaic amphora, found in the *chora* of Metapontum, has been attributed to his hand: see Denoyelle (1997) figs. 11–12.
53 The style of the first Apulian painter, the Painter of the Berlin Dancing Girl, shows a rather eclectic mix of Attic influences. His use of the Doric alphabet for inscriptions is a decisive element for Denoyelle in seeing him as a colonial Greek who travelled to Athens for training: see Denoyelle (1997) 402.
54 McPhee (2018) proposed that the Spinelli Painter, the Chequer Painter, and the Eros and Hare Group all represent migrants from Athens to Campania, with the Chequer Painter probably ending his career in Syracuse. The Dundee Painter may have been another such personage: see McPhee (2015).

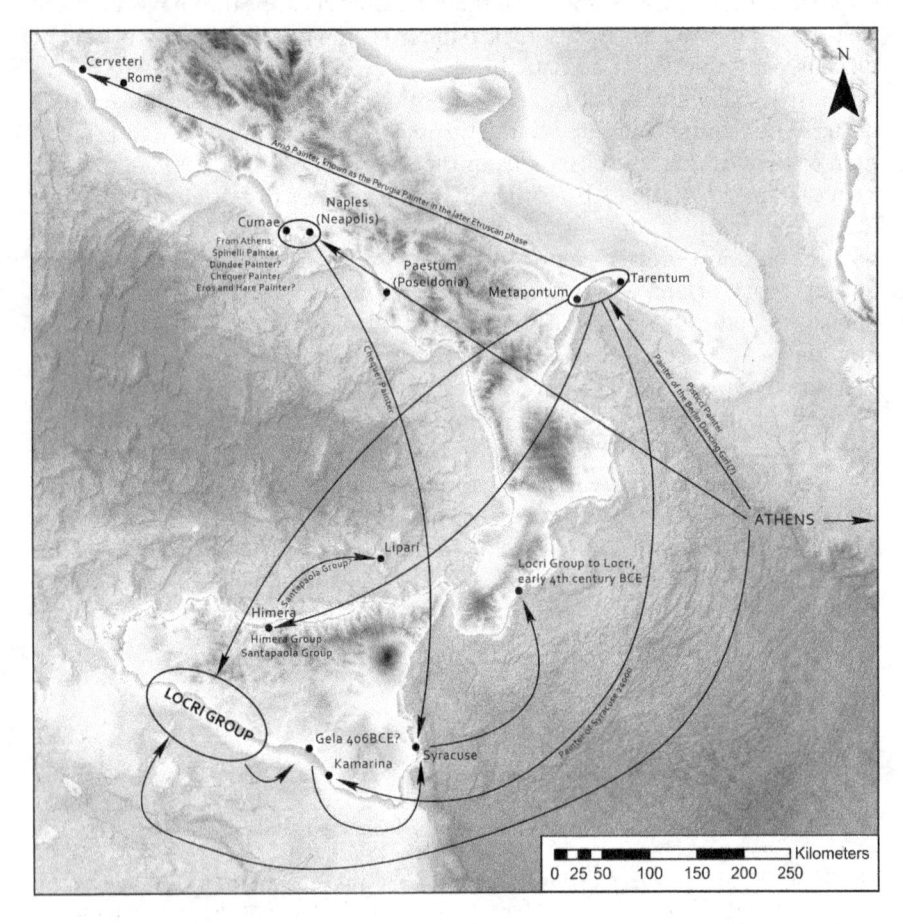

Figure 5.1 Proposed movements of ceramic artisans in southern Italy and Sicily in the second half of the fifth century BCE.

Sicily is an interesting case. In the 25 years since the end of Trendall's career, a good deal of what he wrote has been revised, some of it quite radically.[55] Trendall tended to see the organisation of the Athenian ceramic industry being directly reproduced in southern Italy and Sicily, when the reality was probably quite different. Trendall saw the Chequer Painter, an Athenian migrant to Syracuse (probably via Campania), as what Barresi has termed the *protos euretes* of Sicilian red-figure, the prototype painter from whom all subsequent painters stemmed. But there is, for example, a series of vases found mainly at Himera which Trendall dated to 380–360

---

55 Trendall himself recognised the need for a complete re-appraisal: *LCS* Suppl. III, 267.

BCE on stylistic grounds. The excavators of the site agreed to this date, although perhaps reluctantly, since the sack of the city by the Carthaginians in 409 BCE always provided a much more likely explanation for the highly fragmentary nature of the red-figured pottery found in domestic contexts. Trendall's dating has now been altered through Marco Serino's detailed study of the group which pushes its inception back to the period before the Carthaginian sack.[56] By careful analysis of the shapes, accessory decoration, style, and iconographic schemes used by the Himera Painter, Serino has also shown that, far from originating in the 'workshop of the Chequer Painter' as Trendall had thought, the painter seems to have migrated from southeastern Italy.

The 'Locri Group' is a group of related painters which Trendall had dated, again, after 380 BCE. He placed it in the Lucanian sequence, despite the fact that the group used a number of strange shapes, foreign to Metapontum, and that the earlier vases were almost universally found in western Sicily. The likely migratory path of the Locri Group has now been set out by Barresi:[57] (1) initial training of some painters in Metapontum, and others perhaps in Athens in the late fifth century; (2) the establishment of a workshop in Selinus and/or in other parts of western Sicily; (3) flight from western Sicily with the Carthaginian sack of Selinus in 406 BCE; (4) refuge found perhaps first at Gela;[58] (5) some time spent in Syracuse; (6) a final jump to Locri in Calabria where there is a very consistent production, contained almost entirely in the necropolis of Locri, from the early- to mid-fourth century BCE.[59] These painters clearly had no problem relocating, and doing so quite frequently.

When it comes to the migration of ceramicists from Greek cities to Italic centres, the Arnò Painter is a fascinating example. He was an early Lucanian painter, working in Metapontum c. 400 BCE, with a very distinctive style, especially for the anatomy of male figures. This personal style is what allowed Martine Denoyelle to link him to the work of the Perugia Painter, of the first generation of Etruscan red-figure painters. The Perugia Painter's vases have all been found in Etruria, mostly around Cerveteri. This individual is apparently the same person as the Arnò Painter, who migrated from southeastern Italy to southern Etruria.[60]

At around the same time, Sicilian painters seem to have migrated to Campania and settled at sites like Paestum.[61] This Greek city may have come

---

56 Serino (2019).
57 Barresi (2018).
58 Santostefano (2018).
59 Elia (2018).
60 Denoyelle (1993); now also Gilotta (2014).
61 Trendall (1987) 22–40; Denoyelle and Iozzo (2009) 181–99; Pouzadoux (2017) 194–6 for additional information and changing ideas about the routes of mobility in the Tyrrhenian Sea. The Thyrsus Painter, from Tarentum, may also have spent part of his career in Paestum at this time: see Denoyelle and Iozzo (2009) 184–5; Denoyelle et al. (2018) 8.

under the control of Oscan speakers shortly before the arrival of the first red-figure painters. That control may have been, in part, responsible for the creation of the red-figure industries in these towns; it had always been the Italic people in Campania who were more desirous of Athenian figured pottery than those living in the Greek cities, at least to judge from the contents of graves. The new Oscan elites of the Campanian metropoleis presumably desired new forms of self-representation. As far as the mechanism goes, we should not underestimate the importance of mercenary activity in this period when it comes to the mobility of people, ideas, and technologies. Campanian mercenaries were used extensively in Sicily at the end of the fifth century and this may have been another factor behind the movement of vase-painters.[62] There are, it should be added, a relatively large number of vases of the later fifth and early fourth centuries BCE that have never been attributed to the hands of Attic or southern Italian artisans, and there is reason to believe that there were many more artisans on the move in this period than we can clearly identify from the evidence.[63]

The fourth century BCE sees a tidal wave in the passing of red-figure ceramic technology from Greek to Italic sites in southern Italy. The Choephoroi Painter, in the earlier part of the century, must have been working in Metapontum; his vases are very close in style to the Dolon and Creusa Painters, whose work has been discovered in the *kerameikos* at Metapontum, and he seems to have collaborated with those artisans on some vases.[64] His later vessels are made of a different clay and have mainly been found in the Val d'Agri; local shapes of ritual significance, like the *nestoris*, were often decorated. Clearly this artisan migrated from Metapontum to an Italic settlement.[65] A little later, the Lampas Painter seems to have moved from Tarentum to Canosa.[66] After the middle of the century, many other painters followed, certainly to Ruvo, Canosa, and Arpi.[67] Some of these movements have been confirmed archaeometrically. Several Apulian painters and groups, which were not suspected to have been working outside Tarentum (simply because too few of their products had a provenience to show see a clear local distribution-pattern), used clays typical of Peucetia.[68] A great deal more could still be done using archaeometry to trace the movement of southern Italian vase-painters.

Tarentum became the principal artisan centre of southern Italy in the second half of the fourth century BCE, also supplying vase-painters to Italic

---

62 Tagliamonte (1994).
63 Barresi (2005), (2014).
64 Silvestrelli (2018) 148.
65 Denoyelle and Silvestrelli (2019).
66 Corrente (2005).
67 Robinson (1990); Mazzei (1996); Lippolis and Mazzei (2005); Lippolis (2007); Denoyelle and Iozzo (2009) 157–61.
68 Robinson (2014b) 23–4 and fig. 5, for the Painter of the BM Centaur and certain Gnathia painters probably working in southern Peucetia.

centres in the Val d'Agri, to Metapontum (after a hiatus where red-figure does not seem to have been produced there for a few decades), to Paestum, Cumae, Capua, and eventually, in the third century, to Rome, when artisans decorating pots in added paint, like the Volcani Painter, moved to central Italy.[69]

In these examples of mobility, it may sometimes have been the case that individual painters migrated; more often, much larger groups were probably involved. The ceramic technologies were often new, and the artisans who dug and prepared the clay and gloss, formed the vases, painted the subsidiary decoration, built the kilns and performed the firing may all have been individuals who cannot be identified on the basis of their personal style (to say nothing of the families that may have accompanied them). Study of the remains of the workshops of potters and painters in the *kerameikos* at Metapontum (including an analysis of the fingerprints left in the wet gloss) have given an indication of the size of the workforce.[70]

Discussion so far has revolved around the possibility of the migration of potters and painters from Greek cities, taking their ceramic technology with them. That is, of course, only one possible mechanism, and we certainly have to think about other modes of transfer. One of the minor Late Apulian painters, recognised by Trendall, was someone that he called the Lucera Painter, who was working, it seems, in Tarentum.[71] Trendall recognised that a few of the vases produced by the Lucera Painter were found in Campania, and seemed to have used a non-Apulian clay, and thus he speculated that this artisan had migrated. On one vase, connected to the painter, there is an inscription painted, before firing, under a handle.[72] Trendall provided no translation, but Rucco and Tagliamonte have recently proposed an interpretation.[73] They read the inscription as an artisan's signature, extremely rare in southern Italy: *Stenis Pupdiis*, in Oscan. *Stenis* is a very common Oscan praenomen, while *Pupidiis* is a relatively rare Oscan nomen, found especially in Pompeii and attested rarely in Bruttium and in a couple of other places. If they are right, we have a painter who was an Oscan-speaking Campanian, who travelled to Tarentum to learn his trade (his vases are 100% canonical in terms of Tarentine style and shape), and then went home.[74]

Beyond migration, the practice of itinerancy by vase-painters was surely quite common in southern Italy. There are occasions when one detects a concentration of vases from precisely the same phase of an artisan's career at a particular site, for example, vases by the Iliupersis Painter at Ruvo. Of

---

69 There is a strong 'Apulianising' phase in all the production centres in Campania, through apparent immigrant painters like the Aphrodite Painter, the Libation Painter, and the CA and APZ Painters: *LCS* Suppl. 3.234. For the Volcani Painter in Central Italy, see Green (1976).
70 D'Andria (1997); Cracolici (2003).
71 *RVAp* II 577–9.
72 *RVAp* II 579, no. 181.
73 Rucco and Tagliamonte (2007).
74 Pouzadoux (2017) 198.

course, this could be due to the vagaries of distribution systems; a merchant may have had a relationship with a particular ceramic workshop in Tarentum and therefore took their wares to a site where he had a particular connection, but it is also possible that the Iliupersis Painter went to Ruvo for a period to produce pottery.[75]

Sometimes the presence of itinerant artisans is quite clear. At the site of Roccagloriosa, on the Tyrrhenian coast, a group of chamber-tombs in an elite cemetery of the second half of the fourth century contained vases by a painter whose personal style is distinctive. The Underworld Painter, who seems to have been based in Tarentum, apparently travelled to Roccagloriosa to execute a commission; the vases are made from a clay that is quite different from that which he used for his regular production.[76] The clay is dramatically inferior but, working in a different location, there might not be the opportunity to procure and prepare clays of the desired quality.

Although we cannot always see the mechanism of the transfer of styles (migration, visits for training, itinerancy, etc.), what seems to characterise the southern Italian ceramics industry is amazingly high levels of mobility between and among the Greek and non-Greek centres, perhaps characteristic of a culture in which migration was a founding factor.[77] Barresi saw a 'productive decentralisation'. Unlike Athens, where a centralised industry attempted to adapt its products to the needs of internal and external consumption, in southern Italy we see a transfer of the technologies of production towards the areas of consumption.[78]

Artisan mobility and population mobility

The broader question, provoked by the evidence outlined earlier, is whether these high levels of personal mobility – much higher than we can detect with any other sort of evidence – can be imagined as indicative of the wider possibilities for movement between Greece, Greek cities, and Italic centres. It is hard to be certain, but the more abundant literary and epigraphic evidence from Greece and central Italy demonstrate high levels of personal mobility

---

75 Roscino (2019) for the possibility of the Iliupersis Painter working for periods in Ruvo. A perfect opportunity for testing this hypothesis through archaeometry exists, since the clays of Ruvo are quite different to those used in Tarentum. But if the phenomenon is to be explained by a trade relationship, one thinks of the *negotiatores* with specialised trade routes for the distribution of Italian sigillata, helpfully stamped with the names of the workshop-owners: see Kenrick (1993).
76 Gualtieri (2012).
77 There are, of course, cases of the migration of ceramicists within Greece, especially in the late fifth and early fourth century BCE, when Athenian potters and painters relocated to places like Olynthos, Old Smyrna, Corinth, and Olympia: see MacDonald (1981). The level of movement in these decades is exceptional for Greece. See also now Schierup and Bundgaard Rasmussen (2012).
78 Barresi (2018) 56.

in the fifth and fourth centuries BCE, and it is very unlikely that southern Italy lagged behind in this respect. The strong cultural diversity in southern Italy needs an explanation beyond ethnic hostility and low levels of interpersonal contact. The explanation for persistent cultural diversity between well-connected people is a field of intense interest to anthropologists, and archaeologists would do well to incorporate some of this theoretical work.[79]

In the interests of balance, there are some reasons why the mobility of artisans, and particularly of ceramic artisans, might not be representative of wider populations. Pottery-making was a famously hard and dirty job and, according to Plutarch (*Solon* 24.4), Solon attracted foreign artisans to Athens and made them citizens.[80] The Athenian habit of signing vases makes it easier for us to trace the phenomenon, and there is an astonishing number of artisan-names that are non-Attic (e.g., Myspios, Oltos, Psiax, Amasis), which refer to foreign places (Sikanos, Lydos, Kholkos, Thrax, etc.), or which use non-Attic letters in their signatures (including painters as quintessentially Attic as Exekias and the Brygos Painter).[81] But even if ceramicists had higher levels of personal mobility than most people in southern Italy, the evidence presented earlier shows that 'borders' were a great deal more permeable in southern Italy than has often been thought.

The demonstration of mobility should not be an end in itself but rather serve as a starting-point for asking what motivated people in southern Italy to move around, and what were the consequences for the migrants and their hosts.[82] The 'new mobilities paradigm' with its interest in 'how mobility and control over mobility both reflect and reinforce power' ought to be incorporated better into studies of this period.[83] The politics of mobility is not much discussed in southern Italy. State-level exchanges are virtually unknown; in southern Italy, there is nothing akin to the exchange of specialised artisans between the courts of the Aegean and Eastern Mediterranean in the Bronze Age.[84] The migrations of Greeks into southern Italy in the eighth, seventh, and sixth centuries BCE are now generally seen not as directed, state-sponsored enterprises but as much more random diasporas. The artisans of the first waves of migration, along with the later ceramicists who arrived in established poleis

---

79 Flache (2018).
80 Boegehold (1983).
81 Papadopoulos (1996), (2009); Hurwit (2015) 92–3.
82 van Dommelen (2014) 480.
83 Skeates (2017) 167.
84 Many case-studies can be found in Kiriatzi and Knappett (2016). There is very little evidence in southern Italy for a trade in prestige items (e.g., gold, silver, bronze, or stone vessels), or even in the types of pottery (rhyta, pictorial kraters) that have often been associated with centralised production in Greece (Borgna and Càssola Guida [2005] 500), but a number of Mycenaean vase-painters migrated to southern Italy. Archaeometry has been able to distinguish locally-made vases from imports, and demonstrated that the production of Aegean-type wares in southern Italy was not a matter of simple emulation: see Jones *et al.* (2014); Buxeda i Garrigós *et al.* (2003).

(e.g., Corinthian potters at Tarentum), are generally perceived as individual entrepreneurs. Some of the transfers of Greek ceramic technology to Italic sites, though, may have been negotiated at a more explicitly political level. The *anaktoron* at Torre di Satriano, discussed earlier, was certainly a building for elite activity and the Laconian ceramicists who travelled there to make its terracotta decorations must surely have had experience working on public buildings in Taranto. Their presence in Torre di Satriano might have been brought about by state-level contacts or through the type of elite networks between Greeks and Italians that have been proposed already in the archaic period.[85] In the fourth century BCE, itinerant red-figure painters (e.g., the Underworld Painter at Roccagloriosa) or migrant painters at Italic sites (e.g., in Paestum, the Val d'Agri, Ruvo, Canosa, or Arpi) are quite likely to have been permitted and encouraged by the elites of those regions to supply new modes of self-expression to 'both reflect and reinforce power'.[86] Red-figured pottery almost immediately spread to a much wider part of the social spectrum, although the monumental kraters found in the chamber-tombs of northern Puglia, decorated with mythological themes, probably retained an element of prestige well beyond that of the mass-produced small vases that appeared in the more modest burials. This is worth mentioning, not least because these remarks otherwise have a strong whiff of caricature: independent Greek entrepreneurs versus hierarchy-bound Italic societies, only able to receive new objects, people, and ideas with the consent of their rulers. Those are precisely the sort of assumptions that the study of mobility in southern Italy should invite us to interrogate.

---

85 Robinson (2011). See Armstrong in this volume for artisan attachment to elite networks for bronzeworking.
86 Some idea of the sophistication of the iconographies in use can be gleaned from Pouzadoux (2013).

6 'The potter is by nature a social animal'

A producer-centred approach to regionalisation in the South Italian matt-painted tradition

Leah Bernardo-Ciddio

Archaeologists often grapple with the principles of 'innovation' and 'imitation' in material culture. Those who work on pre-Roman Italy have particularly focused on relationships between Greek and non-Greek forms and between material culture and sociocultural change from a perspective that focuses on consumption choices and identity signalling. There is, however, a critical need to consider material culture change, and the emergence of regional trends, from a production perspective – one that considers the producers of objects, their social worlds, and the way they learn within and across communities. This approach, when carefully undertaken, offers an alternative to viewing consumer demand and/or major migrations as the catalysts for change. In this chapter, I will argue that the social realities and embodied practice of potters are highly important factors to consider when examining ceramic change through time and identifying its origins. Potters are not motivated by solely economic or market-based considerations in their productive or innovatory choices; their choices are instead rooted in their dynamic social worlds and the contexts of their learning. It is only by keeping this in close consideration that we can come to discuss ceramic changes from a producer-centred approach that recognises potters as social actors in their own right and as agents of material culture change.

As a case study, I will focus on these questions in the context of emergent regional change in the matt-painted pottery of Salento, in south-eastern Italy, which has been attributed variously to economic pressures or to mass migrations westward from across the Adriatic. I argue for an approach that is focused on the technological profiles of Salentine matt-painted pottery and on relevant comparanda from outside Italy to assess whether or not regional developments resulted from potter interaction. While this is a restricted case study, the approach and principles can be applied to many other cases in Italian archaeology in which cultural changes are attributed to strictly external and/or economic factors, particularly when dealing with an assumed Greek influence on local production and practice.

The chapter will first introduce this case study by providing an overview of the ceramic class, regional developments in Salento, and past approaches

DOI: 10.4324/9781003120728-6

to this material. Then, I will discuss the methodological and theoretical approaches that support exploration of ceramic evidence from a producer-centred lens. Finally, I will move to my analysis of currently available data and offer pathways for future research.

A case study from the Southern Adriatic: matt-painted pottery in Salento

This chapter offers a case study from south-eastern Italy as an argument for approaching stylistic change, at the local and regional scales, not by cataloguing the economic pressures on producing communities but by accounting for typical patterns of cultural transmission within them and the various mechanisms by which the wider environment encourages shifts in typical behaviours. Here, I will focus on the developmental trajectory of South Italian matt-painted pottery in the Salento area through out the eighth century BCE,[1] when regional traits began to emerge in the local production at Otranto – specifically, new shapes associated with new dining and drinking practices, which bear strong resemblance to vessels produced in the Korçë-Devoll Valley of south-eastern Albania.[2] These changes are variably attributed to sudden local consumer demand for Devollian-style vessels, to potter responses to the presence of foreign goods in local markets that created competition and imperilled their livelihoods, or to a heavy influx of migrants into south-eastern Italy from Albania.

My aim is to counter approaches to these changes that have leaned alternatively towards diffusionist or isolationist rationales for material cultural change and to avoid strictly addressing elite consumption. Rather, I will focus on the potters responsible for the creation of new forms and the social context of innovations in crafting communities that are often driven by social interactions between groups of consumers and producers. At the core of this

---

* I would like to thank the anonymous reviewers who offered robust and helpful feedback on a previous version of this chapter. Many and endless thanks go also to the editors, Sheira Cohen and Jeremy Armstrong, both for their patient guidance through the editing process, and for their organization of the *Exchanging Ideas* conference in Auckland in February 2020, along with Aaron Rhodes-Schroeder. I am deeply grateful to Natalie Abell for multiple rounds of comments, suggestions, and encouragement from a ceramic specialist's perspective. Eliane Brigger and Ted Robinson were both supportive and offered important and much-appreciated help by sharing their work that was not previously available online. My advisor Nicola Terrenato and my colleague Alex Moskowitz thoughtfully read and listened to early versions of this paper and offered crucial suggestions to strengthen and reorganise it. My colleagues Nadhira Hill, Machal Gradoz, and Caitlin Clerkin patiently fielded a barrage of questions as I worked on the final edits. I also would like to thank Dorjan Kallanxhi, Director of the National Archaeological Museum of Korçë, for his warm welcome in 2018 and for his patience with my eleventh-hour requests of him. Finally, I am grateful to the Interdepartmental Program in Classical Art and Archaeology and Rackham Graduate School at the University of Michigan for financial support to attend the Auckland conference.
1 I use the most recently defined chronology, found in Brigger (2007).
2 Yntema (1990); Herring (1998); De Juliis *et al.* (2006); Colivicchi (2014).

re-examination is the intention to define different communities of practice through the traces of similarity and difference in the technical behaviours undertaken during production process for ceramics – that is, through the identification of different or overlapping *chaînes opératoires*.

The *chaîne opératoire* framework allows some initial steps towards the identification of different communities of practice sharing space; the resulting producer-centred approach to South Italian matt-painted pottery provides a greater understanding of the social dynamics underlying its development. Applying this framework to the material from Salento will illuminate the relationships and interactions between local and mobile producers, if those relationships and interactions truly existed. While it is clear from the archaeological evidence that the Adriatic was a nexus of communication and human mobility between south-eastern Italy and the western Balkans,[3] the question of whether potters were mobile within this space, and whether their migration shaped the development of local Salentine style, requires a more rigorous analysis of the matt-painted pottery itself.

Matt-painted pottery was produced in southern Italy from around the mid-twelfth century BCE. The fabric is fine and light in colour, and the manganese oxide–based paint is matt and dark, usually black or brown or sometimes slightly purple.[4] The vessels were typically hand-built or formed partially by hand and partially on a wheel used at medium or low speed.[5] They are typically self-slipped. They are high-fired, requiring a high level of skill on the part of the potters and significant investment in their production, thus explaining their rarity and probably their high value. In the past, the origins and development of this class was considered using 'import replacement theory';[6] it was claimed that the decline of external trade and connections with the Aegean created a gap in the market which indigenous potters managed to fill.[7] Recent statistical analysis indicates, however, that the production and use of matt-painted pottery overtook that of Aegean-type/Italo-Mycenaean pottery at a moment when imports from the Aegean world were still at their zenith.[8] This class was therefore not something local potters began to produce suddenly when they realised that there would be fewer Aegean-style products among them. Rather, it was developed by producers already situated in the local impasto tradition, which is apparent from the morphology of the matt-painted vessels, while also engaging with some production methods of Aegean-style pottery, specifically the high-firing and the application of a dark paint on a light fabric (Figure 6.1).

---

3 Batović (1975); Bass (1998); Forenbaher (2009); Tomas (2017); Forenbaher (2018); Iacono (2018); Recchia *et al.* (2018).
4 Brigger (2007) 16.
5 Boccuccia *et al.* (1995); Brigger (2007) 23–5.
6 Jacobs (1972).
7 Herring (1998) 127–30.
8 Brigger (2007) 588, Fig. 138.

Figure 6.1 Example of a matt-painted vessel, from the Borgo Nuovo deposit. Museo Archeologico Nazionale di Taranto, Inv. 611, 14078.

Source: Photo by author. By permission of the Museo Archeologico Nazionale di Taranto.

South Italian matt-painted pottery from across Apulia, Basilicata, and Calabria did not reflect regionally diverse traits (morphologically or stylistically) through the first few centuries of its production, though there are no suggestions of a centralised industry either.[9] From the eighth century BCE, however, differences in morphology and style emerged within regional repertoires. This is first observed in the Salento region, specifically at Otranto and Taranto. The local matt-painted pottery period, called Salento Middle Geometric (SMG), mostly comprised shapes and motifs that had clear precedent in the earlier South Italian Early Geometric and Protogeometric tradition, and technical features remain consistent. Some new forms and motifs were incorporated into the repertoire in this period, which can be observed in the assemblages retrieved during the Otranto excavations conducted by the University of Lecce[10] and in contemporary assemblages from the Borgo Nuovo deposit at Taranto[11] and I Fani.[12]

While most vessels of the period were morphologically similar to those being produced earlier, some local potters began to produce two forms that have no contemporary or preceding parallels in the matt-painted class, in the repertoire of plain (unpainted) fine pottery, or in the poorly decorated local impasto. The first, a small one-handled vessel, is referred to as the 'bag-shaped

---

9 Brigger (2007) Ch. 2; cf. Dietler and Herbich (1998) 250, n. 5. It is difficult to detect any patterns among the earliest matt-painted pottery of Italy that would allow us to construct regional typologies, but hyperlocal 'microstyles' probably existed due to communication amongst and education between potters.
10 D'Andria (1979); Yntema (1982).
11 Lo Porto (2004).
12 Descœudres and Robinson (1993); Brigger (2007).

Figures 6.2a–d (a) Bag-shaped jug from the Borgo Nuovo deposit. Museo Archeologico Nazionale di Taranto, Inv. 14090; (b) bag-shaped jug from the Borgo Nuovo deposit. Museo Archeologico Nazionale di Taranto, Inv. 14061; (c) two-handled vessel from the Borgo Nuovo deposit. Museo Archeologico Nazionale di Taranto, Inv. 14049; (d) new motifs in SMG pottery – pendent rays (solid and hatched) and hanging ladders.

Source: (a–c): Photo by author. Used with permission of the Museo Archeologico Nazionale di Taranto; (d): adapted from Yntema (1990) 51.

jug'. The second type is typically called either an 'olla' or a 'kantharos', with tall rising strap-handles and an articulated neck. In this chapter I will refer to them as two-handled vessels. While most of the decorative motifs often (but not always) used in this period have precedent in the earlier matt-painting tradition, the pendent rays and the hanging ladders, almost exclusively restricted to these two new forms, are entirely new. Rather than being applied to the upper half of the vessels, as is common in the rest of the SMG forms, these are regularly placed on the lower half of the jugs and two-handled vessels, 'hanging' from a band that traces the widest point of the vessel body.

The source of influence for these changes in the matt-painted wares of Salento seems to have been the influx of Albanian handmade matt-painted pottery from the Korçë-Devoll Valley (south-eastern Albania) and of Greek

Geometric pottery, possibly from Corinth.[13] The forms and motifs I focus on in particular are attributed to the Albanian Devollian products, which do turn up consistently in eighth-century assemblages, although at a low rate (about 1% of any context).[14] There are two explanations that have been given for the sustained presence of Albanian material in Salento and the subsequent enduring effects on the local ceramic repertoires. The first is a proposed migration of Illyrians from what is now Albania to Italy who brought these vessels with them and continued to produce matt-painted pottery once they had settled in Italy.[15] The matt-painted pottery is thus taken as one of multiple signs of significant migration from Albania to Italy.[16] The other explanation offered is both economic and grounded in discourse about material culture as a reflections of identity.[17] Herring, for example, addressed potential motivations of potters and the organisation of their production units, thus conceptualising innovation from a non-diffusionist perspective that instead focuses on internal developments. At times, however, economic-focused explanations have tended to be structuralist and functionalist, focusing on cost-benefit analyses and the social functions of *use* rather than *production*.[18] This approach cannot examine how change occurs within the technical processes and social/cognitive worlds of potters, and the extent to which relationships between potters and their communities drive that change.[19]

Herring proposed that the process of stylistic regionalisation in the matt-painted repertoire reflected a desire of a specific group – Salentine potters – to differentiate themselves from others with whom they interacted and communicate their identity.[20] This implies that stylistic change functions primarily as a mode of differentiation and separation in situations of competition for markets and livelihoods by potters who otherwise were inherently conservative. It is difficult, however, to accept this as fully explanatory of the presence of Devollian pottery in Italy and the absorption of its traits into local repertoires. The total quantity of Devollian pottery present at Otranto is overall quite low, so it is unlikely that local potters could face serious competition. The adoption of the two specific forms – the bag-shaped jug and two-handled vessel – is also not explained.

---

13 D'Andria (1979) 18–22; Yntema (1990) 78–82; Herring (1998) 159.
14 Yntema (1990) 53–8.
15 D'Andria (1984) 340–1; Descœudres and Robinson (1993) 30.
16 See Norman (2013) for a similar argument for influence on funerary commemoration in northern Puglia; see also Barresi (2016) 143.
17 Herring (1998).
18 Such economic explanations have some affinity with New Institutional Economics, see Smith in this volume.
19 Wobst (1977); Hodder (1979); Wiessner (1983), (1990). Herring makes use of texts that Dietler and Herbich (1998) explicitly refute as containing partial arguments that do not fully account for both the structure experienced by and agency exerted by craftspeople.
20 Herring (1998), influenced strongly by Wiessner (1983).

Figures 6.3a–d (a) Matt-painted, two-handled vessel with pendant ray motif. National Archaeological Museum of Korçë; (b) matt-painted, two-handled vessel with pendant ray motif. National Archaeological Museum of Korçë; (c) matt-painted, one-handled vessels. National Archaeological Museum of Korçë; (d) selected motifs typical of Devollian Iron Age pottery in the Barç tumulus.

Source: (a–c): Photos by author, taken in 2018; (d): adapted from Yntema (1990) 56. See also Agolli (2014) 640–1.

To explain stylistic change without leaving craftspeople behind or misinterpreting their choices, we must deploy an explicitly interactionist view. This is especially true when discussing regionalisation, development, and innovation within ceramic repertoires. This approach centres interactions between producers/producer and communities/communities of practice rather than tension between broadly conceptualised and rigidly defined ethnic/cultural groups, or between producers and consumers, or between producers and imported objects. When we understand the social embeddedness of craft production, we recognise that material culture change reflects realities beyond difference – it also suggests exchange, heightened communication, alternating cultural affinities and economic foci, rearranged and reconfigured social and learning groups, and shifting ideologies.[21] Colivicchi's consumption-focused explanation for the appearance of new forms begs for a correlate explanation from a production-focused perspective – a description of the new social engagements arising between producers, direct or indirect.[22]

Illyrians across the Adriatic?

The interactionist model requires addressing the proposed migration of individuals from the Devoll Valley in south-eastern Albania to Italy. The narrative of a large migration from the western Balkans to Italy has been repeated frequently through the years.[23] There is much evidence for material exchange across the Adriatic through prehistory, but the distribution of similar objects and styles does not automatically indicate human mobility. Likewise, even if compelling conclusions can be drawn about human mobility from one set of evidence (e.g., burial customs or personal objects such as fibulae, belts, and pendants), this cannot always be applied unquestioningly to another set of evidence (i.e., pottery). To discuss the current Salentine case study, therefore, it is crucial to consider it in its full geographic and material contexts.

What is typically proposed is that populations moved from south-eastern Albania to Italy.[24] This part of Albania was a nexus of communication within the Balkan peninsula during the Iron Age. Presumably, the presence of Devollian pottery at Otranto indicates communication and travel along the Devoll and Seman River basins down to the coast of Albania and then across the Adriatic. The distance between the Adriatic coasts is not problematic since it was short-enough to be easily navigable. However, there is little contemporary material evidence for direct connections between this specific part of Albania and this specific part of Italy. There is evidence for common metal artefacts, mainly personal adornments found in burials, between north-western and central-northern Albania and northern Apulia.[25] However, no burials have been recovered in Salento that date to the period in question, so whether this phenomenon of shared female costume and burial assemblage extended this far south cannot be explored, nor would it say much about ties with south-eastern Albania. Another present, but limited, sign of exchange between Albania and southern Italy

---

21 See Cohen, in this volume, for a wider discussion of interactionist approaches.
22 Colivicchi (2004), (2014).
23 Andrea (1975); Batović (1975); D'Andria (1984); Pallottino (1984) esp. 53–4, 57, 62, 66, 92; Korkuti (1985); Bodinaku (1990); Barresi (2016).
24 D'Andria (1984) 340–1; Descœudres and Robinson (1993) 30.
25 Iaia (2007b); Kurti (2012), (2020).

in this period comes in the form of evidence for trade of bitumen moving from east to west, potentially across the Adriatic, including at multiple large dolii at Otranto that may have been used to store large quantities of the substance.[26] Although evidence for this potential connection is intermittent, Albania was a well-known location for harvesting this resource, which was exploited long term.[27] However, the sources of bitumen are located in south-western Albania, not from the Devoll Valley, and thus it is probable that this bitumen was part of a wider Balkan exchange network that eventually linked with those on the Italian peninsula. Bitumen and metals, along with pottery, could have both belonged to wider, interconnected Adriatic exchange networks, which certainly required the movement of people, but not necessarily migration.

The material evidence of these trans-Adriatic exchanges is sporadic, but constant through time, and involves various other artefact classes and cultural phenomena.[28] There is little to suggest a major population transfer. The 'maximalist' model of Albanian/Illyrian migration to south-eastern Italy cannot explain the patterns that characterise the material culture of Salento and wider Puglia. This material culture is admittedly idiosyncratic, but to explain it cursorily by proposing major migratory episodes for which there is scant evidence overlooks a more nuanced answer: that the indigenous peoples of Iron Age Puglia communicated with other peoples of the Adriatic region, but that this communication happened at various scales and intensities over time, involving and influencing individuals holding various social roles, including craftspeople. The intention is not to downplay communication or cultural interaction but to understand the multi-scalar nature of both and the integrative nature of these phenomena.

If we examine the hypothesis that Illyrian people, Illyrian objects, or both were present in Salento in the Iron Age, how would that come to affect local ceramic production? It is difficult to accept the suggestion that pure consumer demand would have been suddenly significant and influential enough to create changes in local behaviours and choices. Why would local people want these vessels? What value were they assigning to them? How can imports drive demand if most consumers do not actually know about the imports prior and or do not assign them sufficient value to drive local production? Unfortunately, the lack of burial evidence for Salento in this period means we cannot examine contemporary burial assemblages for clues about if or how these vessels were used as cultural objects.[29] Their production alone, however, does suggest that there were individuals in Salento who

---

26 Guglielmino (2012); Iacono (2018) 181.
27 Morris (2006), (2014); Pennetta *et al.* (2020).
28 Broodbank (2013) offers brief discussion of the phenomenon. Iacono (2018) Ch. 2 provides a cursory discussion of some of the published evidence, however there is no single publication that comprehensively collects all of it.
29 Yntema (1982); Lo Porto (2004).

wanted and used these shapes. Who, then, was producing them? Engaging with research from Albania can help explore this as it provides studies of contemporary Devollian pottery in Albania.[30]

A recent study by Esmeralda Agolli approached the production and distribution of southern Albanian pottery in the Bronze and Iron Ages (2500–500 BCE) in Albania proper.[31] Her research tracked the qualitative properties of the matt-painted pottery of southern Illyria to examine the changing social contexts and the intensity and models of regional and intra-regional networks in the period. Her discussion was not restricted to the Devollian pottery, but also addressed the matt-painted pottery of all parts of Albania. As a result, it is possible to use her conclusions to begin to re-think the relationship between the populations and producers of south-eastern Italy and southern Albania, and trade and mobility between these regions.

Based on ethnographic parallels and systematic analysis of the standardisation and production steps, Agolli argued that, in Iron Age Albania, vessels were produced at the household level by women potters who rarely moved far from their home settlements. At the same time, she noted that the Early Iron Age was a period of change in which the matt-painted pottery became more technically standardised with more attention to varying aesthetic attributes. However, the technological profile of the pottery is consistently one usually associated with household production, and it never reaches the status of a commodity with a sharply increased production scale or assigned value in a formal market.[32] Contrary to assumptions, pottery produced in domestic contexts can be objects of intra- and inter-community exchange,[33] but there is not any strong evidence that this was happening at the inter-regional scale in Iron Age Albania.

While a 'Devollian heartland' in which potters were producing similar vessels with similar techniques of production and decoration could develop through the vertical transmission of knowledge and then subsequent movement of women potters to a new community after marriage,[34] there is little to explain the wider usage or significance of Devollian shapes and motifs into Italy. One possible hypothesis is a general increase in mobility among previously closed/isolated communities. This increased mobility and communication may have allowed the steady change of practices and dispositions widely within the region. Illyrian women may have then travelled to Italy, but perhaps not necessarily those from the Devoll Valley. Another hypothesis is that the vessels produced by these potters were being produced

---

30 Brigger (2007) notes in her dissertation (317–21) that this comparison is absolutely essential; it is unfortunate both that it was written when we had less material available from Albania and that this dissertation has never been published.
31 Agolli (2014).
32 Agolli (2014) 204.
33 Abell (2020) 382–4.
34 As Agolli (2014) argues.

and exchanged somewhere outside of the context of strictly household production for daily use, within wider exchange networks, without the potters themselves being mobile.

There are multiple hypotheses for this journey across the Adriatic, of either people or concepts, that must be tested from a material perspective. The present study forces us to determine whether Illyrian potters were migrating to Italy and producing at the household level, whether Illyrians were bringing/exporting these vessels already made but also creating a demand for similar products among local Italians, whether only the pottery was moving, or some combination of the above. To get the clearest picture, it is important to compare – technologically and compositionally – the imported Illyrian pottery to that from secure contexts in southern Albania as well as to local SMG. However, even before moving to these archaeometric approaches, it is important to identify the questions about production and learning that are most important and to develop a methodology for preliminary analyses. For this case study, then, there are specific theoretical considerations and methodological approaches that can be combined to address these questions. This approach can be also applied to other studies examining issues of stylistic change and migration. A robust understanding of producer agency, learning processes, and social interactions must underlie the necessary close study of the material.

Producer agency and social contexts for material culture change

New styles in artefact repertoires should be understood as the material correlates of different social behaviours that arise and adapt through periods of increased social entanglement as connectivity between microregions ebbed and flowed. In periods of material culture change, it is critical to think through implications of these moments of increased connection on producer communities. Change should be understood as also driven by choices and/or interactions between producers or producer communities rather than solely by consumer desire.

The interpretation of the presence and style of 'high-value objects' and 'prestige goods' is often linked to discussions of 'elite' identity, status display, and personal connection with other elite communities. Stylistic or morphological change through the incorporation of 'foreign' or external styles in local products is usually attributed to these elite individuals, their need to demonstrate their power locally, their desire to communicate some sort of oppositional identity, and their control over local industries or artisans. This, admittedly, is the case in certain contexts, and some elites likely coveted foreign or foreign-looking objects. However, such a generalising model makes broad assumptions about consumer–producer relationships based on a capitalist, rational economic idea and denies the agency of producers. Furthermore, it cannot be applied uniformly to all societies or all periods. Economic preoccupations have also beleaguered attempts to centre the motivations of producers who innovate, leading to conclusions that innovation is not logical, is high-risk, and is undertaken as a reaction to external pressures.[35] The result is a rigid paradigm for ceramic style which is both increasingly external to the context of production and necessarily homogeneous until some economic peril or consumer desire suddenly forces individual potters or communities of potters to change typical behaviours in order to compete on the market. This also supposes that all actions taken by craftspeople during the production process are undertaken with a specific idea in mind for what a consumer should understand and communicate when looking at or using the product.

External factors do have a part to play, but they are not invariably cultural (the need to communicate identity) or economic (the need to compete in the market). There are also external factors that are social and material. Dietler and Herbich's exploration of material culture change made illuminating use of Bourdieu's dynamic and relational concept of *habitus*[36] to argue that the practices of craftspeople are both conditioned by structure and continuously reshape that structure. When we approach material culture change through this lens, we understand that craftspeople exist and develop within a set of material and social conditions that dictate the development of certain dispositions that constitute their *habitus*. This, in turn, structures the way they respond and behave when faced with changes, opportunities, or problems (technical or social) that might be hyper-local or might have a regional or supra-regional origin. In concrete terms, when we think through what this means for the actual process of producing an object, we conclude that these changes, opportunities, and problems force craftspeople to make decisions to respond to them at any, or all, stages of that process.[37] Those responses contribute to, and alter, the material and social contexts of the dynamic *habitus*, which will in turn structure further responses infinitely.

The potential range of responses and decisions that could be made by craftspeople is vast, but the choices made are not random. They are conditioned by various factors, both material and social. Craftspeople are 'social actors' in their own right, and the very actions of not only producing something but also teaching another person how to produce something are social activities. Every choice made at every step of the production process is influenced by, and itself influences, the social world of the producer, the contexts of their teaching, and their own embodied learning. Because craftspeople do not exist as islands but are deeply embedded in their communities, their innovations and their responses to changing material and social

---

35 Wobst (1977); Arnold (1985); Herring (1998).
36 Bourdieu (1977), (1980).
37 Dietler and Herbich (1998) 245–8; cf. Giddens (1984).

contexts have the potential to set off a 'ripple effect' or to themselves be a ripple already formed by some earlier decision and pushing forward yet another. But the process of macro-scale material culture changes does not happen overnight; relying on macro-scale perspectives focused on bounded cultural structures is itself inadequate. Well before changes or innovations can be detected or appreciated at the macro scale, a long series of preceding changes will have occurred within the producers' social world, particularly within their contexts of learning and training. Craftspeople linked within that world, and within those contexts, belong to a 'community of practice'. It is through the ongoing social interaction within and between communities of practice that we can explain how perceivable material culture change can eventually result from a series of decisions and responses structured by *habitus*.[38]

A community of practice is constituted by craftspeople who, due to the shared context of their learning and training, make similar productive and technical choices which are socially embedded and driven by a variety of environmental and cultural factors. In the context of ceramic production, we are referring to choices made when procuring, sorting, and adulterating raw materials, forming vessels, modifying their surfaces in topography and decoration, and so forth. Members of communities of practices typically make consistently similar choices throughout the production process, especially for steps requiring accumulated skill (i.e., wheel-throwing), but innovation and differentiation to varying degrees do occur.

The communities of practice approach is grounded in the idea of situated learning as described by Lave and Wenger.[39] The authors proposed that learning was both a process linked to daily life and interactions and something that was grounded in participation; skills are neither fixed nor only mutable solely in times of flux. Artisans, and the communities of practice to which they belong, are fully engaged and dynamically entwined with their wider, sometimes geographically immediate/local, community; thus, they are bound up in the same changing spheres of interaction as the consumers of their products, experiencing the same shifts in environmental, economic, social, and political realities that structure their actions, their dispositions, and any adjustments. Various episodes of turbulence (in a neutral, not necessarily negative, sense) also forge contacts between producers/producer communities with other individuals, groups, objects, and ideas. These new interactions elicit responses manifesting as material or stylistic change.

In practical and productive terms, multiple communities of practice may co-exist in one geographic place or region (i.e., groups producing different classes of pottery at a single site) and might also overlap (i.e., groups that

---

38 Lave and Wenger (1991); Dietler and Herbich (1998); Gosselain (1998); Wenger (1998).
39 Lave and Wenger (1991).

share the same process for clay processing but not for vessel decoration, groups that use the same method for the production of fine pottery but different methods for large storage vessels).[40] A community of practice is not necessarily restricted to one artefact class – a group of potters may have their own characteristic ways of producing coarse pottery and fine pottery that differ from the production of coarse and fine pottery by other groups of potters. A single community of practice may also be spread across significant geographic distance and, though some elements of their production process may change to adhere to local custom, there are certain habits and gestures that may remain unchanged.[41]

These communities, and their physical productive output, are not static entities. They develop and reorient constantly through interactions within their own group and outside of it, with other producers, with consumers, with their families, and with social peers.[42] They may also be connected to each other indirectly as they become engaged in broader 'constellations of practice' through the agency of boundary objects that connect communities or through individual brokers who exist at the peripheries of different communities of practice and bridge social gaps between them.[43]

While the transmission of technical knowledge tends towards consistency, innovation was a frequent response to interactions, both quotidian and exceptional – between potters, between their loci of interaction, between potters and the objects within their sphere of existence, and between potters and the very materials and resources essential for their craft.[44] Community members could also act as mediators bringing together groups of producers with distinct knowledge bases, allowing for different bodies of knowledge to intersect, for new information to be exchanged, and thus for innovation to occur.[45] This type of brokerage does not necessitate a demand issued by consumer to producer – that is, a standard market-driven approach to stylistic change via a capitalist lens, one that suggests someone who wants a specific type of pot would visit a workshop and commission it on the spot.

The gradual, developmental nature of innovations in ceramic production and the influence on, and from, wider social and cultural phenomena underscore the need for highly contextualised studies of local and regional change. The transmission process of technical or procedural dispositions occurs at the collective level within social groups/communities of practice,

---

40 Gosselain (2016b) reviews an example of the potters of the Niger River Polychrome Tradition, who produce what is typically seen as a relatively homogeneous class but include several variations at all stages of the *chaînes opératoires*.
41 Gosselain (1998) 83, 102–4; Abell (2014) 532, n. 277, (2020).
42 Bowser and Patton (2008).
43 Wenger (1998) 126–7; Davies (2005); Knappett and van der Leeuw (2014) 73; Lyons and Clark (2012); Roddick and Stahl (2016) 10–1; Gosselain (2016b); Abell (2020).
44 Roddick and Stahl (2016); Gosselain (2016b).
45 Knappett and van der Leeuw (2014); Gosselain (2016b).

which are themselves highly dynamic – growing or shrinking, incorporating other groups partially or wholly, adapting to new material and social circumstances.[46] Intergenerational continuities or modifications of the technical traditions can indicate fluctuating compositions of the social components or age cohorts of the community of practice and the dynamic tension involved in that fluctuation, as new members are incorporated or as younger potters with different priorities grow older and assume new statuses in their communities – all against the backdrop of changing sociopolitical realities.[47]

It is thus important to identify and describe co-existing *chaînes opératoires* – the series of operations undertaken in a specific order to transform raw material into finished product – to identify where and how adaptations begin to propel change. The combinations within the sequences of techniques, methods, gestures, and tools employed in the stages of forming finished vessels from raw clay will vary between individuals and between communities of practice, even those existing in proximity, but will also be altered when necessary. The degree of variation and standardisation from a morphological perspective and across these production sequences allows for the identification of homogeneity or variability across assemblages and thus across local producer groups. Sudden changes can suggest an influx of new elements, ideas, and/or persons into the social sphere, or adjusting economic realities. Interpretations can then address the dynamics of social and historical change in new ways that centre producers as agents rather than as passive and reactive.

Analysing SMG pottery: first steps

SMG pottery is a tricky data set to analyse due to the unevenness of publication in multiple respects, including lack of publication, barriers to travel with the purpose of accessing unpublished data, and inconsistency in what kind of information is presented across those publications that do exist. For example, some publications include fabric descriptions while others do not, and some ceramic specialists provide measurements that were not collected or not published by others. This next section will, however, demonstrate possible analyses that can be done with the data that have been published and offer pathways for continued exploration.

Ideal comparative explorations would involve petrological and chemical studies of the material in order to look at the different choices made when selecting resources (clays, tempers),[48] but they would not tell us whether

---

46 Roux (2015) 102–3.
47 Bowser and Patton (2008); Roux (2015) 103.
48 Some of this compositional analysis has been carried out using x-ray fluorescence (XRF) and laser-ablated inductively-coupled plasma mass spectrometry (LA-ICPMS) to test the chemical and elemental composition of matt-painted pottery from both Salento and from Albania. The Salentine material from Otranto, Vaste, and I Fani was analysed by E.G.D. (Ted)

Illyrian potters were present and actively producing in Salento, or whether they interacted with local potters. Chemical and elemental analysis can tell us whether potters were making use of the same clay sources, but exploring standardisation and the steps of the production process can allow for identification of the technical and procedural choices of different potters or groups of potters.

Given the current state of published data, it is possible to consider degrees of standardisation across assemblages in a general way. Examining the morphometric standardisation of the Salentine vessels, and comparing it to those of the Devollian vessels, can offer insight into the metrical and/or conceptual comparability of these shapes across cultures. Approaches to the degree of standardisation usually refer to variation or homogeneity in the materials, dimensions/shape, and/or decoration of an object. The degree of standardisation across a group of objects has, in the past, been interpreted as a reflection of the degrees of economic specialisation, skill (through experience or effort or a combination thereof), and/or intensity of production (i.e., full- or part-time) in pottery production.[49] Higher standardisation, and thus more uniformity, has been taken to reflect higher rates of production by specialised, full-time artisans in routine fashion. However, standardisation or variation can also reflect specific economic, environmental, cultural, and/or social conditions, realities, or constraints.[50] Some attributes that might reflect standardisation or variability are intentional and consciously controlled by the producer – these might include decoration, size/shape, or the specific choice of materials based on knowledge about their properties or intended use that is passed from teacher to apprentice or parent to child. This is not a type of standardisation that comes from simple mimicry but implies a full understanding by the producer of the choices they are making, whether functional or otherwise. Other attributes are mechanical and are unintentionally or unconsciously created, which might include colour differences in fired pots or choice of materials without any specific attention to formal properties (i.e., chosen due to proximity or availability).[51]

Robinson in 2006 (Robinson [2007]). The Albanian material from the Cave of Tren, in the easternmost corner of the Devoll Valley, was undertaken recently (Agolli *et al.* [2020]). The difference in years and in research questions mean that a comparison of the results of these studies is difficult and can only be suggestive rather than definitive. Robinson's results indicate that the pottery he tested shows clear chemical differences from local pottery including Salento Middle Geometric, being noticeably lower in calcium and higher in iron than the other samples. They are thus certainly non-local, though their precise origin cannot yet be determined. The results from the Tren material seem to show similar compositions for these vessels tested by Robinson. Further analysis and the acquisition of comparable data sets would allow for us to confirm whether those non-local vessels are indeed from the Devoll Valley.

49 Blackman *et al.* (1993); Costin and Hagstrum (1995); Longacre (1999).
50 Costin and Hagstrum (1995).
51 Costin and Hagstrum (1995); Roux (2003a).

As ever, archaeological and ethnographical evidence has revealed that we are mistaken to assume too much when we encounter high standardisation or high variability. Low standardisation/high variability is one criterion often considered when trying to determine intensity and organisation of ceramic production, but, as already mentioned, the household–workshop dichotomy is problematic – high variability can emerge from workshop production contexts (especially where multiple specialists share a work space), just as high standardisation can be achieved by part-time, household-based producers.[52] Handmade pottery will often reflect more variability than wheel-made by nature but with simple tools – such as a stick to measure height and diameter – even handmade vessels can be produced in standard dimensions.[53] Ethnographic studies also indicate that even where the wheel is used, there can often be a surprising degree of variation within assemblages, even among vessels of the same general shape or type.[54] From the ancient world, note the interesting example of conical cups at Bronze Age Ayia Irini (Kea) and Phylakopi (Milos).[55] At Ayia Irini, the cups seem intentionally standardised in dimension, but at Phylakopi there is more metrical variation despite also being wheel-made. There is no way to precisely account for the difference, but automatically assuming that Kean potters were more skilled or faced more economic competition is difficult to support. A viable option is considering that at Phylakopi there was no cultural expectation that a conical cup should be of a certain size, or at least that even within a broad 'size class'; consumers at Phylakopi were not bothered with metrical uniformity. In this case study, morphometric standardisation is thus not employed as a direct proxy for production organisation.

Morphometric standardisation

To examine variation within morphometric attributes, such as height, diameter, wall thickness, and handle thickness, the coefficient of variation (CV) for the sample is used, which indicates the degree of variation from the mean expressed as a percentage.[56] A lower CV suggests high standardisation, while a higher CV suggests low standardisation. Eerkens and Bettinger established

---

52 Esposito and Zurbach (2014) 40; Kotsonas (2014) 12.
53 Longacre (1999) provides an ethnographic study from the northern Philippines explored the practices of four potters (two very experienced and two with less experience) who made traditional water jars by hand using the paddle and anvil method before finishing them on the tournette; these vessels were very standardised despite being handmade.
54 Benco (1988); Esposito and Zurbach (2014); Fragnoli (2021).
55 Berg (2004).
56 Coefficient of Variation = (Standard Deviation / Mean) * 100. There are other methods for evaluating standardisation such as the Brown-Forsythe test and jack-knife method, but CVs are adequate for evaluating intra-site phenomena and are also relatively simple to undertake and communicate. Kvamme *et al.* (1996); Longacre (1999); Eerkens and Bettinger (2001); Kotsonas (2014).

that even a specialised and highly skilled potter producing identical objects can and will commit 'scalar errors' when producing multiple objects from memory and that variation below 1.7% was thus not possible unless production was automated or an independent standard of measurement (i.e., use of tools) was implemented.[57] Roux thus suggested that a CV of up to 3% reflects highly specialised local production at high intensity, the 3–6% range reflects a slightly lower scale of production, the 6–10% range reflects small-scale and part-time specialist production, and any figures above 10% suggests that producers were not specialists (see Tables 6.1 and 6.2).[58] Roux's figures do not necessarily provide a simple correlate for production organisation. The most standardised vessels could have been made by producers who produced at a large scale, and whose routine high-volume production might either require or foster an ability to repeatedly recreate vessels of consistent dimensions. Conversely, they could also have been

Table 6.1 Types of specialisation and proposed corresponding levels of standardisation.

Type of specialisation	*Intentional Standardisation*	*Mechanical Standardisation*
Non-specialist	Low	Low
Individual specialisation	Low-high	Low
Community specialisation	Low-high	Low-moderate
Dispersed workshop	Low-high	Moderate
Nucleated workshop	Low-high	Moderate-high
Dispersed corvée	Low	Low
Nucleated corvée	High	Low-moderate
Individual retainer	Low	Low-moderate
Retainer workshop	High	High

Source: Adapted from Costin and Hagstrum (1995).

Table 6.2 Coefficients of Variation associated with varying scales of production.

Scale of production	*Range of Expected CVs*
Large-scale production (14,000 pots a year per potter)	< 3%
Large-scale production or small-scale production (between 14,000 and 4,000 pots a year per potter)	3–6%
Small-scale production or very small-scale production (6,000 pots a year or fewer per potter)	> 6%

Source: Adapted from Roux (2003a) 780.

57 Eerkens and Bettinger (2001) 494–5.
58 Roux (2003a); Kotsonas (2014); Fragnoli (2021).

made by producers who produce less but actively try to ensure standardisation across their products (possibly with the help of tools). Additionally, her study of CVs addressed standardisation across limited production events and thus the resultant models are idealised; we should expect that assemblages and products made across a significant period of time will not exactly map on to her figures directly and might be more variable. This does not mean that these are not useful models to consider, but it does suggest that this kind of analysis must take a flexible approach, especially diachronically.

Metrical data available from various sites in Albania and in Italy, including for the shapes in question, allow for an initial exploration of morphometric standardisation.[59] Agolli reported remarkably low CVs among the two-handled vessels from the Barç tumulus near Korçë. Two-handled vessels from the nearby tumulus at Kamenicë were less standardised than those at Barç but still reflect relatively low CVs.[60] To attempt to compare what are interpreted as analogous, similar, or inspired shapes in Italy, CVs were calculated for the bag-shaped jugs and two-handled vessels at Otranto, I Fani, and Taranto.[61] The results are presented in Tables 6.3 and 6.4 and compared to the CVs from the analogous one-handled vessels at the Barç and Kamenicë tumuli, as well as to the one-handled vessels from Lofkënd.[62] This material was included here because the site is close to the coast and because the matt-painted pottery there does exhibit similarities to that from the Devollian area.[63]

It is a challenge to interpret these figures. Of primary concern is that the sample sizes from Italy (especially from Taranto) are larger than those available from Albania, but some early observations are worth exploring. The low CVs for the two-handled vessels from the Barç tumulus, and similarly low CVs for those from Kamenicë, suggest that at these settlements there must have been a general idea of what size these vessels should be, and there

---

59 Uneven publication of excavations and inconsistencies in terminology and detail across multiple projects' publications mean that a robust exploration of standardisation must wait for further, multi-methodological investigation.
60 Agolli (2014) Appendix 2 584–5. These vessels date to the Early Iron Age period which Agolli identifies as ranging from 1100 to 800 BCE. More precise dating is unclear, but the tumuli have multiple burial events with material dating as early as the Early Bronze Age (second millennium). States of preservation of the vessels were not entirely clear.
61 Lo Porto (2004); Brigger (2007). These are from the same chronological period (dating broadly between 775 and 730 BCE). The material from I Fani and Otranto is from settlement contexts while that from Taranto is from a single deposit of an unidentified nature. States of preservation of the vessels were not entirely clear, though it appears that vessels from Taranto were more complete than those from I Fani and Otranto.
62 A comparison between the data for one-handled vessels at Lofkënd and those in Italy is thus important for exploring whether there might have been an intermediary closer to the coast for the transmission of Devollian styles and Albanian shapes. The Lofkënd vessels come from Phase II-Va at the site, between the eleventh and ninth centuries BCE: this is slightly earlier than the other vessels in Albania and in Italy.
63 Agolli (2014); Pevnick and Agolli (2015).

Table 6.3 Comparison of Coefficients of Variation for bag-shaped jugs from Italian sites and one-handled vessels from Albanian sites. This includes versions with articulated neck and without articulated neck.

Site	Height		Diameter			
Otranto	29.56%		26.42%			
Taranto	19.29%		13.2%			
I Fani	31.79%		19.48%			
Barç	18.28%		16.05%			
Lofkënd	Rim: 10.88%	Max: 13.17%	Base: 6.2%	Rim Int: 8.27%	Rim Ext: 11.71%	Max: 9.79%

Source: Data from Yntema (1982) (Otranto); Lo Porto (2004) (Taranto); Brigger (2007) (I Fani; Otranto); Agolli (2014) (Barç); Pevnick and Agolli (2015) (Lofkënd).

Table 6.4 Coefficients of Variation for two-handled vessels from Italian and Albanian sites.

Site	Height (rim)	Diameter (rim)
Taranto	25.26%	27.78%
I Fani	20.88%	13.3%
Barç	8.64%	3.37%
Kamenicë	14.96%	10.42%

Source: Data from Lo Porto (2004) (Taranto); Brigger (2007) (I Fani); Agolli (2014) (Barç and Kamenicë).

was possibly less tolerance for variability (on the part of either producer or consumer or both). This is also the case for one-handled, fine light vessels at Lofkënd; the sample size is small (six vessels), but the fabrics are so different that they cannot have been made by the same potter. However, across other sites, there was a high tolerance for variability in the morphology of one-handled vessels more generally.

The volume/scale of production and the generally low standardisation overall (cf. Table 6.2) mean that those incidences of higher standardisation were not the result of mass production, specialisation, or routinisation in local production. This level of standardisation could be achieved through the use of measuring implements, but the question would remain: why would so much attention be paid to one specific shape and not others at these Albanian sites? Whether measuring implements were used or not, the data suggest that an effort was made to keep two-handled vessels at a specific size, or capable of holding a specific volume. The reasons for this are unclear and are currently irrecoverable. Comparison in future with examples recovered from non-funerary contexts may yield more answers; it is possible that these funerary goods were modelled on, or the same as, vessels used in life for specific social or cultural practices.

'The potter is by nature a social animal' 119

The boxplots[64] in Figures 6.4a–d are useful for visualising the similarities and differences across these samples in terms of absolute size and size ratio, as well as the degree of variation within each sample group.[65] Interesting patterns emerge when the data are approached in this fashion. There seem to be significant size and ratio differences among the vessels from Lofkënd, while those found elsewhere – from Taranto and Barç and, for one-handled vessels, I Fani – show some interesting and perhaps unexpected overlaps. The data

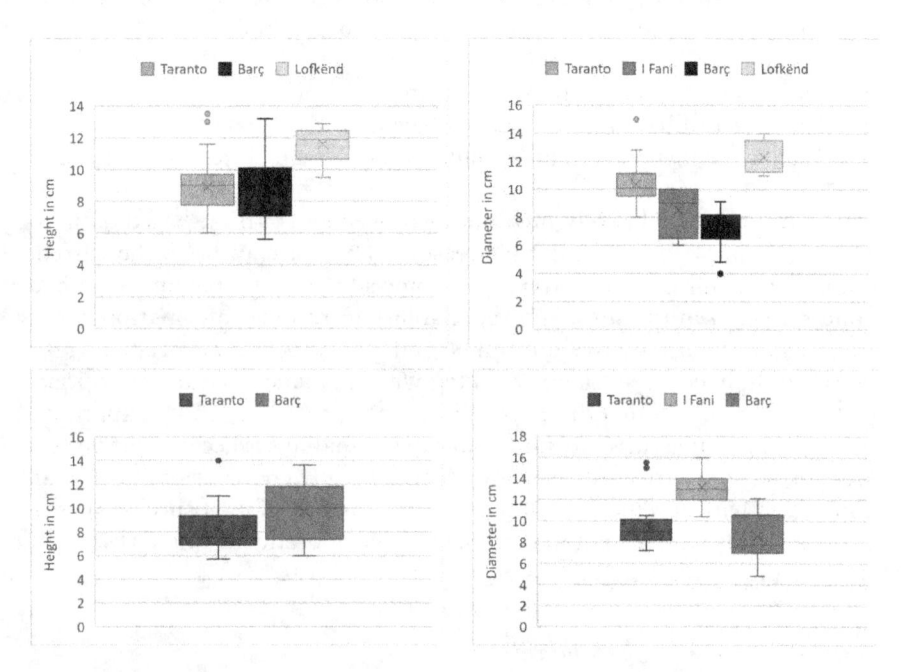

Figures 6.4a–d (a) (Coefficients of Variation CV) for height (to rim) of one-handled vessels; (b) CV for rim diameter of one-handled vessels; (c) CV for height (to rim) of two-handled vessels; (d) CV for rim diameter of two-handled vessels.

64 Boxplots (or box-and-whisker plots) divide the data into quartiles; one quarter of the data is between each line or "whisker" and the top or bottom edge of the box, and within the box two more quartiles are above and below the line that indicates the median. This type of graph is helpful for displaying the dispersion of data across ranges. Taller boxes and longer whiskers suggest more variable data, while shorter boxes and shorter whiskers suggest data that cluster around centre values. Overlaps between boxes and medians suggest some similarity in the data and the groups that they reflect, whereas there are differences between boxes and medians that do not overlap.
65 There is no boxplot for Kamenicë as there is no detailed pottery catalogue published. Otranto has also been removed from the boxplot due to inconsistencies in approach to measurement (reconstructed vs. measurements of sherds); while estimating CVs from this is fine because those measurements are internally consistent, placing them on a boxplot with data obtained differently is inadvisable since these are not congruent metrics.

seem to indicate that, although the vessels in Italy were not as standardised as those from the area around Korçë, the Italian vessels are of similar dimension to those from Albania. Those at Lofkënd are of generally larger dimensions. This offers some early data that might rule out Lofkënd and western/coastal Albania as an intermediary and reinforces earlier hypotheses of a connection with the Devollian pottery specifically. Whether that connection is direct imitation or producer mobility will be further explored in future analyses.

Let us revisit the three significant hypotheses that have been used to explain the new production of these vessel shapes in Italy:

1   There were Illyrian potters in Salento.
2   There were Illyrian consumers in Salento.
3   There were Illyrian pots in Salento, but no Illyrian potters or consumers.

It is difficult to conclusively prove or disprove most of these based on morphometric data alone for multiple reasons. Those are, in brief, the current inability to confirm fabric diversity at some sites, the sharp contrast in find contexts between the sites, and the inability to recover information about use/consumption. Tentatively, it can be said that whoever was producing the vessels in Italy clearly was not working with the same sense of appropriate standardisation, but that there are indications of a similar sense of appropriate size ranges. It is currently impossible to say that this is because the potters were or were not from Albania, or because there were or were not Illyrian consumers with specific expectations, or whether outside of specific sites in Albania it was not relevant to consider size when producing these vessels, or because the producers were simply imitating imports.

Beyond morphometric standardisation

Morphometric standardisation can be a problematic attribute to focus upon alone, especially when approaching partially or fully handmade vessels, and when we cannot access information that would allow us to recover the uses or significance of these vessels in different contexts. Standardisation or variability in technological and production processes, as well as in the actual composition of clay fabrics (reflecting different paste 'recipes'), can therefore provide another approach to understanding the organisation of ceramic production at a site. Compositional and technical choices – of materials, of sequences, of forming gestures – are less visible in the final product but are also deeply embedded in the learning and interactions of potters and are thus important to investigate.[66]

The choices made throughout the process may have, at some point, originated in practical and functional considerations, but through the diachronic

---

66   Gosselain (1998), (2000); Hilditch (2014) 26–7.

transmission of knowledge between potters became characteristic of specific communities of practice. Members of these communities might thus not make the most 'practical' choices when producing vessels. They may instead make choices that were socially contextual and tied to their identities – that is, it was the way they learned to do it and the way they always did it. This is directly relevant to the current case study and to producer-focused studies of material culture change because, when the composition and forming of vessels recovered locally that 'look foreign' (in this case, look Devollian) are closely analysed, it should become clear whether their producers are in fact from a community of practice entirely separate from those responsible for the rest of the local repertoire or belonged to multiple communities of practice and potentially could act as brokers between them. In the former case, the two *chaînes opératoires* would probably have some major differences, while, in the latter case, there would be similarities between the *chaînes opératoires* for different kinds of production, including in elements that are not replicable on the basis of observation of a finished pot.[67] The need to combine approaches when exploring such issues is demonstrated by a comparable study exploring Late Cycladic conical cups and Minoan-inspired ledge-rim bowls at Akrotiri. While the producers of both did make use of a typically Minoan forming method – combining coil-building with smoothing on the wheel – they used typically local clay paste recipes that did not vary sharply from their other products and did not reflect Minoan approaches to clay/paste processing.[68] This combined methodological approach, which included statistical analysis, scanning electron microscopy (SEM), energy-dispersive X-ray spectroscopy (EDS), quantitative evaluation of materials by scanning electron microscopy (QEMSCAN), petrography, and macroscopic analysis, offers a robust example of the various scales at which material must be studied in order to identify and explore local *chaînes opératoires* and technical behaviours to best examine the nature of change.

To approach the current case study, then, some initial analysis of Salentine fabrics can be done. Salentine matt-painted pottery assemblages comprise eight different fabric groups (Groups IV–XI) as identified by Brigger (Table 6.5).[69] These groups co-exist at multiple Salentine sites. Brigger distinguished them from each other based primarily on the size and sorting of inclusions. Each group has a variety of inclusions, including grog, vegetal/organic material, and micas. However, there is a notable divide even among these eight groups in terms of the predominant macro inclusions found in the clay paste.

---

67 Davies (2005); Knappett and van der Leeuw (2014) 73; Lyons and Clark (2012); Roddick and Stahl (2016) 10–1; Gosselain (2016b).
68 Gillis (1990); Hilditch (2008), (2014).
69 Brigger (2007) 20–3. Brigger identified 11 groups; three were from Lipari and thus are not addressed here. These groups are present at I Fani, Vaste, and Otranto. The Taranto matt-painted awaits this analysis.

Table 6.5 Salentine matt-painted fabric groups, as identified in Brigger (2007), 20–3.

Fabric Group	Colour variance	Macro Inclusions	Inclusion Size	Other Inclusions	Surfaces	Slips	Finishing
IV	Grey-brown, beige-brown, beige-yellow, grey-pink, beige-orange, orange	Limestone	1–7 mm	Shell, quartz, vegetal inclusions, grog, micas	Hard, porous, sometimes with deep cracks and holes	Self-slip in similar tones to the paste	Brushed bottom; internal and external surfaces smoothed *a stecca*
V	Beige-orange, orange-brown, orange	Limestone		Iron, sand, micas, grog, plant inclusions	Hard, porous, sometimes with cracks	Similar tones to the paste, or off-white or beige-yellow	Internal and external surfaces smoothed *a stecca*
VI	Beige-pink to pink	Limestone	0.5–9 mm	Iron, mica, quartz, shells, grog, plant inclusions	Hard, sometimes with cracks, **never porous**	Similar tones to the paste or beige-yellow or orange	Internal and external surfaces smoothed *a stecca*
VII	Beige-brown	Limestone	0–5mm	Iron, plant inclusions, micas, shell, grog	Hard, porous, sometimes with cracks and holes	Similar tones to the paste or beige-yellow or light grey	Smoothed internal surfaces.
VIII	Beige-brown, beige-yellow, beige-orange, light grey	Quartz		Iron, mica, shells, grog, plant inclusions	Hard, porous, sometimes with cracks and holes	Similar tones to the paste or green-yellow or light grey	Smoothed internal and external surfaces
IX	Brown-red, beige-orange, orange	Quartz		Iron, mica, shell, grog	Hard, porous, sometimes with cracks and holes	Similar tones to the paste or beige-brown or brown-yellow	Smoothed internal and external surfaces
X	Beige-pink	Quartz, iron, mica		Grog	Hard	Similar tones to the paste or beige-yellow	Smoothed internal and external surfaces
XI	Beige-brown	Quartz, iron, mica		Plant inclusions	Hard, sometimes with cracks	Similar tones to the paste or beige-yellow	Smoothed internal and external surfaces

What exactly do these variations in clay recipe signify? There are multiple answers which potentially interrelate. From a practical and mechanical perspective, the differences in inclusion size and type may be functional choices made by potters. Different inclusions have different effects in a clay body at various stages of vessel manufacture. The firing temperature range of Italian matt-painted pottery is 900–1000° C.[70] At these high temperatures, the minerals and inclusions within a clay body undergo multiple changes. The transformations of quartz can reduce vessel shrinkage during firing, but above 870° C there occurs a second inversion of the quartz that could cause stress on the vessel and result in cracking.[71] Calcareous inclusions, such as limestone, can be even more problematic. Calcium carbonate begins to decompose on heating to 700–900° C and forms lime and carbon dioxide. Upon cooling, lime absorbs moisture from the air, forming quicklime and releasing heat, resulting in the expansion of the clay and stress to the clay body, resulting in cracks, spalling, and even the crumbling of the body and complete vessel failure. Solutions to this problem are possible – the use of finer inclusions, the addition of salt to prevent spalling, and wetting hot vessels with water.[72] Larger inclusions do increase the strength of fired vessels and slow heat transfer through the body, but smaller quartz inclusions can avoid causing stress during firing due to 'thermal dimensional mismatch' in which various minerals expand differentially.[73] There is a delicate balance to be struck.

It is clear that the different fabrics identified in Salento reflect multiple phenomena. While there are colour differences across them, colour is also affected by firing temperature/control and the clay itself and therefore is not the ideal attribute to discuss here. Instead, a focus on what were active choices, and likely not accidental outcomes, is important. First, differential processing of material is evident; the Group VII fabric, for example, shows consistently smaller limestone inclusions, while other fabrics contain these inclusions in different size ranges. Producers of these different groups were accustomed to grinding their limestone to different fineness before including it as temper. Second, some understanding of the different performance of various tempers may be reflected in the choices of quartz (sands) or limestone (crushed rocks). Third, there are some signs of being able to appropriately offset potential problems that could be caused. All of the calcareous fabric groups include vessels with cracks and holes, although some are porous while others are not. This suggests that there were some consequences for the choice of temper (in both size and material), but also that some steps were being taken to mitigate them. Among the quartz fabrics, holes and cracks

---

70 Herring (1998) 37.
71 Rice (2015) 108, 112.
72 Rice (2015) 80, 108–9.
73 Rice (2015) 86, 329.

and porous surfaces are a problem except for Group X, which is described as having a very smooth surface. Fourth, all of the fabric groups describe vessels with a self-slip that appears as a beige-yellow, except for Group IV, which not only has more variable slip colours but also reflects a habit of finishing the bottom of the vessel with a brush (perhaps suggesting that these were dipped upside down into the slip while others were fully dunked). Fifth, three of the groups comprise vessels with surfaces clearly smoothed or burnished (*a stecca*), while the rest were smoothed by another method (perhaps with a cloth or the potter's hand). Finally, the sixth point is not a point of difference but one of general similarity – all fabrics included additions of grog, plant material, and sometimes shell; however, some tended to include all of these, while others tended not to include either plant material or grog at all.

These patterns across the fabric groups are important, and especially so given that all of them are present at multiple sites in Salento and dated to the same period. The overlapping distribution of various fabric groups across multiple settlements in the extreme reaches of the Salentine Peninsula suggests a context in which multiple potters or communities of practice co-existed at one or more settlements or were themselves mobile (or some combination of the two). Robinson's chemical analysis indicates chemical differences between some material from I Fani and Otranto, supporting the existence of local production rather than a strict model of centralised production at Otranto followed by transport to nearby centres.[74] The overlapping of steps in the production process is especially interesting given the clear differences. The image of organisation of production in the settlements of Salento is one in which essentially the same natural resources were exploited to make the pottery, but with different approaches to processing some of them. Given some of the functional implications of these choices – that is, that some of them could cause serious problems for vessel integrity – one might wonder whether potters discussed their choices with other potters in order to achieve an optimal clay recipe. This question, however, assumes that the production steps and technical choices existed only to achieve the optimal product.[75] Approaching this diversity with a robust understanding of communities of practice – how they learned, and what they learned to do – it is clear that some patterns and choices persisted because they are what was learned and taught consistently within those bounded communities. Yet some of these fabric groups might also reflect 'intermediary' practices and choices; the clay recipe of fabric Group VIII shares multiple

---

74 Robinson (2007) 645.
75 Müller *et al.* (2015) undertook an experimental study to assess the addition of phyllite temper to the clay recipes of Bronze Age cooking ware from Akrotiri; they determined that phyllite temper did not increase performance properties of the cookware – it did not increase thermal shock resistance or thermal conductivity. They propose a cultural reason for the change instead, namely Cretan/Minoan influence, as this change in clay recipe coincided with the introduction of a new shape (tripod-leg cooking pot) and of the potter's wheel.

traits in common with groups VI through VII, with the only difference being the choice of quartz-based temper, likely sand, rather than crushed limestone. This fabric group may well be the result of a potter/group of potters interacting with other potters (those who had always used sand) in some way and thus adjusting the recipe. The nature of this interaction is what is difficult to reconstruct.

Let us return to the shapes of interest in this case study. Of the bag-shaped jugs from Otranto and I Fani that Brigger included in her catalogue, about half belong to Group IV and the other half to VIII. Of the two-handled vessels, the majority were also made in Group IV fabric, with a few in Group V. We are dealing with a very small sample – only about a dozen or so vessels of each shape. It is notable that there are plenty of other vessels at these sites that are also made in fabrics IV and VIII – the fabrics of these bag-shaped jugs are not outliers in the context of the local assemblage, despite their 'foreign' shape.

Paths forward

These shapes were produced by potters who were at least partially, if not fully, integrated into the local production sphere, using recipes and fabrics that were common to other shapes. They were also making vessels of vaguely similar dimensions to those from the Devoll Valley. What we do not know is whether there is anything notable (either for similarity or for difference) in the way they were forming these vessels.

There are a number of other methodologies that might be applied to this material to answer further questions, but an analysis of forming techniques of both the Albanian and the Salentine materials is critical to get closer to the fullest possible understanding of the origins of the shapes in Salento. While a potter or group of potters might adapt to new situations post-migration by making use of local resources and learning from other local potters' techniques and recipes, forming methods are an aspect of vessel production that are more resistant to change.[76] If, however, there is a very specific conception of how a type of vessel should be made, local potters might adopt that method and newly arrived potters might continue to produce vessels in the same way even after an episode of displacement or migration. The study of ledge-rim bowls and conical cups at Akrotiri is relevant here again; in that case, it was determined that local potters were using the same paste processing and composition to make these vessels but made use of the wheel for exclusively these two types and not for others. Theran potters thus had had contact with Minoan potters and learned how to use the wheel, but only for vessels that they perceived as Minoan.[77]

76 Arnold (1981); Roux (2011); Gosselain (2018).
77 Hilditch (2014).

We know that the majority of Albanian matt-painted pottery was handmade,[78] and that Salentine matt-painted is generally understood to have combined coil-building with smoothing on the wheel using rotative kinetic energy (RKE). A vessel-by-vessel and attribute-by-attribute analysis of forming is not available in either case, however. This is a major and critical future pathway for the exploration of this case study – the recording of evidence for the shaping, fashioning, and preforming techniques, surface treatments, finishing methods, and tools and instruments that were used for each vessel.[79] This approach would allow not only for the more refined and thorough identification of *chaînes opératoires* within settlements and regions, and the communities of practice they reflect, but also for a very real look at whether there is something different about the forming of the bag-shaped jug and two-handled vessel at Salento. We might want to explore, for example, whether these two shapes were made exclusively by hand without any use of the wheel (and whether that reflects what was happening in Albania contemporaneously), or whether these vessels were formed in the same way as other local vessels. This analysis must go beyond the actual fashioning of the body of the vessel and focus on all other steps in the physical production process. There are multiple ways to attach a handle, for example; at Late Bronze Age Sovjan, handles were attached to the body by means of a clay 'pivot' or nodule, a notably different method than used earlier at the same site.[80] Handles and other appendages would have to be added in different ways depending on whether this was done while the clay was still wet or when it was leather hard,[81] and this might vary between potters. If there are clear differences in the process of physically constructing these two shapes in Salento, this would suggest that local potters had an understanding that these vessels were different and that there were specific ways that they should be made. This would suggest in turn that there was some sort of cultural significance with which they were viewed – whether because they were exposed to some cultural event that involved them, whether they met people who used them, or whether they were producing for customers who wanted to use them in a culturally specific way. This alone would not clarify who these potters were – whether they were local or non-local. If, however, these vessels were built differently than the rest of the assemblage, and if those differences in technique are also reflected in contemporary Albanian matt-painted repertoires, this would be strong evidence to support the presence of Illyrian potters in Salento, or at least of potters who had learned in an Illyrian context.

---

78 Agolli *et al.* (2020) note that there are examples of wheel-made pottery in Iron Age Albania but that the technology was not popular or in wide use.
79 Roux (2016) Ch 2.
80 Gori and Krapf (2015) 97, 101 Fig. 3.
81 Roux (2016) 90.

Conclusions

This chapter has argued for producer-focused, robustly contextualised, and localised approaches to material culture change. Specifically, in the context of ceramic change, I have proposed that close attention to the archaeological correlates of the production process, framed by a disentanglement and description of multiple and possibly overlapping *chaînes opératoires*, is fundamental to this kind of study. My advocacy for this methodology is shaped by the understanding of craftspeople as social actors whose decisions are structured by habits cultivated by their social and material realities. Within this framework, change and innovation are not only possible but undeniable; as craftspeople interact with each other, with their wider communities, with objects, with their 'taskscapes', their choices are shaped by and reciprocally shape infinite possible variables. In this way, material culture change occurs gradually and is driven by choices made by those responsible for producing these objects. The infinite possibility of how change might appear is a function of the dynamism of the *habitus* and the potential for dispositional changes to snowball and result in changes that later, to us, seem sharply divergent.

The changes comprising the regionalisation of Salentine matt-painted pottery are a case study ripe for analysis through this lens. Such analysis must be grounded in the social and material realities of Salentine potters while also engaging with the evidence for high connectivity within Adriatic area – in this case, the southern Adriatic in particular – in the long term. Rather than interpreting the developments of Salentine pottery in the eighth century as a sign of stress and competition, and the formation of regional and local identities as antagonistic or oppositional, we should view material culture changes as unintended reflections or manifestations of identity and belonging rather than necessarily intentional tools for demonstrating it.

Should a fuller comparative analysis reveal that the new vessel shapes – the two-handled vessel and bag-shaped jug – were produced just the same as any other in the settlements of Salento, this is not the end of the road for a producer-driven approach to understanding their production. As it is, there would still be a lack of evidence to support the many hypotheses that could be or have been offered to explain their presence, whether that be those that suppose local potters felt threatened or that local consumers had a sudden appreciation for Devollian-like objects. In this case, we could return to the concept of 'boundary objects',[82] and to the point of this volume – the exchange of ideas, and the ways in which that is codified materially in object form. An object created by one community of practice in one cultural

---

82 Wenger (1998) 103–31; Roddick and Stahl (2016) 10–2.

context may find its way to other producers or consumers in another cultural context, who adapt them for local needs, and invest them with specific and distinct meanings and values. Much like the metal and amber personal adornment from graves in eastern Italy and north-western Albania,[83] these objects may not have been produced by mobile artisans but still materialise the complex histories of millennia of exchange and communication between the coasts of the Adriatic Sea.

---

83 Iaia (2007b); Kurti (2012), (2020).

7 Bronzesmiths and the construction of material identity in central Italy (1000–700 BCE)

Cristiano Iaia

The primary aim of this chapter is to argue that, in the earliest stages of the formation process of urban centres in central Italy, highly innovative and mobile craftspeople actively helped construct new collective and individual identities for emerging social groups, mainly, though not exclusively, articulated along gender lines. Moreover, in this particular context, some craftspeople, and particularly metalworkers – part of an elusive and diverse collective body – were among the agents of intercultural exchange between the 'Etruscan' protourban centres and distant areas, particularly in central and eastern Europe.

Some underlying principles guide this chapter's approach. First is that artefacts are not passive containers of meanings but are active participants in their social context or, indeed, expressions of and participants in a dynamic 'network'.[1] Second is that the technical systems and systemic relationships which existed between producers and consumers in any particular sociocultural context contributed to the shaping of styles and identities that we can recognise in artefacts.[2] In an effort to explore this point and these principles, a selection of artefact classes and related contexts will be examined, with particular regard to the most sophisticated bronze products from the conventionally named 'Villanovan' culture in Etruria (tenth to eighth centuries BCE). For a better contextualisation of this evidence, some comparable artefacts belonging to the 'Latial' culture, immediately to the south, will also be considered.

Before we continue, some caveats are necessary. The evidence garnered from metalwork in the early first millennium BCE in central Italy is inexorably intertwined with the problematic funerary record and, in particular, the idiosyncratic cremation burials common in this period. This issue is not unique to the Early Iron Age (c. 950–730 BCE, henceforth EIA) and is present across many periods

---

* I warmly thank Jeremy Armstrong and Sheira Cohen for inviting me to contribute to their exciting conference, book, and for their excellent editing work. I also owe genuine thanks to the anonymous reviewers, who stimulated what I hope is a decisive improvement of completeness, clarity and consistency of the subjects I discuss in this chapter. All errors and omissions are obviously only mine.
1 Knappett (2005).
2 Dietler and Herbich (1998). See, also, Cohen and Armstrong in this volume.

of human prehistory when the archaeological record is dominated by this one-sided type of evidence.[3] At the onset of the Iron Age,[4] other types of essential archaeological evidence and contexts, well-known in the previous period (the Final Bronze Age, 1150–950 BCE, henceforth FBA), disappeared almost entirely. In central Italy c. 1000–950 BCE, the last 'hoards', that is to say highly diverse assemblages including a comprehensive inventory of metal products (including tools, weapons, etc.), were deposited.[5] This hints at the profound shift in consumption patterns that was taking place during the earliest stages of development of 'proto-urban' centres. However, it also complicates our interpretation of the material deposited subsequently. Following this period, which features significant evidence for metallurgical production linked to daily life, work activities, and the economy, there is an archaeological lacuna of about 100–150 years; this substantially affects our archaeological picture, which will be dominated by a few selected classes of items. A more extensive repertoire of objects reappeared only during the eighth century BCE (in the conventional chronology), or EIA Phase 2, when forms of conspicuous consumption took hold in the ritual sphere. Thus, studying metalwork in this specific period and region means tackling a complicated entanglement between crafts, rituals, and ideology.

In the following pages I shall focus on selected artefact categories that will allow us to trace the relationships between metalwork and group and individual identities, and to survey trans-regional and trans-cultural transfers of models and technologies over broad areas: in particular, weapons (helmets, swords) and fine ornaments (belt plates and ring-pendants). The treatment here constitutes an updating of an argument which I began in a 2005 monograph, in the light of recent discoveries and further reflections.[6]

The construction of warrior material identity at the dawn of the EIA

In contrast to the relative homogeneity of the cremation graves in the FBA in Middle-Tyrrhenian Italy, the transition between the FBA and the EIA, c. 1000–900 BCE, saw a marked divergence in the representation of individuals of different genders within burial assemblages.[7] Metal objects played an important role in this divergence. In this period, grave-sets associated with women, with a few notable exceptions, lacked a specific characterisation while, in contrast, many of those associated with men seemed to go through an increasing elaboration.[8] In particular, an image of an armed man emerged, particularly within the funerary

---

3 On the importance of archaeological visibility for the definition of metallurgical 'horizons' see Hansen (2010).
4 There is increasing evidence (mostly C14 and dendrochronological dates) for the beginning of Early Iron Age in Italy within the tenth century BCE, probably well before 950 BCE. See on this: van der Plicht and Nijboer (2018), with earlier literature.
5 E.g., Fugazzola Delpino and Pellegrini (2009–2010); Lo Schiavo et al. (2013).
6 Iaia (2005).
7 Pacciarelli (2001) 202–16; Iaia and Pacciarelli (2012).
8 The overall picture of southern Etruria is extensively discussed in Iaia (1999a), (2013b).

assemblages in cremation burials, which is varied but corresponds to culturally determined models displayed via carefully selected items and assemblages.

Within this wider phenomenon, there are regional differences visible in Etruria and *Latium Vetus*. These two contiguous regions shared numerous sociocultural developments in the FBA. However, they were characterised by, at least partly, different trajectories towards early 'urbanisation'. Within Latium, this involved the development of a seemingly hierarchical system of villages centred on hilltop settlements and secondary positions, while in southern Etruria we already find more nucleated 'mega-sites', c. 900 BCE.[9] Evidently, in the latter region, more radical and rapid processes of social, political, and spatial centralisation were in action, which in the end led, without interruption, to a landscape dominated by urban centres by the seventh century BCE. To be clear, and in accordance with recent developments in studies on a European scale, in this paper 'urbanisation' is not conceived as a phenomenon with a definite 'start' or 'end', or indeed a 'natural' or inevitable progression, but as a process characterised by continuous developments and changes.[10] In this view, I consider EIA developments in south Etruria as the early stages of a peculiar 'urbanisation' process.

A common type of grave assemblage for a male cremation burial in Latium, between the eleventh and ninth centuries BCE, consisted of complex miniature panoply made of bronze.[11] These sets included an array of types of armour, including 'figure-of-eight' shields, breast-plates, and greaves, along with different weapons, and (possibly) ritual tools, such as knives (Figure 7.1). Sometimes, even miniature reproductions of war chariots were deposited.

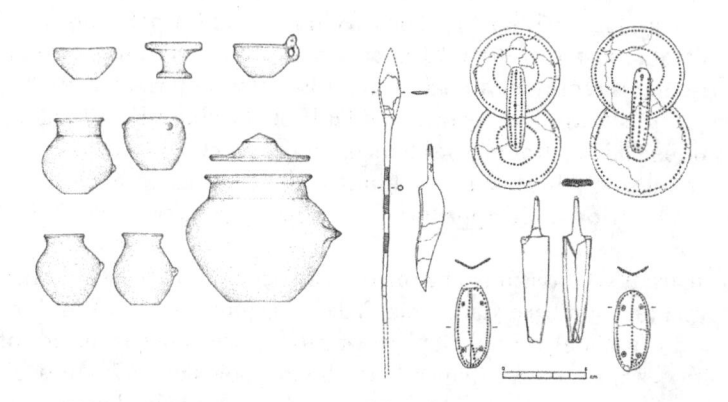

Figure 7.1 Pratica di Mare (ancient Lavinium), tomb 21. Cremation burial with set of miniaturised weapons

Source: Final Bronze Age late, c. 1000 BCE. After Iaia (2013a).

---

9 On the Late Bronze and Early Iron Age settlement system in Latium: Alessandri (2013) 29–33. On the coeval situation in Etruria, with particular regard to processes of urbanisation: Pacciarelli (2001), (2017a). On the funerary evidence: Riva (2009).
10 Fernández-Götz (2020).
11 De Santis (2011); Bietti Sestieri and De Santis (2003).

It is possible that some of the full-scale artefacts which presumably inspired these miniature replicas, and in particular shields and breast-plates, were made of perishable organic materials (namely leather and wood), since no metal examples of them (esp. shields) are known for this period in Latium or Etruria. The socio-ritual context visible within these mortuary contexts and assemblages is characterised by extremely limited access to burial space, including no more than four to five graves per funerary plot. Since these figures certainly did not represent an entire demographic spectrum, there are strong hints that these represent selected elite burials. A. M. Bietti Sestieri and A. De Santis have emphasised this last point, and interpreted burials with miniature panoplies as evidence of a 'chiefdom society' that was experiencing an increasing self-consciousness as a distinctive entity in this period.[12] However, one cannot avoid the impression that these burials, though unusual and carrying a strong symbolical message, are far from impressive in terms of investment of raw materials and techniques. Moreover, the surprisingly high number of these 'chief graves' in Latium, and their codified characteristics, raises the possibility that they represent more of a nod towards an ideal image of an elite-status group in a pre-urban context, as opposed to representing burials of the totality of actual, prominent individuals within a community.

In contrast to the situation in Latium, in the incipient proto-urban centres of Villanovan Etruria (EIA, Phase 1), we find selected metal weapons of full size. Bronze swords, and occasionally helmets and spear-heads, were placed in a small number of burials (e.g., Figure 7.2, nos. 3–6, from Tarquinia).[13] In the very early stages of the Iron Age, bronze bell and hemispherical helmets – whose body was made of sheet with an over-cast apex on top – were adopted (e.g., Figure 7.3, n. 1). Their technical and formal roots are clearly in the metal industry of the FBA in east-central Europe.[14] It is virtually certain these items represent a local re-interpretation and re-contextualisation by local workshops of an 'exotic' model brought about by a long-distance connection. The positioning of helmets on top of cinerary urns – a custom documented solely in this area – hints at their use as an extension of the deceased's body or, more appropriately, as permanent symbols of the heads of warriors.

This martial symbolism is not the only association though. In both southern Etruria and southern Campania (Vulci, Tarquinia, Caere, Veii, Pontecagnano, Sala Consilina), ceramic replicas of cap helmets, used as the lids of urns, frequently feature an apex shaped like a house roof (Figure 7.3, nos. 2–3). In other cases, the entire helmet-lid can be shaped as something akin to a complete domestic structure. A comparable motif can be found in other contemporary media, most notably hut-urns, funerary stone receptacles, and grave-stones

---

12 Bietti Sestieri and De Santis (2003).
13 Iaia (1999a), (2005); Iaia and Pacciarelli (2012); Pacciarelli (2001), (2017b).
14 Iaia (2005) 47–53; Mödlinger (2017) 83–90.

Bronzesmiths and material identity 133

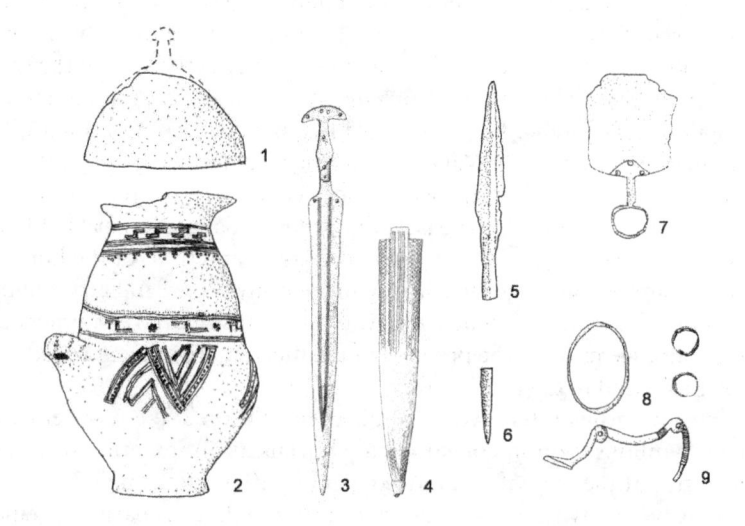

Figure 7.2 Tarquinia, tomb Poggio Selciatello 75, Early Iron Age phase 1A, c.900–850 BCE.

Source: After Iaia (1999a); Bianco Peroni (1970).

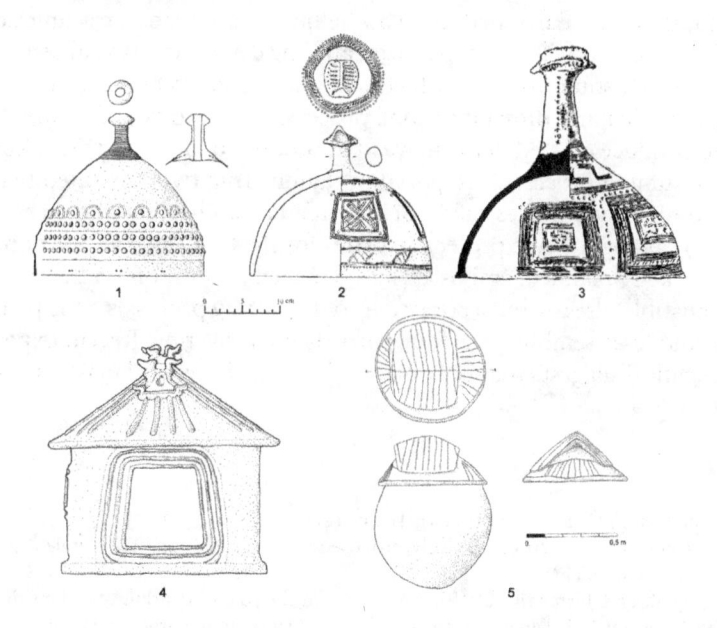

Figure 7.3 Cinerary Urns (1) Tarquinia, Arcatelle necropolis, bronze bell helmet with knob; (2) Tarquinia, Villa Bruschi Falgari, pottery helmet lid with roof-shaped apex; (3) Veii, Quattro Fontanili, pottery helmet lid with roof-shaped apex; (4) Tarquinia, Arcatelle necropolis, pottery hut urn; (5) Tarquinia, Villa Bruschi Falgari, stone receptacle of a cremation burial with roof-shaped lid.

Source: After Iaia (1999a), (2005); Trucco (2002).

134 *Cristiano Iaia*

(e.g., Figure 7.3, nos. 4–5).[15] These 'polysemous objects'[16] may evoke a transparent overlap between the concept of military prowess and authority in war and the notion of the 'house', or the domestic sphere, as the core of the (proto-) urban community.[17] This implies strong metaphorical associations. Interestingly, the adoption of the helmet-lids with a roof-like apex had a significant impact on local cremation rituals. In the Villa Bruschi Falgari cemetery at Tarquinia, graves containing these forms, all made of ceramic, were clustered in the south-western sector of the burial plot. This suggests that some social groups, probably clans, claimed the privileged access to the role of warrior and head of the house.[18] At the same time, these same groups did not include any bronze military equipment (or other prestige items associated with warfare) in their burials – a practice that, in this period, seems to be the preserve of the much more affluent social groups burying their dead in the nearby Arcatelle necropolis.

Corinna Riva has interpreted the absence of a precise equivalent to this funerary symbolisation in coeval female burials as an intentional statement about status, at the cost of a balanced gender differentiation.[19] Even though exceptions were always possible, it is undeniable that the earliest cremation rituals in southern Etruria emphasised one dimension of gender, the male warrior identity, while neglecting others.

In a slightly later phase, innovative metalworkers at Tarquinia created the first crested helmets with pointed caps in the region (e.g., Figures 7.4, n. 1a and 7.5, n. 3A).[20] Early bell and cap helmets were made of a unique, very thick and irregularly hammered sheet, and the decoration was absent or very simple. Overcasting the apex, albeit a sophisticated technique, did not constitute a particularly difficult or long process.[21] In contrast, the *chaîne opératoire* to produce crested helmets was the product of a more painstaking and time-consuming process. It required (a) hammering two separated blanks in order to form two halves made of very regular and thin sheets (less than 1 mm); (b) casting the two protective plates for the forehead and the nape, then adding exactly planned, embossed and punched decoration (in the case of the plates possibly already incorporated into the casting process) to the plates and sheets; and (c) assembling the four parts through riveting. Recent experimental replication suggests that only highly skilled artisans, real masters, have the

---

15 Bartoloni *et al.* (1987); Iaia (1999a); Trucco (2002).
16 This definition has been perceptively proposed in D'Agostino and De Natale (1996) 111. See also, Gastaldi (1998).
17 Cf. Naglak and Terrenato (2019), who focus on the role of continuity of kinship groups ('houses') as critical elements of the social reproduction in the proto-urban and early state situation of Iron Age Latium.
18 Iaia (2013b) 77, fig. 4; Trucco *et al.* (2005) fig. 2.
19 Riva (2009) 74–84.
20 Iaia (2005) 63–112 (with literature).
21 Mödlinger (2017) 158–67.

total control of this entire process and the ability to reproduce such objects.²²
In this respect, we can say that, in the EIA context of peninsular Italy, these
new objects (or rather, new within Italy) may have represented a real technological breakthrough, whose impact was seemingly felt more in the symbolical
and ideological sphere than in the field of warfare.²³

The oldest example of a Villanovan-type bronze crested helmet that can be
dated on a contextual basis, c. 850 BCE, comes from an exceptional burial found
in the aforementioned Arcatelle necropolis at Tarquinia, tomb Monterozzi 3
(Figure 7.4).²⁴ This burial comprised other 'novel' objects that are technically and
stylistically akin to the helmet, most notably a bronze cup, reminiscent of those
found in central Europe, and a miniature bronze table on three legs (Figure 7.4,
nos. 2 and 8). These likely represent an allusion to the importance of feasting for

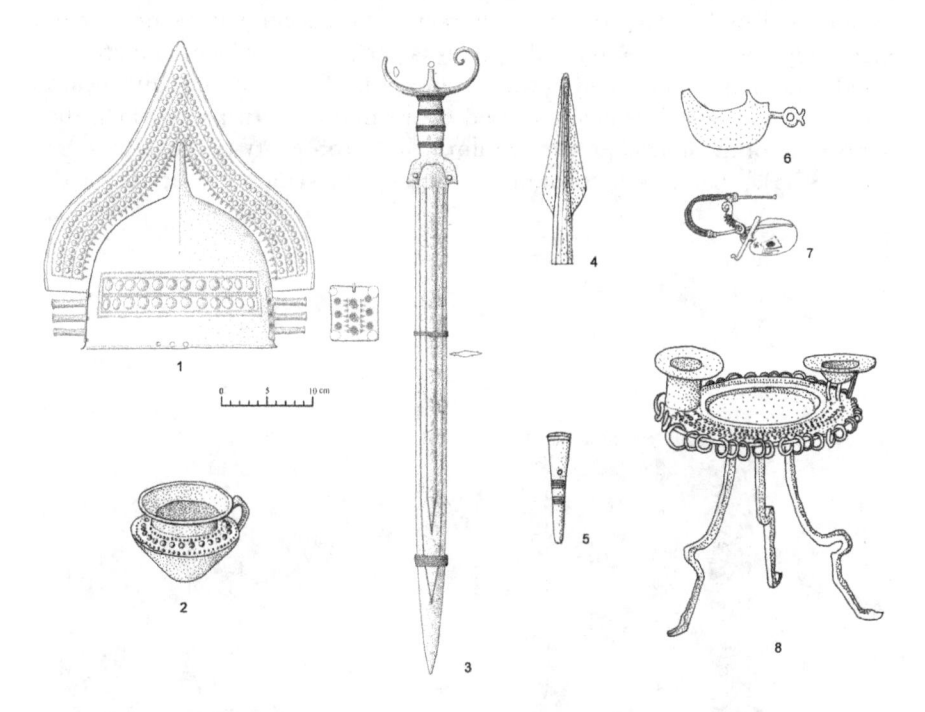

Figure 7.4 Tarquinia, Arcatelle necropolis, tomb Monterozzi 3, Early Iron Age 1B,
c. 850 BCE

Source: After Iaia (1999a), (2005); Bianco Peroni (1970).

22 Retrieved on 20/01/2021 from www.hephestus.net/2019/11/12/etruschi-maestri-artigiani/
23 The innovative nature is due to the complicated process and skill needed in production.
These helmets utilised two distinct production techniques, with two hammered sheets and
cast protective plates. The sheets are very thin with complex, hammered decoration. The
project involves tremendous forethought and complete control of the overall scheme. See
Armstrong in this volume for some discussion of the production process for bronzework.
24 Hencken (1968) 86–8, figs. 73–4; Iaia (1999a) 42, fig. 9b, (2019).

social groups, competing for social prestige and power. It is possible they were both manufactured by the same smith or workshop that produced the helmet; the shaping technique and the embossed decoration of the cup, for example, suggests this. The grave also contained a new type of sword, with possible Nordic associations, which will be commented on later. The Monterozzi 3 grave was part of an area of the necropolis where unusually wealthy graves were concentrated, attesting, for arguably the first time, to the appearance of what might be considered a restricted elite burial ground in the early Etruscan context.[25]

The advent of the Villanovan crested helmets can be argued to mark a shift of meaning of these broad types of artefacts, from symbols of warriorhood in the framework of the nascent proto-urban community to symbols of sociopolitical power. From this point on, bronze crested helmets, as opposed to weapons, would only be found in burials assemblages with other exceptional or highly prominent characteristics, seemingly belonging to incredibly high status individuals.[26] This is particularly evident in a cremation burial dating to the end of the ninth century BCE, the tomb Impiccato I at Tarquinia, which is characterised by a sumptuous ritual in which the deposition of the items appears to mimic the corporeality of the individual (Figure 7.5).[27] This burial, including all of the main symbols associated with

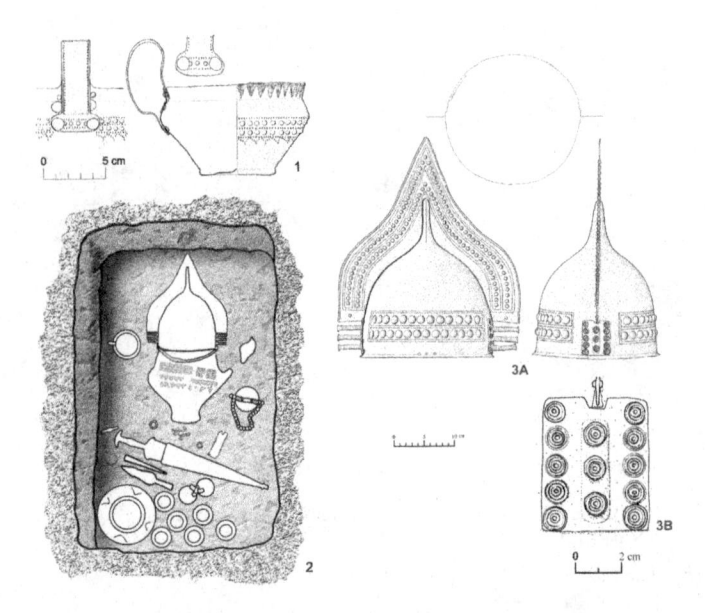

Figure 7.5 Tarquinia, Poggio Impiccato tomb I, Early Iron Age 2A, c. 830–800 BCE.
Source: After Delpino (2005); Iaia (2005).

25 Iaia (1999a) 123, (1999b).
26 Iaia (2005) 132–6.
27 Delpino (2005); Iaia (1999a) 53–4.

individual prestige during this period, such as golden ornaments, a sword with finely decorated scabbard, an exceptionally big spear, part of a chariot and bronze vessels, anticipates the so-called 'princely' assemblages of later EIA Middle-Tyrrhenian Italy. Again, in this burial, an object with strong resemblances to central-European specimens occurs, a bronze cup of the 'Stillfried-Hostomice' group (Figure 7.5, n. 1).

Pottery imitations of the bronze crested helmets also began to appear in numerous burials belonging to individuals of seemingly lower status in the same centre of Tarquinia (Figure 7.6).[28] Some specimens were also characterised by a sort of skeuomorphism, indicated by the application of bronze bosses to the ceramic surface – a detail clearly aimed at imitating the repoussé ornaments on bronze artefacts (Figure 7.6). This suggests a prompt response to this novelty by the Tarquinian community at large: the new artefact class was incorporated into other crafts (pottery), and became an integral part of the burial ritual.

The impact on the ideological sphere of these objects was a lasting one. Figural evidence attests how bronze crested helmets, in the subsequent period of the late eighth and early seventh centuries BCE, became stereotyped icons that helped shape the visual identity of the warrior leaders in vast areas of north-central Italy. Both in Etruria proper and neighbouring areas (e.g., Bologna and the Veneto), warriors wearing this kind of helmets are frequently represented as schematic designs on bronze helmets or bronze figurines applied to ceremonial paraphernalia (Figure 7.7).[29] Later, echoes of a variant of this

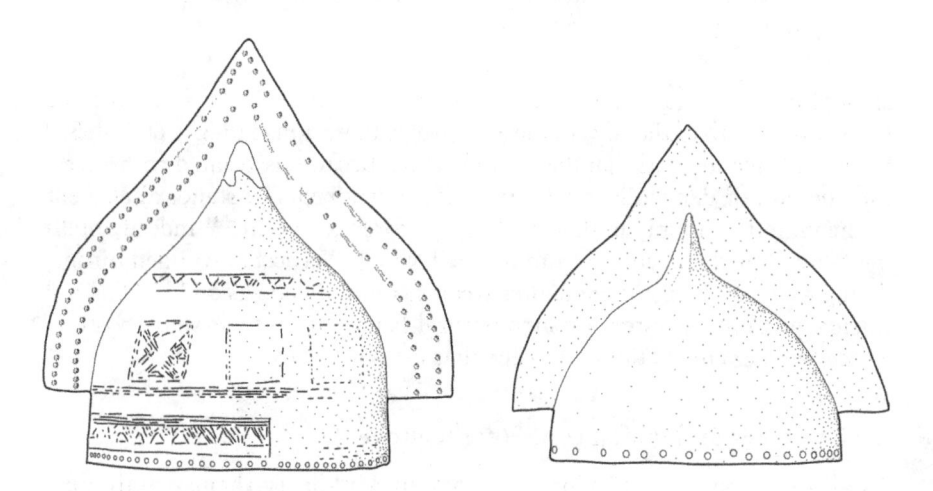

Figure 7.6 Tarquinia, pottery crested helmets used as lids for ossuaries, Early Iron Age 1B-2A, c. 850–780 BCE. The helmet on the left features bronze bosses to imitate the repoussé decoration on bronze prototypes.

Source: After Iaia (1999a), (2005) with modifications.

28 Iaia (1999a), (2005) 112–4; Mödlinger (2017) 134–6.
29 Iaia (2005) 141–9.

138 *Cristiano Iaia*

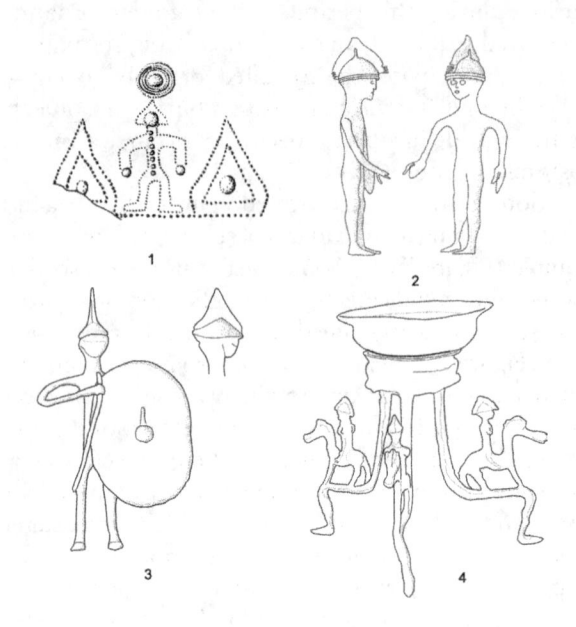

Figure 7.7 The iconography of a warrior wearing a crested helmet on bronze artefacts, north-central Italy: (1) Ornament detail on a crested helmet of unknown provenance (possibly Vulci), Musée du Louvre; (2) Reggio Emilia; (3) Lozzo Atestino (Padova); (4) Tarquinia, Monterozzi.

Source: After Iaia (2005), with modifications.

iconography (warriors mounting horses and wearing crested helmets) can be found even north of the Alps in the Strettweg cult wagon, dating c. 600 BCE.[30] Some evidence suggests that the crested helmet became associated with ancestors, heroes, or demigods, after having been dropped as a standard element of the military panoply in this area, except for at Verucchio.[31] Indeed, a telling piece of evidence comes from the well-known Verucchio wooden throne, dating to c. 700 BCE, where figures wearing crested helmets and holding tall shields, possibly ancestors or supernatural beings given their static posture, watch over an enigmatic ritual scene that is taking place.[32]

Technologies and craftspeople on the move

As already intimated, EIA bronze work in Middle-Tyrrhenian Italy provides some significant clues of technological transfers. This phenomenon emerges clearly in specific branches of metalworking, such as the hammered

30 Egg (1996) 14–61.
31 Iaia (2013b) 83.
32 von Eles (2002) fig. 121.

bronze industry, and in cast swords.³³ In particular, the impressive connections and interdependence of the sheet bronze industry of north-central Italy with that of final Urnfield and early Hallstatt in central Europe attests to the movement of craftspeople, or at least their knowledge, over long distances.³⁴ This needs to be briefly contextualised. For instance, among the most explicit evidence for these connections are the aforementioned bronze cups of the 'Stillfried-Hostomice' group (Figure 7.5, n. 1.), which feature several morphological and technical details, including form and decoration of the attachments of handles, that are highly similar – although not identical – to those visible on central-European specimens.³⁵ The same applies to other sheet bronze artefacts, such as neck-amphorae and biconical vessels ornamented with solar and bird-boat motifs according to a typical northern and eastern-European decorative style.³⁶ Notwithstanding these similarities, the key factor here is that some specific formal and technical details suggest the vast majority of objects were produced locally, although according to 'exotic' stylistic/technological models, while imports of already fashioned items are hard to identify.

In the previous section, I examined the class of bronze cap and bell helmets with apex, whose origin, in terms of shape, ornament style, and technology is evidently connected to, and likely from, eastern-central Europe. In contrast, Villanovan bronze crested helmets cannot be directly connected to 'foreign' prototypes, although this is somewhat debated in scholarship. Since the seminal G. von Merharts' study,³⁷ it has been customary in German-speaking scholarship to consider European bronze crested helmets as a unitary category with geographical and chronological ramifications, whose later manifestations appeared in Italy.³⁸ Undeniably, the earliest specimens of metal crested helmets appeared in temperate Europe at the transition of the Middle to Late Bronze Age (*Bronzezeit* C-D, c. 1400–1200 BCE), or in the FBA at the latest.³⁹ However, the different techno-morphological charac-

---

33 Since an in-depth examination of the relevant Italian artefacts through analytical techniques is still lacking, I will limit myself to typological insights and macroscopic observations. Some comments on technical details are found in Iaia (2005); Lehoërff (2007).
34 On the general topic: Iaia (2005) 238–43, (2017) 745–50.
35 Iaia (2005) 188–201, with literature.
36 Jockenhövel (1974); Iaia (2005) 223–37. On recent finds from eastern Europe that confirm the strong relationship between the Danube-Carpathian sheet bronze craft and the Villanovan one, see Gábor Tarbay (2018).
37 Von Merhart (1940); on the same line Hencken (1971).
38 E.g., Lippert (2011); Brandherm (2011); Mödlinger (2017) 90–126.
39 Only a vague resemblance with the Villanovan specimens can be found in the north Alpine crested helmets of the Pass Lueg type, whose chronology is a matter of controversy, due to the problematic find contexts. However, there is no doubt that these helmets are much older than the Italic ones: Egg and Tomedi (2002) date them to *Bronzezeit* C; Lippert (2011) to the Final Bronze Age; Mödlinger (2017) 106–7, to *Bronzezeit* C/D. This means we should think of a date around 1350–1150 BCE at the latest, while the Etruscan specimens do not appear before 900–850 BCE. The French-German helmets of the types Bibesheim and Bernières

teristics of the older transalpine examples, and the huge chronological gulf between these and the peninsular ones (about two centuries for most types), are such that any direct relationships, in terms of 'genetic filiation', between the two groups appears unlikely. The issue needs to be addressed in a different way. On one hand, the Villanovan crested helmet was the product of craftspeople who operated within the framework of an artisanal tradition, hammered bronze work with embossed decoration, which existed within a broader transregional framework and network which went back to at least the FBA and included regions as far afield as central Europe.[40] On the other hand, some morphological features and details of the decoration of the Villanovan helmets can be only contextualised within a very local tradition. For instance, the hemispherical shape of the cap with pointed apex is completely absent in the central European crested helmets of the LBA, yet it is reminiscent of the local, Italian helmets with a hemispherical cap (on which see earlier). Additionally, the decorative ornaments of punched concentric circles, that occurs frequently on the highly peculiar protective plates (e.g., Figures 7.4, n. 1; 7.5, n. 3B), are well known in other locally produced products from earlier periods.[41] Thus, the creation of this class of artefacts seems a complex process of creative hybridisation and re-contextualisation of artisanal knowledge, combining local and interregional influences, and cannot be explained in purely diffusionist terms.

Later developments within the same class of item reveal a different scenario. While initially restricted to a small area of southern Etruria in the ninth century BCE, the Villanovan-type bronze crested helmet became a transcultural element in the eighth century and the artefact type is shared by different groups across the broader region, some of which seem to have been otherwise unrelated to each other (Figure 7.8). This suggests that its producers played a special role as vectors of technological and cultural transmission beyond their local region. Specimens were deposited, since the early eighth century BCE, into burials in regions historically linked to Etruria through a range of connections (including material culture, trade, epigraphy, etc.): Fermo in the Marche, Capua and Sala Consilina in Campania.[42] Among these findings, we can also recognise helmets which seem to be imported from Etruria as well as locally made imitations. At Verucchio in Romagna, for instance, recent studies have made it possible to discriminate between a

---

    d'Ailly are also completely different, particularly in terms of the cap and decoration (which is usually absent): Mödlinger (2017) 109–23.

40 In particular, compare the large bosses recurring on the decorative schemes of the caps in the oldest examples from Tarquinia with those occurring on the bronze flasks of the type Blanot: Thevenot (1991) fig. 9–10.

41 See, for instance, the same ornaments on the spear heads and knives from the Goluzzo hoard (northern Etruria), dating to the tenth century BCE: Fugazzola Delpino and Pellegrini (2009–2010) tab XX, 1–2; tab. XIII, 1; tab. XXIV, 1.

42 Iaia (2005) 245–50.

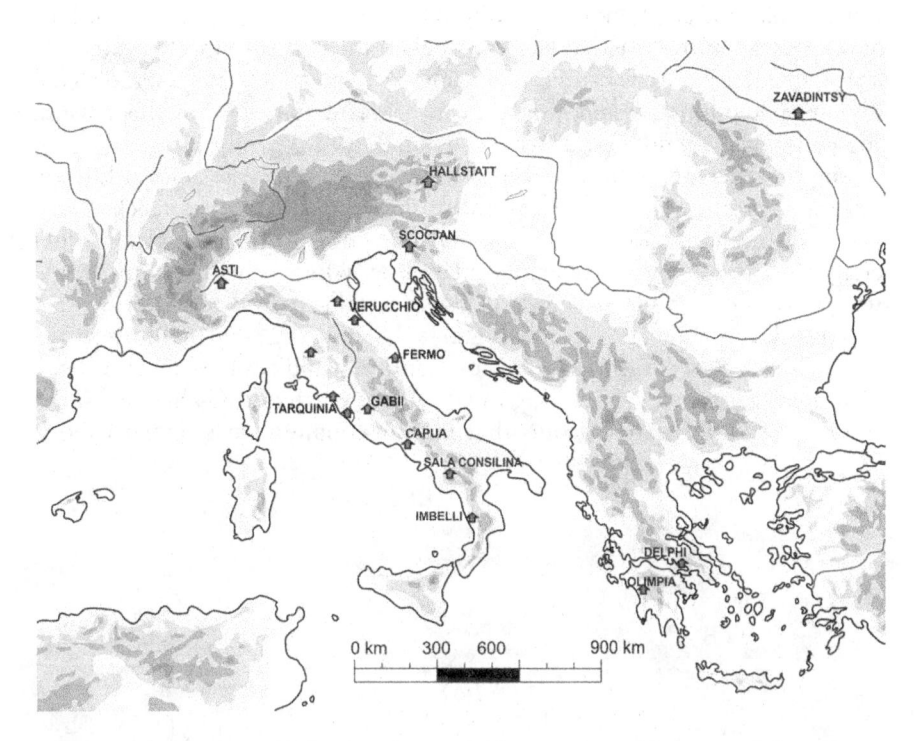

Figure 7.8 Map showing the distribution of bronze crested helmets of the Villanovan type.

small number of earlier specimens, directly dependent on southern Etruscan prototypes, and numerous later developments that attest to the emergence of a local manufacturing tradition.[43] In regions further from Etruria, crested helmets, either of possible Etruscan manufacture or local imitation, have also been found in what appear to be sacred depositions. Examples have been found in the river Tanaro near Asti (Piedmont), where the artefact was probably an import from Etruria,[44] and in a cave used for cultic purposes at San Canziano-Škocjan in Slovenia. In the latter case, at least three of the crested helmets were, given their formal idiosyncrasies, manufactured by workshops that were not in the Italian peninsula.[45] Small fragments of crested helmets and shields of southern Etruscan manufacture have come to light in Greek (or Greek/Italic) sanctuaries as well: Delphi, Olympia, and

43 Negrini *et al.* (2018) 12–3.
44 Iaia (2005) 83, n. 31, fig. 26.
45 Iaia (2005) 87, n. 33, fig. 27; Teržan *et al.* (2016) 129–32, tab. 18.

Imbelli near ancient Temesa in southern Italy.[46] However, this is contentious as we do not know whether objects reached the cult sites intact or already as fragments, since the custom of offering scrap metal as raw material to the divinities is amply attested in archaic Greek sanctuaries.[47] For this reason, these findings will not be further commented on.

The presence of Villanovan-type crested helmets in east-central Europe raises important questions. A variant of these crested helmets reached surprisingly remote regions, including Hallstatt, north of the Alps, and especially the eastern Carpathians, now Ukraine, where a helmet comparable with those from San Canziano-Škocjan and Hallstatt was found in the late nineteenth century at Zavadintsy (Figures 7.8 and 7.9).[48] Furthermore, three new helmets, almost identical to the one from Zavanditsy, have recently been identified from the black market in Ukraine.[49] Parts of these helmets show technical and decorative details that hint at a manufacture by workshops

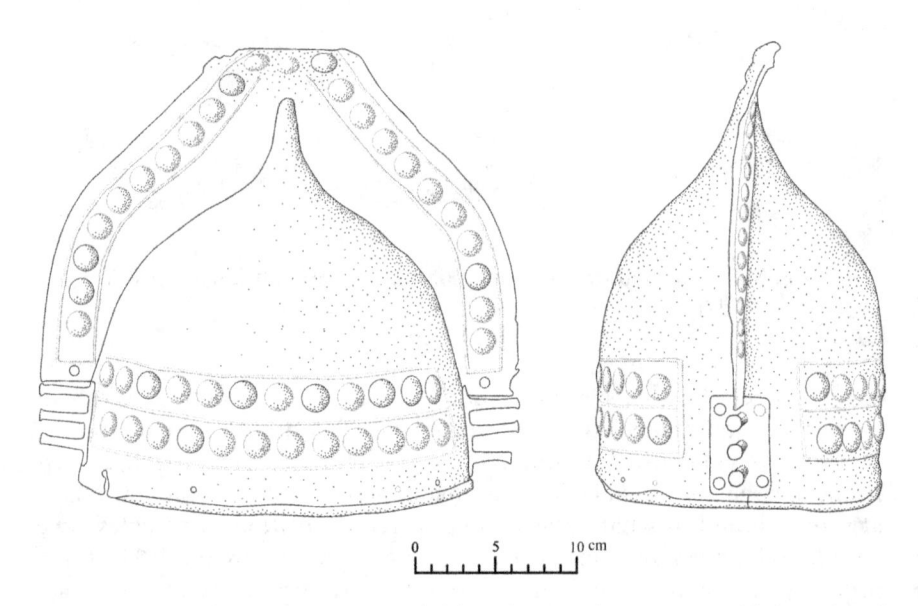

Figure 7.9 Zavadintsy (Kamenets-Podolsky, Ukraine), bronze-crested helmet found in the nineteenth century CE, formerly preserved at the Musée Massena, Nice.

Source: After Iaia (2005).

46 von Hase 1997 (with previous literature); Iaia (2005) 245–9, fig. 100; Mödlinger (2017) 126–36; Naso (2006).
47 Baitinger (2018) with literature.
48 Iaia (2005) 88, fig. 27 ('Elmi crestati tipo San Canziano').
49 In addition to the specimen cited in Mödlinger and Tsirogiannis (2020) 331–2, two other crested helmets of Villanovan type have recently turned up in the Ukrainian black market (I owe the information to the courtesy of Marianne Mödlinger).

distinct from those in peninsular Italy,⁵⁰ but the similarity in the overall design with the southern Etruscan specimens is nonetheless impressive and suggests a direct connection between Etruria and this area.

Swords are another significant case in point. Here we can observe an intriguing relationship between 'local' and 'foreign' shapes. In Villanovan Italy, short swords with a flanged T-shaped hilt (e.g., Figure 7.2, n. 3.) correspond to a local type, visible from the FBA to the EIA.⁵¹ Swords of this type are mainly found in rich burials, although they are not exclusive to them. Different workshops situated over a wide area, including southern Campania (Pontecagnano), seem to have produced these bronze swords, along with fine scabbards with incised decoration.⁵² In contrast, swords with a solid handle, most of them belonging to the so-called 'antenna-hilted' group, were introduced into Italy in the late tenth to early ninth century BCE, seemingly through central European connections.⁵³ The earliest known specimen from Etruria is that from the aforementioned tomb Tarquinia-Monterozzi 3 (Figure 7.4, n. 3). These swords were made by casting them in two separate parts, the hilt and the blade. Analytical work on some specimens confirms that at least the hilt was made by the lost-wax technique, while the blade could have been made by using a clay mould;⁵⁴ a similar procedure was probably also applied for shaping the blade of the Tarquinian sword, since, technically speaking, the regular and deep grooves on it could hardly be made in the post-casting stage. Seemingly made for the purpose of use in combat, the blade was probably also hardened by hammering but, since we do not possess archaeometric analyses of the Italian specimens, this detail can only be reconstructed in theory. Importantly, the lost-wax technique was only used intermittently for creating solid-hilted swords in northern Italy in the Middle/Late Bronze Age, and was utterly unknown in the rest of peninsular Italy until the EIA.⁵⁵ Hence, it is possible to conjecture that antenna-swords represent the product of a different set of innovative metalworkers who specialised in this manufacturing technique. Antenna-swords are indeed a transcultural type, whose distribution covers vast areas of Italy and central Europe.⁵⁶ Even in this case, considering the broad extent of its spread and the relative homogeneity of the artefacts, it is difficult to imagine other ways

50 For instance, in the Hallstatt-Škocjan-Zavadintsy specimens (e.g., Fig. 7.9) the outward folding of the rim of the cap, and the decorative panels consisting of ribs (*Leisten-Buckel Zier*), instead of the classical rows of dots, are characteristics unknown in the Italian crested helmets: Iaia (2005), fig. 27, 33a, 35, 36.
51 Bianco Peroni (1970); Bietti Sestieri and MacNamara (2007).
52 Gastaldi (1998).
53 De Marinis (1999) 542–7.
54 This technical procedure is confirmed by archaeometrical observations (X-ray analysis) of an antenna sword from Terni preserved at Essen, Germany: Brandherm and Sicherl (2001) 228–31.
55 Bianco Peroni (1970).
56 Baur (2019) sums up the discussion and the rich previous literature on this topic.

to transmit the special knowledge necessary to produce these objects other than through the mobility of craftspeople and direct interaction between members of different artisanal traditions.

As suggested by ethnographic observations, the transmission of detailed artisanal knowledge, including, in this case, the ability to craft highly elaborate products is something that cannot be conceived without a long and intense apprenticeship;[57] this implies a direct training relationship between masters and apprentices, which cannot be surrogated only through imitation of finished artefacts. A corollary of this is that the circulation of models and artisanal knowledge is expected to be as important as the mobilisation of artefacts. Vectors of these transfers could be highly skilled craftspeople, who were probably pushed to travel by strong attractors, such as powerful élites and/ or emerging central places, and eventually induced to settle in new areas.[58]

This must be considered as one aspect of a wider phenomenon, which deserves to be briefly sketched here. Evidently, basic metalworking in EIA central Italy, for instance that devoted to producing bronze fibulae, working tools, and other common artefacts, was in the hands of average resident smiths, who were likely well-integrated into local communities.[59] The classes of artefacts discussed here, however, belong to a different level of production, which implies superior skills, a measure of mobility, and stronger relationships with elites – the consumers of such goods. In this, the model differs from Childe's classic model of Bronze Age metalworkers as 'itinerant smiths',[60] which assumes that metalworking, in general, was practiced exclusively by outsiders who were holders of mysterious, quasi-religious knowledge; this model has been rightly criticised in the past or even overtly dismissed.[61] In particular, while the religious nature of metalworking is impossible to demonstrate in most cases (although it cannot be rejected in principle), the model of generalised mobility does not account for the evidently strong integration between local societies and settled smiths in Europe from the Late Bronze Age onwards. Conversely, a degree of limited mobility of specialised craftspeople has been assumed for the Bronze Age in continental Europe by some scholars who relate this phenomenon to the emergence of social stratification and interconnected 'chiefdoms'.[62] Travelling smiths could be elite-attached

---

57 Nørgaard (2018) 270–2 on the importance of long and face-to-face apprenticeship for 'quality-oriented' craft.
58 On this, see also Armstrong in this volume. Bernardo-Ciddio in this volume discusses similar issues around the movement of ceramic styles and production techniques.
59 For an overview of metal production in the Villanovan context: Iaia (2017) 741–52.
60 Childe (1930).
61 Rowlands (1971). For an updated discussion on this subject, with an intentional aim at deconstructing the notions of the Bronze Age smith as specialist and owner of a superior knowledge, see Kuijpers (2018a) 24–6
62 An extensive treatment in Nørgaard (2018) 360–5 (with literature). A different view is proposed in Dietrich (2012), who suggests the possible mobility of smiths producing more common type artefacts (axes) with the purpose of serving large areas.

specialists, who produced rare prestige goods in order to bolster the power and social prominence of their patrons, even on a regional or interregional scale. They would therefore have especially moved through areas where raw materials and artisanal skills were rare and concentrated in particular places.[63] However, the specific case of Villanovan bronze workers has further implications: in particular, the smiths played an active role as vectors of long-distance connections by introducing technologies and stylistic features deriving from distant areas, namely transalpine and eastern Europe.[64] Thus, this phenomenon goes beyond the interactions between local neighbouring communities and small networks of villages, and presupposes the existence of wider network and set of dynamics. This is probably dependent on the nature of early Etruscan central places and related communities, which are huge proto-urban agglomerations, with high population density and considerable centralisation of wealth, individual power, and economic functions. Textual and archaeological evidence from ancient civilisations, for instance Late Bronze Age Egypt and the Near East, amply demonstrate that mobility of craftspeople was an important aspect of interconnectedness between archaic states, in the form of forced resettlements, gift-exchange between courts, and as a facet of trade relations.[65] Exchanges of special artisans might have been an integral part of alliances between ruling elites and powerful individuals. In particular, it is conceivable that, behind the movements of craftspeople across large swathes of the peninsula, and across the Alps, there was an exchange of sought-after raw materials, such as copper, salt, and amber.

Epilogue: the construction of material gendered identities in the eighth century BCE

As illustrated in the opening sections of this chapter, the funerary record of the tenth and ninth centuries BCE in south Etruria saw a concentration of high-quality metalwork in a few prominent burials, mainly cremations housing the burnt remains of male individuals. This reflects an increasing hierarchisation of power and wealth, partially enhanced by the illusory 'egalitarian' attitude of the cremation ritual. During the eighth century BCE, the gradual emergence of inhumation rites corresponded with a radical transformation of the depositional patterns of metalwork and luxury objects. This phenomenon occurs alongside a general intensification of metalworking (and other crafts) within the framework of gradual 'urbanisation'. Generally

---

63 Nørgaard (2018) 364–5.
64 Technologies and style are here intended as synonymous, that is to say specific ways of making things by means of techniques: cf. Lechtman (1977); Lemonnier (1986); Dietler and Herbich (1998).
65 Moorey (2001); Nørgaard (2018) 365–7.

speaking, inhumation, and to a lesser extent cremation, entails an emphasis on the display of the corporeality of the dead. The shift to inhumation burials resulted in an increase in the quantities of goods deposited in connection with the body itself, either as dress accessories and equipment linked to social roles (weapons, working tools, etc.), or as vessel-sets for commensal activities. From a consumption viewpoint, the utilisation of prestigious metal artefacts in mortuary contexts in the eighth to early seventh century BCE can be understood as a form of 'sacrificial economy',[66] whereby ever-greater quantities of valuable objects were taken out of circulation by depositing them in the grave.

In this period, and for the first time in Etruria, the mortuary record seems to indicate the existence of a sort of military hierarchy in which metal weapons played a prominent role.[67] We can roughly distinguish between burials containing simple associations of spear, javelin, and knife, possibly corresponding to lower social levels, and more elaborately equipped leaders, associated with offensive weapons, several elements of armour, horse harnesses, and parts of chariots. In the most extreme cases, many coming from the cemeteries of Veii,[68] grave assemblages seem to emphasise aesthetic values (an ambiguous 'warrior's beauty') through the display of splendid armour, suggesting parallels with the Homeric 'men of bronze' celebrated in the Iliad.[69]

Within this social setting, dress accessories in metal seem to have taken on a new importance in signalling various forms of group membership within female burials. It is probably not by chance that the most elaborate sets of metal ornaments correspond with the new inhumation rites: transformations in ritual practice, an emphasis on the body as social locus, and a quantitative rise in the production of metalwork all seem to be interlinked phenomena. As an example, we can explore two cases which will allow me to sketch the expression of female material identity through metal objects.

Lozenge belt plates, made of thick bronze sheet, constitute a remarkable class of items that feature prominently in the eighth century BCE (e.g., Figure 7.10). In this context, these appear to be considered jewellery and are found as part of the ceremonial clothing in wealthy female grave-groups.[70] Seemingly originating in southern Etruria, the class of artefact subsequently appears in a much wider set of contexts, apparently imitated by local workshops in central-eastern and north-eastern Italy.[71] Accordingly, they may plausibly be considered a typical product of early Etruscan manufacture and type, later transmitted to other areas. They are characterised by abundant ornamentation,

---

66 Bachhuber (2011); Wengrow (2011).
67 Pacciarelli (2001) 261–76, (2017b) 767–75.
68 E.g., De Santis (2005); Iaia (2013b) 85.
69 Treherne (1995). A collective re-assessment of this seminal paper: Frieman *et al.* (2017).
70 A complete corpus of this class is still lacking. For partial syntheses see: Lucentini (2009); Naso (2020) with literature.
71 Naso (2020) abb.3.

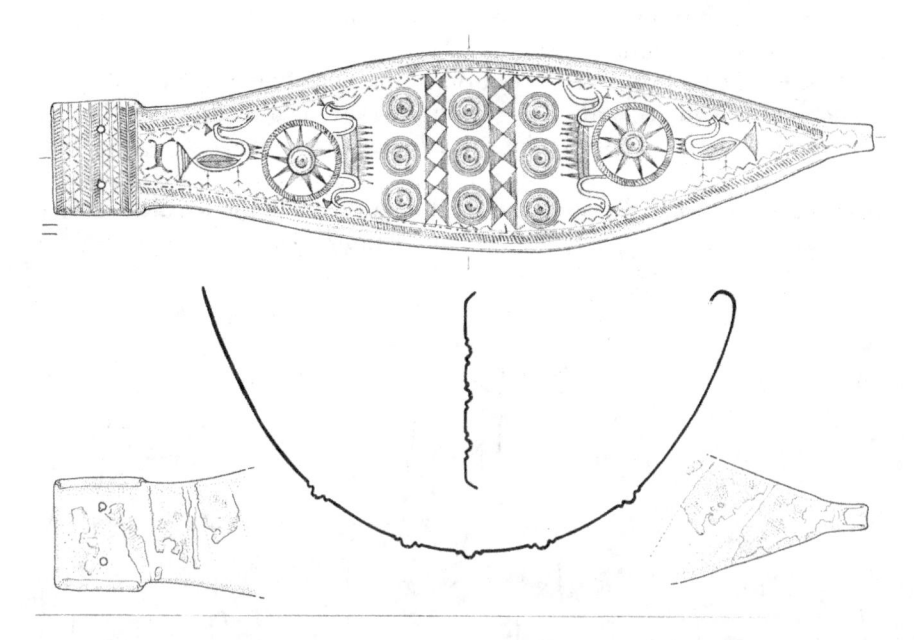

Figure 7.10 Bronze lozenge belt from Veii, tomb Quattro Fontanili OP 4–5, early eighth century BCE.

Source: After Bartoloni and Pandolfini (1972).

made principally by engraving, punching, and embossing, in a wide variety of decorative schemes. The most widely used decorative motif was a cosmological representation utilising traditional Late Bronze Age iconography. Nine relief bosses in the middle of the belt are flanked by heraldic allusions to the wagon of the sun pulled by birds. The chariot's divine connection is also highlighted by the use of solar elements, albeit ambiguously, representing wheels.[72]

Solar and bird-boat motifs occur in a wide range of prestige bronze artefacts in Villanovan contexts, mainly as decorative elements on armour and vessels. It can be considered a stylistic trait of an emerging status group, and carries strong central-European linkages.[73] However, lozenge belts carry a particularly intricate version of the sun-wagon motif, which has no parallel in other classes of metalwork, both from a technical and stylistic point of view. This suggests that they were tailored to the specific taste of female members of certain elite social groups. Interestingly, the vast majority of female burials, identified as elite and sub-elite, in Etruria during the eighth

72 Zipf (2006).
73 Iaia (2005) 224–36.

148 Cristiano Iaia

century BCE include a lozenge belt, which therefore may represent a visual marker of identity in a very general sense and possibly an emblem of a nascent 'ethnic' or cultural distinction.[74]

A second example of this sort of ornamental class of items in female burials across the Middle-Tyrrhenian region involves the use of series of bronze rings, mostly rhomboid or circular in section, known as *anelli da sospensione* (suspension rings). As a rule, they lay suspended from one fibula, whose placement was originally upon the chest or the belly of the female deceased (the range of variability is exemplified in Figure 7.11).

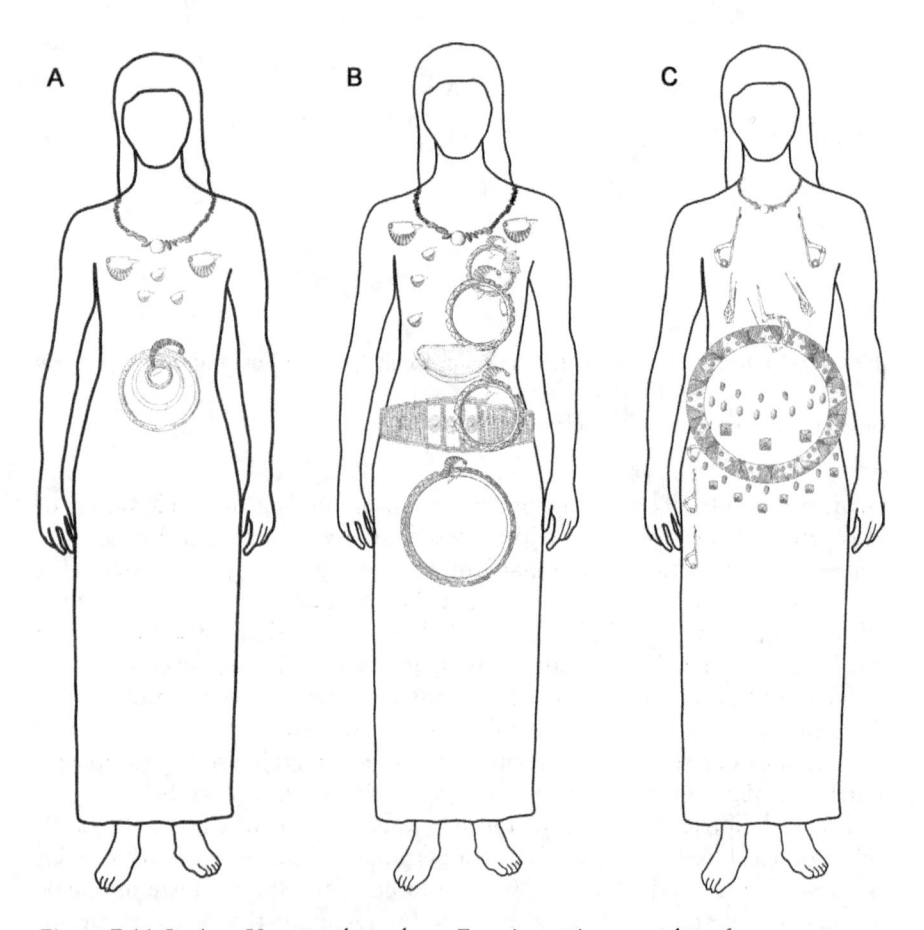

Figure 7.11 Latium Vetus and southern Etruria, main examples of ornament sets including bronze suspension rings, eighth to early seventh century BCE.
Source: After Iaia (2007a).

74 A similar view has been recently argued by Naso (2020).

At the onset of the Iron Age, *anelli da sospensione* occurred only in the historical region of Latium Vetus and only subsequently, in the eighth century BCE, crossed the River Tiber to be adopted in the southernmost district of Etruria and neighbouring areas.[75] Compared with the artefact classes examined earlier, this one shows a more extensive distribution in burials and could be considered a general 'folk custom' in the ceremonial attire of women. These objects belong to a different sphere of craft production and consumption than the fine belts described earlier, not to mention helmets and swords. Albeit finely ornamented, they represent a far simpler and standardised artefact, which neither requires outstanding skill from the bronze workers nor does it indicate a particularly close relationship with the very highest levels of society.

Some years ago, I proposed that the movement of this class of item may be connected to a corresponding inter-regional and inter-cultural marriage network, involving family groups moving and residing across the traditional boundary between Latin and Etruscan territories.[76] Whether this hypothesis is accepted or not, the distribution map of these ornaments strongly suggests some sort of directional social interaction, which also involves the contribution of metalworkers: most specimens concentrate east and south of the River Tiber, but they are also present in Caere's territory, in the *Ager Capenas*, and in Sabine territory, while completely absent in the rest of South Etruria. This absence is especially striking when considering the area around Veii and the *Ager Faliscus*, which are obviously in the same region and share many other connections. This selective distribution hints at the possibility of specific relationships and alliances between female members of the households of some early Latin and Etruscan centres – something that anticipates later phenomena.

Conclusions

This short overview has hopefully managed to stress the crucial role which metalwork had in shaping the material identities of both genders in burial contexts of the EIA in central Italy. The deposition of different metal artefacts in burials emphasised the dichotomy between masculine, war-dominated imagery, and the feminine sphere, in which adorning the body with elaborate adornments was symbolically important. The use of metal objects in this way is a phenomenon which emerged gradually, between the Early Iron Age Phase 1 and 2. It corresponded to a transformation in the realms of funerary practices and, in the end, of ideology and beliefs.[77]

Special artefacts, such as helmets, lozenge belts, and suspension rings have an essential feature in common: they all correspond to, and enhance, a body

---

75 Iaia (2007a) with literature.
76 Iaia (2007a). Cf. Fulminante (2012) for a comprehensive overview of questions of ethnicity in protohistoric Latium Vetus.
77 On the strong relationship between burial practices and beliefs: Rebay-Salisbury (2012).

part – helmets to a warrior's heads, lozenge belts and suspension rings to the torso and chest. Furthermore, these artefacts show a dual nature: on one hand, they were standard markers of individual status; on the other hand, they tended to function as emblems of new collective entities, possibly 'ethnic' or cultural groups.

The strong iconic character of these artefacts, and their aesthetic strength, relied on the ability of highly skilled artisans to both craft the items and to serve as a conduit for new techniques and shapes, either imported or locally derived. Specialised technical knowledge incorporated into these objects by master craftspeople provided additional value. At the dawn of the Iron Age, given the impressive technological and stylistic parallels with central and eastern European metalwork, it is likely that some artisans moved from and between those areas. The alternative, that these parallels were the result of trade in finished artefacts, is at the moment both unconvincing and lacking in any concrete evidence. In contrast, while most metalwork in the Late Bronze and Early Iron Ages was almost certainly produced by local practitioners with standard levels of competence and skills (this is demonstrably the case of those making fibulae and working tools), some specific branches of production, because of their level of complexity and transcultural connections, may have been dealt with separately. For instance, we could imagine producers of sheet bronze artefacts and swords were elite-attached or connected specialists who were moving across long distances, not necessarily through direct paths but via intermediate nodes, and who settled in distant areas giving way to new artisanal traditions. This mobility of master artisans and the transfer of knowledge was not a rare phenomenon, but a structural one. Hints of two-way movements indicate this. From 950 BCE onwards we witness the introduction to Italy from central and east-central Europe of two distinct technological/stylistic 'packages', including shapes, decorations, and technical recipes. In an earlier stage, a group of workshops (or individual smiths) were manufacturing hammered bronzes with embossed decoration (helmets, vessels), while others, apparently holding a different expertise that presupposes a mastery on casting techniques (lost-wax and similar techniques), were crafting solid-hilted antenna swords. Both seem to owe their know-how to older metalworking traditions of continental Europe. In a slightly later stage (eighth to early seventh century BCE), a reverse, but more selective phenomenon occurred: a transmission of specific types of crested helmets (and other shapes) from Etruria to Northern Italy, eastern Alps and east-central Europe (helmets from Škocjan, Hallstatt, and west Ukraine).

In conclusion, this chapter has argued that technological innovation by craftspeople, perhaps coming from distant areas, likely exerted a real 'transformative capacity'.[78] In the period c. 1000–700 BCE, the emerging

---

78 Maran and Stockhammer (2012).

proto-urban centres of Etruria functioned as a powerful catalyst and nexus for people, new technologies, and cultural traits. This resulted in a burst of creativity and cultural hybridity in the field of metalworking. Craftspeople, artisans, specialists, and the objects they created, were essential for the legitimation of emerging elites and were actively sought after. Technologies and craftspeople provided an effective form of symbolic and economic capital for these new centres of power. I have limited my inquiry to metalworking, but other forms of craft production could be usefully considered in this regard, such as ceramics which are considered elsewhere in this volume. Furthermore, this phenomenon started a domino effect as we see further echoes of these forms and technical solutions through northern Italy and further north. Thus, bronzesmiths in this context played not merely the role of passive recipients of elite inclinations and wills, but instead can be considered autonomous agents of innovation and transculturality.

8 The 'Bradano District' revisited
Tombs, trade, and identity in interior Peucetia

Bice Peruzzi

Apulia has long remained a marginal area in the scholarly debate on pre-Roman Italy. Yet, in antiquity, this region was far from being part of the periphery. In the fourth and third centuries BCE, it was the stage for major events of Mediterranean history – from the arrival of Alexander the Molossian and the other *condottieri*, to the Samnite Wars, to the Battle of Cannae. Furthermore, Apulian burials show evidence of enduring long-distance trade and complex social organisation, while the iconography of Apulian red figure pottery hints at a discerning population who understood and appreciated Greek literature.

In the past few decades, some Apulian populations – the Messapians, for example – have received increased attention, although other communities remain understudied. Among these lesser studied people are the inhabitants of the central part of Apulia, traditionally known as the Peucetians.[1] The Peucetians left no written accounts and were largely ignored by the writers of the ancient literary sources. Moreover, because of the continuity of life in this part of Apulia, many settlements have remained largely

---

* This chapter is a revised version of the paper that I presented at the conference held in Auckland in February 2020. I am very grateful to Jeremy Armstrong, Sheira Cohen, and Aaron Rhodes-Schroder for asking me to participate and to T.H. Carpenter, Fabio Galeandro, Valentina Natali, and Marisa Corrente for their help. In the months between the conference and the publication of this volume, both Douwe Yntema and Ettore Maria De Juliis passed away. This paper could not have been possible without their life long dedication to the archaeology of Apulia.

1 Several important central Apulian sites have been published in the past couple of decades: e.g., Small (1992); Ciancio (1997); De Juliis (2007); Riccardi (2003), (2008); Ciancio and L'Abbate (2012); Ciancio and Palmentola (2019). However, the only monograph-length study on pre-Roman central Apulia remains Claudia Greiner's (2003), which covers only the period between the eighth and fifth centuries BCE. Even the proceedings of the 2009 University of Bari's conference on central Apulia (Todisco [2010]), whose aim was to assess the state of the discipline, read more as a series of case studies than an attempt to create a complete narrative on Peucetia. Douwe Yntema's (2014) recent book on south-eastern Italy largely ignored Peucetian sites.

DOI: 10.4324/9781003120728-8

unexcavated; thus, their necropoleis are our largest data set to study their worldview.

This chapter investigates the definition of cultural identity in central Apulia between the end of the sixth and middle of the fourth century BCE on the basis of geographical variability in burial customs. The distribution patterns of certain classes of artefacts show substantial differences between the sites closer to the Adriatic Sea and those in the interior portion of the region. By comparing the composition of grave assemblages across Peucetia, I will explore whether these differences gave expression to the identities of sub-regional groups or if they reflected patterns of trade and connectivity. Between 525 and 350 BCE, Peucetian communities saw the emergence of new social groups which used funerals as arenas to negotiate status. Thus, understanding Peucetian funerary practices will give us better insights into the movements of goods within central Apulia and nearby regions, and will shed light on the relationship between the consumption of material culture and the construction of identity during a time of social restructuring.

Cultural background

Apulia, the 'heel' of the Italian peninsula, was lightly touched by Greek colonisation. The only Greek city in Apulia was Taras (Tarentum), which controlled a *chora* with a radius of c. 15 km². The rest of the region was inhabited by Illyrian-speaking people who have been defined in scholarly literature alternately as 'indigenous', 'native', and, more recently, as 'Italic'.[3] The existence of three local styles of pottery, and different burial customs, shows that, at least from the mid-seventh century BCE, the inhabitants of Apulia can be plausibly divided into three archaeological cultures, conventionally known as Daunian in the north, Messapian in the south, and Peucetian in the centre. These names have been borrowed from Greek and Roman sources; however, attempts at reconciling ancient tribal designations with recognised archaeological and linguistic cultures have been only partially successful. While mentions of the Peucetians have been found already in fifth century BCE works, there was no consensus among the earlier authors about their precise location or even exact name. Furthermore, Strabo in the sixth book of the *Geography*, after defining the land of the Peucetians,

---

2 Whitehouse and Wilkins (1989) 107–9. For the debate on the *chorai* in Magna Grecia, see also the proceedings of the 1967 and 2000 Taranto conferences (Aa.Vv. [1968], [2001]).
3 Although the population cannot be defined as 'Italic' *sensu stricto*, as these people did not speak an Italic language, this is the term that is used in this paper, as it has become common in scholarship on south Italian pottery to distinguish the non-Greek populations from the Greek settlers or Italiotes.

claims that the name Πευκέτιοι was not used by the local populations, except maybe in earlier times.[4]

In this chapter, I will continue to use the label 'Peucetian' to identify these communities, because this term has become conventional in scholarship. However, I am not implying that the Peucetians were necessarily an *ethnos*. As Sian Jones has recognised, ethnicity is not just the reflection of the sum of all the shared characteristics of a culture; rather, ethnic groups 'are self-conscious/self-defining groups, which are based on the perception of real or assumed cultural difference'.[5] As the inhabitants of Peucetia have left no written accounts, we are not able to determine if, and how, they identified themselves. Therefore, the label 'Peucetian' is intended, in this study, to represent an archaeological culture that shared common behaviours and practices – however, as Cohen and Armstrong argue in this volume's introduction, this is but one way of considering a population.

The land of the Peucetians is identified with the part of Apulia that ran along the Adriatic coast between the Ofanto River and Egnatia (Figure 8.1).[6] Inland, the town of Gravina di Puglia (ancient *Sidin/Silbion*), has been traditionally considered as the westernmost Peucetian settlement, following Strabo's description; however, archaeological work in the province of Matera and the ongoing survey of the Basentello Valley have revealed that Peucetia might have extended further inland.[7]

Between the seventh and the middle of the fourth century BCE, the region was populated by small, scattered sites, in which small groups of houses coexisted with open areas for agriculture and burials.[8] The second half of the sixth century BCE saw a period of great activity and change in central Apulia: permanent domestic architecture appeared across the entire region, settlements seemed to be organised in regular grids, and new burial practices were introduced.[9] These changes, which indicate profound social transformations,

---

4 The first mention of the tripartite subdivision of Apulia is found in Polybius (3.88.3–6). For mentions of the Peucetians, see, e.g., Hdt. 7.170; Paus. 10.10.6; Pherek. *FGrH* 3F 156; Herodoros *FGrH* 104; Dio 1.12; Strabo 6.3.8. In Roman times, there was no triumph on the Peucetians in the *Fasti triumphales*, while all other Apulian populations are mentioned; Nikander (*Ant. Lib.* 31) and Trogus (Justinus *Epit.* 12.2.12) both mention the Peucetians, but otherwise the term disappears completely by the Imperial period, and they were not even included in Pliny's list of the populations of Regio II; see, e.g., Grelle (1989) 111–6; Peruzzi (2014) 33–9; Fioriello (2017).
5 Jones (1997) 108.
6 There is no consensus on the nature of Egnatia, which has been considered both Peucetian and Messapian; see, e.g., Cocchiaro (2002) 10; Mannino (2006) 17; Galeandro (2005), with previous bibliography.
7 Strabo 6.3.8; Lo Porto (1973) 149–251; Ciancio (1989) 48; Fioriello (2002) 75–136. Cf. De Juliis (1995); Ciancio and Riccardi (2005) 57–60; Mannino (2004) 333–55. Small (2014a) 13–35.
8 On Peucetian settlement patterns, see, e.g., Galeandro (2010) 195–206. It does not seem that areas for domestic architecture were separated from tombs, as tombs appeared in areas that were previously allocated to settlement, and houses were built in areas originally dedicated to tombs. See, e.g., Ciancio (2008) 895–918; Ciancio and Palmentola (2019).
9 Small (2014a) 13–36.

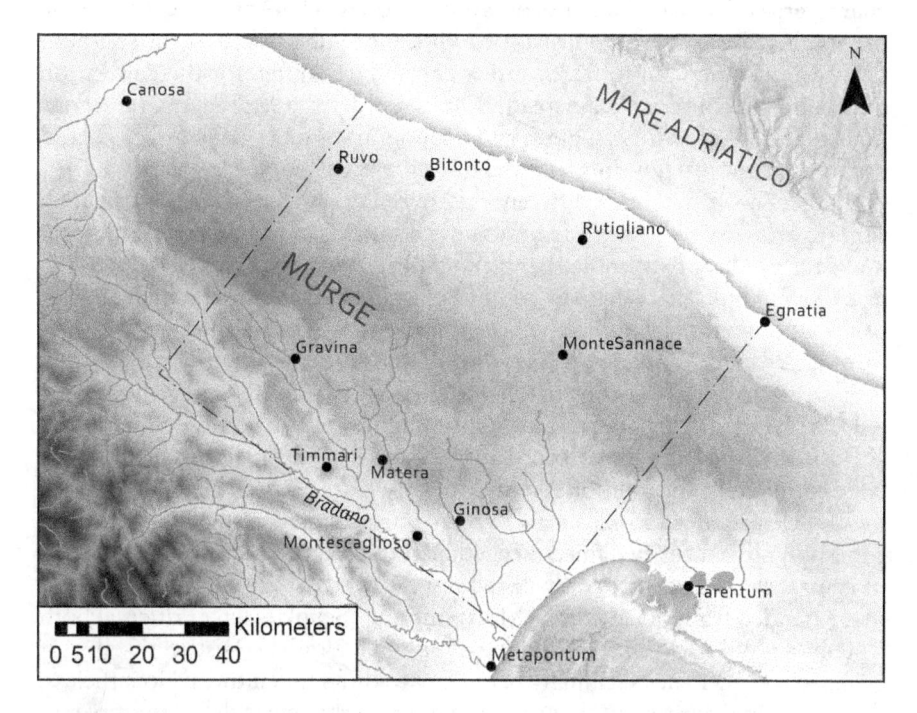

Figure 8.1 Map of Peucetia
Source: Adapted from De Juliis (1995) Carta A by Joshua Emmitt.

fit within broader patterns noticeable in all of south-eastern Italy.[10] Another moment of boundary creation, illustrated by extensive changes in Peucetian material culture, is visible in the second half of the fourth century BCE. This period was characterised by a substantial increase in the number of tombs and the size of the assemblages; a change in feasting behaviour, as indicated by the introduction of new shapes in the pottery repertoire; and the disappearance of locally made, matt-painted pottery in the funerary assemblages. Furthermore, there was a profound shift in the settlement pattern, with the progressive abandonment of many sites and the construction of circuit walls around most of the surviving ones.

The current state of published evidence does not permit us to speculate on the existence of a hierarchy among Peucetian settlements; however, there seem to be visible differences in the settlement patterns between the coastal area, which was more densely populated by smaller sites, and the interior region, which had fewer, but larger, settlements.[11] This arrangement might be at least partially explained by looking at the landscape, as central Apulia is

10 Yntema (2014) 160–4.
11 Galeandro (2010) 195–7.

characterised by two distinct geographical zones. The Adriatic coastal zone (now called Terra di Bari) consists of a Pliocene plain crossed by the southern tributaries of the Ofanto River and is particularly suited for the cultivation of cereals. The interior is, instead, dominated by the Murge, a Cretaceous limestone massif, whose typical karst topography must have affected land use, settlement distribution, and the movement of people.[12]

Scholars have noted that differences between the Adriatic zone and the interior are also visible in the distribution of certain classes of pottery, both local and imported. For example, Peucetian sub-geometric wares were attested in central Apulia between the middle of the seventh and the first quarter of the fifth century BCE. Production comprised a limited number of shapes (primarily *ollae*, *kantharoid* vases, *askoi*, and *amphoriskoi*) in two distinct decorative styles: monochromatic, with geometric motifs, and polychrome, with both geometric patterns and stylised figures.[13] The first type was found almost exclusively at sites closer to the coast; in contrast, polychrome pots were common in the interior. As this latter style of ceramics had closer ties to the vessels produced in Basilicata, Yntema argued against the existence of a cohesive cultural entity named 'Peucetia', and instead considered the interior of central Apulia as part of the 'Bradano District' – a rather eclectic region that extended from the Murge to Metapontum.[14] Scholars have criticised both Yntema's typological clusters and the notion of a 'Bradano District' itself, as it grouped together sites seemingly belonging to different cultures. Nonetheless, there is general agreement that the circulation of the two styles of pottery had very little overlap, and that Peucetian polychrome sub-geometric pottery was found at sites in the valleys of the Rivers Bradano and Basentello.[15]

Similarly, the popularity of Attic imports varied between the coastal area and the interior of Peucetia. As Katia Mannino and Claudia Lucchese have observed, there were almost four times as many Attic black and red figure vases in the

---

12 Under Vespasian, the Adriatic zone was largely centuriated and many sites located in this area became *municipia*. Contrarily, the interior area became a *saltus* under the Romans and was used primarily for sheep raising and other activities connected with animal husbandry, such as textile production. Small (2014b) 53–64.
13 Yntema (1990); De Juliis (1995); Herring (1998).
14 Yntema (1990) 16; 45–85; 236–50. Yntema reprised the concept in his 2014 book, dividing central Apulia into several districts, including a 'Bari district,' defined as a '20 km wide and 25 to 35 km long coastal strip' which included the sites of Ceglie, Rutigliano, Noicattaro, Bari, Bitonto, and Conversano. His proposed 'Bradano-Basento district' consisted of the 'lower Basento and Bradano with their gently sloping hills' and included the sites of Monte Sannace, Santeramo in Colle, Gravina di Puglia, Altamura, Ginosa, Palagiano, L'Amastuola, Montescaglioso, Timmari, Difesa S. Biagio, Cozzo Presepe, Metaponto, Pisticci, Ferrandina, Pomarico Vecchio, Miglionico, and Garaguso. See Yntema (2014) 41–2.
15 De Juliis (1995) 21–2. Greiner (2003) 55. Both De Juliis and Greiner have criticised the idea of a 'Bradano district.' However, De Juliis sees ties between the two styles of pottery (monochromatic and polychrome) found in Peucetia and admits influences from the nearby Basilicata – see De Juliis (1995) 80–1. Greiner, in contrast, believes that the pottery found in interior Peucetia has followed a completely separate stylistic evolution – see Greiner (2003) 193.

Adriatic zone as there were at inland sites. Furthermore, in the coastal area, there was a distinct preference for larger shapes, in particular kraters, while in the interior, Athenian imports consisted primarily of smaller vases (cups, *kantharoi*, and *oinochoai*).[16] Such a stark contrast between the two zones, however, is diminished if one considers that well over 60% of the catalogued Attic vases from the Adriatic zone were decontextualised pots from nineteenth-century excavations at Ruvo.[17] Therefore, this data likely speaks more to the exceptionality of this site in antiquity rather than any true regional patterns.

In order to determine whether the interior part of central Apulia had distinctive cultural characteristics, I will now turn to the necropoleis and discuss the grave goods in their archaeological context and 'context of use'. The context of use is here intended as the purpose, occasion, and users of the objects found within and around the tombs. The purpose of the objects includes both their practical function (e.g., storage, defence, decoration) and their cultural use (e.g., the banquet). This type of analysis offers a better understanding of the assemblages as organic units and shifts the focus from the artefacts to the people who used them.

The potential of burial practices to reveal an individual's affiliation to a particular social or cultural group has long been assumed. However, more recently scholarship has highlighted how the relationship between material culture of the tomb and cultural identity has to be read as an evolving dialectical discourse made of practices.[18] In other words, artefacts derive value and meaning from being employed in different social contexts, and, at the same time, their materiality is engaged in the very structuring of practices.[19] In fact, although material culture stores the 'codes of signification' that can be drawn upon in social exchanges, an object (e.g., a pot), after being deposited in a new context of use (the tomb) during a prescribed set of actions (funerary rituals), might acquire a different meaning from what it had in other social processes and contexts. The movement of the vase – both the material product, and its symbolic value – from one type of social practice to another was possible because the agents shared a common frame of reference.[20]

---

16 Mannino (1997) 389–99; Lucchese (2010) 299–306. For the importance of specific shapes in Apulia, see, e.g., Carpenter (2003) 1–24; Colivicchi (2006) 117–30. On general trends of Attic imports in Apulia, see Giudice (2007) 411–24.
17 Ruvo di Puglia, identified with ancient *Rubi*, is a town about 40 km northwest from Bari and 15 km from the sea. After chance findings at the end of the eighteenth century revealed many rich burials, this site attracted the interest of local antiquarians and international collectors alike. As a result, from the first half of the nineteenth century Ruvo suffered what scholars have called a 'systematic sack' of the necropoleis, the looting of which has continued well into the twentieth century. For a study of Ruvo's necropoleis and an attempt to reconstruct ancient contexts from archival documents, see Montanaro (2007).
18 Chilton (1999) 2, with previous bibliography.
19 The arguments borrow notions from Pierre Bourdieu's practice theory and Giddens' duality of structure; see, e.g., Barrett (2001) 151–4.
20 Barrett (1987) 468–73.

What is considered significant in social interactions depends on such a shared conceptual framework. The idiosyncratic 'way of doing things', specific to each society, informs behaviours in the social arena, often unconsciously, on a daily basis. It both shapes, and it is shaped by, repeated actions and knowledgeable decisions about what can be done in any given situations – at a funeral, for example – and it is these shared, often subliminal, dispositions that are at the basis of the construction of cultural identities among the users of items.[21] In order to investigate such behaviours, I will pay particular attention to the ceramic analysing them both according to class and to the function they might have had (e.g., drinking, offering, mixing).

Evidence from the necropoleis (525–350 BCE)

This chapter will explore four sites as case studies: two from the Adriatic zone (Rutigliano and Bitonto) and two from the interior (Gravina di Puglia and Monte Sannace). Beyond their topographic locations, these sites were selected because they have been excavated with modern methodologies, have been more extensively published than other sites, and because they offer a representative image of the social hierarchy, since they contain burials of individuals from different strata of the population.[22]

More than five hundred Peucetian tombs have been published from the territories of these sites, about a third of which were dated to the period considered in this chapter (525–350 BCE).[23] They were virtually all inhumations, with the bodies buried in the *rannicchiato* position (i.e., on their side, flexed) or on their back with the legs contracted.[24] The most common type of burials were *fossa* tombs, closed by one or more slabs of calcareous stone;

---

21 There is a vast bibliography on this notion, usually known as *habitus* – see, e.g., Bourdieu (1977) 261–2; and Dornan (2002) 305; Jones (1997) 128; Barrett (2001) 141–64; Dietler and Herbich (1998) 232–63. See Bernardo-Ciddio in this volume for a discussion focused on the production of vessels, rather than their use; see also Cohen in this volume for an alternative approach to community which draws on similar concepts of *habitus*.

22 Rutigliano: see, e.g., Lo Porto (1976) 736–45, (1977) 501–4; De Juliis (1980) 425–42, (1981) 468–9; Damato (2001); De Juliis (2007). Bitonto: Riccardi (2003), (2008). Gravina: Small (1992); Ciancio (1997); Whitehouse et al. (2000). For Monte Sannace: Scarfì (1961); Ciancio (1989); Ciancio and Palmentola (2019).

23 This chapter considers data from 46 tombs from Monte Sannace, 55 from Gravina di Puglia, 70 from Rutigliano, and 20 from Bitonto.

24 Cremation is almost completely absent in central Apulia, and only very few exceptions are known: one tomb from Monte Sannace (tomb 8/2003 dated to 600–575 BCE), one from Bari, loc. Punta della Penna (575–500 BCE); one from Gravina Botromagno (DA S7/1969, difficult to date) and one tomb from Timmari (tomb 33, 350–300 BCE). The individuals from Monte Sannace and Bari Punta della Penna are usually interpreted as foreigners – see Montanaro (2010) 185. The cremation from Gravina Botromagno is in a chamber tomb that has been used from the late fourth until the second century BCE – see Small (1992) 80. Tomb 33 from Timmari is an exceptional burial that the excavators have hypothesised was the tomb of Alexander the Molossian – see Canosa (2007).

higher expenditure tombs included monolithic sarcophagi and *semi-camera* tombs with painted walls.[25] Tombs may or may not have featured permanent markers on the surface; nonetheless, the communities must have maintained knowledge of their location, as tombs were routinely reopened and reused.[26] At both Rutigliano and Monte Sannace, sarcophagi tombs often also had a *ripostiglio* – a secondary, rectangular pit dug at the foot of the burial. This smaller space was usually lined with thin slabs of calcareous stone, and it was used to hold ceramic grave goods.

The assemblages found in these tombs were composed primarily of pottery and a few metal artefacts (weapons, ornaments, and, rarely, banquet paraphernalia). The 'standard set' seems to have been a combination of local forms, a limited number of imports from Athens, Corinth, and Etruria, and a larger quantity of vases produced in the nearby Greek colonies. Elements that pointed towards personal identity or achievements were very rare, and usually limited to ornaments (e.g., pendants and fibulae).[27] Weapons have been found in all tombs that have been identified as containing adult males by anthropological analysis.[28] They consist primarily of spears and bronze belts, although more complete panoplies have been found at Rutigliano; unfortunately, looting – both in antiquity and in modern times – has meant that fewer metal objects have survived at Gravina and Monte Sannace.

Analysing the pottery found at the four sites, some patterns emerge (Figure 8.2). Among ceramic vases (2119), 12 classes of pottery were represented: Peucetian sub-geometric, matt-painted (banded and mixed), brown slipped, Attic black figure, Attic red figure, south Italian red figure, Gnathia, overpainted, black gloss, *acroma*, and cookware.[29]

---

25 Ciancio (1997) 70–2.
26 The exceptions could be three tombs on the Acropolis of Monte Sannace (104/1960, 2/2002, and 3/2002), dated to the end of the sixth century BCE. Tombs 2/2002 and 3/2002 might have used a vase as a *segnaculum*: respectively, a sub-geometric *olla* and a middle-Corinthian krater attributed to the Memnon Painter. Tomb 104/1960 might have had a structure built on top, which Nevio De Grassi believed was a *naiskos*. See Capozzi *et al.* (2012) 55–92.
27 A staggering 23% of all amber found in pre-Roman Apulia comes from Rutigliano. No other site comes close. The second richest site was Canosa (11%) in Daunia. See Montanaro (2015) 35–64.
28 Belts appear also in tombs of sub-adults. For the importance of belts in Apulia, see Herring (2017) 22–30. There are also two tombs from Bitonto (7/2003 and 3/2003) and one from Rutigliano (84/1978) with weapons that were associated with adult females. See Riccardi (2008) 20–1, 27–31 and De Juliis (2007) 229–31.
29 Percentages expressed in the graph refer to the total of vases found at each site. A very small percentage of Corinthian imports (less than 1%) was found both at Rutigliano and at Monte Sannace. Corinthian pottery at Monte Sannace was more common in the period between 625–575 BCE (e.g., the very fine middle Corinthian krater attributed to the Memnon painter mentioned above). Corinthian imports must also have inspired a very interesting hybrid pottery style; four *ollae* have been found at Monte Sannace, whose shape resemble local sub-geometric production, while the decoration – in particular, the long rays at the bottom and the Σ patterns – uses different motifs known from proto-Corinthian pottery. See Gallo (2019) 170–3.

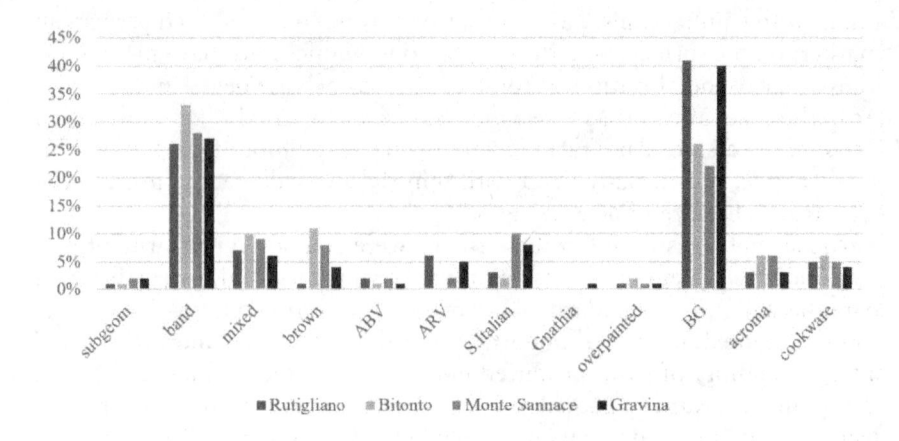

Figure 8.2 Distribution of pottery classes at the four sites (525–350 BCE).

Comparing the distribution of classes between the sites in the interior and the Adriatic zone reveals both similarities and differences. For example, the most common classes at all sites were black gloss and matt-painted fineware, decorated either with bands or with a mixed style of bands and phytomorphic motifs. In contrast, we find fewer Attic imports at Gravina (6%) and Monte Sannace (4%) than at Rutigliano (9%), although there was no real difference in the chronology and authorship between the vases found in interior Peucetia and those found at sites closer to the coast. It appears, in fact, that the same painters were attested across the entire region.[30]

Peucetian sub-geometric pottery was found in very small quantities. However, the analysed grave assemblages confirm that the polychrome style was attested only at Gravina and Monte Sannace, even if monochromatic vases were present at all four sites. Furthermore, the percentage of sub-geometric pottery from sites in the interior was double that of Rutigliano and Bitonto, illustrating a less decisive break with the previous pottery tradition in this part of central Apulia. On a similar note, there were fewer black gloss vases at Monte Sannace than the other sites, as its inhabitants seem to have preferred locally produced, brown-slipped pottery, in particular for drinking vessels.[31]

A traditional interpretation would just explain these differences in distribution away as a sign of fewer interactions with the Greeks. According to the old

---

30 The oldest Attic import in interior Peucetia is a fragment of Siana cup (MG 1467), attributed to Lydos (560–550 BCE) from Monte Sannace, *CVA Gioia del Colle* [Italy 68] pl. 24 [3071]:1. For a complete list of the Attic painters found in Peucetian sites, see Lucchese (2010) 302, with previous bibliography.
31 8% of all vases attested at Monte Sannace were brown-slipped *kantharoid* vases, while, at the other sites, this shape makes up 4–5% of the total pottery.

principle of diffusionism, which postulates that different forms of borrowing had to be equated with different depths of cultural assimilation, the people in internal Peucetia would simply have to be considered less 'Hellenised' than their counterparts in the Adriatic area. Yet, excavations of the earlier phases of Monte Sannace – and to lesser degree at Gravina, località Jazzo Fornasiello – have revealed long-standing exchanges with Siris and Metapontum.[32] Furthermore, Gravina and Monte Sannace had proportionally more south Italian red figure pottery, and indeed were among the first sites to adopt it as the presence of early works of proto-Lucanian and proto-Apulian painters illustrates.[33] Similarly, some of the first examples of overpainted pottery in all of central Apulia, dating to the late fifth century BCE, were found at Monte Sannace and Gravina, often in association with early Italiote vessels.[34]

It is also interesting to note that, despite the disparity in sample size, there are closer parallels between the general distribution of classes at Rutigliano and Gravina – and Monte Sannace and Bitonto – than between the pairs of sites that were geographically closer, weakening the hypothesis of the existence of two internally cohesive but distinctive cultural zones.

Furthermore, in order to determine how the inhabitants of Peucetia styled themselves in death, as well as what social, cultural, and behavioural norms they embedded in the items they used, it is necessary to understand both what their grave assemblages looked like and how they were used during funerals. This is because meaning is not a characteristic inherent to the artefacts themselves; rather the message objects carry is (re)negotiated every time they are deployed, both by the individual who uses them and others in the community who recognise them to be meaningful. Some performative aspects of the rituals might remain ephemeral, although the analysis of the spatial distribution of human remains, grave structures, and artefacts reveals traces of the *gestes funéraires* that were carried out.[35] Similarly, while pots

---

32 Gallo (2019) 165–81; Lambrugo (2018) 62.
33 Scarfì (1961) 230–46; Gargano (2019) 631; CVA Gioia del Colle [Italy 68], pls. 34 [3081]: 1–2; 35 [3082]: 1–4; 37 [3084]:1; Ciancio (1997) 204–96; Schierup (2014) 191–215; Ciancio (2005) 50–1.
34 E.g., in tomb 4/1957 at Monte Sannace, there was an overpainted *kantharos* of the Xenon group, associated with a proto-Lucanian bell krater attributed to the Amykos painter (430–410 BCE) and a Saint Valentin *kantharos*. The tomb also contained a banded column krater, two brown one-handled bowls, one banded cup, two black gloss *skyphoi*, a black gloss cup, a brown-slipped miniaturistic *kantharoid* vase, a trefoil *oinochoe* decorated in silhouette, an Apulian red figure *pelike*, two black gloss *oinochoai*, a black gloss plate, two *chytrai*, an Apulian red figure *askos*, a banded *stamnos*, a banded *lekythos*, mixed *kalathos*, black gloss *lekanis* base, black gloss *askos*, and an *acroma* basin. There were also a bronze *lebes* of possible Etruscan manufacture, eight iron fibulae, and parts of four more. See Gargano (2019) 631; Scarfì (1961) 230–46; Robinson (1996) 447–52; De Juliis (2002) 176.
35 As demonstrated, in particular, by archaeothanatology, an approach that relies on the collaboration between anthropologist and archaeologists. See, e.g., Duday (2009). For *gestes funéraires*, see Scheid (2000).

might have had more than one use, information can be extrapolated from a vessel's mechanical performance characteristics (e.g., fabric, size, shape, technological details), which limit the ways it could have been utilised.[36] A taxonomy based on the assumed function of the vases, therefore, is a useful framework to investigate practices when we lack emic knowledge about the cultural environment. For example, in a Greek context, a *hydria* or a *kalathos* carries specific, gendered connotations. This does not seem to apply to their Peucetian counterparts, as these shapes have been found in both male and female burials; nonetheless, they remain, respectively, a vase to pour liquids and a storage vessel.

Organising the vases on the basis of which behaviour they most likely facilitated shows that virtually all Peucetian burial kits, for both male and female adults (and many found in burials of sub-adults), include a decorated mixing vessel, vases for serving and drinking liquids, a small vase for libations, a number of pots, and implements for food preparation and consumption.[37] The number of vases per tomb varied between five and more than one hundred. However, even the richest assemblages can be broken down into repetitions of this module, with the addition of storage vessels for small quantities of solids and liquids, and metal artefacts.[38] This point can be easily illustrated by comparing two sarcophagus tombs with *ripostiglio* (Figures 8.3a–b) dated to the second half of the fifth century BCE – one from the acropolis of Monte Sannace, the other from Rutigliano, località Purgatorio (Table 8.1).[39]

Comparing the assemblages found at sites in the interior with those from the Adriatic zone gives an impression of general uniformity (Figure 8.4). Despite some preferences for specific shapes, they all seem to illustrate the same behaviours, again with some closer parallels between Rutigliano/Gravina, and Bitonto/Monte Sannace. The most noticeable pattern is the high percentage of drinking vessels at all sites. Speculatively, it is possible that the repetition of the same shapes in some funerary kits was not indicative of

---

36 There is a vast anthropological literature on the theoretical implications of imposed systems of classification. See, among others, Adams and Adams (1991) 157–68; Ruby (1993) 289–320. For taxonomies based on vases' functions in Apulia, see De Juliis (1995) 25–46; Lanza Catti (2011) 265–79; Pace (2014) 75–106.
37 Some uniformity is visible among mixing vessels. The most popular shape of this type of vessel, by far, was the column krater. Among drinking vessels, *skyphoi* and the *kantharoid* vases were the most common. Serving vessels for wine (pouring and storage vessels) appeared in a great repertoire of shapes, with some represented by just a few examples. The most popular shape was the so-called Type 8 *oinochoe*, which was attested both in black gloss and in matt-painted pottery, followed by matt-painted pitchers.
38 About 15% of all the pottery was made up of storage vessels not necessarily connected with communal drinking. Most numerous were shapes intended to hold small amounts of liquids (*lekythoi, askoi,* and *gutti*). Vases, possibly used to contain solids (such as *lekanides, kalathoi, stamnoi,* and *ollae*), became more popular in the fourth century.
39 For Monte Sannace 5/1957, see Gargano (2019) 631. For Rutigliano, see Lo Porto (1977) 739.

Figures 8.3a–b Pottery assemblages from 5/1957 at Monte Sannace (Archivio fotografico – Museo Archeologico Nazionale di Gioia del Colle) and 17/1976 at Rutigliano (after Lo Porto [1977] tav. CIX).

Source: After Lo Porto (1977) tav. CIX.

the deceased's wealth, especially since we cannot be sure of the value of these vases in antiquity. Rather, the multiple vases might have indicated the number of people who were – actually or symbolically – present at the funeral, and they might have even been provided by the mourners themselves.

The vast majority of the pottery found in these funerary contexts consisted of shapes connected with the consumption of wine and food. It has to be

164 Bice Peruzzi

Table 8.1 Comparison of the pottery assemblages from tombs 5/1957 at Monte Sannace and 17/1976 at Rutigliano, divided by function.

	Monte Sannace 5/1957	*Rutigliano 17/1976*
MIXING	Matt-painted column krater	Attic red figure column krater
OFFERING	two black gloss one-handled bowls	two matt-painted one-handled bowls; three black gloss one-handled bowls
DRINKING	black gloss skyphos; black figure skyphos; brown-slipped miniature kantharoid vase	Peucetian sub-geometric monochrome kantharoid vase; Attic black gloss skyphos; black gloss cup-skyphos; four black gloss cups
SERVING	Two black gloss type 8 oinochoai; black gloss trefoil oinochoe	Matt-painted trefoil oinochoe; four black gloss type 8 oinochoai
EATING	Matt-painted stem plate; black gloss stem plate	Matt-painted plate
COOKING	chytra	chytra; mortarium
STORAGE	Matt-painted kalathos; matt-painted stamnos with lid; black gloss aryballic lekythos	Attic black gloss lekanis
OTHER		Matt-painted kothon
METAL		bronze griff-phiale; bronze cauldron; bronze colander

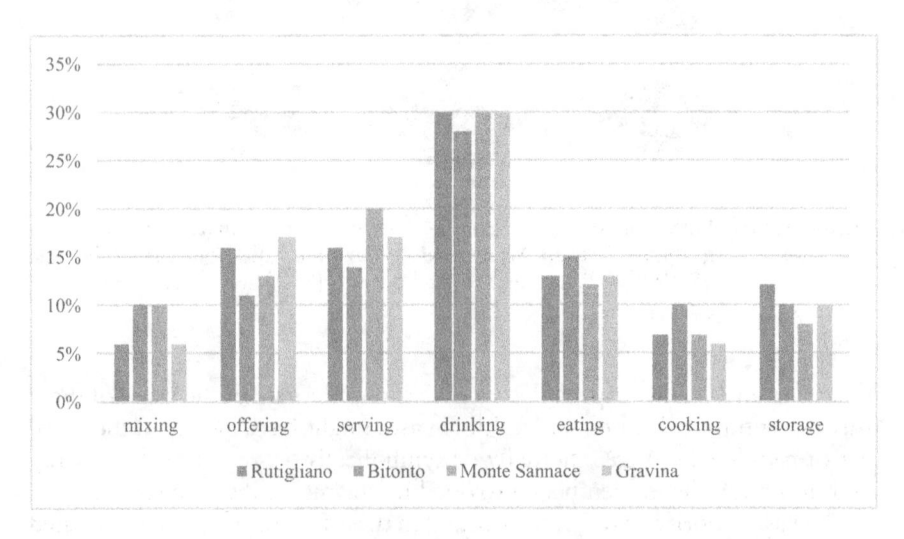

Figure 8.4 Distribution of pottery by function at the four sites (525–350 BCE).

noted that, although these 'banqueting sets' might share equipment with the Greek *symposion*, the type of feasting illustrated by Peucetian tombs shows some different characteristics (e.g., consumption of food, participation of women, funerary occasion) and goals.

Banquets were diacritical events meant to create relationships within social groups, in part by the exclusion of outsiders; they involved the assertion and negotiation of status through the provision of both wine and food; and, when performed at funerals, they attest to the well-being of the survivors.[40] The general uniformity of the assemblages, coupled with the preponderance of objects related to communal activities, demonstrates that a crucial part of the representation of the deceased was their membership in a group, separated from the broader population. Essentially, the introduction of the new burial kit in the last quarter of the sixth century BCE visually divided the people who shared the new practices from everybody else. Thus, if the inhabitants of Monte Sannace and Gravina were sending a 'message' through their funerals in this moment of boundary creation, it was one of kinship to their peers in the Adriatic communities and not separation.

Movement of people, goods, and ideas

It remains to be investigated how practical conditions (e.g., geography, state of roads, and closeness to centres of production) might have affected the distribution of Attic imports, Peucetian sub-geometric, south Italian red figure, and other classes of pottery at sites in the interior part of central Apulia.[41]

The presence of the Murge massif, which physically separates this region into two parts, must have played an important role in the circulation of goods. Besides a road directly along the coast, the two major routes of communication in central Apulia crossed the region longitudinally on the two sides of the plateau (Figure 8.5). The first road, which would become the *via Traiana* in the second century CE, followed the Adriatic coast and passed through Ruvo, Bitonto, Ceglie, and Rutigliano.[42] The other route was shorter and went through the *Fossa Bradanica*, a deep tectonic depression between the Murge and the Apennines.[43] This second road, which would become

---

40 For ethnographic comparisons on the role of feasting in creating and maintaining social relationships, see Dietler and Hayden (2001). The issue of feasting in the Mediterranean has also been explored at length in scholarship on the Aegean Bronze Age; see, e.g., the conferences held in Athens in 2004, Wright (2004), and in Melbourne in 2008, Hitchcock *et al.* (2008).
41 Differences between the two zones are also visible among later productions of overpainted pottery and Gnathia – see De Juliis (2002) 186–90; Lanza Catti (2011) 275–6.
42 *Itinerarium Antonini* 310.5–315.6. This road has sometimes also been called *via Minucia* in scholarship. The confusion comes from a passage in Strabo about the roads from Brindisi to Rome; as an alternative to the *via Appia* he mentions a 'ἡμιονική' (*via Minucia*) or 'ἡμιονική' (mule-track). Strabo 6.3.7; Marin (1981) 220.
43 Livy (9.2.6) specifically mentions that the *via Appia* went through Gravina. On the road system between central Apulia and Basilicata, see, e.g., Vinson (1972); Bottini (1979) 77.

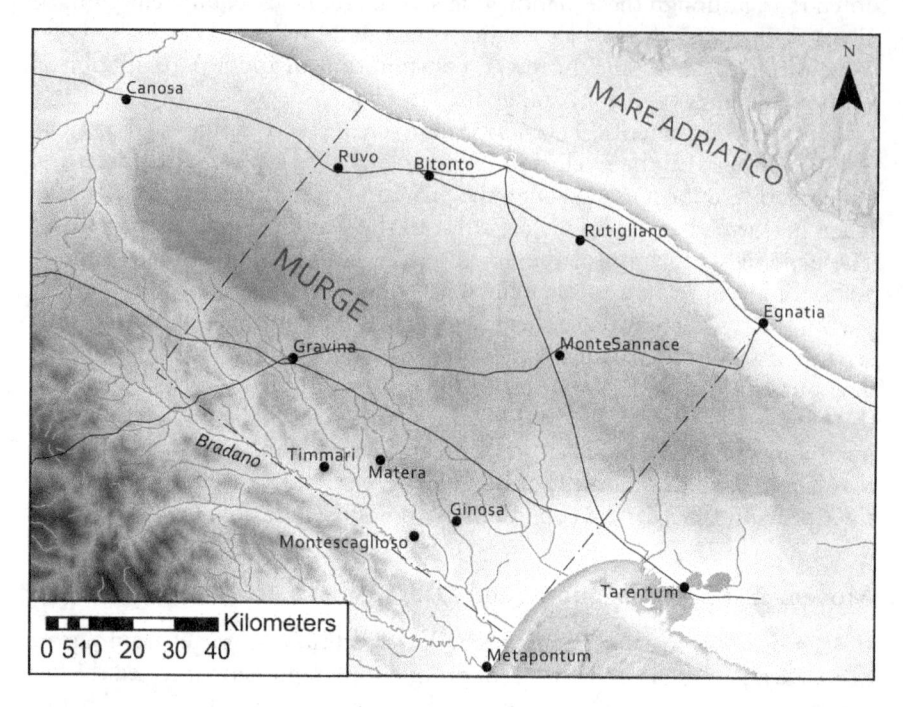

Figure 8.5 Map of road system in Apulia.
Source: Produced by Joshua Emmitt. Road data from McCormick *et al.* (2013).

part of the *via Appia*, connected the Gulf of Tarentum with the northern part of Basilicata, and served the sites in interior Peucetia, as it went through Gravina, Altamura, and Laterza.

A system of drove roads, some of which survived into the twentieth century, clustered around these two major arteries. Geology affected the path of the secondary routes as well; in the Adriatic zone, many of them seem to follow the *lame*, the deep karst erosions that ran west to east, from the Murge to the sea.[44] In the *Fossa Bradanica*, instead, communication seems to have been facilitated by the presence of the Basentello and Bradano rivers and their tributaries; by navigating these waterways – or even just travelling alongside them – it was possible to safely reach the Adriatic coast from Gravina, going through the territories of Timmari and Montescaglioso.

Thus, goods likely moved within central Apulia on two parallel trade networks: one connecting the sites on the coast, the other linking the eastern

---

44 Some scholars have hypothesised that a portion of the shorter road that connected Bari and Tarentum, described by Strabo (6.3.8), might have run within one of these *lame*; Uggeri (1983) 312.

side of the Murge and the *Fossa Bradanica*. This hypothesis is supported by the origin of the pottery found in the necropoleis at Gravina and Monte Sannace. Unfortunately, the location of the production centres of Peucetian sub-geometric is still largely unknown, especially for the monochromatic pots. However, some evidence is available for polychrome sub-geometric; remains of kilns and ceramic wasters of this type have been found at Montescaglioso.[45] Furthermore, the very limited circulation of some decorative motifs, in addition to the more spread-out settlement pattern in interior Peucetia, has allowed scholars to hypothesise the existence of workshops at several sites, including one at Gravina and one in the territory of Monte Sannace.[46]

The production of proto-Lucanian and Lucanian pottery can be safely placed at Metapontum, whose *kerameikos* has been extensively excavated in the past fifty years.[47] This site might also have been the location of the earliest workshops for the production of overpainted pottery, even if this class of material is completely absent from Metapontine tombs and might have been made exclusively for the Italic market.[48] The main production centre for early Apulian red figure vases, instead, is traditionally identified with Tarentum, although workshops might have later been established at other sites.[49] In sum, all the pottery that seems to be more common at Monte Sannace and Gravina was made either locally or at Metapontum and Tarentum. Given their location, it may have been easier for the inhabitants of the internal part of Peucetia to look west to acquire their pots.

Interestingly, the sites that were closer and better connected to the Greek colonies were also the ones with fewer Attic imports. Clearly, Athenian vase trade in this region did not need the mediation of Tarentum and Metapontum. As Filippo and Giada Giudice have argued, the vessels must have arrived directly on the central Apulian coast through the Adriatic, and were then distributed to the other Italic centres through land routes.[50] The majority of the pots were moved along the predecessor of the *via Traiana*, with Ruvo having a prominent role in this network. Not only was it the destination of a very large number of Attic imports, as we have seen already, but it might have also served as a staging area for the trans-Apennine trade that

---

45 Lo Porto (1988–1989) 388–93.
46 De Juliis (1995) 81–2. Remains of several kilns have been found at Monte Sannace; the earliest of these was located on the acropolis and is dated to the second half of the fifth century BCE. Unfortunately, the type of pottery fired at this kiln is still unknown. See Del Monte (2019) 62, with previous bibliography.
47 See, e.g., D'Andria (1975) 356–77.
48 Robinson (1990) 262–5, (1996) 448; more recently, Calandra (2008) 7–8.
49 On pottery production at Tarentum, see, e.g., Carpenter (2009) 28–30; Fontannaz (2014) 71–95; see also Robinson in this volume.
50 On the Adriatic trade route, see, e.g., Giudice (2002) 171–210 and Giudice (2007) 311–16; 385–9. Tarentum, instead, might have been the distribution centre for Corinthian pots; see, e.g., Ciancio (2010b) 291–7. Canosa (2014) 11–20.

brought vases from the Adriatic coast to Campania.[51] A smaller quantity of Attic vases were brought further inland, most probably using a drove road within the so called Frassineto Canal, which connected the coast (either at the point of Egnazia or Polignano) with Monte Sannace and Gravina, and continued to Serra di Vaglio, in Basilicata.[52] This hypothesis would explain both the presence of works of the same painters across all of central Apulia, and the smaller quantities of Attic imports at sites in the interior.

Conclusions

In conclusion, the analysis of the necropoleis of Rutigliano, Bitonto, Gravina, and Monte Sannace reveals an image of general uniformity among Peucetian graves. There were substantial parallels in the distribution of classes between coastal and interior sites (in particular, between Rutigliano and Gravina, and Monte Sannace and Bitonto). Furthermore, despite some preferences for specific shapes, all assemblages seemed to illustrate the same patterns of behaviour. It follows that the same funerary customs had been adopted across the region, which belies the possibility of the existence of two sub-regional zones.

Ease of access seems to be the primary cause of the variability in the material culture between the interior and the Adriatic part of central Apulia in this period (525–350 BCE). Although the evidence does not support the argument that the people of the 'Bradano District' belonged to a cohesive and distinct cultural group, it does support the existence of an identifiable social and economic network. Evidence suggests that there was a Bradanic 'trade corridor', which saw a stream of products, people, and ideas moving through the communities of the *Fossa Bradanica*, from the Ionic coast to the Upper Melfese.[53] The everyday interaction between different cultural groups along this corridor naturally brought a certain level of hybridisation in the material culture, which is observable as far north as Baragiano.[54] However, this did not affect the funerary practices of Gravina and Monte Sannace. Instead, it appears that

---

51 The distribution pattern of vases by the workshops of the Meidias, Nikias, and Meleager Painters seem to support this hypothesis; see, e.g., Giudice (2007) 379; 396; Curti (2000) 25–34. An intense connection with Campania is also suggested by the fact that Ruvo was the only site in the entire Adriatic basin that has yielded examples of Nolan *amphorae*, which were produced primarily for Capua and Nola. Similarly, some of the gold jewellery and the bronze basins found in Ruvo's necropoleis, can be safely traced back to sites in Campania featuring a strong Etruscan influence. On these, see Montanaro (2006).
52 The road was identified using aerial photography by Dino Adamesteanu in the 1950s; however, the portion of the route that connects Monte Sannace to the sea is still debated by scholars and there are at least two possible variants – see, most recently, Del Monte (2019) 40–2, with previous bibliography. See Heitz in this volume for discussion of these drove roads and transhumance in cultural transfer.
53 See, e.g., Pace (2014) 75–106 for a study of the diffusion of the one-handled bowl.
54 The northern part of central Basilicata is sometimes identified in scholarship as the territory of the *Peuketiantes* a population similar to the Peucetians. There is only one reference to the

inhabitants of these sites, in particular the elites, were interested in strongly showcasing their ties to the wider Peucetian tradition through their behaviour, even if they used the ceramics that were more easily available to them.[55]

In the end, it cannot be denied that choosing a particular style of artefacts for the grave assemblages conveyed information about the deceased; yet, formal variability in the material culture should not be the only criterion to identify social and cultural groups. Different communities might have used the same objects in different ways, and imbued them with different meanings. This is particularly true for fluid, liminal, or border zones, like the Bradanic corridor. Therefore, if we truly want to leap from the study of pots to that of people, we must move away from some traditional frameworks, and think about how objects functioned in the different contexts. Only this way, we might be able to shed light on the identity of their consumers.

Πευκετίαντες in Hecateus of Miletus, who calls them neighbours of the Oenotrians. Hekat. *FGrH* 1F 89. See also Bottini (2011) 5–14.

55 Massimo Osanna has noted that the funerary practices of the Apulian populations in the Bradano area remained distinguishably 'Peucetian' still in the third century BCE, even if some other religious aspects progressively assimilated to local practices. See Osanna (2013b) 641.

9 Etruscan trading spaces and the tools for regulating Etruscan markets

Hilary Becker

Virtually every facet of the economy of pre-Roman Italy is debated in modern scholarship, from how we conceive of it functioning on a grand level, to the nitty-gritty of the production, movement, and deposition of items – all of which are touched on in this volume. The dynamics of the tools and places of exchange in Etruria merit further consideration. What were the mechanisms that facilitated the movement of products across Etruria? How did goods move around and between consumers, and what spaces and tools might have facilitated the commercial exchange of goods? The average Etruscan farmer or artisan, whether they lived in the town or in the countryside, did not produce everything that they needed, so one of their day-to-day concerns would have been the ready ability to acquire the products of others, especially foodstuffs. Of particular interest for this volume are the means and mechanisms by which an early Italian consumer could have satisfied these needs and so participated locally, regionally, and potentially globally, within their economic sphere.

Trade in Etruria

It is a truism that Etruscans of every type, class, and profession would have, in order to augment what they did not produce, engaged in trade and exchange of some type. They could have traded locally with neighbours, with several people in turn (down the line), or, particularly if they were members of the ruling class, could have participated in gift exchange from time to time for prestige items, perhaps over long distances.[1] In addition, an itinerant merchant might have also exchanged products with an Etruscan consumer, thus linking them into a wider network with connections which spread across the Mediterranean.[2] Trade was a vital, linking principle which bound all Etruscans together, and to the wider world.

---

1 Cristofani (1975); Riva (2009) 42–3, 173–5. See also Mauss (2016).
2 An example of an iterant merchant might be Arruns, the merchant from Chiusi who inadvertently started a war with the Gauls by selling Etruscan products (along with sharing information). See Livy 5.33.2–5; Dion. Hal. *Ant. Rom.*13.10.3–13.11.2; Plut. *Vit. Cam.* 15.3–17.4. See also de Ligt (1993) 108; Smith (2005b); Perkins (2012). For different trading scenarios, see the masterful survey by Renfrew (1975).

DOI: 10.4324/9781003120728-9

Exchanges happened in a wide range of locations. Neighbours could trade with each other at the house door or farm gate. A myriad of smaller sites and urban centres could have hosted opportunities for the exchange of products and services. A potential site for trading may be found at a possible workshop or shop at the North Etruscan site of Gonfienti (discussed further below). In addition, there were a variety of workshops at Marzabotto, ancient *Kainua*, (southwest of Bologna), a site that was ideally positioned to accommodate traders given its location at the exit of the Apennine mountain passes, and evidence assessed in this chapter will demonstrate one way in which the site accommodated regular exchange.³ With all of these possibilities for trade in practice in mind, this chapter surveys the evidence for Etruscan physical markets and is primarily interested in whether the Etruscans consciously developed mechanisms to facilitate marketplace exchange.

This chapter will therefore explore the evidence for physical markets in Etruria, focusing especially upon marketplaces or, following Garraty, 'any regular and predictable loci of market exchange, [that] offer a formal setting for market exchange'.⁴ It is hypothesised that another characteristic of many Etruscans markets is that they were held on a predictable schedule.⁵ Thus, exchanges at marketplaces could be optimised by tying them to a calendar, as then the markets could be scheduled so that more merchants might be present on a given day, providing options to both sellers and consumers. Such markets lowered transaction costs because, instead of negotiating with many individual producers or farmers who were steadily trying to exchange one product for another, they allowed for a greater variety of products to be available simultaneously.⁶

This chapter will also review markets that appealed to the different commercial needs of Etruria, starting from those that accommodated foreign audiences (*emporia*), then moving to trading opportunities that attracted the largest, long-range, and more culturally diverse audiences (i.e., interregional markets taking place at religious festivals), and finally shifting to more

---

3 Maggiani (2002) 173–80; Sassatelli and Govi (2013) 291. I thank an anonymous reviewer for pointing out that a Transalpine road has been hypothesised, based on archaeological and literary evidence, that would have connected the Tyrrhenian coast with the Adriatic (Spina) crossing sites like Gonfienti and Marzabotto. Such a road would have served as a trade route for metals, a *via etrusca del Ferro*. Some traces of an Etruscan glareate road have been found in Frizzone, near Lucca, which is dated from the sixth to mid-fourth century BCE (Ciampoltrini Zecchini [2007]; Emiliozzi [2017] 418; Centauro [2020]). This may be the road mentioned by Pseudo-Skylax in the fourth century BCE which took three days to travel (*Periplus* 17; Shipley [2020] 59, 107–8).
4 Garraty (2010) 9.
5 Shaw (2012) 122.
6 Smith (1974) 169; Garraty (2010) 17; Hirth (2010) 236–47. Kenneth Hirth elaborates on the utility of marketplaces further, stating that 'what the marketplace does is make household provisioning more efficient by reducing the amount of time needed to procure resources through reciprocal house-hold exchange networks.' See Smith, in this volume, for an alternative view.

local, periodic markets. The first two categories will be surveyed briefly, as their existence is not debated, in order to focus more upon the literary and archaeological evidence for both permanent and periodic markets.

Throughout, attention will be paid to the evidence for the institutional framework (e.g., locations, scheduling, standards) that might have made centralised spaces feasible marketplaces. It is will also be useful to consider how such a hypothetical institutional framework might have facilitated a system that could be utilised and understood by consumers, whether they lived in the centre or the periphery. Comparisons with other cognate civilisations that had such periodic market systems can be useful for learning how to recognise (or cautiously predict) a market archaeologically, as well as providing useful parallels for understanding the institutional mechanisms that facilitated markets. Throughout, the focus will be on places that would have provided opportunities for Etruscans to meet and acquire a range of commodities, as well as the tools that could have facilitated such encounters.

Etruscan *emporia*

Emporia are coastal ports of trade found at Etruscan sites such as Pyrgi (Caere) and Graviscae (Tarquinia). They are externally oriented trading spaces,[7] where artefacts, including the bilingual Phoenician and Etruscan golden plaques dedicated at one of the sanctuaries at the *emporion* of Pyrgi or the votive anchor dedicated at Graviscae by a Greek trader named Sostratos, document regular trade with Greeks and Phoenicians.[8] Such imports are also celebrated on the wall of the 'Tomb of the Ship' at Tarquinia (mid-fifth century BCE), which depicts a merchant ship approaching a shore while a man waits for him.[9] The *kylikeia*, a stand full of different types of Attic vases, standing next to the Tarquinian seems to emphasise the imported objects his labours and connections had wrought.[10]

Sanctuaries were integral to *emporia* and would have mediated and protected trade. Indeed, trade could have occurred within the sacred space of the

---

7 Nijboer (2004) 147, 149–50; Michetti (2016) 83.
8 Demetriou (2012) 64; Becker (2017a) 1018.
9 Moretti (1960); Petrarulo (2012); Becker (2017a) 1019. Note that Colonna (2003) emphasises that this scene, instead, is a reminder of one route of the journey to the underworld – see also Riva (2021) 158. Note that Gabriella Petrarulo (2012) 126 has reanalysed the painting and does not see a ship in distress and so would interpret this scene as it has been in the past, in so far as the 'cargo ship represents an autobiographical element that not only celebrates the deceased and his social status but also his probable role in the field of maritime trade'.
10 For the possible status of external trading partners see Torelli (1986). Corinna Riva (2010) 221 hypothesised that it was 'likely that Etruscan intermediaries managed trading activities in the *emporion* for notable local families'.

sanctuaries themselves.[11] Laura Michetti observed that the emporic sanctuary at Graviscae was 'flourishing next to a market placed in a key location for communication and international trade'.[12] Etruscan traders at such a site would have then worked to both facilitate the trade and distribution of imported goods and, at the same time, collect goods (including metal, wine, and olive oil) that could have been exported.

These *emporia* were inexorably connected to nearby major cities, under which they operated.[13] Connections between these trading cities (and their *emporia*) were likely strengthened by treaties and bilateral agreements, such as the reported treaty of 509 BCE between Rome and Carthage.[14] Another important element of this trade concerns the local people who facilitated, or even regulated, exchange at Etruscan trading sites. Power dynamics at these sites are still uncertain. When considering trading at *emporia*, it is not clear whether dominant aristocrats were in charge, or whether, as Torelli suggested, there may have been a town-herald or clerk ultimately in charge of each *emporion*, such as the Punic magistrates officiating at Punic sites in the aforementioned treaty between Carthage and Rome.[15] This chapter explores who might have officiated at different types of Etruscan markets in order to better understand the extent to which each of these trading spaces was integrated within a larger sociopolitical framework. While the governance of Etruscan *emporia* might not be a question that can be resolved, a line of argument through this chapter considers who might have officiated each different type of Etruscan market. Such a theme contextualises the extent to which each of these trading spaces was integrated within a larger sociopolitical framework.

Festivals and low-frequency periodic markets

One type of hypothesised market in Etruria and central Italy happened infrequently and pulled from a large catchment area, and provided a place where a religious celebration or festival might have offered a context for mercantile exchange. Periodic festivals or fairs, around the world and in different periods, often hosted markets as well. So many people gathering in a single place would naturally create a good market opportunity for itinerant merchants, or even fairgoers with their own wares. An example of this would be the rituals at the *Fanum Voltumnae*, the shrine of Veltumna (Latin Vortumnus or Vertumnus), which hosted an annual religious, pan-Etruscan

---

11 After all, a significant amount of metal processing occurred within the sanctuary at Graviscae. See Torelli (2004) 122; Haack (2014).
12 Michetti (2016) 83.
13 Riva (2010) 211; Michetti (2017).
14 Polybius 3.22–3; Colonna (2010); Michetti (2016) 78.
15 Fiorini and Torelli (2010) 43. See also Bresson (2000) 288–9.

festival celebrating the Etruscan deity Veltumna.[16] Elite men from the leading cities of Etruria attended this festival for sacral activities and games, and this fair likely attracted an intraregional and even interregional audience as well.[17] Such a festival offered an opportunity for people, with a wide range of social and economic backgrounds, to converge and discuss and react to contemporary political and martial affairs in central Italy. When Veii asked other Etruscan cities for assistance at a meeting at the *Fanum Voltumnae* in 434 BCE, the Romans heard about this from merchants who were present.[18] An interpretation of this historical episode, recounted by Livy, suggests a gathering from across Etruria at the shrine, at which merchants were also present.

While the political or religious importance of the festival at the *Fanum Voltumnae* is often considered, its commercial aspect should not be overlooked. Whereas Etruscans could be expected to have sourced most of their daily needs locally, an annual fair would have provided the opportunity to acquire a wider range of items. Low-frequency fairs, such as the one possibly held at the *Fanum Voltumnae*, might have involved the trade in materials related to the annual religious celebrations (such as food, votives, and sacrificial animals), but also (analogous to medieval fairs) might have offered a far wider assortment of sellers, goods, and services than were typically available in one's local region.[19] The religious context of such a transregional fair would have also provided a particularly optimal location for commercial exchange, plausibly mediating any military or political tensions, providing a protected neutral safe trading place, and serving as a 'hinge between economies otherwise not in dialogue'.[20]

Ancient authors did not record where the *Fanum Voltumnae* was located but important evidence is provided by Propertius, who identifies the god Vertumnus with the Etruscan city of Velsna (ancient Volsinii, modern Orvieto).[21] A Constantinian rescript also refers to an annual festival occurring near Volsinii, according to ancient custom (*CIL* 11.5265). Excavations led by Simonetta Stopponi at Campo della Fiera, just to the west of modern Orvieto, have revealed a site that may have hosted the religious festival at the *Fanum Voltumnae* for centuries.[22] This sacred site was active from the sixth century BCE into the Roman imperial period. Campo della Fiera was a nodal meeting point at the foot of Orvieto's plateau, where the roads connecting

---

16 Stopponi (2013a) 632; van der Meer (2013) 104; Gori (2014).
17 Colonna (1985) 25.
18 Livy 4.23.4–4.24.2; Becker (2013) 364.
19 de Ligt and de Neeve (1988) 399; Cherici (2012) 301, 304.
20 Cherici (2012) 299–311 (direct quote from 301). See also Cohen, in this volume, for discussion of the role of festivals and fairs in facilitating economic and social interaction.
21 Livy (4.23.5, 4.25.7, 4.61.2, 5.17.6, and 6.2.2) mentioned the *Fanum Voltumnae* but does not mention where it was located. See Stopponi (2013a) 632.
22 Harris (2007); Stopponi (2011), (2013a) 633, (2013b); Massa-Pairault (2016).

the Tiber River valley, Bolsena, and Chiusi met, and, indeed, this area is still a major transportation crossroads today.[23] No traces of commercial stalls have yet been found at Campo della Fiera, but temporary, wooden stalls might have once accompanied the preserved remains of temples and votives.[24] The site was used for fairs into the medieval period, a usage preserved in its name, Campo della Fiera, or 'fairgrounds field'. Further, a medieval church there was known as S. Pietro *in nundinis*[25] and was located in the *campus nundinarum*.[26] The Latin term *nundinae*, which will be explored in more detail below, connoted 'market days'. As interpreted, the site of Campo della Fiera embodies well the saying, 'no human settlement is more difficult to supplant than an established market' since it seems that marketing activities persisted at this site for many centuries.[27]

An annual religious festival/market also occurred at *Lucus Feroniae* in the territory of Capena. Livy mentions that Roman traders were supposedly captured at the fair in the reign of Tullus Hostilius, although votives date religious activity at the site only as early as the sixth and fifth centuries BCE.[28] As with the *Fanum Voltumnae*, the location of this site made it ideal for people from many different regions to congregate and trade – the site was located at an important crossroads that predated the creation of the *Via Flaminia*, one which linked the *Via Tiberina* and a road leading to Capena, and was about 3 km from the Tiber itself. As such, this festival and its markets would have been near to, and connected with, the territories of Etruscan, Latin, Sabine, and Faliscan people.[29] Filippo Coarelli noted that it was little wonder that a *grande mercato*, connected with the sanctuary of Feronia, would be located here, since the goddess was revered by both Latins and Sabines.[30]

It is typical for modern, low-frequency markets, such as these, to have some sort of administrative apparatus – for instance, to coordinate trade and organise the overall festivities. If there was administration, such a mechanism would help to make sure that exchange was fair; this was even more important if people from different regions were all temporarily intersecting in the same space. The only potential evidence for this comes from Livy (5.1),

---

23 Stopponi (2007) 502.
24 Françoise-Hélène Massa-Pairault (2016) 109 expressed she would also like to know more about the fair and the commercial functions of the sanctuary but also the deities who looked over such commerce; evidence offered by an inscribed weight at Caere (discussed in the following pages) may shed light on two gods who seem to have been connected to Etruscan commerce and market spaces, see Capdeville (1999).
25 Stopponi (2013b) 145; Massa-Pairault (2016) 140.
26 Stopponi (2007) 501.
27 Sir Halford John Mackinder, quoted in Bird (1958) 464; Bromley et al. (1975) 531.
28 Livy 1.30.5; Gabba (1975) 155; Moretti Sgubini (2006) 126; Di Fazio (2012) 339–42.
29 Coarelli (1975) 164; Frayn (1993) 136; Zifferero (1995) 334. On this point, Livy (26.11.9) wrote: *Capenates aliique qui accolae eius erant . . .*, 'The people of Capena and the others who were the town's neighbors . . . '
30 Coarelli (1975) 164.

who discusses the election of a chief priest for the annual celebration of the *Fanum Voltumnae*. The king of Veii apparently lost this election in the late fifth century BCE and withdrew the game performers whom he had promised for the communal celebration. Perhaps it was the priest and/or a combination of leading men who contributed to the festivals that might have helped to regulate the secular activities at the fair.

Etruscan high-frequency periodic markets, calendars, and nundinae

The markets that occurred at festivals like the *Fanum Voltumnae* and *Lucus Feroniae* were low-frequency periodic markets. It is worth considering whether other periodic markets, which would have met more regularly, also existed in Etruria. Periodic markets are generally found in economic contexts where there is a low, but constant, demand for goods and a similarly low level of supply.[31] They are often found in rural contexts and are useful for disposing of agricultural surplus. Periodic markets, like a modern farmer's market, have existed in various historical contexts, both ancient and modern, around the world.

Such high-frequency, periodic markets are often regulated according to a calendar. Speaking about similar markets over time, Ross Hassig observed, 'one of the basic concerns of market scheduling is simplicity. It is crucial that buyers and sellers alike know when the markets are held. Consequently, schedules that fit the fundamental units of time of a given calendrical system are best and most easily remembered'.[32] The schedule of Roman periodic markets could be easily followed and remembered thanks to a multimodal calendrical system, which allowed for reckoning of days of the month (e.g., *Kalends, Nones*) and feast days, as well as tracking the market schedule. Periodic markets were observed in Rome and in other Roman settlements and were known as the *nundinae*. *Nundinae* stems from the Latin words *novem* and *diem*, for the market took place, according to the inclusive Roman reckoning, every ninth day.[33] They were originally held every eight days and organised so that farmers who lived in the countryside could have dependably appointed days on which to sell their wares in a nearby town. Macrobius (*Sat.*

---

31 de Ligt (1993) 109; de Ligt and de Neeve (1988) 402. It is important to note that permanent markets and periodic markets are not evolutionary variants of one another but could coexist (de Ligt and de Neeve [1988] 411).
32 Hassig (1982) 347. See also Bromley *et al.* (1975) 531.
33 Michels (1967) 27–8, 84–9; de Ligt (1993) 51, 112–17. Varro (*Rust.* 2. pr., 1–2): *Itaque annum ita diviserunt, ut nonis diebus urbanas res usurparent, reliquis septem ut rura colerent*, 'Accordingly, they divided the year in such a way that they practised their town business on the ninth days, so that they cold tend rural matters on the remaining seven days.' See also Columella *Rust.* 1, pr. 18; Dion. Hal. *Ant. Rom.* 2.28.3; Plin. *HN* 18.3.13–14; Plut. *Quaest. Rom.* 42; Macrob. *Sat.* 1.16.28–36.

1.16.33) explains that Servius Tullius created the *nundinae*, 'so that people intending to set both their urban and their rural interests in order would gather in the city from the countryside'.[34] As Macrobius saw it, it is at these markets where the boundaries between city and countryside were blurred.

The Roman periodic markets were predicated on a fixed calendrical system and the Etruscan calendar has parallels that suggest a similar cycle was also at work in Etruria. For example, there were fixed points within each Etruscan month equivalent to the Roman *Kalends*, *Nones*, and *Ides*, and Macrobius even believed that the word *Ides* was derived from the Etruscan word *itus*.[35] Further evidence from Macrobius suggests that the nine-day system, which the Romans used, also had resonance with the Etruscans. According to Macrobius, 'among the Etruscans, several *nonae* were observed, because on every ninth day they paid respects to their king and consult (with him) about their own business' (Macrob. *Sat.* 1.15.13).[36] Agnes Michels suggested that when Macrobius used the term *nonae*, he was not referring to the *Nones*, which fell nine inclusive days before the Roman *Ides*, but to the *nundinae* – and she noted that Macrobius occasionally confused these two words.[37] That the Latin also says 'on every ninth day' seems to support Michels' reading. Michels suggested in her discussion of Roman *nundinae* that the observation of the *nundinae* may have originated with the Latins or the Etruscans. A case, then, might be made for crediting the Etruscans with the invention of the *nundinae*, rather than the Romans. The *Liber Linteus* of the Zagreb Mummy (written between the mid-third to the early first century BCE) demonstrates that the Etruscan calendar adopted a numerical daily system. The 26th day of the month of Celi (September), for example, shows the integrated system at a time when the contemporaneous calendar of the Romans did not have it.[38] Thus, the Etruscans had an intrinsically numerical approach to their calendar and such an approach could very well have led to the regular counting of nundinal days.[39]

---

34 Trans. Kaster (2011) *ut in urbem ex agris convenirent urbanas rusticasque res ordinaturi*. Charles Good (1975) 51, who was thinking about the periodicity of modern markets, noted, 'marketing calendars are social and cultural in origin. They not only regulate the frequency of a market and define the length of the "market week" for a given area but also often have a pervasive, subtle impact on other aspects of economic and social life which are only remotely associated with markets. The commingling of city and hinterland for a market, that would have served more than just marketing needs, was a part of this.

35 Edlund-Berry (1992) 331; Cherici (2012) 307. Edlund-Berry interprets certain words associated with months as these fixed points. In addition, see Macrob. *Sat.* 1.15.14, where for example the word *Ides* is thought to derive the from Etruscan term (*itis*).

36 ... *apud Tuscos Nonae plures habebantur, quod hi nono quoque die regem suum salutabant et de propriis negotiis consulebant.*

37 Michels (1967) 191–2. *Nundinae* is the feminine plural of the adjective *nundinus* (*novem* and the root **dinom* [day] – every 9 days). For this reasons, Latin terms such as *nundinor* and *nundinatio* signify 'holding a market' or 'buying'.

38 Roman market calendars reflected a seven day of the week system only by the Augustan period (if not before), see Michels (1967) 89, 192.

39 This suggestion was kindly made by Mario Torelli when he heard my early work on this topic.

Etruscan priests were responsible for maintaining their varied calendars. The aforementioned *Liber Linteus* prescribed religious rituals for different divinities for each day.[40] The Capua tile (*Tabula Capuana*, mid-fifth century BCE) offers a similar Etruscan calendar that also kept track of the different rituals for the gods on each day and was found at S. Maria Capua Vetere in Campania.[41] Both calendars recorded regular feast days.[42] The Brontoscopic calendar was a tool (or even a reference table) formulated by priests to help interpret thunder. If it thundered on any given day, a look at the calendar would reveal what was portended for that day.[43] The text would have been composed by a small group of priests who collected observations and transmitted them to future priests in their town.[44] Thus, there is ample circumstantial evidence to connect Etruscan priests with tracking time on calendars for a variety of different purposes.

A calendar is important for revering the gods, so that humanity's relationship with both the divine and natural worlds can be maintained. But if the Etruscans were also using a nundinal calendar to coordinate regular commercial exchange at periodic markets, such a practice would add a vital socio-economic layer. A calendar was a tool to which people of all ranks would have needed to be attuned, whether they lived in the town or country. A related corollary is that, if a calendar helped to regulate an important quotidian institution, there would have needed to have been a social (or even political mechanism) in order to share scheduling information.[45] In later societies, information about prices (or even relative valuation) at a market may have been a vital component to disseminate. But before even that, knowledge about the cyclical schedule of the meetings would have been essential to the success of periodic markets for any society that maintained such a tradition.

---

40 Edlund-Berry (1992) 331; van der Meer (2007), (2009); Turfa (2012) 5; Agostiniani (2013) 460–1.
41 Edlund-Berry (1992) 332; Turfa (2012) 23; Agostiniani (2013) 461.
42 Edlund-Berry (1992) 333, 336–7.
43 Turfa (2006), (2012) 4. This late antique Greek text (sixth century CE) was recorded by Johannes Lydus and it is a copy of a mid-first century BCE Latin text by P. Nigidius Figulus, which was itself a copy of an Etruscan original. The original text is thought to have been composed in the early seventh century BCE, if not just before.
44 It is helpful to recall here that Etruscan calendars were likely regional. The Brontoscopic calendar states at its conclusion, 'the brontoscopic almanac Nigidius claimed was not universal, but was only for Rome' (trans. Turfa [2006] 190). The observations of cause and effect of thunder might be different indeed for Perugia compared with Rome, and so this specificity is important for religious reasons – although Turfa notes that the climate is similar for these adjacent areas (Turfa [2012] 106). Edlund-Berry's (1992) important survey of Etruscan calendars discusses the evidence for individual calendars (with potentially different names for months and different local gods) specific to each city.
45 Garraty (2010) 8.

The placement of Etruscan markets: assessing range and demand

It is helpful to situate the discussion of periodic markets within the real needs of the Etruscan population and with respect to their settlement patterns, while also considering the limitations of product transport. Not every villager or farmer would have lived within easy travelling distance of a major Etruscan city and its market(s), especially in northern Etruria where the territories were large and the cities were located at a considerable distance from one another. In addition, some products would not be transported very far from their point of origin (i.e., range of products), since each product has a distance beyond which buyers will not be willing to travel in order to acquire it (Figure 9.1).[46] Perishable products, such as fresh vegetables and produce,

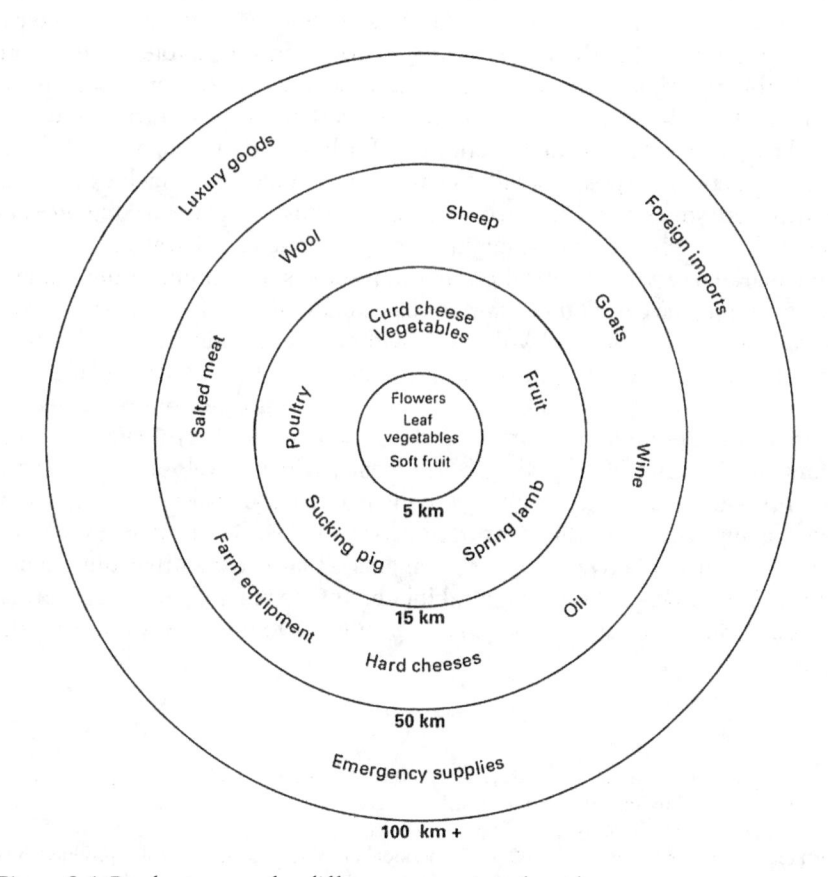

Figure 9.1 Product ranges for different categories of products.
Source: After Frayn (1993) 77, figure 7.

46 Smith (1974) 181–2, (1976) 12–3; de Ligt and de Neeve (1988) 401; de Ligt (1993) 7–8. Range is determined by factors such as need, price, transport cost, and frequency of use.

tend to travel not more than 5–10 km to reach a market.[47] Some products, such as luxury items, have a greater range.

The principal corollary to 'range of products' is the 'threshold' of demand, which is defined as the area containing enough consumer demand for a good to enable the supplier to survive in a fiscal sense.[48] Periodic markets allow each tradesperson to carry out their work and only take one day off in every eight, at most, for marketing needs. In the countryside, there would likely not be a sufficient demand threshold to warrant a permanent market (although there would have been a much more intense concentration of demand in urban centres). Such periodic meetings would allow for a consumer to have a much greater choice among products than they might have had in casual trading among houses and villages in their village. These guidelines for the movements of products and people present a hypothetical model for what could be possible across Etruscan landscapes. Such a model is not predicative, but it is useful to think about how far commonly available products can profitably move, such as leaf vegetables (5 km) or cheese curds and fruits (15 km). In such a case, it seems fair to predict that not every Etruscan would need to travel to their nearest major city for basic provisioning.

For practical purposes, smaller centres in each territory (such as *castella*, which were small, fortified settlements on hilltops and plateaus), villages, or convenient meeting grounds, might thus be theorised as logical sites for periodic markets serving the local population of the surrounding countryside.[49] For example, the *castellum* Cetamura Del Chianti lies more than 30 km from Siena, Fiesole, Arezzo, and Volterra.[50] Although Cetamura is a small site, it might have been a convenient gathering place for the smaller villages and farms in its area; there might have been a sufficient threshold for a market that occurred periodically. Alternatively, one could think of the survey results from the Albegna Valley, where settlements, which developed in the later seventh and sixth centuries BCE, are distributed about every 10 km.[51] Phil Perkins suggested that this distribution was a reflection of the market economy that existed between these settlements – that is to say that the spacing of these settlements allows for rural inhabitants to reach the nearest market, which is close enough that perishable products would not spoil during the

---

47 Frayn (1993) 76. This model considers distance and does not consider topographic variation that might impact time devoted to travel.
48 Smith (1974) 181, (1976) 13; de Ligt and de Neeve (1988) 401.
49 Hodder and Orton (1976) 58–60. Rural periodic markets also allow surplus produce to be collected (by merchant middlemen?) so that it can be used in the city. I thank Nicola Terrenato for drawing my attention to the historical and archaeological phenomenon of Etruscan *castella*.
50 de Grummond *et al.* (1994) 84–5; Becker (2002–2003 [2006]), (2008).
51 Perkins (2000) 96 and similarly, for the Albegna valley; see also a similar spacing nearby in Rendeli (1993) 173.

journey.⁵² So, considering the distances that common products might travel, small settlements such as these might have provided efficient meeting points for exchange, but more evidence than just spatial locations will be needed.

Poggio Civitate (Murlo), has been posited as a possible market site and its location, 20 km away from nearest large city of Siena and near the Crevole River, fits within this scheme of periodic markets serving the surrounding villages.⁵³ Ingrid Edlund-Berry, in her analysis of Etruscan market territories, proposed a market catchment for Murlo that likely reflects the sale of more ubiquitously available products, such as vegetables and the abundant meat and milk products that the site produced.⁵⁴ For those who lived near Murlo, perhaps this was sufficient for a market every week. However, more unique items, such as bone, ivory, and bronze objects, were produced in the 'Orientalising Workshop 2' (c. 675–600 BCE) at the site.⁵⁵ In addition, the presence of more than 1,600 textile implements from this period indicate that fine yarn and textiles (especially tablet-woven textiles or borders) may also have been a specialty of this site.⁵⁶ Such evidence suggests that Murlo had the potential to have served as a high-end market, offering specialty products which could have attracted buyers from further afield, perhaps on a more intermittent schedule than the regular market for foodstuffs.

There are issues, however with this interpretation of Murlo. Despite the wealth of items noted earlier, very few imports were found at Murlo, which may indicate that this was not a site that attracted long-distance exchange and that its market could not have accommodated sustained demand.⁵⁷ Additionally, few materials that could be securely sourced from Murlo have been recognised beyond the site.⁵⁸ Further, scientific analysis of the bone, horn, clay, and metal ores at Murlo seem to indicate that these materials were sourced locally. Thus, in spite of its geographic and resourceful promise, perhaps Murlo was not a market for the materials produced in its workshops and was instead a largely self-sustaining centre that 'catered primarily to

---

52 Perkins (2010) 107. Colin Renfrew (1975) 52 observed, 'Evidently the study of settlement distribution can give clues about the organization of trade, even if these will need corroboration by other evidence of organization and by the traded good themselves'.
53 de Grummond (1997) 37.
54 Edlund-Berry (2006) 123–4, fig. VII.7; Trentacoste et al. (2020); Tuck (2021)151.
55 Nielsen (1995); Tuck (2021) 149–51.
56 Cutler et al. (2020) 20–1 which estimates that there could have been as many as 113 workers if there were five tools for each spinner.
57 Trentacoste et al. (2020); Cutler et al. (2020) 25–6. Clearly, the ivory found at the site was imported.
58 Nielsen noted ivory and bone artifacts with similarities at sites north of Murlo: Quinto Fiorentino, Monte Calvario in Castellina in Chianti, and La Montagnola (Nielsen [1983] 340–3, [1984] 398–9; Tuck [2021]152). These sites are within 80 km of one another. I thank Tony Tuck for talking to me about this topic and for sharing materials. Similarly, for the bucchero produced at or near Murlo, this fabric did not travel far from the site at all, see Berkin (2003).

182 Hilary Becker

internal consumption'.⁵⁹ Certainly, some of these craft products could have occasionally travelled singularly, as objects of gift exchange among elites or singular barter exchange, but there is currently no evidence to support a regular periodic market in the commodities manufactured there.

Etruscan marketplaces: the archaeological evidence

While it is clear that periodic markets would be advantageous for the settlement pattern in Etruria, especially for the smaller settlements that were further away from their nearest urban centres, the archaeological record does not always provide clear evidence for confirming suppositions about these markets. It seems that the sanctuary itself may have served a vital function in the exchange of items at *emporion* sanctuaries, such as Graviscae, although temporary stalls are also a possibility at sanctuary sites. Temporary stalls would have been useful for low-frequency festivals, such as that held for the *Fanum Voltumnae*, and potentially even at nundinal markets. Indeed, it is probable that most markets did not require any permanent buildings and used open-fronted workshops or temporary stalls, which would have left little trace in the archaeological record.⁶⁰

There is little archaeological evidence to support the idea of permanent shops in Etruscan urban centres, but the building case for Etruscan markets, however, has been potentially expanded thanks to the discovery of a house with two shops or workshops at Gonfienti (in modern Campi Bisenzio). This Etruscan site facilitated the iron trade coming from Elba and destined for Felsina and Spina.⁶¹ A large house (1,400 square meters) was found in an excavation area labelled Lotto 14 (Figure 9.2).⁶² This house, built within the orthogonal urban grid of Gonfienti, included two rooms on the side of the structure that faced onto the street, thought to be craft workshops or commercial shops, which were constructed in the late sixth century BCE and abandoned by the second half of the fifth century BCE.⁶³ Four weights were found in and around this house at Gonfienti – weights which could have been used in support of the shop or workshop there. Thus, Gonfienti may have hosted the only archaeologically visible Etruscan workshops or shops known to date.⁶⁴ The impact of this discovery on the issue of Etruscan markets is, at present, still unclear. It is clearly possible that other shops existed in Etruscan urban centres, but it is also possible that periodic markets and interpersonal, reciprocal exchanges were sufficient to satisfy the quotidian

---

59 Cutler *et al.* (2020) 26. See also Tuck (2014), (2016) 108, Tuck (2021).
60 Frayn (1993) 5, 101; Ellis (2018) 6.
61 The ancient name of this Etruscan center is not known – see Poggesi *et al.* (2005) 272; Gori (2007).
62 Poggesi *et al.* (2005) 270–5.
63 Poggesi *et al.* (2010) 130; Maggiani (2012).
64 Note that this is stated with caution, as these rooms may have been workshops.

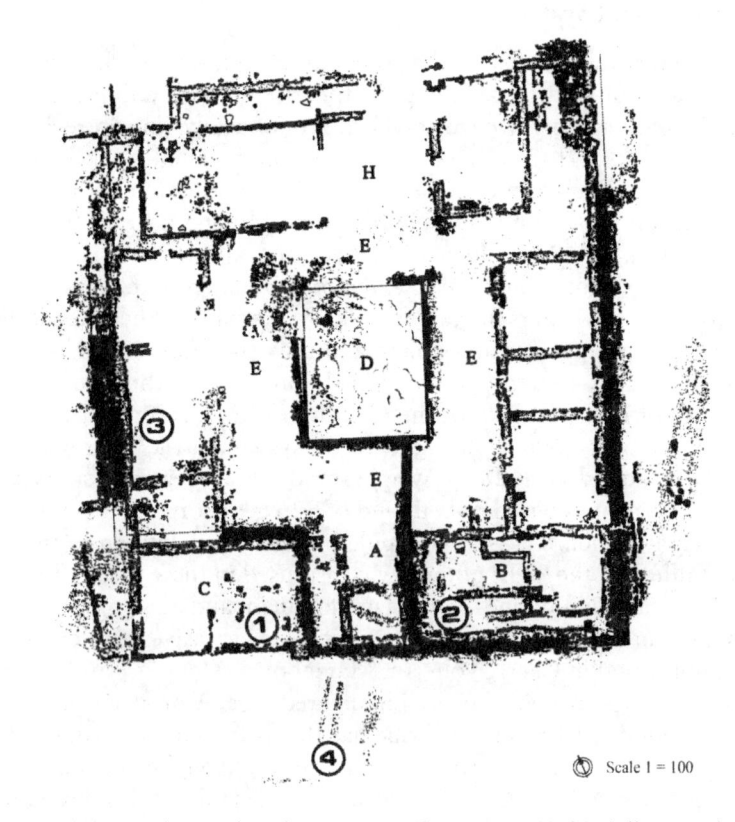

Figure 9.2 Lotto 14, late archaic house at Gonfienti (Prato), plan following the 2002 season (scale 1000:1). Locations of the weights found are marked with numbers.

Source: After Maggiani (2012) figure 3.

needs of Etruscan urban dwellers and that fixed shops and markets did not develop in Etruria, especially in smaller urban centres.

This leads to further questions about markets in urban centres. There is evidence to suggest that periodic markets existed at Etruscan urban centres (i.e., Caere, discussed below), but could there have been more frequent, even daily, markets where there was sufficient demand? Claire Holleran, considering the Roman economy, notes, 'in smaller urban centres, the market for locally produced food and other goods may have been adequately supplied by such periodic markets, but the size of the market at Rome means that from a relatively early date, the *nundinae* were supplemented by more frequent periodic and daily markets'.[65]

---

65 Holleran (2018) 466.

184 Hilary Becker

Etruscan weight systems

It has been fruitful to consider the potential schedules of markets that could have operated in Etruria, as well as to theorise about the range that different kinds of goods might have travelled economically, and to review some of the archaeological sites that may have accommodated markets. It also is useful to examine another category of evidence in order to explore Etruscan markets and how they might have operated. Moving beyond the physical spaces of markets, archaeological evidence also allows us to consider how tools such as weights could have served to facilitate and regulate exchange in Etruria.[66] Such weights make it possible to animate further the mechanics of Etruscan marketplaces and where and how they functioned. There was a standard weight system that was largely preferred within the traditional boundaries of Etruria, south of the Arno River, but also further north. This weight standard, known as the light weight system, or the 'light pound', has the Etruscan pound set at 287 g. Weight standards are regional, so the weight system of Rome was based on a pound of 326 g.[67] North of the Arno, a different weight standard was also popular, set at 358 g, known as the 'heavy pound' (although the 'light pound' was also used in these areas).[68]

The Etruscan 'light pound' was the predominant and most common weight system used in Etruria;[69] this weight system was pervasive, with examples of this weight found in Caere, Volterra, Marzabotto, Mantova, and other sites (see Table 9.1).[70] Five weights are highlighted here. A bronze weight with a lead core found at Chianciano Terme has the form of a janiform head. This weight depicts a woman's face on both sides and weighs one 'light pound' (265 grams, originally 286.5 g).[71] Another bronze janiform head weight, also from Chianciano Terme, was shaped in the form of a silen on one side and a maenad one the other. This weight was 576 grams and weighs two 'light pounds'. A lead weight on this standard, which is held in a private collection, weighs half the 'light pound'; the weight is dated to the third century

---

66 Regional standards have been worked out by scholars such as Cattani (1996) and Maggiani (2001a), (2002), (2009), (2012), (2017) by looking at the corpus of Etruscan weights.
67 Maggiani (2016) 476.
68 358.128 g. Fifth-century coinage from Populonia is also tied to this standard. Cattani (2001) 92–4; Maggiani (2002) 173.
69 Some Etruscan coinage (e.g., Volterra, some of Tarquinia, and central Etruscan towns) is based on this standard – see Maggiani (2016) 477. Many more weights, including others in this study, have been found that were set to this light system – see Maggiani (2002). These five weights were highlighted because they all have a shared religious context or association and that presents a nice cross-section. Two of them at least, are associated with a likely market location, as will be clear later.
70 Maggiani (2002), (2017) 478 fig. 28.4
71 Maggiani (2001a), (2002) 165–6, (2017). Both weights date to the late fourth century-third century BCE.

Table 9.1 Weights on the Etruscan 'light pound'

Details and find spot	Weight in grams	Equivalency to the light pound (286.5 grams)
Bronze weight with lead core in the form of janiform female heads, Chianciano Terme. Late fourth to early third centuries BCE.	265 (originally 286.5)	1
Bronze weight with lead core in the form of janiform heads (silen/maenad), Chianciano Terme. Late fourth to early third centuries BCE.	576	2
Bronze weight with lead core without suspension ring, Caere (S. Antonio). Fourth to early third centuries BCE.	716.28	2.5
Cuboidal bronze weight, Caere (S. Antonio). Second half of sixth century BCE.	11.465	0.04
Lead weight in a teardrop shape, provenance unknown. Private collection, USA. Third century BCE.	143.9	0.5
Spherical lead and bronze weight, Pian d'Alma, after modification (or shaving) of a larger weight. Found in a layer with material dating to the second half of the sixth to mid-fifth centuries BCE.	287	1
Stone weight, number one, Gonfienti. Second half of the fifth century BCE?	574	2
Stone weight, number three, Gonfienti. The original weight has been partially restored; the weight is now in two parts with small pieces missing (Maggiani 2012). Second half of the fifth century BCE?	861	3

Source: From Maggiani 2002, 2012, 2017.

BCE due to the orthography of its inscription.[72] An oval weight from Caere (fourth to early third century BCE), weighs 2.5 'light pounds' – while a smaller weight, found in the same area (but dated to before the end of the sixth century BCE), is one twenty-fifth of the 'light pound' (Figures 9.3 and 9.4).[73] The two Caeretan weights will be returned to below. Weights such

---

72 Maggiani (2002) 167, (2017); the weight lacks provenience.
73 The earliest coinage in Etruria (the Volterran series and the Thezi series [Vulci area]) are set on the same standard as this weight, see Maggiani (2002) 180; Catalli (2017) 463; Becker (2017a) 1022–3.

Figure 9.3 Inscribed weight from Caere (fourth to early third centuries BCE).
Source: After Maggiani (2001a) figure 35.

Figure 9.4 Bronze weight from Caere (second half of sixth century BCE).
Source: Museo di Villa Giulia. After Maggiani (2002) tav. XXVIIIc.

as these all follow the same standard, even though most of them ostensibly come from different contexts.

In the late sixth to early fifth century BCE, Vetulonia seems to have had its own weight standard based on 315 g.[74] This weight standard is attested by

---

[74] Maggiani (2009) 139–43, (2012). These weights were found in the Quartiere di Poggiarello Renzetti in Vetulonia. Maggiani classifies this system as 'standard V'.

Table 9.2 Weights set to the Vetulonian weight standard, dating from the late sixth to early fifth centuries BCE.

Details and find spot	Weight in grams	Equivalency to the Vetulonian pound (315 grams)
Spherical stone weight, Follonica (loc. Rondelli)	315.41	1
Stone weight with a biconvex shape, Vetulonia. Original weight reconstructed.	626	2
Stone weight resembling a parallelepiped, Vetulonia	157.84	0.5
Stone shape with a cylinder shape, Vetulonia. Original weight reconstructed.	788.046	2.5
Stone weight roughly resembling a parallelepiped, Vetulonia. Original weight reconstructed.	1569.44	5
Spherical lead and bronze weight, Pian d'Alma, before ancient modification (or shaving) of the weight.	317.9	1

Source: From Maggiani 2002; Maggiani 2012.

six examples that have only been found within Vetulonia and its hinterland (Table 9.2). A weight made from lead and bronze, found at a habitation at Fullonica (near Vetulonia), was based on this standard.[75] One of the weights from Vetulonia, carved from stone, weighed about 626 g originally, and was valued at double the Vetulonian local weight standard, thus perhaps it is not surprising that this weight had the numeral 'II' inscribed upon it.[76] Yet another stone weight from Vetulonia, resembling a parallelepiped in shape, weighs half the standard.[77] Two additional weights from Vetulonia that weigh, respectively, two and a half times, and five times this local standard.[78] The final member of this group is a lead and bronze spherical weight, dated to the late archaic period, which was found at the farm of Pian d'Alma, near Vetulonia (dating to the second half of the sixth to the middle of the

---

75 Maggiani (2002) 169 n. 8, (2009) 141. The weight has a 'V' inscribed upon it.
76 Maggiani (2009) 139, 141–3, Vetulonia n. 1, inv. 8969. This weight from Vetulonia was not found in a dateable context. The current value of this weight is 610.24 g but this weight's surface was chipped, thus the original weight of this object was reconstructed.
77 Maggiani (2009) 139, 141, 143, n. 2.
78 Maggiani (2009) 141, 143, n. 3, 4. These weights are estimated by Maggiani to have originally weighed 788.046 g and 1569.44 g respectively.

Figure 9.5 Weight from the farm of Pian d'Alma (second half of the sixth to the middle of the fifth century BCE). Museo Archeologico Nazionale di Firenze

Source: After Maggiani (2002) tav. XXVIIIf.

fifth century BCE) (Figure 9.5).[79] There are indentations on this weight, and areas where the patina is different, which indicate that this weight had metal removed from it to reach a final weight of 287 g. According to Maggiani, the original weight, before the metal was removed, was about 317.9 g and therefore in line with the local Vetulonian pound.

The six weights found in the area of Vetulonia show that a local pound was popular there, which speaks not only to commercial standards but also to political power and its reach. The weight found at Pian d'Alma offers some insight into this interplay between the different weight standards. This weight was originally based on the Vetulonian local weight standard but was seemingly updated to the Etruscan light standard at a later date. The owner of the Pian d'Alma weight recalibrated it, removing some metal so that it would weigh 287 g, thus bringing this weight in line with the 'light pound'.[80] The house at Pian d'Alma dates from the mid-sixth to mid-fifth century BCE, so the weight had to be adapted by that point.[81] Maggiani assumes that by the middle or late fifth century, residents in and

---

79 Maggiani (2002) 169–70; Becker (2017b) 1134–5. This is weight standard V.
80 Maggiani (2002) 169–70, (2009) 142–3, (2012).
81 In his most recent chapter dealing with this weight, Maggiani (2012) states that the weight needed to have been adapted before the end of the fifth century BCE.

around Vetulonia adopted the wider regional standard. Clearly, at each point in time, the owner of the Pian d'Alma weight was aware of whatever prevailing convention was utilised in their area and found utility in making an update so that they could continue to participate in commerce. Thus, this weight had two economic-political identities – at one time the weight was in line with a local standard and later it was adapted to match the changed needs of a presumably larger economic orbit. It is unclear whether merchants and farmers decided such a shift would benefit their trade or if the shift was encouraged at the political level.[82] If the latter, this would hint at the power of central authority.[83] In either case, the life story of this weight reveals the connectivity between town and country. The Pian d'Alma weight certainly finds parallel to the later *mensa ponderaria* at Pompeii whose volumetric standards were adjusted from the Oscan standard to the Roman standard when needs and the economic-political situation eventually demanded.[84]

The site of Marzabotto, in contrast, allows us to explore how multiple weights could be used in one place. An archaeologically visible market space has not been identified at Marzabotto, but more than 60 stone weights, dating to the sixth and fifth centuries BCE, have been found there. At least 10 different weight standards have been detected among the multiple weights found at Marzabotto.[85] These weights included those calibrated to the Etruscan 'heavy pound'. The relatively short lifespan of occupation at Marzabotto makes it unlikely that the different weight standards utilised at the site can be dated to different periods.[86] Instead, one, or possibly two, different scenarios seem to have been at work at this site.[87] The first is that different types of products or industries used different weight standards (such as

---

82 Certainly, regular trade and itinerant merchants, as well as periodic markets and intraregional fairs, might have provided opportunities for such standards to spread.
83 Berrendonner (2009) 352.
84 Frayn (1993) 111–2; *CIL* 10.793. It seems that in the Roman period, reference weights were being shipped out from the capital to deter fraud (Berrendonner [2009] 352). At least, by the later Imperial period, there is explicit evidence that that was the case (*Cod. Theod.* 12.6.19; *Cod. Iust.* 10.70.9). Likely such standard weights could be replicated by local officials responsible for maintaining the standards in their towns and colonies (Corti [2001] 192). For attempts to standardise weights in medieval England in spite of national standards – see Davis (2014) 190–6.
85 Maggiani (2002) 177–8. Incidentally, the one weight standard that has not been yet identified at Marzabotto is the aforementioned Vetulonian archaic pound.
86 The site of Marzabotto was active for a relatively short period of time. It was established in the second half of the sixth century BCE and assumed its characteristic orthogonal layout in the early fifth century BCE (Sassatelli and Govi [2013]). The site was conquered in the mid-fourth century BCE.
87 Maggiani (2002) 174; Becker (2017a) 1025.

Figure 9.6 Stone weight from Marzabotto, inscribed with tally marks reading '4' and '10'.

Source: After Maggiani (2002) tav. XXIXa.

grains versus metals). The second is that the different weight standards were observed in different areas, since Marzabotto was ideally located to facilitate trans-Apennine traffic. Whether a customer utilised the 'light pound' or the 'heavy pound' (the latter, popular in the north), they could have their goods measured according to a standard that was familiar.[88]

In some cases, the weights could be used to translate between different weight standards. One such example is a stone weight that weighs 1,432 g (Figure 9.6).[89] On one side the weight bears an inscription denoting the number ten and, if the stone's weight is divided by ten, that equals 143.2 g, which is half of the 'light pound'. The other side of the stone bears the numeral four. If the stone's overall weight of 1,432 g is divided by four, the weight standard represented is 358 g, one 'heavy pound'. Thus, this weight could have been used to convert between weight standards popular in both the north and south. This weight provides persuasive evidence that some of the many different weight systems found at this site responded to a need for translation. Thus, the weights at Marzabotto would have facilitated both local and intraregional exchange.

Let us return to the aforementioned four weights found at the northern Etruscan town of Gonfienti.[90] Two stone weights (weights one and two) were

---

88 Becker (2017a) 1024–6.
89 Maggiani (2002) 175 n. 32; Becker (2017a) 1025.
90 Maggiani (2012).

found in the two front rooms of a *domus*, which may have been craftsmen's workshops or commercial shops. Maggiani cautiously suggested that these weights date to the second half of the fifth century BCE. Weight three, which is co-eval to the others, was found in an adjacent room thought to be the kitchen. Weights one and three are both based on the Etruscan 'light pound', whereas weight two is based on the heavy standard. Thus, at least two different standards were in use at the same time at Gonfienti. Maggiani wondered whether these two types of weights were used for different goods, but again, as with Marzabotto, they may have also served a local and export market. A marble stone weight (weight four) was found in a pit, just in front of the house, and it is thought to be dated earlier than the others (before the end of the sixth century BCE).[91] This weight follows a different standard than the other weights at Gonfienti, known as standard VI (343.95 g) – a weight standard which is also present at Marzabotto, Vetulonia, and on the early sixth-century Giglio shipwreck.[92] It is possible that this was a weight standard observed at this earlier time. If the house at Gonfienti accommodated a shop, these weights highlight the spatial possibilities for organised trade in Etruria. If there was not a shop, these weights nevertheless demonstrate the different choices, in terms of weight standards, that artisans may have utilised contemporaneously and over time.

To summarise our understanding, there were regional weight standards, as well as other weight standards which may have been reserved for specific categories of goods. Multiple weight standards may have been used at a single site simultaneously in order to facilitate trade with people from different regions, or to help convert between different standards. At least one weight standard – the local Vetulonian standard – fell out of favour over time and was replaced with a standard more popular for a larger region. The weights, which were based upon these standards, were made of stone or metal and can be found in all kinds of contexts, whether at a workshop, in a shipwreck, or a farm suggesting a diffuse engagement with trade and connections between city and countryside.

Regulation of trading spaces

The use of weights, and weight standards, also provides insight into the regulation of trading spaces, particularly at sanctuaries where, among other purposes, weights could be used for the weighing of dedications. But weights may, in turn, have had an additional function, as official public weights used to facilitate markets held on or near the sanctuary grounds.

---

91 Weight four was found below the beaten pebble and gravel road built in phase with the house.
92 Maggiani (2009) 144, (2012). Weight 4 weighs 2931 g. There was chipping on the stone, so its original weight is thought to have been 3444.45 g. Maggiani notes that these weights were based on a system close to the *libbra italica*, which was set at 341 g. For standard VI: the Giglio weight 11 (352 g), Vetulonia weights 5 (682.87 g) and 6 (1026 g), according to Maggiani's numeration. The Giglio weight is dated to the early sixth century BCE.

192   *Hilary Becker*

The five weights chosen to exemplify the Etruscan 'light pound' standard all seem to have shared a religious character (Table 9.1). Two are from Caere and found in the sacred area of S. Antonio at Caere's Temple A.[93] This sacred area is sited strategically at the southwestern edge of Caere's plateau, overlooking a road travelling up to the city.[94] One is an oval bronze weight with a lead core, dating to the fourth to early third century BCE; the other is a cube-shaped weight, dating to the archaic period. The two weights from Chianciano Terme (late fourth-third centuries BCE) were found in a sanctuary fill at Fucoli and both have the faces of gods.[95] The fifth weight (third century BCE), lacks provenience, but its inscription explains that the weight was dedicated to the goddess *Catha* (or the mother of *Catha*).[96] This inscription connects this weight to the sacred world, so it is possible that this weight was also once used at a sanctuary.

Further information can be discerned from the lengthy inscription on the oval weight from Caere. The objects stated its own weight – with the numerals '*IIC*', or two and a half.[97] The weight weighs 716 g, which is two and a half times the Etruscan 'light pound'. This inscription is reminiscent of some of the weights at Marzabotto that also declare how a particular weight measured in relation to a certain weight system. This weight, like the others, ostensibly conveys that its calibration to an official standard has taken place.[98] But the Caere weight does not just state numerals but also includes the addition of the term *tece*. This term was also found inscribed on the foot of an Attic black figure amphora, which reads *tece X* which Agostiniani has posited as a term of measurement, the Etruscan version of the Latin term *libra*.[99] Using this amphora as a parallel, it seems that the Caeretan weight declared that it weighed 2.5 pounds.[100] The inclusion of the hypothesised

---

93 Temple A at S. Antonio has a phase in the late Archaic period and a second one that begins in the early Hellenistic (late fourth century BCE or just after). See Maggiani and Rizzo (2001), (2005) 179; de Grummond (2016) 150, table 13.1.
94 Maggiani and Rizzo (2001) 143, (2005) 177.
95 Rastelli (1993) 474; Maggiani (2001a), (2002) 165–6; Becker (2017b) 1135.
96 Bonfante (1994) 269–70; Maggiani (2001a) 67, 72, (2002) 166; Bonfante and Bonfante (2002) 145; Becker (2017b) 1135. Catha is a goddess related to Fufluns (Maggiani [2001a] 72).
97 Maggiani (2001a) 69, (2002) 168, (2012); Agostiniani (2016) 159; Becker (2017b) 1135.
98 Agostiniani (2016) 159.
99 *ET* OI 0.4; Cristofani (1996) 48.
100 Agostiniani (2016) 159–62. The amphora's inscription *tece X*, in turn, may read '10 measures', (specifically *librae* (*mensurales*)). Agostiniani wondered whether this numeral would be the measurement of the capacity held by the Attic amphora. The amphora is 40cm tall and Agostiniani estimated that its total capacity might have been just over eight liters. He suggested a possible scheme where this number represented volume, but he was not able to reconcile the numbering. Using the ideas of Alan Johnston, Agostiniani posits that this vase was shipped to Etruria empty and that the inscribed measurement may have been the quantity of oil or wine, etc. the vase was filled with.

term for a pound itself underscores the official standard that this weight represented.

The official form of this weight was further underscored by the remaining inscription. This inscription explained that the weight was dedicated to *Turms*, the Etruscan corollary of Mercury, and *Rath*, who was associated with Apollo.[101] The Greeks believed that Mercury was the inventor of weights and measures, and from this weight it seems possible that *Turms* had a similar association for the Etruscans.[102] The inscription further stated that that it was dedicated here (*thui*) in the city (*methlum*) – a phrase that may have added an official tone, as Agostiniani noted.[103] Indeed, this specificity finds parallel with the *Liber Linteus*, a ritual text that applied to the city for which it was written. Similarly, this text was tied to the place in which it was meant to be executed.[104] Other examples of this geographic specificity can be found on the Brontoscopic calendar, the observations of which, as stated earlier, were specifically valid for Rome,[105] and the *Tabula Cortonensis* (late third to early second century BCE) which stated, 'During the zilathship of Larth Cusu, son of Titinei, and Laris Salini, son of Aule, in this area here of Lake Trasimene (*tarsminass*)'.[106] Thus, the inscription on the Caeretan weight explains that the weight's relevance and power was to be exercised in that place, at Caere. The weight's inscription further states that the weight was dedicated by L(ar)c(e) Penthe and Vel Lape when Larth Nulathe was serving as a *zilath* (*zilc*).[107] The *zilath* is the chief magistrate of an Etruscan city-state and his office would have helped to date this weight. It is also possible that including the *zilath*'s name not only gave an eponymous date but also gave this weight an official character. Thus, the previously cited two local *zilaths* on the *Tabula Cortonensis* provided an eponymous date to that legal negotiation.[108] Whether it is one of the aforementioned calendars or an inscription on a weight by a local magistrate, what this written evidence

---

101 Cristofani (1996) 43, 45; Maggiani (2002) 167, (2012). While *Rath* was originally viewed as a possible epithet to *Turms*, Maggiani (2012) and Agostiniani (2016) suggest there was an asyndeton.
102 Dio. Sic. 5.75.2. Maggiani (2001a) 73, (2017) 479. Apollo is also associated with weights in Greece as his name is sometimes written on weights.
103 Cristofani (1996) 45, 47; Becker (2013) 361; Agostiniani (2016) 169.
104 The *Liber Linteus* was a ritual text that was especially relevant 'for the sacred fraternity/priesthood (*sacnica*) of the citadel (*cilth*), for the city-state (*spura*) and for the city (*methlum*) of *ena* (of whomsoever)' (van der Meer [2009] 217–8).
105 This calls to mind the possibility that Etruscan calendars also had regional variations as mentioned above – see Edlund-Berry (1992).
106 Trans. van der Meer (2014) 163, 176. For more on for Section part 3, sec. VII of the Cortona tablet, see Maggiani (2001b) 105, 107; Wallace (2008) 211, 213. van der Meer (2014) 176 noted that the term *celtinei* is 'in this area here', formed from the adjective *celthi* 'here'.
107 Maggiani (2001a) 72–3, (2002) 167–8.
108 Maggiani (2001b) 107; Wallace (2008) 206, 210, 212–3; van der Meer (2014) 176; Becker (2020) 172.

(e.g., ritual texts, a weight with a local tie) shares in common is that they are products of leading men in a particular city.

Why did Larce Penthe and Vel Lape dedicate the weight and then choose to mention these official circumstances? In Roman practice, the dedicants of official weights were the ones who guaranteed that the weight was set to a correct standard and were often the ones responsible for administering it.[109] An inscription naming the local aediles, Marcus Articuleius and Gnaeus Turranius, guaranteed a bronze weight balance from Herculaneum (47 CE).[110] Another inscription from Herculaneum honours the duumvirs, a father and son both named Marcus Memmius Rufus, who dedicated weights (among other benefactions) to the town and who would be responsible for managing the weights for the town in perpetuity.[111] Thus, it is possible that Larce Penthe and Vel Lape performed a similar function to the Rufi in that they donated a weight. These Etruscans may have been the individuals that were responsible for administering the weight when it was newly donated.[112] This inscription, therefore, indicates that some portion of the elite class, and thus by extension the city-state of Caere, seems to have been involved in the standardisation of exchange, something that would have been useful for person-to-person exchange and markets.

There is another artefact that provides evidence for the official regulation of weights by an Etruscan state. A small piece of misshapen bronze from Suana (Sovana), weighing 14 g and dating to the Archaic period, has been variously identified as a piece of *aes rude* or a weight (Figure 9.7).[113] This piece was inscribed on one side with three tick marks. Much like

---

109 Corti (2001). Carla Corti (2001) 192 notes, 'come garanzia del controllo effettuato veniva apposto sul peso il nome del magistrato incaricato dell'operazione,' 'as a guarantee of the implemented control, the name of the magistrate responsible for the transaction was affixed to the weight'.
110 CIL 10.8067.2; Bertinetti (1985) 209; Corti (2001) 192; Cooley (2013) 104. That is, this was the standard that the *aediles* had verified and shared.
111 CIL 10.1453; Frayn (1993) 110; Berrendonner (2009) 357, 360. This weight is thought to be Augustan in date (or earlier). Cooley and Cooley (2013) 182, no. F88. The Latin text also stated that they remedied faults in the weights and that this (along with many other benefactions) was in line with their generous fulfillment of their magisterial duties and their desire to take care of their city.
112 Maggiani (2001a) 72–3, (2012). Agostiniani (2016) 169 did not believe that these men were magistrates responsible for validating an official weight, although he does not state why. The parallels drawn by Maggiani between the Caeretan weight and the Roman state weights (and their dedicants) are persuasive.
113 Maggiani (1972); Colonna (1988) 19; Becker (2010) 135, 144 n. 23. This bronze is now in the storerooms of the Museo Archeologico Nazionale di Firenze and has been examined by the author.

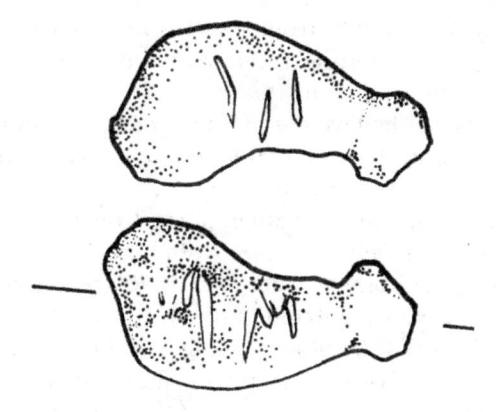

Figure 9.7 Inscribed *aes rude* from Suana.
Source: Museo Archeologico Nazionale di Firenze. After Maggiani (1972) 409.

the inscribed weights at Marzabotto or at Caere, these tick marks can be decoded to reveal the ponderal system to which this piece of bronze was tied. If the weight of the bronze is divided by three, it becomes clear that the ponderal unit upon which it is based is 4.68 g.[114] An inscription on the reverse reads '*SP*', likely an abbreviation of *spural,* which marked this piece of bronze as property of a city-state.[115] If pieces of *aes rude* were exchanged on the basis of weight, which seems probable, it could be that this piece was used as a defined ponderal measurement against which others could be measured.[116] While this would be useful to standardise exchange on an individual basis, it could also have been useful at a market. If the

---

114 This is a standard weight found elsewhere, as there are pieces of *aes rude* from Orvieto (of varying weight) which are all divisible by 4.68 (Maggiani [1972] 409). This weight is tied into the Etruscan light ponderal weight. Maggiani originally wrote that this weight was equivalent to 1/60th of the light ponderal weight (which, in 1972, he set at 268.4 g). Maggiani later set the light ponderal weight at a different number – 286.5 g. It can be noted that 268.4 g is one of the weights that can be found amongst Populonian coinage (late fourth to early third century BCE) (Maggiani [2002] 185), so this weight is most likely a small denomination, tied into the light standard.
115 Becker (2010) 134–6, (2013) 360.
116 Cattani (1988) 206: 'Che l'uso delle unità ponderali e probabilmente anche l'impiego dei frammenti di *aes rude* fosse organizzato e sottoposto al controllo di un sistema centrale, ce lo fanno supporre i passi degli storici latini relativi alla funzione monetaria del bronzo in età arcaica,' 'The passages of Latin historians, relating to the monetary function of bronze in the Archaic age, makes us suppose that the use of ponderal units and probably also the

interpretation of this piece is correct, what this small weight shares in common with the inscribed weight from Caere is that they both indicate that an Etruscan city-state was setting public standards that would facilitate the exchange needs for the community.[117]

Returning to the inscribed weight of Caere, the inscription states that the weight was dedicated in the sacred area of *Hercle* (Hercules). The storage of this weight, which has clear public import, in a sacred space in the city of Caere finds parallel in later Roman practice. Roman official weights and measures were stored in a *ponderarium*.[118] In both Rome and Greece, such weights were kept close to the marketplace. In Rome, the *aediles* (and later the *praefectus urbi*), who regulated markets and made sure that weights were standardised, stored the official public weights in sacred spaces such as the Capitoline temple or the Temple of the Dioscuri.[119] These weights were typically inscribed with some, or all, of the following information: the magisterial date, the actual weight, the location of the sacred place which the weight was stored, and the magistrates who donated the weights. If the fourth century BCE weight from Caere can be compared to these in function, then Larce Penthe and Vel Lape were the magistrates charged with ascertaining the accuracy of the weights on behalf of the city-state. Like Roman magistrates, these men made a gift of the very tool they would need to use in the very building in which they would use it.[120] Adriano Maggiani thus describes one of the functions of Temple A at S. Antonio at Caere as akin to a Roman *ponderarium*. The archaic weight from Caere was found on the grounds of the precursor to Temple A, within the area of the small archaic three-room building. Although the earlier structure remains enigmatic, Maggiani argued that it may have been a house for the priest and possibly also served as a *ponderarium*.[121] Even if this is not correct, there seems to have been a long association between weights and sacred space in this context.

---

use of *aes rude* fragments was organised and subjected to the control of a central system.' See also Catalli (2009).
117 Because of its small size (roughly 3cm by 2cm), this weight might have been used to check the weights of coins (in minting or in trade?), or it could have been a makeweight – the Etruscan word for which was *mantis(s)a* (Paul ex Fest. 103, 1L: *Mantisa, additamentum dicitur lingua Tusca, quod ponderi adicitur, sed deterius et quod sine ullo usu est*, 'Mantisa,' is how it is put in the Etruscan language – a makeweight that is an addition added to the weight, but which is a rather poor addition and without any utility.). See D'Aversa (1994) 33. On the Latin use of this word, see Kleijwegt (2002).
118 Frayn (1993); Corti (2001); '*Ponderarium*' BNP.
119 Maggiani (2001a) 73; Bertinetti (1985) 109; Corti (2001). See Cic. *Ad fam*. 8.6.4; Juv. 10.101.
120 As an anonymous reader rightly pointed out, presumably the magistrates were also sacralising the weight to give it divine authority as the possession of gods.
121 Maggiani and Rizzo (2005) 182; Maggiani (2002) 180, (2012); Biella (2019) 39.

In the Roman world, these *ponderaria* were especially tied to commercial transactions. For these reasons, it is possible that Temple A at S. Antonio at Caere, or its environs, might have hosted a market over a long period of time. Furthermore, if there was a nundinal calendar curated by a priest, this might have been publicly displayed or consultable in some form at such a sacred space.[122] Indeed, such a sacred space, especially one thought to be explicitly connected to Hercle, would have been well suited to serve as a trading space, just like the area sacred to Hercules in the Forum Boarium at Rome or the late Republican Temple to Hercules Victor outside of Tivoli, with its market shops that were built over an ancient sheep market.[123] Similarly, the sacred space of S. Antonio – or the area just adjacent to it – may have been used as a market over a long period of time. As noted earlier, the site of S. Antonio was located at the edge of the southern plateau of Caere near one of its gates and would have been ideally suited to traffic either within or beyond the city.[124] It is worth hypothesising whether both weights found at the site, and not just the one discussed in depth earlier, served a commercial function and, indeed, whether other weights found at or associated with Etruscan sacred sites were also tied to a market held in such locales.[125] Importantly, in a survey of sites that could have hosted commercial exchange, sacred sites are prominent. At *emporia*, temples served to mediate a neutral space and make traders from any nationality feel more welcome. At the aforementioned *Fanum Voltumnae*, this annual religious fair was known to have merchants, and likely served as a much-anticipated regional fair in addition to its sacral, and at times political, functions. Albert Nijboer commented that 'the early markets for internal exchange in the primary centres of Etruria are yet to be defined'.[126] Sites, such as the sanctuary at Satricum or the sanctuaries at S. Omobono in Rome, Nijober argued, seem to have acted like incipient *fora* which had 'religious, public and market functions'.[127] Did the Temple A of S. Antonio at Caere, as well as certain other sacred sites elsewhere in Etruria, host periodic markets, which would have not only served as an important central place for the exchange of goods, but also an intrinsically important sociopolitical opportunity as the community came together?

---

122 Indeed, the calendar recorded on the Capua tile demonstrates that calendars could have been posted publicly – see Turfa (2012) 23. To consider the different formats an Etruscan calendar might have taken (e.g., wax tablets, linen books, bronze or terracotta plaques) – see Turfa (2012) 132–5.
123 Coarelli (1987) 85; Zifferero (1995) 334; Winter (2006) 203.
124 Cristofani (1986).
125 Maggiani (2012) also cites two weights from Tarquinia that may have been from the Ara della Regina; Biella (2019) 39. See Romanelli (1948) 266 n. 82, 270.
126 Nijboer (2004) 147.
127 Nijboer (2004) 150.

The institutional structure of Etruscan markets

Christopher Garraty observed that 'market exchange is worthy of study – and archaeologically visible – once it becomes socially *institutionalised* as a common and prevalent practice'.[128] Evidence for Etruscan trading spaces has not been synthetically studied before, but there is clearly a variety of evidence, whether historical, epigraphical, or archaeological to support a discussion of the varied trading spaces that likely existed in Etruria. Whether periodic markets were being held within cities, *castella*, or a natural meeting place, some institutional framework, including hypothesised community calendars with a nundinal schedule, as well as weights, and a leader to oversee it all, would have facilitated the regular traditions of the market. What, then, were some of the other institutionalised aspects that support evidence for markets in Etruria?

Was specific architecture needed for periodic markets?

The archaeological record at present suggests that no permanent building was necessarily needed to accommodate the markets posited at sacred sites. As Charlotte Potts recognised, 'architecture was not a prerequisite for ancient marketplaces and trading posts. Commercial sites could be enhanced by the provision of shelter places to store or display goods, and ways to secure animals and materials from damage or loss, but all served to attract traders and customers rather than meeting essential needs'.[129]

In Bernadette Cap's study on Mayan markets she considers what some of the archaeological correlates were for a physical marketplace for Mayan contexts. For her very different archaeological context, some of the strongest correlates included macroartefacts, such as currency, weights, as well as dense concentrations of the same artefact type.[130] For Cap, weights represent one of the strongest correlates for a market. As stated, weights can be used for many different purposes in Etruria – but the two weights from S. Antonio at Caere were found within a sacred location. Importantly, the archaic weight was found in a small archaic building that may have been some kind of house for the priest and may have served as a *ponderarium*, as well.[131] In this light, it can be hypothesised whether weights were stored in specific special spots at certain Etruscan sanctuaries – storing the weights for perhaps many potential uses, one of which was a periodic market.[132]

---

128 Garraty (2010) 6.
129 Potts (2015) 115.
130 Cap (2015).
131 Maggiani and Rizzo (2005) 182; Maggiani (2002) 180, (2012); Biella (2019) 39.
132 That Etruscan sacred spaces could have been used in many ways, including the hypothesised periodic markets, calls to mind the working of iron at the sanctuary at Graviscae, discussed above.

Here, Marshall Becker's work on Mayan marketplaces provides help because Mayan markets are temporary, periodic affairs – whereas a 'built market suggests daily use'.[133] Such comparanda is constructive, because in Etruria, beyond this one suggested *ponderarium*, there is no physical evidence for the commercial spaces that hosted periodic markets. Etruscan periodic markets were temporary periodic occurrences that we can anticipate may have taken place perhaps in a large open space near a sanctuary (cf. the *ponderarium* and the calendar).

Market fees?

In this hypothetical model of periodic markets in Etruria, a natural question is whether merchants were required to pay a market fee or dues in order to use the space. Such a fee or indirect tax is a common feature of periodic markets, across time and cultures.[134] A market fee might serve to help in terms of the management of the market and space. To this end, a related question has been asked whether a *portorium*, or commodity tax, was charged at Etruscan *emporia* as occurred at Greek *emporia*.[135] Gabriele Cifani has also noted that ancient sources record a *portorium* paid by Romans at the end of the regal period, but it is not clear if this was historically accurate.[136] Thus, this is an open question that Etruscan evidence cannot currently negate or support. If there were such charges at Etruscan *emporia*, or long-term or short-term periodic markets, this would add another layer of institutional structure to Etruscan markets.

Coinage at Etruscan markets?

In the course of considering the tools and institutions that may have facilitated markets in Etruria, it is worthwhile to consider to what extent coinage might have been operative at such markets. The first evidence for the production of coinage in Etruria dates to the end of the sixth to early fifth

---

133 Becker (2015) 92. For the Mayans, 'market areas using temporary tents or awnings are far more common than built markets'.
134 MacMullen (1970) 334; Gabba (1975) 153; Blanton and Fargher (2010) 213; Garraty (2010) 2; Hirth (2010) 235. A sampling of different markets at which taxes were charged includes: a tax at 16th century markets in the Yucatan (Shaw [2012] 129); the Mayans charged a fee (Shaw [2012] 129), as did the Aztecs (Hirth [2016] 76–9), medieval England (Davis [2014] 146); modern rural periodic markets in China (Rozelle et al. [2003] 23), in Uganda (Good [1975] 57); Quinto, Ecuador (Bromley [1964] 62), etc. Stall fees are. of course, a standard part of American farmer's markets (e.g., Farmers' Market Federation of New York. 2009. 'Farmers Market Manager Training Manual'). https://static1.squarespace.com/static/5e70ea6d10d5dc73a27d1184/t/5e7cce0170ce646e64cd7877/1585237545837/NYFM_Training_Manual.pdf, Accessed June 23, 2020).
135 Purcell (2005) especially 207 fn. 18; Riva (2010) 222; Cifani (2016) 163, (2021) 151–6.
136 Cifani (2016) 163; Liv. 2.9.6; Dion. *Ant. Rom.* 5.22.2.

century BCE from Populonia. It consisted of silver coinage and silver bars, and it was found in a hoard in Volterra along with coins from the Greek city of Massalia, demonstrating that the idea for coinage was spread along with international connections.[137] Not a lot of coinage was produced in the first period of Etruscan coinage, such that the first productions are thought to have been intended to satisfy the needs of gentilicial groups rather than 'state'/community needs.[138] These coins were evidently used for storing value and not for regular exchange and these sets of coins have 'low numbers, high face value and a restricted area of circulation'.[139] Populonia eventually minted its own state coinage by the third quarter of the fifth century BCE, and included low denominations.[140] There is no evidence for Etruscan commodity prices. Was Populonia's coinage ever suitable for small change? Could an Etruscan coin have ever used to buy a leg of mutton or fresh vegetables at a market? Etruscan coinage was likely not used, or intended, for the majority of market transactions at Etruscan *emporia*.[141] Further, coinage was never pervasive in Etruria. Caere never minted its own coinage and Tarquinia only minted coinage very briefly in the late fourth century BCE.[142] Therefore, when imagining Etruscan marketplaces, many transactions would not have been greased by the transfer of monetary instruments (e.g., coinage, *aes signatum, or aes rude*) but by the exchange of goods in kind and barter.[143]

Market administration

Whether it is a night market in Taiwan, a periodic market in Tanzania, or a local farmer's market in America, market administration is a basic expectation in the modern era.[144] Market administrators secure space and assure

---

137 Catalli (1990) 33–5; Parise (1985); Catalli (2001) 89; Riva (2010) 222; Catalli (2017) 464; Becker (2017a) 1023. To this end, note that Catalli (2017) 465 assumes that these coins had 'high values'.
138 Parise (1985) 260–6; Catalli (1988) 469, (2001); Riva (2010) 222; Catalli (2017) 465; Becker (2017a).
139 Catalli (2001) 89.
140 Catalli (1988) 470, (1990) 41–59, (2001) 90, (2017) 465; Becker (2017b) 1136.
141 Haack (2014 207) discusses the exchange for metals produced at Gravisca, where Greeks would have exchanged imported goods for worked metal – see also Riva (2010) 222. Fiorenzo Catalli (2001) 90 discussed how one function of Populonia's coinage (and it should be pointed out that does not exclude others) may have been to facilitate 'wages and other costs' stemming from the 'internal market' devoted to the Elban iron industry, see also Catalli (2017) 465.
142 Becker (2017b) 1136–7.
143 Catalli (1990) 35; Nijboer (2004) 150, 153, (2017) 910; Becker (2017a) 1022. Maria Cecilia d'Ercole (2017) 158 noted, 'this suggests that most Etruscan trading did not involve monetary exchange but was based on other forms of payment'. The term barter is used to signify, 'a form of exchange that does not employ media of exchange' (Garraty [2010] 8). See Hirth (2016, 72) for an account of Aztec bartering, where goods are exchanged for one another or cacao beans (which served a monetary function); see also Shaw (2012) 122–3.
144 Garraty (2010) 10.

adherence to laws (whether weights and standards, tax, sanitation, etc.). However, when considering market administration when looking back to a past culture, extreme caution is required, in terms of not equating modern phenomena with ancient practice. At the very least, the inscribed Caeretan weight speaks to the probability of some oversight.

What were the sociopolitical structures in which Etruscan periodic markets were embedded and which allowed them to operate?[145] Another tool that would have supported the market are hypothesised community calendars into which market schedules were tied. For Macrobius, the Etruscans met every ninth day for a variety of reasons (Macrob. *Sat.* 1.15.13). These reasons, as explained earlier, included a periodic market – one day of a long week when everyone might take off for provisioning and social interaction. In Macrobius' account, the king was a part of this, because this periodic coming together is a great way for town and country to reinforce connections and for the *zilath* to check in with the larger populace. In Rome, the origin story of the market was credited to a *rex*.[146] In the late fifth century BCE a king of Veii had hoped to be the sponsor of the celebration at the *Fanum Voltumnae* for that year as a priest (Liv. 5.1.2–7). Livy recorded that because he did not receive this position, he withdrew performers that he would have sponsored. In Etruria, would such a leader, as well as elites from the other participating city-states, have also helped to administer the market at the celebrations of the *Fanum Voltumnae*?

There were a variety of different types of magistrates whose titles are recorded epigraphically. While the function of the chief magistrate of a city-state, the *zilath*, is reasonably understood to have covered military and political obligations, the orbits of many Etruscan titles are not always clear.[147] To this end, it would be fruitful to know if there were Etruscan magistrates, akin to the *agoranomoi* of Athens or the *aediles* (or later the *praefectus urbi*) of Rome, who were responsible for regulating Etruscan periodic markets?[148] Were the individuals who dedicated the weight at Caere such magistrates? Having an official regulate the market, who can enforce the use of weights and measures and discourage cheating, in essence would have reduced transaction costs at the marketplace and would have made such a commercial experience more efficient and fair for all.[149] If the Etruscan weights from Caere, in particular, have been interpreted correctly, by at least the archaic period there was utility in having weights to support and reinforce fair trading at such markets. Importantly, these official weight standards would have likely been sponsored and curated over time by Etruscan leaders, who were

---

145 Becker (2013).
146 Macrob. *Sat.* 1.16.32–33: Romulus or Servius Tullius.
147 Becker (2013).
148 Arist. *Ath. Pol.* 51.1–4; Arist. *Pol.* 6.1321b; *Lex Irnitana* 19; *Dig.* 19.2.13.8 (Ulpian).
149 Manning (2018) 209.

perhaps even magistrates. Throughout in this study, there has been attention to the institutional mechanisms that regulated exchange in dedicated commercial spaces, whether they were held at *emporia*, or long-term or short-term periodic (nundinal) markets. These mechanisms could have included weights, calendars, and perhaps market fees. Paying attention to these institutional mechanisms and how Etruscan city-states and their magistrates (and priests) might have facilitated trade across a number of different types of spaces is in line with the concerns of New Institutional Economics (NIE). NIE is attuned to looking at, *inter alia*, how social, legal, and institutional frameworks can facilitate or even hinder an economy.[150] The markets themselves may have been managed by elites and there may even have been a fee to use the markets.[151] Such elements, along with weights, and even the calendar, were some of the 'background constraints' that this study posits were at work in these varied Etruscan marketplaces.[152]

Conclusion

Etruscan marketplaces varied in terms of their local, regional, or interregional coverage, as well as their periodicity. Synthesising such information over time and space makes it more possible to imagine where and when Etruscan commerce was transacted.[153] Considering how such commerce was regulated and protected, learning what we can about the mechanics of that commerce is also a vital part of the picture. Above all, some of the most persuasive evidence coalesces around the institutions and infrastructural tools that facilitated markets. These include a possible nundinal cycle and weights, as well as officials to make sure that those weights and the market itself were fair. In Rome, the *aediles* regulated commerce at markets (especially in order to counteract fraud) and one wonders whether there would have been some sort of official presence at an Etruscan marketplace. The idea of this official and public presence is also carried further by the suggestion that the periodic markets occurred according to a schedule likely set by priests and maintained upon a calendar. All of these ingredients help us to understand better the ways in which the orbits of Etruscan priests and political officials might have impacted trade and daily life.

Such a constellation has further implications seen in the breadth of this study, which is why it is fruitful to look at different types of Etruscan trading places together, however varied. It is possible that at least some periodic

---

150 Frier and Kehoe (2007).
151 The occupants of temporary merchant stalls near the amphitheatre of Pompeii were using the space *permissu aedilium*, 'by the permission of the aediles' (*CIL* 6.1096, 1096a, 1097b, 1115; Della Corte [1965] 222, 397–8 nos. 852v, 852c; Frayn [1993] 5).
152 North (1991). See also Frier and Kehoe (2007) 113.
153 To quote from Garraty (2010) 10, 'equally important to the question of "what is a market system" is "when is a market system"'.

markets in Etruria were held at religious sites, and the calendar and the five weights of a religious nature tie into this. Additionally, the *emporia* and the long-cycle periodic markets that have been hypothesised to have accompanied the religious festivals held at the Etruscan *Fanum Voltumnae* (likely near Orvieto) and the festival at the Capenate sanctuary of *Lucus Feroniae*, all demonstrate the suitability of conducting exchange in neutral, religious spaces.

The Etruscan market, whether permanent, periodic, or accompanying a festival, is a lens through which Etruscan society is mediated. A market, as Macrobius wrote, was an opportunity for people to meet their king and this sociopolitical opportunity could be extended to include aristocrats meeting their dependents, as well as craftspeople meeting farmers, the urban populace meeting the rural one, and so on. Along with the commercial convenience, a marketplace creates a social and political nexus wherein information was exchanged, a calendar could have been consulted, and new people could have been encountered. The focus of this study has not been as much interested in a top-down perspective focused on high-ranking members, but rather a middle-up look asking how the average person in any Etruscan locale might have acquired products and participated in networks of exchange, both material and sociocultural. Too little is understood about the public mechanics of daily life in Etruria. Compounded with that, very little is understood about Etruscan public spaces. Speculating about the markets and where and when they occurred, as well as how they worked, allows for the daily lives of ordinary Etruscans, as well as politicians, to be fleshed out further.

10 A mobile model of cultural transfer in pre-Roman southern Italy

Christian Heitz

Scholarly reflections about mobility, during the period from the eighth to fifth century BCE in the central and western Mediterranean, have traditionally focused on the movements associated with 'Greek colonisation', that is the presence, movement, or settlement of people of eastern Mediterranean origin (Greek and Phoenician) further west than the Adriatic. This myopic focus on travellers and migrants from the east has resulted in an imbalance in our understanding. While the settlements founded during this period of colonisation are among the best archaeologically investigated sites of southern Italy, and the reasons for their erection, the provenience of their inhabitants, and their urban development have been explored in detail, the amount of research on the indigenous populations of this area, and the character of their interaction with the *apoikiai*, is comparatively limited.[1] This is despite the fact that the survival and prosperity of the new settlements, at least in the first few decades, would have likely relied on the connections to, and (good) relations with, the peoples and communities already present within the area.[2]

The following chapter deals with a specific feature within this wider set of issues that has important implications for our understanding of this cultural exchange. I will argue for the importance of mobility, not only as a singular act by the settlers from the east, but also as a permanent way of life for major parts of the regional population of central and southern Italy.[3] In particular, the chapter will emphasise the importance of animal husbandry, especially in its mobile form. This economic model, and way of life, helped form the vast circulatory system of ancient Italy, allowing and encouraging the flow of people, objects, and ideas within the peninsula. When the travellers arrived

---

1 It is impossible to list the countless studies on this topic; to name just a few prominent ones: Pugliese Carratelli (1996); Mertens (2006); Tsetskhladze (2006), (2008) and many others.
2 This bias is enhanced by the fact that, due to the development and division of academic traditions, the various regions, cultural complexes, and kinds of evidence are subject to different modern disciplines: on the part of the Italian population – Archaeology and Anthropology (Anglophone countries), Paletnologia (Italy) or Ur- und Frühgeschichte (Germany); on the part of the Greeks – Classics, Archeologia (classica) or Klassische Archäologie, respectively.
3 See Isayev (2017) on mobility in Italy more broadly, and also Cohen in this volume.

DOI: 10.4324/9781003120728-10

from the east, they did not step out onto a stable landscape, but a fluid one – mobility met mobility.

Transhumance as a historical economy

Mobile pastoralism is, historically, well-documented in many regions of Europe and has long represented both an important branch of the economy and also a very specific way of life. This statement certainly includes Italy, as well as the rest of the Mediterranean basin, and this type of activity was indeed considered a major element of the *longue durée* in the work of Fernand Braudel.[4] Archaeological investigations into this lifestyle have been perennial, but their systematic inclusion into a wider scholarly debate has traditionally been rather limited in Mediterranean archaeology, although several sources suggest that it was common from an early period on.[5] In Greece, the most prominent testimony is the story of the young Oedipus who, on the order of his father king Laios, was taken by a Theban shepherd to his summer pastures on mount Kithairon. Unable to expose the baby prince to certain death by sun or beasts, the shepherd passed the child on to another herder from Corinth, seasonally using the same pastures (Soph. *OT* 1132–1139). The end of the story is well known – but it is noteworthy that this passage seems to testify to the practice of transhumance in Sophocles' own time, projected back into the heroic past.[6]

Mobile pastoralism, in the form of transhumance, is characterised by the seasonal movement of flocks between two regions of different climate. Different to nomadism, the phase of actual movement is typically only measured in days or weeks, while the stay at the seasonal grazing areas themselves lasts weeks or even months.[7] The term 'transhumance' was coined by French geographers in the late eighteenth century when describing the Spanish *mesta*,

---

4 Braudel (1972) 120–34.
5 Studies of the topic that in the last decade received renewed and augmented interest include Whittaker (1988); Collis *et al.* (2016); Costello and Svensson (2018), to name but a few; the hesitant reception of this research was/is mainly due to the scarcity of direct archaeological evidence (in comparison to sources for agriculture, both in ancient literature and material remains). Another reason for the marginality of research into ancient (mobile) pastoralism probably lies in its present marginal status in the modern nation-state Mediterranean economy.
6 For a recent account of transhumance in ancient Greece, see Cardete (2019). She however reiterates the assumption that transhumance on a larger scale, and as a system separate from agriculture and animal husbandry, was not possible until the Middle Ages; this is problematic both in the chronological sense as well as in the assumption that, for such a specialisation, a complete separation of these fields was necessary – and even possible, considering the enormous variability in herding strategies, cf. Dyson-Hudson and Dyson-Hudson (1980), and also the assumption that the ancient household economy was completely self-sufficient and only focused on subsistence is debatable, especially when new circumstances offered easy possibilities of surplus production; Cardete (2019) 107–8.
7 See, e.g., Carrier (1932) 8; Hütteroth (1959) 38; Waldherr (1999) 565.

one of the oldest and largest examples of historical, horizontal (i.e., long-distance, as opposed to short, vertical, mountain) transhumance.[8] The *mesta* was set up in 1273 CE and developed from regional forerunners into a national institution involving the annual migration of flocks of sheep from Andalusia to Castile. Including approximately 3000 cattle breeders, it was beneficial for all sides by facilitating the corporate negotiation of long-term leases with the pasture owners as well as the control and taxation of animals. In the fifteenth century, almost three million sheep took part in these movements. A very similar system, the *dogana della Mena delle Pecore di Puglia* was inaugurated by Alfonso I of Aragon in 1447 CE in the Kingdom of Naples.[9] In principle, the *dogana* had the same tasks as the *mesta*, most notably the taxation of the animals to fill the royal purse. The drove roads utilised by the *dogana* (called *tratturi*) reached far up into central Italy, where the summer pastures in the Abruzzi – and also the traditional homes of the herds and livestock owners – lay. The winter pastures were situated in the Tavoliere di Puglia. In 1604 CE, more than five million sheep were moved, often over several hundred kilometres. At the end of the eighteenth century, more than 40,000 individuals were directly dependent on the *dogana*-system, with many more indirectly linked to this economy (as farmers supplying agricultural products to shepherds, craftsmen specialising in shepherd's products, traders, etc.).[10]

Although the *dogana*-system was officially abandoned in 1806 CE, transhumance pastoralism retained its importance as a way of life in Italy into the twentieth century, when some mountain villages were still entirely inhabited by shepherd families, seasonally moving with their herds.[11] Yet the long-distance *dogana* movements were not the only system employed by southern Italian shepherds. Much shorter routes were also used, only partly coinciding with the royal *tratturi*. One such practice, operational until the twentieth century, is the so-called *statonica* in modern-day Basilicata and Apulia (Figure 10.1). In this historically attested case, the shepherd families involved were originally based in the uplands and thus practised an 'inverse' type of transhumance typical for the Italian peninsula, that is with the home-bases and permanent residences in the upland summer pastures and seasonal travel to the lowland winter pastures.[12] However, over time, most of the populations involved in the *statonica* relocated their main base to the lowland, Apulian winter pastures. The system mediates between the area dominated by the

---

8 Zöbl (1982) 1–2; cf. Hütteroth (1959) 40–1; Rudenko (1969) 16–17.
9 Organised by the *mesta*-experienced Catalan Francesco Montluber; Heitz (2020) 252.
10 Lombardi (1999) 26–7.
11 These movements were still witnessed in the second half of the nineteenth century by the historian Ferdinand Gregorovius who vividly described the large flocks of sheep and cattle, guarded by intimidating men and dogs, he encountered during his travels, especially through the regions of Molise and northern Apulia; cf. Gregorovius (1978) 401, 608, 623–4.
12 Carrier (1932) 8; Hütteroth (1959) 38; Waldherr (1999) 565; Carrer (2015) 10.

Murge, a karstic limestone massif, and the mountainous Apennine interior.[13] In modern times, more than two-thirds of the stock kept in the area took part in these short (c. 30 km) movements of the *statonica*.[14]

In Roman times, literary and epigraphic sources attest to the practice of transhumance between central and southern Italy.[15] Maybe the earliest hint is a passage in Frontinus (Frontin. *Str.* 1.7.4, written in the second half of the first century CE) who noted that in 290 BCE the Roman consul Dentatus led his troops along *obscura itinera* from Samnium to Sabina,[16] suggesting that these 'hidden tracks' were capable of quickly leading a whole army through the Apennine region. These might be tentatively identified with pastoral routes (named *calles* in Latin, sg. *callis*). Explicit reference to pasture can be found in the *Lex Agraria* of 111 BCE, granting wealthy livestock-owners the use of common land (*ager publicus*) for free pasture and moving herds.[17] In the first century BCE, Varro reports that his flock of sheep was driven from Reate in Latium to winter pastures in Apulia (Varro *Rust.* 2.2.9), and that Publius Pontianus had his flocks driven from Umbria to the pastures of Metapontum and then to the markets at Heraclea (Varro *Rust.* 2.9.6). The fate of a transhumant shepherd family of the Imperial period might be illustrated by the tombstones of what appear to be two brothers, set up by their parents at the distant sites of Sulmone in the Abruzzi and Canosa in Apulia, areas of transhumant summer and winter residence respectively.[18] The most famous evidence for Roman transhumance, however, is an inscription of the second century CE at one of the gates of the city of Saepinum/Altilia (modern Sepino in the Molise region). It reports the problems that the shepherds occasionally had with the inhabitants of the cities they passed – interestingly it was not the townspeople complaining about the shepherds, but the shepherds complaining about the townspeople who often (wrongfully) accused them of being thieves and harassed them.[19] The name of the town, Saepinum, probably derives from the Latin term *saepta* (corral/pen) and a historical *tratturo*, likely a successor of an older *callis*, runs right through the city centre, possibly witnessing the development of the site from a seasonal transhumance stopover-point to a permanent small rural settlement.[20]

---

13 Sprengel (1971) 135–40 with fig. 29–30. See also Peruzzi, in this volume, for discussion of the relationship between the Murge region and both the coastal and Apennine zones.
14 Their southern- and western-most summer pastures are in the region around Pescopagano, between Cairano/Calitri and Muro Lucano.
15 Zöbl (1982) 20–3.
16 Cf. Santillo Frizell (1996) 67; Camerieri and Mattioli (2014) 333.
17 *CIL* I², nr. 585, see esp. sections ii.14–15 and 25–26. See Carrier (1932) 32–8 and also Cohen in this volume.
18 *CIL* 9.3113; Chelotti et al. (1985) no. 78.
19 *CIL* 9.2438.
20 Magnani (2003) 53; cf. Van Wonterghem (1999) 427 fig. 16.

A frequently proposed argument, against the assumption of early transhumance in southern Italy, is that mobility and long migratory movements would not have been possible without the political unity that only existed from Roman times onwards.[21] However, in pre-state societies, it is not the political unity of the territory that matters but the rights of use and passage that are agreed between shepherds/flock-owners and farmers/landowners along their routes. The success of these negotiations is the decisive factor for unhindered migration. As late as the early twentieth century, herdsmen travelling with their flocks concluded contracts in the form of oral agreements with the landowners whose territory they crossed.[22] Seasonal migratory movements necessitated, and perhaps even generated, supra-regional networks, the maintenance of which was of vital importance for the undisturbed annual rhythm of the peoples and communities involved. They had to be secured by the accompanying renewal of mutual obligations and dependencies that thus were an integral part of these networks. Thus, encounter acted as a prerequisite and warranty for mobility and vice versa.

Beyond the historical sources

Did the Romans simply regulate and channel activities carried out in earlier times by the pre-Roman communities of Italy, just like Alfonso I did in the fifteenth century CE?[23] The importance of this question, and the topic of ancient transhumance in general, are highlighted by the fact that it keeps popping up in scholarship – and most notably several contributions in a recent volume on pre-Roman Italy – without any clear evidence.[24] Already in 1959, Puglisi suggested that the 'Apennine culture' of the late Bronze Age practised mobile pastoralism as a major branch of its subsistence.[25] Apart from the natural support of climate and geography for this economy, he argued that the absence of stable settlements, as well as cultural similarities between coastal and inland sites (especially pottery vessels suitable for cheese-making, as well as wooden objects used for stirring), can be taken as indicators of this practice. He also suggested that some of the upland

---

21 Cf. Santillo Frizell (2009) 27. The structure of ownership and use of land in pre-Roman times is largely unknown and was probably completely different from modern conceptions; even until the early imperial period, large areas of Italy were still *ager publicus* (i.e., not privately owned), but probably nevertheless subject of a more or less clear idea of the right to use them, executed by local or regional bodies/elites. For the effects of changing use rights on rural communities and economy, see, e.g., Stagno (2019). See also Cohen in this volume.
22 Not only in cases of long-distance travel did pasture arrangements have to be made, see Santillo Frizell (2009) 34. 43–4; cf. Wagner-Hasel (2000) 226–34, (2002). In Portugal, the chief shepherd (*maioral*) responsible for the planning and arrangement of contracts regarding transit rights travelled the route long before the herds; Jorge Dias (1969) 801.
23 E.g., Camerieri and Mattioli (2014) 334.
24 See, e.g., recently Farney and Bradley (2018) 181, 285, 308, 428, 514, 524, 588 etc.
25 Puglisi (1959).

sites, which would have probably been deeply covered in snow in winter, must have been seasonal summer camps. Similar reasoning was employed by Pearce on the area of Trentino – he argued that a pastoral economy, and the production of hard cheese in the Bronze Age, would have been appropriate for an area characterised by intensive mining activities, since the numerous workers at these sites had to be supplied with meat and cheese, and would have simultaneously created grazing areas by clearing forests for fuel.[26] However, both lines of reasoning were (necessarily) based on assumptions, speculation, and 'common sense' rather than on sound archaeological or ethnographic evidence.

The main difficulty in exploring this sort of economic system using archaeological evidence is its very light archaeological footprint. For obvious reasons, mobile shepherds preferred to use light and mostly perishable materials, both for living and dwelling. In terms of objects, this means that breakable materials like pottery were not practical for travel and containers or tools of wood or leather would have been preferred.[27] Therefore, large-scale pottery production is not to be expected, ruling out one of the most important archaeological sources of evidence. Ethnography has shown that pottery can usually only be found at sites of more frequent and stable transhumant presence, and with a clear focus on dairy products.[28] But even then, hardly any vessel shapes exclusively used in the context of milk processing can be identified. Ethnographic observations indicate that iron tripods and copper cauldrons are often used for heating the whey and producing cheese.[29] Yet, despite being archaeologically well attested in many areas, such vessels are, in modern scholarship, generally associated with banqueting activities instead (mainly based on depictions and literary accounts/records associated with the Greek area). The material legacies of pastoralists who specialised in wool and/or meat production are even more ephemeral. Textile production

---

26 Pearce (2016).
27 cf. Cribb (1991) 75–9; for a representation of typical and almost entirely wooden objects and tools used for cheese production in the twentieth century Carpathians, see Földes (1961) fig. 5.
28 Migliavacca *et al.* (2013) 223; Carrer (2015) 16, (2016).
29 It is important to note that, when practiced on a smaller scale, the necessary tools can be entirely made of perishable materials like wood, leather, or cloth; cf. Simonjenko (1961) fig. 1–2. This is true also for the vessels used for heating and/or rocking the milk in cheese and yoghurt production. Ethnographic observations indicate that iron tripods were, in modern times, common tools in the production of cheese; Mientjes (2004) 179. Copper cauldrons are attested in Moravia, the Carpathians, and Transylvania where they were used for heating the whey and producing cheese; Földes (1961) 302; Kopczyńska-Jaworska (1961) 421; Štika (1969) 282; see also Kindstedt (2012) 105. An interesting iconographical suggestion for cheese production in seventh century BCE Italian vase painting has recently been forwarded by Guggisberg (2017) who interprets the object behind Polyphemus on the Aristonothos crater as a cheese harp, symbolizing not the everyday craft but the economic wealth of the cyclops.

was, in ethnographically observed cases, only practiced on a small scale by mobile pastoralists. The bulk of the wool would typically be sold to other groups and cloth or clothing bought readymade on the markets, testifying to the mutual dependence of mobile pastoralists and more sedentary communities.[30] Large quantities of loom-weights on a site are therefore more indicative of sedentary weaving, while spindle-whorls, distaffs, or weaving tablets are compatible with a mobile lifestyle.[31] In archaeological contexts, however, it is not always easy to correctly identify distaffs, which are frequently categorised as 'sceptres,' as Gleba has shown.[32]

A second major issue in analysing transhumant populations is the difficulty in identifying specific concepts or forms of mobile pastoralism and the blurring and overlap which often occurs between them. There is a very wide range of styles and models of transhumance pastoralism, from the whole community being on the move with the herds, to the herds accompanied only by a few specialised shepherds. This has major implications for the level of sedentism and, even within a single approach to pastoralism, the boundary between sedentism and mobility is likely indistinct and fluid.[33] In many transhumant societies, women, elderly people, and children live in stable dwellings and practice agriculture. Dwellings like tents or huts of organic materials are often preferred, as they can be erected and dismantled quickly, or more ephemeral buildings with stone walls which resemble, for an archaeologist, ruined houses.[34] As for special constructions connected to pastoralism, there is hardly any evidence; structures, such as corral fences, were often constructed of only light poles or even shrubs. Not even the production of dairy products, like cheese, necessarily required stable buildings with clearly identifiable installations – although it should be noted that, in historical south-eastern Italy, the characteristic, often very simple, dry-stone-walled and vaulted constructions (like the later *trulli* of Apulia and the *pinnette* of Sardegna) are attested as having served this purpose.[35] At places with high pastoral activity, including those used for longer stays or stopovers, some kind of enclosure or fence is to be expected for safeguarding the animals from beasts, theft, and to prevent escape – although these were likely of even more ephemeral construction than the dwellings. Apart from many ethnographic observations, this is also attested by Roman authors (Varro, *Rust.* 1.14.1–4; 2.2.9). Such installations might go together with corrals with

---

30 e.g., Barth (1961) 8–9.
31 e.g., Marinow (1961).
32 Gleba (2011).
33 e.g., Hütteroth (1959) 72; Salzman (2004) 34; Chang (2008); Mientjes (2004), (2010).
34 For the case of Turkish pastoralists see Hütteroth (1959) 64–7; this ephemeral kind of construction was still practised in the 1930s by the Italian shepherd communities of the Pontine plain/southern Latium before the area was drained and on Sardinia; Zaccheo (2006).
35 cf. Morandi (1999) 196 fig. 3; Manfredi-Selvaggi (1999) 216 fig. 8; Santillo Frizell (2009) 122.

A *mobile model of cultural transfer* 211

a narrowing neck allowing for the separation of the animals and facilitating the control over milked and un-milked animals.[36]

Zooming in: identifying mobile pastoralists at Ripacandida

With all these considerations in mind, let us now turn to the evidence of these communities and populations in the pre-Roman era. If it existed, it seems likely that pre-Roman transhumance took shorter routes than the later Roman and *dogana* tracks; Roman expansion is typically thought to have brought a much larger scale to this activity. It is, nevertheless, helpful to take these historical/modern examples as a starting point for the investigation.

The recently studied site of Ripacandida is situated in the area of the Melfese, along the course of a *tratturo* of the *statonica*-system (Figure 10.1). It has been suggested that this particular *tratturo* is the successor of a *callis* from the middle to late Republican period, connecting Venosa and Atella and passing about 2 km southeast of the site (loc. La Veglia).[37] In the course of rescue excavations in the 1970s and 1980s, a small necropolis of the seventh to fifth

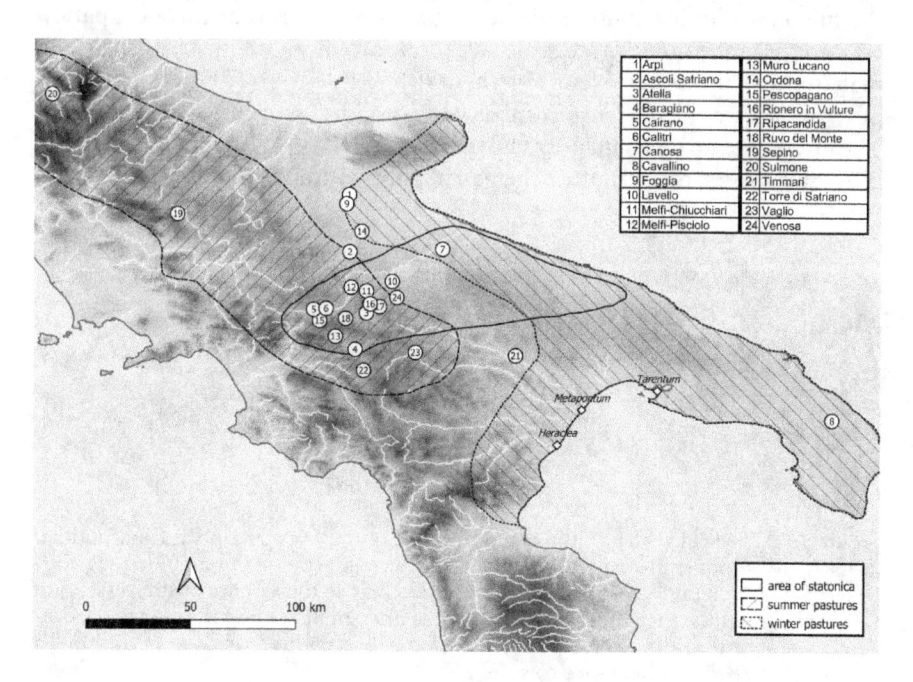

Figure 10.1 Map with sites mentioned in the text and area of the modern *statonica*-system.
Source: © S. Hye/author.

---

36 cf. Barth (1961) 16; Congès and Leguilloux (2012).
37 Volpe (1990) 147.

century BCE was discovered on the hilltop. All of the graves were simple pit inhumations. No dwellings contemporary with the necropolis have been found.[38] Noteworthy is the very limited amount of pottery found in the earliest burials, while jewellery was well represented. Already Yntema's study of the regional pottery tradition has revealed that the Melfese area lacked distinctive pottery production.[39] Most of the pottery found at Ripacandida comes from the wider region, especially from the adjacent 'north-Lucanian' area to the west (Ruvo-Satriano ware) and from northern Apulia to the east ('Daunian' ware). The first imported Greek vessels, occurring as early as the sixth century BCE, are 'Ionian' B2 cups. This shape was replaced in the following century, according to the general fashion, by simple black-glazed *kylices*. Other shapes, like kraters and trefoil jugs, were imported or imitated locally. Local pottery production started only one or two generations after the earliest burials, from the second half of the sixth century BCE onwards, and was practised on a small scale, probably restricted to just a few shapes (Figure 10.2).[40]

Loom weights and spindle whorls in some tombs suggest that the individuals buried there were engaged in textile production. However, according to the number and distribution of these objects, it seems that this occupation was not practiced on a large scale. Weapons are more frequent, probably in male tombs, and never occur together with textile tools. The vast majority of weapons are spears; close-combat weapons like swords occur very rarely. The graves are grouped in loose clusters (Figure 10.3). Within the early phase of these clusters, there is often the pairing of two tombs of adult individuals

Figure 10.2 Typical vessels of the bichrome local pottery production at Ripacandida. From left to right: *olla* with triple zig-zag motif on the shoulder; jug with 'spherical' lines and inscribed stars on the lower part of the vessel; jug with alternating horizontal bands and small zone with lozenge decoration at the widest point; squatted *askos* with vertical spout and bull's head protome (not to scale).

Source: © Author.

---

38 But wells pre-dating the graveyard are attested; Carollo and Osanna (2009) 394–409.
39 Yntema (1990) 16 fig. 3.
40 Setari (1999).

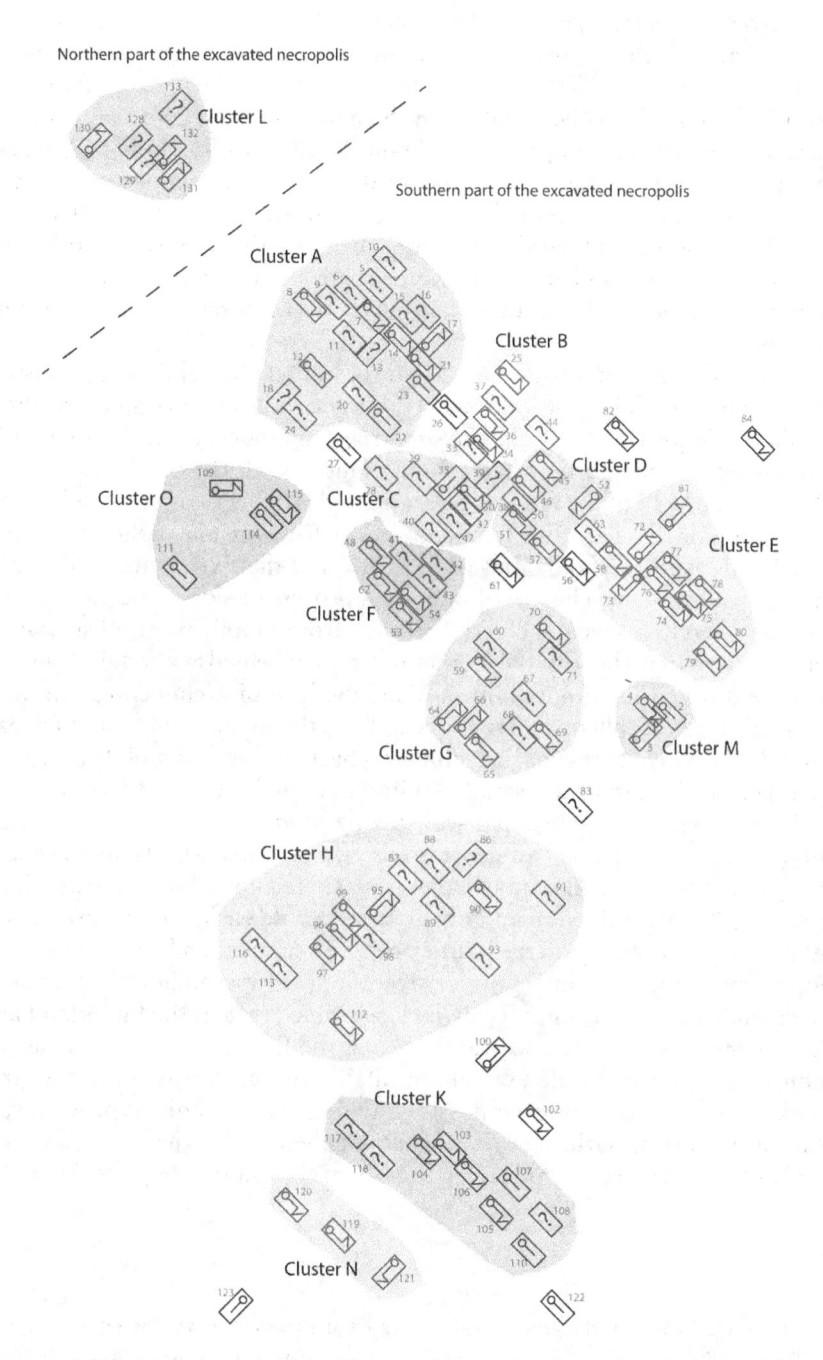

Figure 10.3 Schematic plan of the Ripacandida necropolis with indication of burial clusters.

Source: © Author.

of different genders, suggesting the existence of marriage-like partnerships.[41] Combined with the representation of almost all age and gender groups in each cluster, it seems likely that the clusters represent small, core, family or household units. Initially, members of three to four household clusters were buried, later increasing up to a maximum of 13. Careful estimates suggest that the average number of residents at the site over the entire period was 22, with a maximum of 33 in the second half of the sixth century BCE. The size of each household would therefore have been three to five people. This seems a very low number, casting some doubt on the permanent presence of the community at Ripacandida, or at least its full representation in this necropolis.[42]

Cross-cultural comparison shows that the household is the basic organisational unit of mobile pastoralists. It typically consists of a couple and their children (Figure 10.4). After a son's marriage, an independent household is established, forming a new basic family unit.[43] With the death, senility, or illness of the head of the family, the household is likely to dissolve unless the widow and/or a son are able to take over. Furthermore, the earliest deceased individuals at Ripacandida, buried at the turn of the sixth century BCE, are probably all women. This could indicate a process of slowly increasing sedentism, whereby (typically elderly) women from mobile pastoralist groups did not take part in the seasonal journey or were left behind at a certain point – a practice attested in ethnography.[44] While the lack of architecture can only indirectly suggest ephemeral types of dwelling, the small community of Ripacandida shows traits resembling ethnographically observed mobile pastoralists; specifically, it indicates small, egalitarian household units of armed men and of women engaged in small-scale textile production. That local pottery production started some two generations after the first burials might reflect the fact that (a) a seasonal stay neither necessitated nor allowed the development of pottery production and/or (b) vessels could easily be procured from other sources, probably on the journey between summer and winter pastures. Furthermore, the spectrum of pottery recovered at Ripacandida changes over time: while in the sixth century BCE close connections to the hinterland are documented (Ruvo-Satriano-ware), during the fifth century BCE 'coastal' influences (imports, banded ware) prevail, indicating increased links to (the markets at) the coasts or even possibly, analogous to historical processes, a shift of the (main) settlement sites of the shepherds from the uplands to the lowlands (i.e., change from inverse to normal transhumance pattern).

---

41 The determination of the gender of the deceased at Ripacandida was based only on the position of the corpse and the grave goods, since the bones were not available for study.
42 Heitz (2021).
43 Barth (1961) 18; Hütteroth (1959) 49–50; cf. Mientjes (2010) 157; Chang (2000) 128.
44 Hütteroth (1959) 53–74.

Figure 10.4 Image of a Latin shepherd family, taken on May 19, 1935 at Carpineto close to the dam of Rio Sermoneta.

Source: Zaccheo (2006) 163 (Archivio Consorzio di Bonifica dell'Agro. Pontino: http://image.archivioluce.com/foto/high/PONTINO/BOR001511.jpg).

In the typical northern 'Apulian'/'Daunian' pottery production, the enigmatic shape of the *askos* features prominently a vessel with a globular or squat body to which at least one, often two, vertical spout is attached. This shape is also one of the few vessel types produced by the small local workshop, apart from characteristically decorated *ollae* and two types of jugs (these vessels are however stylistically more related to the northern-Lucanian Ruvo-Satriano ware).[45] While the general function of the shape is still unknown,[46] the locally made *askoi* show an interesting detail (Figure 10.5): their rear spout was transformed into a figural applique in the shape of a bull's head – iconography reminiscent of pastoralism. The same is true for ram- or dog(?)-shaped pendants found in some tombs of the site. A recent analysis of the locally preserved textile remains of Ripacandida has also

---

45 Setari (1999).
46 Organic residue analysis is currently executed for examples recovered at Ripacandida and other sites of the region (J. Dunne, Organic Geochemistry Unit/University of Bristol). For the time being, the shape might be compared to the *čepák*, a vessel equally equipped with a round spout and used in eighteenth and nineteenth century Moravia to collect cream; Kunz (1969) 724 fig. 11.

216 *Christian Heitz*

Figure 10.5 Askos of the local Ripacandida ware and zoomorphic bronze pendants (not to scale).
Source: © Author.

revealed that most of the fabrics were woven in what could be described as a 'Greek manner', that is, as weft-faced tabbies, while some were equipped with typical indigenous tablet-woven borders.[47] If these were attached to textiles obtained from Greek markets, this would fit well with the typical production and consumption pattern of mobile pastoralists.

Zooming out: regional elites and networks

Having identified features that might point to a non-sedentary pastoral lifeway for the local community of Ripacandida, it is necessary to put these observations into a wider frame of reference and look for further indications of the existence of seasonally mobile populations within the region. A prominent category of evidence are the so-called 'princely' tombs (*tombe principesche*) that have been identified as the burials of the most prosperous members ('elites') of their respective communities. The very definition of these tombs as 'princely' often refers to the presence of objects indicating long-distance contacts, both inland and to the coastal areas.

At several sites of the region, in the sixth to fourth century BCE, burial grounds emerge whose structure and grave assemblages display high interregional connectivity between the mountainous hinterland and the coasts. Some 10–15 km north-northwest of Ripacandida, the necropoleis of

---

47 Gleba *et al.* (2018).

Melfi-Chiucchiari (on the present settlement hill) and Melfi-Pisciolo (in the plain on the southern bank of the Ofanto) are situated.[48] At both sites, the earliest burials, placed in sixth century BCE according to the grave goods, are mostly women. Just a little later, tombs of armed males also occur. The richest furnishings are found in tombs of the fifth century BCE. At Pisciolo, tombs 43 and 48 contained rich indigenous jewellery as well as Attic tableware,[49] while tombs B and F of Chiucchiari featured mixed indigenous-Greek assemblages including high-quality imported pottery (e.g., Little-master cups) as well as bronze vessels and items of Etruscan origin (e.g., a *candelabrum*), combined with chariot wheels.[50] The assemblage thus suggests far-reaching connections to the Tyrrhenian coast and/or central Italy, as well as contacts to the *apoikiai*. An equal mixture is represented in some contemporaneous tombs of northern Apulian Lavello.[51]

The sixth- and fifth-century BCE necropolis of Ruvo del Monte, some 15 km southwest of Ripacandida, is situated exactly in the area where the *statonica* took place and only ten km east of its westernmost point (modern Pescopagano). The hilltop site controls an easily accessible valley crossing between the Valle del Vulture, the high valley of Ofanto, and the small river Atella.[52] Again, the earliest tombs were largely those of lavishly equipped women.[53] The pottery consists mainly of indigenous wares from the northern Apulian lowlands in the east to the Campanian highlands in the west.[54] In the fifth century BCE, a pair of large tombs (64 and 65) are of particular importance, with goods indicating access to wide-ranging exchange networks, again spanning from the Tyrrhenian coast (a *candelabrum* from Vulci) to the Ionian coast (a crater of the Pisticci Painter from Metapontum).[55] Some sites even suggest the emergence of a hereditary chiefdom, or at least an attempt by the local elite to establish such a system: Baragiano occupies a hill with command over the surrounding territory, as well as the valleys of the Platano, Avigliano, and Tito.[56] Tombs of the rich necropolis of the seventh to fifth

---

48 Due to *clandestini* activities and the discovery of the remains during construction work, followed by quick and rather unsystematic rescue excavations, the documentation of these findings is quite problematic; Mitro and Notarangelo (2016) 23–6, 71–7, colour pl. I-III.
49 Aa.Vv. (1971) 118–20, 125–8; Bottini (1990) 9; Mitro and Notarangelo (2016) 27–39.
50 Bottini (1988) 132–3, (2013); Mitro and Notarangelo (2016).
51 Ciriello *et al.* (1991).
52 Bottini (1981); Scalici (2009).
53 Scalici (2009) 41–5. Another rich female tomb, according to the grave goods (ornaments like rings and amber), from the first half of the sixth century BCE (tomb 70) has recently been published by Scalici (2013).
54 Scalici (2009) 44, 51.
55 Bottini (1980) 344, (1990); according to Scalici (2009) 47 both tombs date to the last quarter of the fifth century BCE.
56 Some 30 km from Ripacandida; Russo and Di Giuseppe (2008) fig. 3; Bruscella (2009) 29–32; Russo (2008a) 33; Bruscella and Pagliuca (2013) 272. A site plan is given by Di Lieto (2008) 42 fig. 20; the Archaic tombs seem to be aligned along a road.

centuries BCE, including those of children, were equipped with numerous goods of high quality – in addition to horse-riding gear, they contained many indigenous Italian vessels and a number of Attic products like band-cups, eye-cups,[57] and many bronze vessels of Etruscan, or even Laconian, origin.[58] This is suggestive of a local elite with excellent connections within both the surrounding territory as well as along the coasts.[59] The roughly contemporary tombs of the small necropolis at Braida di Vaglio equally show a mixture of prestigious indigenous and Attic pottery, bronze vessels, meat skewers, graters, as well as weapons, horse-riding and chariot gear.[60] A young girl was even equipped with a golden, Greek-style diadem while the rich, indigenously produced amber jewellery points to connections with the Adriatic area. Especially interesting is a bronze cauldron bearing an Etruscan inscription. Torelli's reading of the text is *'mi petut[ies] . alic[u .] lavies . ricenas'* which he translates as 'I [was given] by Betutis to Laive Ricena', identifying Betutis for onomastic reasons as a chief from the Samnite/Hirpine area and the second person as the local chief at Braida.[61] This suggests that the local elite was part of an exchange network with direct links to the Etruscan-Campanian/Samnite area.

Meeting places as nodes for feasting and contract-making

The burial evidence shows that, within the wider regional social network of southern Italy, powerful regional lineages developed in the sixth and fifth centuries BCE, able to accumulate and display an impressive amount of social prestige. Architectural remains that sometimes occur in direct relationship with the elite tombs also seem to point in this direction. The prestigious graves of Braida di Vaglio are located in the immediate vicinity of a building (originally called a 'sanctuary') with a very atypical construction method for the indigenous inland (Figure 10.6): it has a rectangular layout of 12 by 24 metres, and the walls rest on wide stone foundations supporting a tiled roof. Its lifespan was only a few decades in the sixth century BCE, making it one of the oldest known stone buildings in the southern Italian hinterland – at the time of its use, the nearby settlement of Serra di Vaglio was still characterised by simple huts.[62] The most remarkable element of the building is its terracotta frieze, clearly evoking Greek norms, decorated with two armed 'duellists', behind each of which a mounted 'squire' is holding another horse, probably that of the warrior. For good reasons, Mertens-Horn has suggested that it was not a sanctuary, but rather a kind of meeting place – although the two labels need

---

57 Almost all cups can be assigned to two Attic workshops, i.e., the Group E of the Little-masters; Russo (2008b) 73.
58 Russo (2008b) 46–54.
59 Russo (2008b) 61; cf. Montanaro (2012).
60 Bottini and Setari (2003).
61 Torelli (2003) 116.
62 Lo Porto and Ranaldi (1990) 297.

not be mutually exclusive.⁶³ Its primary role as a meeting place, however, is supported by the presence of numerous banqueting vessels, including a large number of imported 'Ionian' B2 cups, but also Italian/indigenous pottery such as large *pithoi* and drinking and eating utensils.⁶⁴ Steininger argued plausibly for the interpretation of the building as a place of banqueting and feasting.⁶⁵

A much better preserved, but very similar, structure may provide some insight into the Braida building: the so-called *anaktoron* at Torre di Satriano, recently excavated by Osanna and his team. Equally associated with rich tombs (although significantly less luxurious than those of Braida di Vaglio),⁶⁶ it was erected around the middle of the sixth century BCE, featuring an almost identical terracotta frieze. The walls were built of rammed earth on stone foundations and the core building measured approximately seventeen by eight and a half metres (see Figure 10.6).⁶⁷ It had a wide entrance hall/

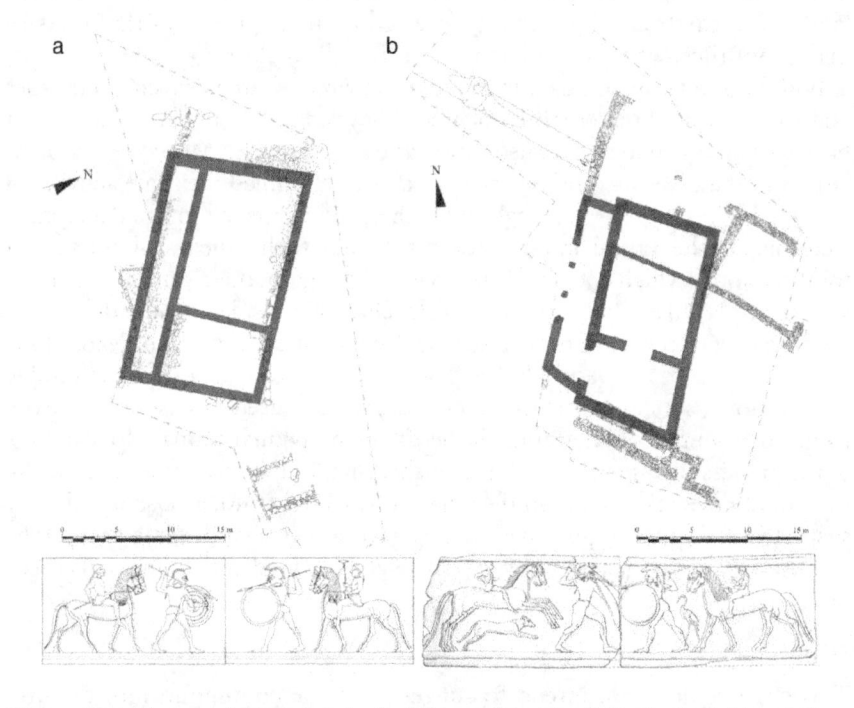

Figure 10.6 Plans and friezes of the buildings of Braida di Vaglio (a, left) and Torre di Satriano (b, right).

Source: Compiled from Osanna (2010) 32, Lo Porto and Ranaldi (1990) 300 figure 4 and Osanna (2009) 163 figure 8.

63 Mertens-Horn (1992) 79–80.
64 Lo Porto and Ranaldi (1990) 297; Russo Tagliente (1992) 79–81.
65 Steininger (1996) 262–4.
66 Osanna (2013a) 55–63; Baglivo (2013).
67 Serio (2009) 117.

portico along one of the long sides, in which looms were set up, based on the number and position of several loom-weights recovered. In the eastern part of the so-called 'vestibule', a circular stone structure was situated, close to which a large amount of banqueting pottery, alongside iron objects (a curved blade and a so-called temple key), were found. Some of the vessels preserved palaeobotanical traces (hazelnuts) and plant remains, hinting at rituals and ceremonies, such as food offerings and libations, and supporting the designation of the structure as an altar. Also, in the so-called 'ceremonial hall', separated from the vestibule by a monumental door, a large amount of tableware was found. Here, banquets associated with the prestigious pottery likely took place.[68] At the end of the sixth century BCE, further rooms were added to this core building. Some of them, like room 4, were seemingly used for storage, indicated by the discovery of *pithoi*. As at Braida, the involvement of Greek craftspeople in the construction is not only suggested by the layout and the frieze, but actively attested by inscriptions on the backs of many roof tiles, written in a Laconian-Tarentine dialect.

Both buildings, at Braida and Torre di Satriano, share basic characteristics and a great deal of (externally procured) knowledge, labour, and wealth must have been invested in their construction and development. Moreover, the similarities in the associated objects suggest that they framed the same activities – presumably prestigious meetings and gatherings connected to ritual actions.[69] Returning to the central argument of this chapter, within the transhumant pastoral economy which was likely in place in the region, these central structures may have played a vitally important role. Directly outside of, and adjacent to, the core part of the *anaktoron*, a strange-looking narrow corridor leads along the outer wall of the vestibule (see Figure 10.6). According to ethnographic observations, similar bottleneck constructions are used in pastoral environments for counting or separating the herds and individual animals, for example in the process of systematic milking or shearing. In the case of the *anaktoron*, this could have taken place in the adjacent yard (room 6), as Osanna already suspected.[70] Furthermore, pollen studies have shown that the area around the *anaktoron* was characterised by extensive grazing land at the time of its use.[71]

Discussion

This chapter does not intend to suggest that the communities of the pre-Roman southern Apennines entirely consisted of transhumant pastoralists and that a mobile seasonal lifeway was shared by all its inhabitants. It rather

---

68 For the *anaktoron* see Osanna et al. (2009) and Osanna and Capozzoli (2012).
69 Cf. Osanna (2015), although, as this paper argues, with a lesser focus on feasting and commensal politics in order to create asymmetrical relations of social power, and rather as an act intended to seal or consolidate economic as well as social agreements.
70 Osanna (2013a) 61–3; cf. Busana et al. (2012) 153; Marinow (1961) fig. 23.
71 Florenzano and Mercuri (2013).

aims to address and discuss the possibility that pastoral transhumance, as a way of life and economy, and as a driving force for social and even settlement development, might hitherto have been underestimated.

Many of the highlighted features in this chapter could also be reflective of sedentary communities – and indeed transhumant and sedentary should not be seen as mutually exclusive modes of existence. This applies to material objects as well as networks/connections – a *candelabrum* can illuminate elite residences, whether tents or houses, and bronze vessels might have been carried around on wheeled carts and used to heat whey as well as holding mixed wine for *symposia*. It does, however, need to be stressed that all the sites mentioned in this paper are situated along the course of historically attested long-distance tracks. Only a few metres north of Braida di Vaglio runs a later *tratturo*,[72] and likewise Baragiano was, in modern times and very possibly in ancient times, an important waypoint of transhumance.[73] Equally, various *tratturi* passed through the Melfese, with an important ford over the Ofanto River at Melfi-Pisciolo.[74] Indeed, a main track of this medieval-modern network of grazing paths is *tratturo 5*, descending from Melfi to Castellanata on the Gulf of Taranto.[75] While a congruence of medieval *tratturi* with Roman *calles*, or even pre-Roman droves, cannot necessarily be assumed, the fact that Roman settlements and *villae* (like at Torre degli Embrici at Rionero in Vulture) are also located along the known *tratturi* indicates that these routes could have had a very long existence, mainly determined by the natural conditions of topography, vegetation, and accessibility, factors with a high degree of temporal and spatial continuity.[76]

As the rich burials in these rural areas show the regional rootedness of these communities, it is very likely that these routes were used, organised, and controlled by the indigenous inhabitants of southern Italy. The appearance of buildings like the *anaktoron* at Torre di Satriano and the so-called 'sanctuary' of Braida di Vaglio reflect the power of the indigenous elites to hire specialised craftspeople from the *apoikiai*. Yet these buildings were not merely copies of coastal practices but specifically served the needs of the local communities and played a central role as a social arena for intra- and possibly also inter-cultural encounters. It can therefore be shown that, in the wider regional environment of southern Italy, regional elites enjoyed an outstanding social standing which developed over time. Within this larger,

---

72 Greco (1980) 385 n. 24; Russo Tagliente (1992) 79 regards the site even as the junction of several *tratturi*.
73 Russo (2008a) 33.
74 Kok (2009) 65.
75 Sprengel (1971) fig. 9. According to personal communication, some older inhabitants of Melfi can even remember the transhumance movements in this area that lasted until well into the twentieth century. For the pastoral routes in this area see also Di Bisceglie (2015) 67.
76 However, at least between the sixth and eight/ninth century CE, the long-distance transhumance routes might have been interrupted; Waldherr (2002) 436.

increasingly hierarchical, social fabric, the smaller, more egalitarian, and arguably pastoral, community of Ripacandida was probably a sub-segment.[77]

But where did the wealth of the elites come from? How did their interconnectedness to the Greek *poleis* develop, from which both the elites and less prosperous communities, like at Ripacandida, obtained items (the latter, mainly plain pottery)? The number and diversity of Greek/imported objects found in tombs of all gender, age, and status groups in the hinterland of southern Italy suggests individual acquisition of objects was the norm, rather than organised trade. It is uncertain what the indigenous communities exchanged for these goods in the absence of natural resources or any substantial number of Italian objects in the *apoikiai*. It has been suspected that Greek goods were traded for perishable (agricultural and pastoral) goods, labour, and maybe slaves.[78]

It is also unclear whether the Greek coastal cities were able to ensure the supply of secondary products independently (and indeed why they would have wanted to seek autarky). Their rather small *chora* was hardly suitable for extensive livestock farming, especially in combination with cereal cultivation.[79] Nor did they have the possibility of transhumance as that would require access to the inland plateaus. This made them ideal markets for indigenous surplus production – a huge economic opportunity for the pastoralists. As Mientjes has recently shown, pastoralists are able to adapt quickly to rapidly changing politico-economic conditions and customer demands.[80] Since pastoralism is a high risk/high reward venture, under favourable conditions it might not have been too difficult to respond to the increasing demands of the Greek markets. Within this context, the pastoralists would have acted as very active agents in the cultural transfer of the area. It would have been the pastoralists who carried the new objects, sometimes serving as symbols of wealth, into their summer pastures and residences. Such movement might, if not mutually agreed upon through oral arrangements or contracts between the mobile pastoralists and the residential farmers along or at the seasonal routes or pastures, pose a constant threat to landowners, especially when

---

77 Heitz (2021).
78 cf. Whitehouse and Wilkins (1989) 114–5. Even in more recent accounts like Yntema (2013), the question of what exactly was exchanged between the indigenous groups and the inhabitants of the *apoikiai* remains unsolved.
79 With liminal sanctuaries and a rather small subdivision of the plots, see Mertens (2006) 52–5, 332–3. Zooarchaeological evidence from the area of Metaponto suggests that cattle and sheep/goat at many sites were for a long time strongly predominant, while, for example, at Incoronata already from the sixth century BCE also pig became prominent; Bökönyi *et al.* (2010). It is however important to consider the character of the site (or rather, the findspot of the bones) since this might gravely influence the composition of the bone sample (e.g., sanctuaries with preferred sacrificial animals etc.); generally, cattle and especially sheep/goat in Archaic/Classical times clearly predominate the faunal assemblage of southern Italian sites, both indigenous and Greek; Veenman (2002).
80 Mientjes (2004).

the whole shepherd community was on the move and therefore including a strong force of armed men.[81]

The worlds of pastoralists and farmers are often mutually dependent. This is not only restricted to close trading contacts, with each part supplying the other with raw materials or specialised commodities that the other can or does not produce. The interrelation, and indeed division, between these two ways of economy and life is far more complex, and mobile pastoralists might even give up their seasonal travels and become entirely sedentary farmers. In many of the ethnographically documented cases, however, this was often the result of economic success, as land was purchased as private property (in contrast to the widely used common grazing land) by very rich flock-owners in order to invest the surplus gained from their herds. On these plots, usually located on either of the seasonal grazing areas, at least parts of the family of the successful herder became sedentary. The decision to take part in the seasonal migrations or not was now up to the flock-owner. Instead of travelling with the flocks, the responsibility for the animals on the migrations might be given to poorer, less successful, herders/shepherds. Agricultural work on the land of the rich flock-owner was likewise carried out by impoverished shepherds who lost, or had never owned, a sufficient number of animals to be economically independent.[82] This situation may have, at least partly, contributed to the pastoralist view of sedentary farming as being somehow inferior – hard agricultural labour on the soil in the eyes of successful flock-owners (i.e., the ideal every pastoralist was aiming for) was a task that only unsuccessful, poor ex-shepherds who were no longer free to choose their lifeway had to carry out (as 'slaves' of the soil and their master). The superiority of mobile herding, and their preference for this way of life, might (at least in the view of the pastoralists) also be based on notions of independence in terms of freedom to make decisions regarding the planning of the migrations and overall herd management. Unlike sedentary farming, mobile herders had the possibility to react to, or avoid, natural constraints as well as hostile encounters. Thus, by making smart decisions and showing prowess in contract-making and conflict (both against beasts and enemies/robbers), and at the same time carrying less burden than the arduous agricultural labour, they were able to make greater profits than the farmers. All this might have added up to a certain sense of pride and a feeling of superiority towards the latter.[83]

Returning to the question of mobility, the model for social change in southern Italy in the period of 'Greek colonisation' forwarded in this chapter postulates a higher degree of movement on the part of the Italic populations than

---

81 This might even give agriculture in the area of winter pastures a difficult standing, as still witnessed by Hütteroth (1982) 210–4 in southern Turkey; cf. Magno (1999) esp. 52–3.
82 See, e.g., Barth (1961) 108–9; Rudenko (1969) 18; Bežkovič (1969) 99.
83 See, e.g., Alizadeh (2008) on the self-conceptions of shepherds in the Zagros mountains.

on the part of the newcomers. Whereas the Greek settlers only moved once, and then became attached to a rather small area surrounding the new place of residence, they possibly encountered a regional environment in which a larger part of the population was roaming around on a seasonal basis. This number may have even increased as the Greek settlers triggered new possibilities for the sale of surplus production by the indigenous population. For the shepherds, the new settlers emerged as a key market for their products and a source of profit, thus provoking more extensive herding on the inland pastures, to which only they had access.[84] This might have enhanced further processes of internal wealth accumulation and social stratification among the indigenous communities, as well as a reorganisation of landscape use and settlement patterns, such as the investment of surplus into land ownership or private pastures and the creation of new and more stable settlement sites at places of seasonal habitation. This is also, perhaps, visible in further architectural features, albeit scarce and ephemeral. From the seventh century BCE onwards, large enclosures were erected in historically attested areas of winter pasture – where, interestingly, no Greek-style *apoikiai* were established. At Arpi, close to the medieval *dogana*-hub Foggia, a seventh-/sixth-century BCE walled ditch-and-bank system circumscribed a vast, almost empty area of approximately ten square km.[85] The structure seems too weak to serve as a stronghold in case of armed conflict – but to impede flocks from leaving or predators or thieves from entering the enclosure, it would have sufficed.[86]

Future directions

A thorough investigation concerning the age, extent, role, and importance of mobile pastoralism demands much further study. The consistent application of scientific methods and techniques, like zooarchaeological analysis, is a necessary prerequisite to gain further insights into this topic, and new research possibilities like isotope analyses, especially of tooth enamel, provide a promising new way to approach the question of herd mobility.[87] However, in particular, the problem of seasonal shift of pasture and the multiple

---

84 Cf. Carrer (2015) 10; for the increasing development of a market economy in first millennium BCE Italy inextricably linked with livestock management see Trentacoste (2020). However, the model forwarded here for increased sheep/goat or cattle transhumance might only apply on a larger scale until the fourth/third century BCE when the faunal spectrum of many sites becomes dominated by pigs; Veenman (2002).
85 Whitehouse and Wilkins (1989) 117.
86 Quite analogously to the *riposi* or *posti* of the *dogana*-droves serving as communal stopover and resting sites; cf. Sprengel (1971) 52–3. The highly dispersed settlement structure at sites like Ordona, although no surrounding enclosure has been detected, might indicate a similar use of space, cf. Mertens (1995) 36 fig. 13. The function of the huge Archaic enclosure (69 hectares) of Cavallino seems open to debate, cf. Yntema (2013) 118–23.
87 See, e. g. Ventresca Miller and Makarewicz (2018).

influences affecting Sr, O, C, and N ratios still pose difficulties.[88] That being said, not just the up-to-date analysis of animal remains, but also anthropological analysis might provide useful hints: many individuals buried at the Iron Age necropolis of Timmari showed muscle and tendon attachments indicating a high level of stress comparable to features of modern-day runners.[89] Combined with the fact that a historic drove-road to the Ionian coast passed by the site, this might possibly point to a mobile lifeway of some of the members of this community.

However, despite the clear need for further scientific study, even the reconsideration of already known material and archaeological features might yield hitherto unseen evidence. As revealed earlier, when placed in a new context and paradigm, existing evidence can take on a new flavour – revealing vibrant and fluid lifeways which exist outside of the traditional urban focus on ancient world studies.

The study of mobile pastoralism therefore not only calls for archaeologists to employ state-of-the-art scientific analyses on 'fresh' material but also to keep this question in mind and consider any material in this respect, with an open eye towards the function of items (for example, sceptre versus distaff, use of tripods or cauldrons), as well as to the social features of the local community. Only with data resulting from a collective effort of both archaeologists and different specialists will it be possible to adequately evaluate of the role of pastoralism in order to understand further, culture- and socio-anthropological developments in this highly dynamic period and region.

---

[88] Although a recent study of Etruscan sites using a combination of different isotope ratios has not been able to discern larger-scale herd mobility in central/northern Italy, it explicitly states that in other regions like Puglia different mechanisms of pastoralism might have been practised; Trentacoste *et al.* (2020).

[89] Marchi and Borgognini Tarli (2002); F. Immler (AnthroArch GbR, Munich) observed similar features on some skeletons at Ascoli Satriano (pers. comm.).

11 Mechanisms of community formation in pre-Roman Italy

A latticework of connectivity and interaction

Sheira Cohen

The landscape of archaic Italy is populated with dozens of ethnonyms; it is a mosaic of different groups, each with their own unique and complicated historiography. The present volume is full of them, as various authors have explored the social, economic, and productive relationships which exist between areas and peoples. Some, like the Latins and the Samnites, occupy an outsized place in both ancient texts and modern scholarship, while others, like the Hernici or the Volsci, rarely merit dedicated treatment or attention.[1] This is not to say these less studied groups are not important. The complex political and military manoeuvrings of this cast of often marginalised ethnic groups still feature prominently in the ancient accounts of Rome's earliest years, first as antagonists before finally being incorporated into Rome's seemingly inevitable empire. Annual raids by a long parade of culturally 'Othered' outsiders form the dramatic backdrop to the 'Struggle of the Orders' and act as the anvil against which a cohesive and identifiable Roman civic identity was forged. Modern scholarship, although often eschewing the ethnic framework of the ancient sources in favour of a more nebulous 'social identity', has still largely followed this historical model in which external pressure drove internal cohesion, and thus Roman identity, throughout the first millennium BCE.[2] This in-group/out-group paradigm of community formation, employed across the ancient

---

* This chapter is the result of many long and spirited discussions with colleagues and friends over the past several years as I have wrestled with issues of identity, ethnicity, and community. I would particularly like to thank Nicola Terrenato, Jeremy Armstrong, J. Troy Samuels, Leah Bernardo-Ciddio, Joseph Frankl, and Matt Naglak for their wisdom, support, and probing and provocative questions on these issues. Thanks are also due to the attendees at the 'Exchanging Ideas' conference in Auckland for their stimulating questions and discussions, and to Elena Isayev, Natalie Abell, Brittany Vasquez, Kelly Wheeler, James Faulkner, members of the UM Roman Republic Reading Group, and all my IPCAA colleagues for their helpful feedback and support. Special thanks to the anonymous reviewers for their thoughtful comments and suggestions. All errors that remain are my own.
1 Although, recently, see di Fazio (2020) on the Volsci.
2 Sherwin-White (1973) 21, 32; Alföldi (1965) 365–77, esp. 373; Cornell (1995); Armstrong (2016a) 147ff. Ethnogenesis as resistance to the 'Other' is also discussed in relation to the emergence of non-Latin ethnicities in opposition to expanding Roman hegemony in Italy, see Dench (1995).

DOI: 10.4324/9781003120728-11

Mediterranean, argues for the activation of identity markers in response to an external threat or opposition. Thus, it is only when an individual or group comes into contact with others who stand in opposition to themselves (i.e., the 'Other') that their own communal sense of identity solidifies.[3]

This vision of identity formation, found in Livy and Dionysius and largely followed by modern scholarship, begins *in medias res*, focusing on the activation of a certain configuration of communal identity within a specific context. The social conditions that allowed for such an activation are less clearly articulated; identity claims are largely assumed to emerge from pre-existing and natural configurations of distinctive groups – often conceived as ethnic or linguistic in nature.[4] However, as now widely accepted in scholarship, all identities are socially constructed and performative rather than an inherent or natural characteristic of an individual or group of individuals.[5] Identity claims are thus not neutral bystanders to events, nor are they reflective of a vague sense of belonging. Rather, these claims are active and dynamic components within the construction of political and historical narratives. Social and ethnic identities might gain purchase and influence in the collective social psyche at certain points and in certain interactions while, in other contexts, they may be of minor or no importance in the structuring of interaction or behaviour.[6] As such, any specific identity or ethnicity is ill-suited as a structuring principle for exploring community formation itself.[7] Instead, identity should be considered as one possible variable or outcome within a larger context of community formation and social interaction.

As discussed elsewhere in this volume, the high degree of connectivity across Italy, attested in the archaeological record and visible beneath the surface of our historical sources, indicates that the supposedly distinctive groups within our historical record were part of complex and overlapping systems of connection – economic, social, religious, political, etc. – that defy the simple binaries that rigidly separate one group from another in the literature.

---

3 For discussion of the 'Other' in identity construction, see, e.g., Hall (1989), (2002), cf: Gruen (2011). Barth (1969) is often credited with shifting the focus of ethnic construction to the boundary between groups, rather than focusing on the 'stuff' contained within. On boundaries and frontier zones as the locus of identity creation, see Neil (2012); Bourdin (2012) 429–39; and various studies in Cifani and Stoddart (2012).
4 Bradley (2000b); Gruen (2020) for bibliography.
5 The literature on ethnicity and identity as social constructs (commonly classed as instrumentalism or constructivism, although a strict political interpretation is not always followed) is considerable. Key works in the field include: Barth (1969); Smith (1986); Bentley (1987); Eriksen (1993); Jenkins (1997); Jones (1997); Brubaker (2004). This socially-constructed aspect makes archaeological identification of ethnic groups difficult, especially in prehistoric periods, as discussed in this volume's introduction; see, for example, Shennan (1989) and Emberling (1997). See Lucy (2005) for overview and further bibliography.
6 See Farney (2007) for discussion of how ethnicity was actively invoked in Roman politics during the Republican period. For Umbria: Bradley (2000a). For Samnium: Dench (1995).
7 Brubaker (2004) 7–11.

This creates a tension within the scholarship as to how to reconcile our dichotomous models of socially constructed and oppositional identity with the connective networks we find in the archaeological record. A new paradigm is needed. This chapter will therefore put aside, for now, the complex and difficult task of exploring and deconstructing the character of particular social and ethnic identities in archaic Italy in favour of a broader lens that steps outside the familiar historical narratives and addresses the underlying mechanisms of community formation. While conflict and opposition to the 'Other' may have been one avenue by which communities sought to differentiate themselves in a particular moment, these moments of identity activation emerged from, and were allowed by, a wider, underlying lattice of connections and interactions. Connectivity and the study of interactions therefore provide a useful access point for studying these overlapping communities and beginning to trace their contours at a regional level.

This chapter will explore the wider landscape of connections that structured interaction between people and communities in pre-Roman Italy. This includes both the foundational structures of life in western central Italy and their implications for interaction – such as subsistence patterns, access to resources, and the importance of personal relationships in mitigating risk and facilitating cooperation – as well as specific institutions that developed to deepen social and economic interaction across the region – such as religious festivals, markets, sanctuaries, and political alliances. Where people come together, marriages can be made, trade relationships established, information transmitted, and bonds renewed through shared rituals and practices. These practices and structures formed the primary linkages through and by which technology, objects, and people moved around the region. These structures, and their effects, can therefore be traced in both the archaeological and historical record, allowing us to use the full range of evidence at our disposal to trace the shape of this latticework of connections over time. Approaching community formation as a product of, and contributor to, these underlying patterns of connectivity at all levels of society – from the regional to the individual – allows us to move beyond simplistic, incomplete, and dichotomous constructions of Italic communities. This more balanced and representative view thus encompasses the experiences and realities of elites and non-elites, urban and non-urban, Romans and non-Romans. It reveals the vast social, cultural, and economic infrastructure which supports the creation of both objects and identities.

From connectivity to community to identity (and back again)

It is widely accepted in modern scholarship that identity (whether ethnic, social, or civic) is both socially constructed (largely through performance) and context-dependent, as opposed to inherent or natural.[8] An interactionist

---

8 See above, fn. 5.

or communicative model of identity builds on this idea and posits that it is the quotidian interactions between individuals and families over time that form the social and economic relationships that are essential to community formation and, eventually, identity formation.[9] These interactions occur both vertically and horizontally and provide the necessary framework to create and maintain a shared sense of solidarity and cohesiveness. Critically, external pressure and differentiation from the 'Other', while important factors, are insufficient mechanisms for the creation of identity *ex nihilo*. External pressure, elite rhetoric, or warfare cannot create community among individuals who have no pre-existing connection, and any attempt will be necessarily short-lived.[10] Rather, such tactics for identity formation depend on an underlying lattice of connectivity that connects individuals and families via multiple overlapping networks.[11] Only when the idea of community is reinforced by repeated interactions between individuals and families can a cohesive sense of identity emerge. The activation and elevation of these networks, or rather of certain configurations and combinations of networks, in specific moments is therefore only the second half of the equation and, arguably, often of secondary importance with respect to broader patterns of social change and development.[12] A narrow focus on specific moments of identity construction not only obscures the myriad of potential identity configurations that might have emerged from this underlying connectivity, but also draws attention only to the most visible identities in the historical record – in this case the elite, male, urban conceptions of Roman identity and the Roman state. The undocumented and un-activated (or less intensely activated) networks of connection, however, still have profound impacts on the development of ancient identities and societies, as they structure behaviour across all segments of society and provide the connective foundation upon which identity claims can flourish.

Language in archaic Italy provides one arena in which the difficulties of separating out underlying patterns of behaviour from performative identity habits have been the subject of considerable research. While scholars have

---

9 Blake (2013); (2014) 71.
10 Brubaker (2004) 20–7. Armstrong (2016b) notes the limitation of warfare as a unifier in isolation and its probable dependence on other social bonds (such as kinship and religion), see discussion below.
11 In contrast to the 'lattice of connectivity' approach advocated for here, Blake (2014) used an interactionist approach and social network analysis to look for regional groupings in the Bronze Age that may have been the precursors to groups attested in the historical period. Blake drew on Smith's (1999) distinction between ethnic categories and ethnic communities and, although taking a broader view of identity, argued for a similar two-stage process in which some regional groupings set in motion a degree of path dependence that eventually solidified as named groups.
12 Brubaker (2004) coined the concept of 'groupness' as a distinct variable for understanding ethnicity and identity, that can be understood both as a continuum and as a distinct event, here described as 'activation.'

traditionally linked onomastic and epigraphic choices to the cultural identity and/or spoken language skills of the individual author, recent work has complicated these correlations and has warned against this 'onomastic fallacy', especially in multilingual societies.[13] Deliberate linguistic choices can take on a performative character in certain contexts, both spoken and written, and are not necessarily reflective of an individual's or group's identity, language facility, or use in other contexts.[14] This has long been recognised in the complicated relationship that Roman magistrates had with speaking Greek abroad, despite their undoubted fluency in the language, and the loaded symbolism visible in the linguistic choices of Rome's earliest writers.[15] Ennius, for example, famously declared himself to have *tria corda* (three hearts) representing the three languages he spoke – Greek, Oscan, and Latin – but, nevertheless, he chose to write his epics in Latin.[16] The epigraphic record, likewise, indicates a high degree of multilingualism across the peninsula throughout the mid-first millennium BCE.[17] It was this widespread multilingualism that provided the necessary conditions for overt linguistic differentiation to emerge as a political or cultural statement.[18] For instance, the self-conscious use of Oscan as an epigraphic language during the Social War, and concomitant rejection of Latin and Greek, was an amplification of a subset of one linguistic network, one of many possible identity markers, in a politically fraught moment. These moments of activation, however, are usually short-lived and are not necessarily characteristic of the entirety of the underlying linguistic context, where multilingualism and linguistic connectivity predominated. In archaic Italy, language was not a meaningful barrier to connectivity or communication and cannot be used as a proxy for social groups. Rather, language is one of many interlocking layers in the connective latticework upon which communities are built.

A similar short-lived and context-dependent activation of identity is visible in the sphere of military conflict. Although late Republican historians anachronistically framed Rome's early military conflicts in existential terms and focused on territorial expansion, these conflicts are often better understood as intermittent raiding for portable wealth (and defence against such raids

---

13 McDonald and Clackson (2020) 77–9; Bourdin (2012) esp. 51–9. On onomastic identifications of ethnic origin or ancestry, with varying methodologies: see Farney (2007); various studies in Clackson *et al.* (2020).
14 Fishman and Garcia (2010) provide an excellent introduction to the sociolinguistic literature on language and ethnicity in the modern context. See also Lytra (2016).
15 Sciarrino (2011); Feeney (2016).
16 Gel. *NA* 17.71.
17 For a general discussion of bilingualism and multilingualism in Italy, see Adams (2003); cf: Mouritsen (1998). For epigraphic evidence, see, for example, Bourdin (2012); Tolosa (2017).
18 Langslow (2012) 300–1 made a similar point on language and identity in highlighting the importance of choice when assessing bilingual inscriptions as evidence of general bilingualism as opposed to as indices of identity.

by others).¹⁹ As Armstrong has argued elsewhere, these economic incentives likely contributed to a short-lived 'task-based cohesion' on the battlefield, which built upon the more diffuse and irregular foundational ties provided by kinship, religion, or other social relationships. This short-lived military cohesion, which we might consider a form of identity, did not appear to have contributed to, nor arisen from, long-term social or political cohesion between soldiers or in the wider community.²⁰ The switching of allegiances and fickleness of allied troops (and Roman troops) suggests that 'enemy' designations were largely contextual; the sharp divisions between groups on the battlefield appear to have dissipated quickly and did not significantly impact connection and interaction in other spheres. These intermittent battlefield divisions were later fixed by our sources into stable ethnic designations for different groups, proliferating across the historical narrative and taking on a solidity and timeless quality that would likely have been incomprehensible at the time. These early, neighbourly conflicts existed in a radically different sociopolitical context from that imagined by Livy and his contemporaries; an early context in which deep social and economic ties existed in tandem with annual raiding, and in which Rome was connected to her alleged enemies almost as closely as she was connected to her supposed allies. Warfare was just one of the many institutions that connected disparate communities in a series of constantly evolving and overlapping configurations.

At Rome, these multivariate connections are often overshadowed in our historical sources by a narrow political and legal perspective on Roman identity that excludes large segments of the population – especially slaves and women. To be Roman was to participate in the political and legal framework of Rome; the struggle for legal recognition, whether by plebeians, Latins, or Italians, was the struggle for inclusion into the Roman political body.²¹ This political identity has likewise dominated modern scholarship which has centred Roman identity as unique and central to Rome's imperial success.²² The broader networks of connection and interaction that existed across the peninsula, however, were essential to Rome's long-term survival and success as a polity.²³ They provided the preconditions for moments of intense identity

---

19 Armstrong (2016a) 98–102, 141–5.
20 Armstrong (2013); (2016b), see also Helm (2020) on how different configurations on the battlefield and within the camp both aided and undermined cohesion within the army at different levels.
21 Isayev (2017); see also Sherwin-White (1973); Cornell (1997) 10; Armstrong (2016a) 185–211.
22 The characterisation of Roman identity has varied – from belligerent to open – but the centring of the political structure at Rome as the unique foundation for expansion still remains. See, for example, Terrenato (2019) with bibliography.
23 This is not unique to Italy and Rome but is arguably a feature of many large polities. Honeychurch (2014), and Porter (2012) have both convincingly argued for the importance of internal connectivity, facilitated by mobility of all or a segment of the population, as a major factor in state formation and cohesion in the Eurasian steppe and Near East.

activation and, even when 'un-activated', provided the social mechanisms necessary for maintaining relationships over relatively long distances. Differentiation from the 'Other', by contrast, was a limited phenomenon that was constantly renegotiated in light of changing circumstances. As Rome expanded its cultural and political boundaries, the interface between 'us' and 'them' was likewise shifted – first the 'Other' was the Sabines, then the Latins, then the Volsci and Aequi, then the Samnites and so on. Yet, the underlying lattice of connections crossed these putative boundaries, tying people together regardless of the political rhetoric and involving repeated interactions across the entire community. Once the frontier of Roman hegemony had moved beyond them, the latticework of connections remained and was the foundation for long-term social cohesion and identity in this now expansive polity. Indeed, as the community grew, harnessing and facilitating that underlying connectivity became increasingly important for maintaining a shared identity that goes beyond one's immediate neighbours.[24] The repeated economic interactions between herders, farmers, urban artisans, traders, and other professions, as well as the social and ritual relationships that accompanied them, provided the connective fabric within which Roman communal identity formed. A civic or political model of identity, centred around Rome and its political institutions, obscures the importance of these underlying connective mechanisms in eventually facilitating Roman hegemony across the peninsula.

This extensive connectivity was therefore important, but, as other contributors have noted, connectivity also has a tendency to be used as a 'catch-all' explanation for similarities or congruencies that we see in the archaeological record. The picture is often one of an endless background churn of interaction, an undifferentiated jumble of connections that describes everything, yet lacks strong explanatory power. The latticework-model deployed here, however, does allow for internal structure and differentiation – not everything is equally connected at all times, but rather we have nodes and areas of relatively stronger interaction alongside fissures and areas of weakness. Different domains – economic, social, ritual, etc. – reveal different internal structures that combine to create a complex picture of multiple overlapping connectivities. This approach to tracing connectivity builds on earlier social network analysis in archaeology which used shared material culture as simple proxies for interaction, but instead takes a holistic and qualitative approach which focuses on specific connective mechanisms.[25] The remainder of this chapter will focus on distinct mechanisms and institutions of connection that existed across western central Italy through the archaic period, highlighting some key structures of this connective lattice. Two domains – the relationships (economic and social) between pastoral and agricultural economies, and festivals and religious institutions – clearly demonstrate the structure of this lattice of

---

24 Honeychurch (2014) 284, 294.
25 Blake (2014).

connectivity and highlight how connections criss-crossed putative boundaries that we see in the historical record (i.e., ethnic or political groupings).

Landscape as a structure for connectivity

The landscape and geography of a region is an important structuring element for interaction, especially economic interaction. Without advocating for environmental determinism, it is important to acknowledge the ways in which behavioural choices are constrained and otherwise influenced by the environment. For example, the subsistence behaviours available in a region, and access to natural resources, can lead to the development of trade relationships, or other social relationships, to mitigate the risks and challenges presented by the environment.[26] Exploring the recursive relationships between landscape and behaviour requires a certain degree of conjecture to build out the picture provided by ethnography, landscape reconstruction, archaeological analysis, and historical accounts. Ordinary economic activities, particularly those that occur outside urban cores or involve natural resources, are often overlooked in elite-focused textual sources and can prove difficult to reconstruct in detail from archaeological evidence (although not impossible, as Heitz discusses elsewhere in this volume).[27] This section will therefore draw on a wide range of evidence, including historical and ethnographic studies of modern Italian shepherding and farming families, in order to sketch out some fundamental environmental constraints that would have structured interaction over time.[28] Small-scale vertical transhumant pastoralism – the seasonal movement of flocks between upland and lowland pastures as part of a mixed agro-pastoral economy – emerges as one important structuring mechanism for interaction that would have required, and facilitated, economic and social ties between diverse populations.

Western central Italy is a highly differentiated landscape with numerous microregions, each with a distinctive environmental history and potential for human exploitation. Broadly speaking, the volcanic soils of the Latin plains

---

26 Braudel (1972). While this approach owes much to palaeoeconomy and human behavioural ecology in considering human risk management and adaptive behaviour, it eschews any assessment of 'natural' use of a particular region or the assumption that individuals would employ the most efficient strategy for subsistence. Similarly, the social, economic, and political context also structured and constrained behaviours that were possible or profitable, but were not isolated from environmental factors.

27 The agronomists (e.g., Cato, Varro, Columella) only provide a window into particular forms of agriculture and animal husbandry relevant to their rhetorical purposes. The material traces of transhumant shepherds did not change significantly for centuries and are difficult to detect or differentiate from other forms of animal husbandry archaeologically; see, e.g., Heitz in this volume; Chang and Koster (1986); Barker (1989); Barker *et al.* (1991).

28 My use of ethnographic analogy is not based on assumptions of continuity of practice (historical analogy), but rather ecological analogy (Carrer [2015]) due to the broad similarity of the environmental constraints and structures over time.

provided excellent agricultural land (once cleared), although access to water was limited in the dry summer months when seasonal streams dried up and river levels dropped. To the south, the Pontine plains were dominated by a series of marshy lagoons (now drained) that would have been abundant fishing and hunting zones, but ill-suited to any sustained occupation or intensive exploitation in their natural state. The higher marine terraces along the southern coast would have provided space for settlements and agricultural production as well as suitable ports for sea trade. The foothills of the Monti Lepini and the Apennines were well-suited for olive and wine production as well as grazing of sheep and goats on the steep slopes. The same can be said of the region of the Colli Albani, where the volcanic lakes provided access to water year-around and fertile soil for agriculture in flatter areas. Further inland, the wide Sacco-Liris Valley was also suitable for agricultural exploitation despite the slightly higher elevation and provided the main land route south to Campania.

None of these regions were self-sufficient or independent; they were part of a densely interconnected economic web that is visible in ethnographic and historical accounts.[29] While the higher mountain areas of the Monti Lepini, the Colli Albani, and the Apennines further inland would have provided excellent summer pasture for sheep and goats, the cold winters would have required the movement of flocks to lower elevations. For the lowland farmer, wintering animals on agricultural land would have provided much needed manure for fertilisation and weed-cropping, but pasture was limited during the dry summer months. Small-scale vertical transhumance was thus mutually beneficial to both shepherd and farmer. Dependent on local circumstance and preference, the movement of flocks between different elevations at varying distances could occur on a regular basis (daily or weekly) or could be seasonal, with animals wintered in lowland pastures and taken into the mountains during the summer. The flexibility of the system was a key factor in its success, as shepherds could adapt to changing environmental, economic, or social conditions.[30] When placed in the historical context of archaic Italy, pastoralism, and specifically the small-scale, vertical transhumance model described here, emerges as an important facet of a mixed agro-pastoral economic system.[31] It was compatible with, and developed

---

29 Barker *et al*. (1991). For a critical review of ethnoarchaeology studies of prehistoric Greek pastoralism: Cherry (1988).
30 Barker *et al*. (1991) indicates that both *pastori stanziali* and *pastori transumanti* could co-exist in the same landscape and use the same drove-roads and campsites, varying the range of their transhumance and choice of pastures over time. See also Stagno (2019), although note that rigid typological divisions between different forms of pastoralism can fail to capture the flexibility and variation in pastoral practices across a region and through time which is evident in ethnographic and historical accounts.
31 Chang and Koster (1986) 102–4. Cf: Lewthwaite (1981) who argues that pastoralism can, at best, be considered a tactical adaptation only in use during the Medieval period in the western Mediterranean, focused largely on manure provisioning, and not in use during earlier periods.

alongside, the more extensive agricultural exploitation and emerging urban markets of the archaic period. As the urban population increased, settlements looked beyond the immediate hinterland for their subsistence needs; the small-scale, intensive, mixed-farming model possible during the Neolithic and Bronze Age would have been insufficient for the urban need for meat, dairy, and wool.[32]

Pastoralism and pastoral economics were therefore important structuring factors for intra- and inter-regional connectivity, both in terms of the physical mobility of humans and livestock and in the informal social interactions that negotiating such mobility necessitates. Some scholars have argued that transhumance requires the existence of a unified political system to facilitate the movement of flocks through different territories, and thus could not predate Roman hegemony.[33] This was certainly the case for the large-scale transhumance of Medieval Italy and Spain, which relied on special grants from aristocrats to protect their right of passage along *tratturi* (drove-roads) and access to winter grazing.[34] The situation was more complex for the earlier periods, however, and these later state-sponsored systems should not be simply retrojected. Under Roman rule, similar protections for shepherds are evident, such as the *Lex Agraria* (*CIL* I², nr. 585, see esp. sections ii.14–15 and 25–26) which allowed limited grazing on public land as well as free movement along public roads and *calles* and free grazing for flocks in transit.[35] But while the expansion of agriculture and increased urban occupation in the mountains may have brought these two groups into greater conflict, there is no indication that accommodation was only possible because of Roman political unification. Rather than establishing new prerogatives or protections, the famous second-century CE inscription from Saepinum (*CIL* 9.2438) indicates that the focus was on preserving the traditional rights of shepherds to move along public drove-roads without harassment or

---

32 The early to mid-first millennium BCE in Italy sits at a transitional period between prehistoric non-urban societies and the fully urban and market-oriented Roman period. Thus, there would have been increased demand for primary (meat for consumption and sacrifice) and secondary products (wool for textiles, milk for cheese) of animal husbandry in large settlements and cities, if not to the extent visible in the late Republic and Imperial periods. This transitional period is often overlooked in the more commonly cited studies on Greek pastoralism, see esp. Halstead (1996), (2006).
33 Toynbee (1965) 286; Trentacoste et al. (2020) 2; cf. Skydsgaard (1974). Pasquinucci (1979) 88 notes that political unification helps but fragmentation is not an inherent obstacle. Frayn (1984) suggests that there was no transhumance between the sixth and third centuries BCE due to a lack of Roman control, although she doesn't extend this to the pre-sixth century BCE.
34 On medieval *tratturi* and the extraordinary power of the *Dogana di Foggia*: Braudel (1972) 85–102; Marino (1988); Thompson (1989) 95–107.
35 The type of public land referred to in this law is debated, see Crawford (1996) 113–80 for text and commentary.

accusations of banditry.[36] Disruption of legitimate economic activity was detrimental to the government purse through lost tax revenue (such as the *scriptura*) and loss of state-owned animals. In contrast to the expansive medieval system, the smaller scale and shorter distances of vertical pastoralism in Roman and pre-Roman Italy did not require such a degree of political control or protection.[37] Informal agreements between farmers and shepherds to allow passage on private land and to winter flocks are attested, with disputes referred to some mutually agreed-upon local arbiter.[38] Similar informality was present in the organisation of seasonal wage labour, which would have also contributed to overall mobility across the peninsula.[39] Thus, while the Roman legal system would begin to insert itself into existing economic transactions over time, trade and mobility undoubtedly existed prior to the emergence of this centralised legal framework.

The dynamic tension between mobile, semi-mobile, and sedentary individuals, and the harnessing of the connective power of more mobile individuals (whether traders, herders, or seasonal workers) is fundamental to the development and maintenance of large polities – both socially and economically. Alizadeh's concept of 'enclosing nomadism,' developed to describe the role of pastoral nomads as mobile facilitators between sedentary communities, might also be usefully adapted here as 'enclosing pastoralism'; agricultural and sedentary occupations were embedded into a culture in which small-scale and baseline mobility was the norm.[40] In archaic Italy, large cities and permanently settled populations were outliers; a relatively new phenomenon that emerged out of a more fluid landscape over several centuries and indeed

---

36 See Corbier (1983) for the full text of the inscription. Generally, conflict over pasture rights in the Republic appear to have focused on competition over who could use the public pasture, as evidenced by the fining of *pecuarii* (e.g., Livy 10.23) and the passage of the Lex Licinia-Sextia (*lex de modo agrorum*), rather than conflict with farmers over the transit of flocks or access to winter grazing on private land. Competition between shepherds and farmers was largely limited to the distribution of newly acquired land or *ager publicus* as part of land reforms (e.g., the *elogium Pollae CIL* 10.6950). For discussion, see Pasquinucci (1979) 92–151; Thompson (1989).
37 Skydsgaard (1974) 17; Pasquinucci (1979) 87–91. Movement of flocks just 10 km could easily provide 500m variation in elevation in stark contrast to the long-distance highly-specialised transhumance of the Medieval period that spanned the entire peninsula, see Barker (1989); Barker *et al.* (1991); Braudel (1972). Thompson (1989) 138 argues, through his historical analysis of Sardinian pastoralism, that minimal regulation was needed for smaller flocks and those making shorter movements.
38 Cato *Agr.* 149 provides a sample contract for winter grazing on private land. A *vir bonus* serves as the primary arbiter, with the Roman courts only necessary in the event of a major dispute. Pasquinucci (1979) 100–2. For historical examples, see Koster (2000) on Greece; Stagno (2019) 315–16 on Ligurian uplands; studies in Costello and Svensson (2018).
39 On seasonal labour for farming: Cato *Agr.* 144–5. Seasonal wage labour was also needed for wool working, at harbour towns for porters and rowers, in public construction, and, it could be argued, for warfare, see Isayev (2017); Roselaar (2019) 38–9.
40 Alizadeh (2010).

one whose sedentary and stable character should not be overstated.[41] The constant small-scale, stochastic mobilities and blurry divisions between sedentary and mobile that characterised Italy's agro-pastoral economy were a central mechanism for connecting diffuse communities across the landscape.

Institutions of connectivity

While a certain level of economic interdependence may have structured interaction across western central Italy during the archaic period, it is not automatic that these economic interactions resulted in deep and profound social connections. Social integration between groups could have been resisted or undermined.[42] That being said, a closer analysis reveals that this was not always the case, and indeed multiple structures appear to have existed to facilitate, and perhaps even encourage, positive connections between different groups.[43] These socially embedded institutions of connectivity further structure the connective latticework, serving both as nodes of interaction and revealing diffuse mechanisms and opportunities that are able to structure interaction between individuals and families.

The symbiotic economic relationship between farmers and shepherds in Italy's mixed agro-pastoral system was made possible, and further reinforced by, social relationships between individuals and families. Ethnographic research into modern Italian shepherding families, as well as comparative evidence from other Mediterranean and Near Eastern cultures, indicates that shepherds and farmers were often different branches of the same extended family structure; different ethnic or kinship groups do not correspond with different subsistence practices.[44] Individuals could also move between different occupations depending on their age – shepherding flocks in the high mountains in their youth and running a small farm in middle-age – thus diversifying the economic base of even a fairly small family group.[45] This can even, arguably, be seen expressed in the mythic life of Romulus, whose early years were spent as a shepherd, before later assuming the leadership role within a community. Trade was therefore mediated through, and served

---

41 Isayev (2017).
42 Indeed, it is possible that the endemic raiding of the archaic period was related to, and arguably reliant on, these very same networks and relationships – especially the movement of pastoralists, whose livestock seem to have been a common target.
43 For later periods: Roselaar (2019); studies in Roselaar (2012).
44 Barker *et al.* (1991); Alizadeh (2010); Porter (2012); Christie *et al.* (2007). The ubiquity of farm sales and shifting occupations are visible in Cato's *De Agricultura* and Plautus' plays, see Isayev (2020). It is also important to remember that the mode of subsistence does not indicate where an individual or family made their home-base. A shepherd could consider their travel to the lowlands in the winter to be a return to their home, a departure from it, or they could consider a third location their primary residence despite their frequent absence.
45 Barker *et al.* (1991). This economic flexibility and diversification seem key to the survival of these communities, see Stagno (2019).

to reinforce, social relationships that were formed between individuals in different subsistence groups, thus allowing for greater long-term stability and access to trade goods or seasonal labour; the marriages brokered in the Republican period between the Eumachii of Pompeii and the Numistrii in Lucania, for example, were aimed at securing their control of the lucrative wool market.[46] Where social ties did not already exist, or where they were weak, they could therefore be created or strengthened. It should be remembered that shepherds were not perennially mobile individuals but often settled for periods within, or adjacent to, agricultural communities (such as during the winter grazing) and this would have provided opportunities for social and economic relationships to develop. Social ties could also be created through marriage or through the incorporation of new individuals and families into the extended family through fictive kinship structures.[47] While many individuals may not have travelled far to make marriages, others would undoubtedly have looked outside the confines of their settlement, ethnic group, or primary occupation for a suitable match.[48] As individuals moved between households and regions, they had to navigate the merging of different practices and cultural differences on issues as diverse as ritual, food preparation, language, birth and death practices, household organisation, production of material culture, resource management, and forms of social or political interaction within the group. Further interactions between families would be made easier by this new knowledge of local custom. Thus, intermarriage was both a testament to, and reinforcer of, social and economic interaction between different groups.

Regional sanctuaries and festivals were important facilitators for such interactions as people came together for joint rituals, and they provided a neutral arena for commercial and social exchange, including the brokering of marriages and other alliances, all under the watchful eye of a deity.[49] Commercial exchange likely included markets and fairs held at or around sanctuaries, such as at the Lucus Feroniae (Dion. Hal. *Ant. Rom.* 3.32.1)

---

46 Roselaar (2019) 48–9; Terrenato (2019).
47 Smith (2006). Italic groups may have practiced patrilocal marriage, in which the woman moved to the household of her husband, evidenced by the use of patrilineal descent in later practices (Corbier [1991]) and interpretation of contemporary funerary evidence (Bietti Sestieri [1992] 146–7, 154, 236). However, this is not definitive; matrilineal descent was also celebrated among the Etruscans, for example. Diverse marriage practices cannot be ruled out and there is no indication that familial bonds were severed by relocation in marriage – the opposite is more probable (Cohen and Naglak [2020]).
48 While some physical anthropologists (Bondioli *et al.* [1986]; Rubini [1996]; Rubini *et al.* [1997], [2007]) have suggested some degree of endogamy was practiced in the Italian population, based on studies of different skeletal traits from individuals in Alfedena and Tarquinia, the evidence is not clear-cut due to small sample sizes and distribution across the region; further analyses using aDNA are needed.
49 Glinister (1997) 78–9. On ritualised exchange, divinely-protected marketplaces, and the purpose of monumental temples at marketplaces: Potts (2015) with bibliography.

and at the Temple of Voltumna near Volsinii (Livy 6.2.2), and temples were often located in proximity to urban marketplaces and ports (i.e., Pyrgi, Gravisca, Forum Boarium at Rome).[50] While direct archaeological evidence of commerce within the sanctuaries themselves is minimal, evidence of production near cult sites, including kilns (at Lavinium) and textile production (at Francavilla Marittima and Lavinium) suggests that commerce did develop around sanctuaries, likely to serve the specific ritual needs of worshippers.[51] Trade and ritual were thus topographically intertwined, each reinforcing the other and capitalising on the influx and concentration of visitors that the other provided. Within the regional landscape, sanctuaries served an important connective function by simultaneously acting as liminal zones between communities and as central places for interaction.[52] As Potts has recently demonstrated, the choice of deity (esp. Herakles), decoration, and monumental architectural form of these sanctuaries appears as part of a deliberate strategy of fostering links between locals and international visitors; the diverse origins of votives in Italian sanctuaries testifies to the success of that strategy.[53] The placement of sanctuaries along major communication and transit routes and at the intersection of trade routes (i.e., Forum Boarium at Rome), however, suggests that this connective strategy was also aligned with patterns of terrestrial mobility and movement, linking different local communities together within Italy.[54] In this respect, sanctuaries and festivals afforded moments of punctuated interaction, at designated times and places, and thus facilitated social and economic connections between diverse, and often semi-mobile, communities across the landscape.[55]

Sanctuaries also allowed the integration of far-flung and individualised social networks through ritualised descent and mythical aetiologies and genealogies. In this way, cult spaces acted as focal points for the negotiation of different identities and connections between communities, not just between the community and the gods.[56] Social, economic, or political connections could thus be solidified through reference to a shared origin narrative in which different groups claimed the same deity or mythic figure as an ancestor or founder (e.g., Herakles, Diomedes, Odysseus, Aeneas). Our historical sources preserve centuries of these overlapping mythic claims, while

---

50 On Roman markets: De Ligt (1993); Roselaar (2019) 46–9; Becker in this volume. On *emporia*: Malkin (2011); Demetriou (2012).
51 Roselaar (2019) 40–6. On textiles: Gleba (2009). See also Becker in this volume.
52 For liminal or frontier sanctuaries marking the extent of the urban hinterland or as regional frontiers: De Polignac (1995); Riva and Stoddart (1996); Cifani (2012) 155–6; Lomas (2012). On rural sanctuaries as central places: Stek (2009); Pelgrom and Stek (2010).
53 Potts (2015). For votive deposits: e.g., Bouma (1996); Diffendale et al. (2016) 13–4, 19–20. On Hercules: Bradley (2005).
54 For transhumance routes and sanctuaries of Hercules: Van Wontherghem (1999); Gros (1995); cf: Bradley (2005). On the river harbour at Rome: Brock (2016).
55 Honeychurch (2014) 310.
56 Potts (2015). On sanctuaries and political leagues: Bourdin (2012) 335–8.

others are hinted at in material culture, especially iconography (coins, vase painting, tomb painting, votives, architecture).[57] Dissecting these different mythological narratives reveals a complex discourse on identity and connection that is constantly reinvented, locally variable, difficult to interpret, and rarely maps onto other networks of identity – mythological or otherwise.

A brief digression into the issue of defining Latinity through ritual serves to demonstrate this tension between ritual configurations of identity and the role of sanctuaries and festivals as institutions of connectivity and loci of community formation. The cult of Jupiter Latiaris, and its associated annual festival (the so-called *Feriae Latinae*), has been cited as a key religious event that distinguished the Latins from their non-Latin neighbours.[58] Despite the etymological link between Latiaris and Latinus (the mythical king and namesake of the Latins), the attendees at the *Feriae Latinae* do not appear to be exclusively Latin – at least in the traditional sense. Dionysius of Halicarnassus (4.49) specifically notes that both the Hernici and two Volscian cities (Ecetra and Antium) joined in a league of friendship with Rome and the Latins under the Roman *rex* Tarquinius Superbus, and that the cult was set up to act as a focal point for this alliance. Dionysius' divergent list of attendees, not present in other accounts, has largely been discounted in scholarship from Mommsen onwards as it contradicts the essentially tribal or ethnic nature of the cult – a circular argument which has proven remarkably resilient in scholarship.[59] That the Volsci and Hernici were later additions, however, is difficult to imagine as the festival itself was celebrated in Dionysius' own time and became strongly linked with Latinity; to add non-Latins to such an account would be counter to our expectations for an authorial retrojection and thus lends some credence to Dionysius' list.[60] While the complex and often highly political historiography of Latinity, from antiquity to the modern period, deserves more attention than can be given here, Dionysius' broader list of attendees at the *Feriae Latinae* clearly complicates attempts to define Latin identity with reference to a series of exclusive cult practices. A similar lack of concurrence on a political or mythological definition of Latinity highlights the fluid and contextual nature of identity and its construction out of a complex latticework of connectivity, in which ritual networks were one layer among many.[61] Thus, shared ritual activity or mythical genealogies, although important institutions and mechanisms for facilitating and solidifying connectivity and social interaction, should be

---

57 E.g., Malkin (1998), (2011); Herring (2009); Farney (2007), (2008); Wiseman (1974); Ceccarelli (2012); Torelli (2018).
58 Cornell (1995) 294–5, (1997).
59 Fowler (1899) 95–7; Alföldi (1965) 11–12.
60 Although certain rituals at the *Feriae Latinae* may have been limited to those who claimed Latin affiliation, it is not clear how such identification would have been adjudicated.
61 Alföldi (1965); Smith (2007); Bourdin (2012) 278–98.

understood as context-dependent and variable rather than as proxies of an enduring identity, ethnic or otherwise.

The degree of connectivity visible in the ritual sphere highlights how connection and interaction in archaic western central Italy was not constrained by putative boundaries between Latins and non-Latins, whether conceived of in political, ethnic, or religious terms. Instead, the lack of a singular proxy that effectively defines any one group exposes the complexity of the connective picture and the multiplicity of overlapping layers within this latticework. For ritual, the disjuncture between identities named in the historical sources and connective networks is particularly clear because we are dealing with specific institutions whose list of participants have been recorded in some fashion. For the economic sphere, environmental constraints on subsistence choices and structuring of trade interactions also allow us to see the interconnections that must have existed. Through a combination of ethnographic analogy and historical comparison, we are able to reconstruct something of the connective networks that would have arisen from, and helped support, the mixed agro-pastoral economy of Italy at this time. In both instances, active choices are being made to connect. Environmental conditions may constrain subsistence choices but they do not determine them; likewise, economic decisions may be supported by certain connective institutions but they do not require them. Rather, the latticework of connectivity that this wide-ranging evidence reveals is a result of human agency at multiple levels of society as people chose to connect. It is the necessary precondition of identity activation, and the foundation upon which it is built.

Moving forward

Connectivity has long been a buzzword in classical archaeology and history but, as the papers in this volume have demonstrated, identifying the material correlates of that connectivity and mapping the implications of different types and degrees of connectivity on societies and communities is much more complicated. The strongly oppositional character of our historical sources and the prevailing discourse on identity construction has limited our ability to effectively model and analyse the archaeological evidence of high levels of connectivity that we uncover. In particular, the link between connectivity and identity construction is often lost in discussions of hybridity and cultural contact, and the activation of identity claims in moments of conflict becomes conflated with the formation of communities themselves. A complex historiography has emerged which attempts to reconcile the overlapping and contradictory networks of interaction, searching either for the perfect metric for tracking connections between communities or a clear narrative of social development towards some vision of unified identity. Yet, we have struggled to move on from our typological impulses and find a new model with which to understand the relationship between connectivity and identity that is accessible via the material record. This chapter has presented an alternative paradigm of community formation that addresses this deficit by arguing for the importance of connectivity and interaction as a precondition for community formation, and for a regional view that focuses on the latticework of connectivity that criss-crosses putative boundaries and provides a foundation for identity development.

Through discussion of the mechanisms and institutions of connectivity, this chapter has demonstrated the utility of the connective model of community laid out in the introduction of this volume and taken up, in various guises, throughout. My fellow contributors have employed archaeological evidence to understand networks of production, trade, and consumption, eschewing conventional labels to varying extents and seeking to understand the underlying connections in human behaviour across the landscape of pre-Roman Italy. Each analysis thus contributes some structure to the latticework discussed here. Connection is not undifferentiated but constrained by a variety of factors – whether that be availability of resources and expertise, or the different structures of trade networks and exchange practices. Combined, these allow us to particularise connectivity at the regional scale and embed it within models that allow for individual and small-group agency. It also provides a structuring mechanism that, arguably, can replace existing models of unitary groups by grounding the 'fuzzy' boundaries that scholars espouse with a more nuanced understanding of the contiguous nature, or not, of specific domains of interaction. Rather than a group with fuzzy boundaries, we can speak of overlapping networks which, at a very basic level, have no boundaries at all but rather intensify or fade at different times, in different places, and in different aspects of society. The mechanisms and institutions which structure connectivity give shape to this latticework, pulling back from an undifferentiated churn of connection to a model which can provide a way forward in our analyses, bridging the gap between the local and the regional.

By refocusing on the latticework of connections and the institutions that structure communities, it is evident that our networks of interaction do not map perfectly onto each other and were not constrained by supposed political or problematic ethnic divisions. Rather, widespread baseline mobility and the existence of numerous mechanisms for supporting social interaction were the norm, and it is through these connective institutions – trade, intermarriage, markets, festivals, and sanctuaries – that the contours of community emerge. It is also these networks of interaction, as much as the rhetoric of identity visible in historical sources, that would allow for the development of a large polity like Rome. These connective institutions and mechanisms, often informal and outside of the political sphere, were the backbone of social cohesion and retained an important role over time. This model challenges us to rethink our definitions of community – rather than simply an urban zone, a region, or the participants in a particular material practice, a community is a collection of connected individuals. Society is thus made up of multiple overlapping communities; these communities are structured in disparate ways, whether around specific nodes or institutions (a shared festival, temple, market, pasture) or through diffuse networks of social and economic relationships. These communities and their connections are dynamic; they predate, support, and also develop alongside the political organisations and identity activations which have come to dominate the historical discourse. While much work remains to be done in tracing all of these networks – ritual, linguistic, social, economic, etc. – and their interrelationships over time, the framework outlined here provides a way forward that places our evidence of connectivity into dialogue with community and identity formation.

Epilogue
Writing of connectivity at a time of isolation

Elena Isayev

The possibility of intersecting with people in the same physical space – to exchange goods, share knowledge, create together, and allow for chance encounters that lead to new ideas and innovation – relies on the ability to move. Yet, in our current moment in the twenty-first century, chances for this kind of connectivity – as distinct from virtual connections through screens and other technological interfaces – have, all of a sudden, become a precious commodity.[1] It is as if such encounters were a distant vision of a privileged existence that was possible in the more innocent past and whose resurgence we look towards in the hopefully not too distant future. The COVID-19 pandemic has resulted in the most extreme period of immobility for people (although not of goods, nor of weapons) across the world in recent history. Crucially, it has reduced the ability of individuals and civilian groups to physically gather and intersect (although this has not prevented ongoing war and conflict). The consequences of such forced isolation will take years to fully emerge as this first requires recognition of the necessity of physical intersections to engender creativity and transformation – the realisation that knowledge is created in transit and that we constantly define and redefine who we are through our connections.[2] The coming together of knowledge-bearers, and the products and frameworks of those processes, within the context of ancient Italy are the main interests of the authors and editors of this volume. At the core of their investigations of connectivity is the mobility of people, whose dynamic intersections have produced a rich body of material, leaving traces in the landscape, inscribed in stone, and in the writings of ancient authors. The studies do not only showcase the presence of

---

* I am grateful to the editors of this volume Jeremy Armstrong and Sheira Cohen for their invitation that has given me the precious opportunity to think together (even if not in person at the moment) and to explore the potential of material evidence to address new questions, not least those which arise from the challenges of the present day.
1 This epilogue was written in 2021.
2 *Knowledges in Transit: Linnaeus's Laplandic Journey (1732)* is an exploration currently being conducted with Staffan Müller-Wille: https://linnaeus-in-lapland.net/, (funded by BA/Leverhulme 2019–20), see Isayev and Müller Wille (2022). As one of its points of departure it uses Secord (2004).

DOI: 10.4324/9781003120728-12

that mobility but critically analyse its diverse forms, drivers, and products. Although it was not the intention, through their analyses, the authors address precisely the question of what may be lost in the current twenty-first-century moment of severely restrained possibilities and restricted spaces where there is potential to engage with others in-person.

Throughout this volume, connectivity is approached carefully to ensure it does not become an all-encompassing term that loses all meaning – an issue most directly confronted by Cohen, Armstrong, and Bernard. It is not presented as something that simply exists, but is investigated through its agents – the people who move and those who facilitate the spatio-temporal opportunities for connections, through the development of infrastructure and institutions. These developments affect the configuration and intensity of the resulting connectivity and need not be orchestrated by ruling authorities. The premise is that mobility is not exceptional in the setting of the ancient Italian peninsula, where the investigations take place. Rather, the evidence suggests that mobility should not be envisioned as a singular act, as that of a settler, but as something ongoing, open ended, and potentially cyclical. For some inhabitants of Italy, mobility would have been a permanent way of life – as for the pastoralists of Heitz's investigation. Decades of debate have focused on whether such people would have been able to move seasonally across extensive territory in pre-Roman Italy, and also the exceptionality of this mode of life. Both Heitz and Cohen challenge the assumption that any long-distance transhumance and migratory movements would have not been possible prior to a unified Roman Italy. Instead, they each present a framework of interdependence, and argue for the prevalence of oral contracts and agreements in the negotiations of rights of use and passage between shepherds/flock-owners and the farmers/landowners along their routes. In the earlier period, in what are termed pre-state societies, such agreements would have mattered more than any political territorial unity. To take these propositions seriously means to rethink how we understand such directives as those inscribed on the famous second-century CE inscription from Saepinum (*CIL* 9.2438). Cohen and Heitz demonstrate that, rather than seeing it as introduction of new protections for the shepherds, it is about preserving the traditional rights of movement for pastoralists, without experiencing harassment from farmers and other landowners – rights, and patterns of using and moving through the landscape, that would have gone back centuries.

Part of such rethinking requires us to envisage a largely fluid landscape, out of which the permanent settlements and cities of archaic Italy emerged. These were, as Cohen suggests, likely outliers well into the archaic period. Such a positioning has a profound impact on how we understand the appearance of centralised settlement conglomerates – the later cities, especially of Etruria, Campania, and Latium, and the Greek-speaking *poleis* on the coasts. It also allows for a better understanding of the role of such vast archaic settlements as Arpi in Puglia. The site features a walled, ditch-and-bank enclosure encompassing some 10 km^2 of what appears to have been unbuilt land with scattered settlement clusters. As Heitz observes, the protective enclosure seems inadequate to repel military attack but would have served well enough to prevent flocks from leaving and to keep out intruders. Here may be an example of a stable or sedentary structure designed for mobile communities, perhaps of pastoralists and their herds to use seasonally, or as part of a life-cycle that anticipates moments of sedentism for certain age groups, or along gender lines. Whoever its inhabitants were, the creation of Arpi and the nearby communal burial grounds are evidence of collective decision-making and the joint investment of resources and labour. Drawing on such mobile-oriented approaches to sites and material, Heitz's study ambitiously explores the transformations in the form of wealth accumulation and social stratification among Italic communities, and the way in which increasing private land ownership and pasturage affected landscape use and settlement. Communal burial grounds appear to signify increasing sedentism and some – those at Ripacandida, for example – have evidence indicating that the earliest burials were associated with women, alongside children and the elderly. These members of a predominantly mobile community were the ones more likely to live in longer-term stable settlements. Defining a settlement as belonging to more sedentary or more mobile communities is challenging, as people on the move are more difficult to track, and it is precisely the accoutrements associated with a sedentary lifestyle that provide the greatest visibility in our material and historical records. People who spend a considerable part of their time moving are less likely to develop their own substantial pottery or weaving industries which are less conducive to mobile lifestyles. Instead, we could imagine acquisition of such objects from markets when needed, the establishment of smaller household-size production units, and the use of more perishable and transportable material such as leather. These observations challenge us to find new approaches to understanding our evidence base. To identify an object as a distaff or a sceptre – as Heitz illustrates – is to commit ourselves to different story lines.

   True to their aspirations, the studies here do not revert to considering isolated histories of individual settlements. Sites and regions are not seen as end points of accumulation but presented as part of what Tim Ingold might term 'meshworks' – dynamic intersections of lifeways and interconnected networks.[3] The material culture of the Bradano Valley, for example, is not examined by Peruzzi to identify a particular group as ethnically or culturally coherent. Instead, it is used to showcase the diverse social groupings of the inhabitants. The region, it is argued, formed a corridor that channelled people, goods, and knowledges between the coast and the interior. There is a resistance to any assumptions that the direction of this channelling was *into* the interior, instead focusing on the diverse roles that the different landscapes allowed for. Engaging with such passage of resources and people seems to

---

3 Ingold (2011) 63–94.

correlate well with urban development, yet we should resist the temptation to assume that it was culture 'in' and raw materials 'out'. It is notable that Rome and Veii, two of the powerhouses of Archaic central Italy, were facilitators of routeways and the passage of resources through the interior, while the few sections of Italy's Tyrrhenian coast that were suitable for deep water harbours were overseen by such coastal sites as Caere and Cyme.[4] Peruzzi's investigation of patterns on the Adriatic side of Italy further cautions against assuming that sites in the interior were less connected, thus challenging spatially coherent cultural zones. She showcases how the value of artefacts is derived from the diverse social contexts within which they are used and that in turn their materiality structures the practices that shape these contexts. This is in line with other recent studies, most recently by Pitts, that focus on objectscapes as a way to understand sociocultural patterns, transfer of knowledge, and innovation.[5] Interaction is central to these processes, and as foregrounded in the introductory chapter by Cohen and Armstrong, there is now increasing recognition, including in Gruen's latest work,[6] that more care was given to common cultural traits than lineage or regionally derived ethnic ties. These approaches expose the way connectivity is central to identity construction. Objects are not treated as exhibitions of identity, but rather as bundles of connectivities – defined by their interactions as Cohen and Armstrong note, rather than their self-perception or performance. Such modes of social construction allow for distinction from moments of identity activation that prevail during conflicts, which, as Cohen shows, are often conflated with the formation of communities in discussions of hybridity and culture contact. How then does an infrastructure, such as citizenship, emerge out of this dynamism? As a form of persistent 'identity' activation, it provides a mode of contractual, and hence seemingly more binding, allegiance. But, as Smith observes, it also provides non-personal identities that allow for neutral trading relations. This is distinct from a system that relies on personal agreements, as found in forms of gift-exchange, and through reciprocal hospitality contracts, like those symbolised by the *tessera hospitalis*.[7] Investigating citizenship through the connectivities expressed in this volume, as witnessed in communities of practice, is an exciting prospect that new research is already embracing, such as Corinna Riva's most recent project, just begun, on precisely these issues.[8] The studies here will be essential for such investigations.

The mobility of artisans confronted here is presented as pervasive, but with the recognition that such movement took different forms, and could be

---

4 Isayev (2017) 71–87, for overview of the positioning of such sites, routeways, and interconnectivity.
5 Pitts (2019).
6 Gruen (2020).
7 As for example mentioned by Plautus in his comedy *Poenulus*, 1047–55. For overview see: Isayev (2017) 100–4.
8 In relation to the new project see Riva's preceding publication (2020).

either autonomous or tethered, which could also mean forced – especially in contexts of slavery. It is particularly difficult to understand, from the evidence of this early period, how individual movement, such as that of entrepreneurs or freelancers, would have fit into wider networks of dependency, obligation, and responsibility. How exceptional were the imagined scenarios presented by later ancient authors who envision, for example, craftspeople forming part of substantial troupes, like those of Demaratus who were to have accompanied him on his exilic journey in the eighth century BCE from Corinth to Etruria.[9] We would expect some to have moved for training, some as slaves or indentured labour, while others would have travelled as dependent groups with patrons. The evidence does allow for the investigation of other aspects of that mobility. It shows not only that the artisans were highly mobile but, as Robinson indicates, it is the diversity of their origins that characterises the ceramics of early sites, which runs counter to the narratives of single-origin incomers that pervades literary accounts. But to what extent is artisans' mobility reflective of more general mobile trends? Robinson's question is beginning to be addressed most directly by bioarchaeological studies, which are increasingly able to identify whether individuals were locals or incomers to the place where they were finally buried. They are also able to signal relative distance between the final resting place and the regions where the individual originated. There is still substantial honing of the bioarchaeological methods needed before we can fully understand what the results reveal – as the findings from the site of Metapontum and its surrounding countryside show.[10] Still, the cumulative analysis so far points to high rates of population turnover in most communities, and various projects are in preparation to test the parameters of these fluctuating rates – preliminary evidence suggests that having one third of a buried community made up of people not born at the site as a norm may be reasonable.[11]

In this volume, the ability of people from diverse regions to come together without restrictions is taken for granted. This is in line with what we find in the ancient historical narratives, which mention ports of free trade and treaties that create privileged exchange conditions. Despite the apparent existence of restrictions on trading goods, they provide little evidence to suggest authorities imposed constraints on free-people from abroad coming together, whether for work or celebration.[12] This is not to deny the variety of interdependent relationships and ties that would have dictated the ability of

---

9 The story of Demaratus is recounted in various versions: Livy 1.34–5; Dion. Hal. *Ant. Rom.* 3.46–9; Strabo 5.2.2; Polybius 6.11a.7; Pliny *NH* 35.43.152. For overview see Cornell (1995) 122–30; Walbank (1999) 672–3; Isayev (2017) 98–105.
10 For Metapontum, see studies by Rathman *et al.* (2017), (2019), with commentary by Robinson in this volume.
11 As an example of current projects, see Altschul *et al.* (2020), and in relation to ancient Italy the proposition and overview is here: Isayev (2017), Chapter 2.
12 Isayev (2017), for example, 220–7, 305–7, 335–8, 370–7.

individuals to move. Against this backdrop, the question of who, and what forces, drove the connectivities remains. Even commercial movement, as Bernard observes, cannot be fully explained through the simple availability of, or demand for, resources. We need to envisage more complex and varied needs and competing interests, which resulted in long distance trade of such commodities as olive oil and wine, despite their availability in most regions around the Mediterranean. At the other end of the spectrum, value could be assigned to the distance over which objects and technologies had travelled to reach the recipient, giving them real or perceived exotic value. As Helms' studies show, knowledge of that distance and 'the far away' could be intrinsically linked with power.[13] There is power, then, in controlling connectivity. The issue of how connectivities were catalysed is framed in this volume by critically examining the traditional roles assigned to craftspeople and elites, whereby the former is at the behest of the latter. To conceive of artisanal production as relegated to the commissioning impulses of the elites, however, would be to negate the innovation at work in craft production and its ability to shape the attributes of status and identity. Instead, the studies here recentre the role of the maker and address Smith's call to look deeper into the way artisanal and craft activity constitutes and transforms the notion and reality of power. This does not ignore the fact that elites were also producers as well as consumers, as highlighted by Cohen and Armstrong. Nor is it to negate the potential that elites had to catalyse opportunities, through patronage and investment in sites, infrastructure, and resource accumulation, as well as brokering exchange through contracts or treaties. Rather, the studies showcase the way craftspeople, as social agents and culture bearers, were not only conditioned by structures but shaped those structures in turn. This is made visible, for example, in the particular choice of styles of matt-painted pottery that Bernardo-Ciddio depicts as a discourse with communities across the Adriatic. This allows a deeper look at the mechanisms by which the mobility of people may transfer into visible changes in material culture. Focusing on the funerary deposition of metalworkers' handiwork, Iaia shows the way these knowledge bearers, in transferring culture, affected identity formation in Etruria through a distinction of status centred on differentiation along gender lines. He traces the interrelationship between transformations in ritual practice, the body as social locus, and a rise in metalwork production, to showcase the role of bronzesmiths in constructing new collective and individual identities for emerging social groups.

These transformations occurred against a backdrop of settlement centralisation and 'urbanisation' (in 'scare quotes', as Smith notes) in the tenth through eighth centuries BCE; sites which, in turn, allowed for higher densities of interactions and innovation through the transfer of different symbolic and knowledge systems. They also led to more intense and larger group

---

13 Helms' (1988), (1993) influential studies, as noted by Smith in this volume.

conflicts. The development of iron ore is central to these forms of power display and resulting conquest, but its relation to trade and sociopolitical transformations still remains debatable. Bernard, in his exploration of the interdependence of different forces, suggests that in relation to Etruria – a key iron exporter – the involvement of its elites in conflicts appears to have driven the demand and search for quality iron, rather than the discovery of iron ore deposits, which then led to the Iron Age elites becoming commercialists. The access to metal resources, and with it the know-how to produce better weaponry, allowed for increased control through coercion, territorial acquisition, and the creation of centres of exchange and production. Such hubs of production and exchange – whether in centralised habitations, at sanctuary sites, or mobile workshops – form part of an infrastructure of innovation and trade relations. Here they are investigated less as stand-alone sites, but as communities of practice, or what Bernardo-Ciddio calls taskscapes. Armstrong's analysis of metalworking environments depicts the way these constitute overlapping *chaînes opératoires*, and the possibility for the co-existence of smaller and mobile production centres – even including smelting sites which required particular resources and raw materials – alongside larger, more centralised operations. The dynamic nature of workshops, Armstrong argues, is what contributed to the rapid dispersal of techniques and styles in relation to bronze working around the Mediterranean. This mobile network appears to have even extended into Europe, as Iaia's analysis demonstrates. These also allowed for the existence of multiple networks and diverse nodes of control, without which it is hard to imagine how, for example, large military endeavours, that required a rapid response, would have been operationalised. We may presume that Dionysius I's need of 140,000 shields would have used the communication channels provided by such meshworks to enlist and, through elite nodes of control, coerce the vast number of craftspeople necessary to carry out the job.

Underpinning this reconstruction of the ancient environment are flexible working practices and spaces, as well as concentrated moments of meeting that provided the best possibility to encounter the widest range of people, skills, and thus heightened the potential for exchange. Key to creating moments of concentrated encounter would have been investments in infrastructure, whether by making routeways safe and easy to travel, creating a calendar of markets and festivals, or constructing sites with the necessary provisions, including that of sacred protection. Temples and sanctuary sites played a significant role in this infrastructure and, as Smith notes, formed an important part of trade relations. In conjunction with such sites, Becker and Cohen investigate how periodic gatherings at festivals or markets allowed for the simultaneous presence of diverse knowledge bearers and those who, through products and symbols, conduct and circulate that knowledge. As Becker notes, the presence of a widely recognised calendar, which allowed for regional and supra-regional markets and festivals, is one of the multiple structures that facilitated and encouraged interconnectivity between groups.

It provided for what Cohen terms 'punctuated moments of interaction', and as such we need to revisit the role of such festivals as the *Feriae Latinae*. These are usually explored through the lens of exclusive identity formation, yet its primary role was perhaps just such an intersection, as it was not exclusively Latins who were its attendees. Sanctuary sites that were not directly connected to any single settlement, such as Rossano di Vaglio in Lucania, present a multiplicity of provenances for the votives and dedications deposited there, indicating its use by multiple communities. This is also evident in the locations of early religious sites, and Potts' studies have shown the ways in which many Archaic temples were positioned to privilege access from routeways, rather than city-centres.[14]

Introducing connectivity as a driver for understanding the processes of settlement centralisation and monumental construction projects provides a counter to explanatory models that use sedentism as a starting point for the emergence of such sites. If we take seriously the evidence showcased in this volume, which positions mobility and opportunities for connectivity at the core of societal transformation, then the challenge is to understand how sedentary practices fit into this imaginary landscape. It means to move away from narrow definitions of sedentism, and see it too as something more dynamic or, at the very least, as predicated on intersections and the movement of people. Massey's observations about place as a cultural system come to mind here. She argued for seeing place not as a site, but as an intersection of lifeways, a coming together of stories so far. She asserts that it is 'not through some visceral belonging (some barely changing rootedness, as many would have it) but through the practising of place, the negotiation of intersecting trajectories; place as an arena where negotiation is forced upon us'.[15]

In our current, twenty-first-century moment of constrained free-movement – which the COVID-19 pandemic has pushed to an extreme, but which the proliferation of borders (physical, virtual, and offshored) has been increasingly inhibiting for decades – the challenge is how we re-create and argue for the importance of communities of practice, the opportunities to experiment and learn by doing through being in-person with each other, and to enliven the widest possible connections. There is no doubt that innovative virtual interfaces and new technologies have been a lifeline, for sustaining creativity, co-working, knowledge-sharing, and forms of distanced social existence. But to what extent do these provide opportunities for chance encounters and the unexpected, which themselves allow for experiencing other modes of knowledge production in situ? What kind of innovations do they lead to and what is lost without them? The value of knowledge in transit may not be visible yet, as we are still drawing on the reserves of such encounters prior to isolation. But how long will the reserve last, and how long will it take to replenish it?

---

14 Potts (2015).
15 Massey (2005) 154. For thinking about ancient mobility, connectivity, and place through the relational approach of Massey and others: Isayev (2017) 390–4.

Bibliography

Aa.Vv. (1968), *La città e il suo territorio; atti del Settimo convegno di studi sulla Magna Grecia, Taranto 8–12 Ottobre 1967.* Naples.

Aa.Vv. (1971), *Popoli Anellenici in Basilicata. Catalogue of an exhibition at Potenza 1971.* Naples.

Aa.Vv. (1981), *L'Etruria mineraria.* Florence.

Aa.Vv. (2001), *Problemi della chora coloniale dall'Occidente al Mar Nero: atti del quarantesimo Convegno di studi sulla Magna Grecia, Taranto, 29 settembre-3 ottobre 2000.* Taranto.

Abbingh, G. and A.J. Nijboer (2014), 'Auf des Messers Schneide: "Stahlproduktion" im 7. Jh. v. Chr. in Italien?', *Beiträge zur Ur- und Frühgeschichte Mitteleuropas* 75: 111–31.

Abell, N. (2014), *Reconsidering a Cultural Crossroads: A Diachronic Analysis of Ceramic Production, Consumption, and Exchange Patterns at Bronze Age Ayia Irini, Kea, Greece.* PhD Dissertation. University of Cincinnati.

Abell, N. (2020), 'Rethinking Household-Based Production at Ayia Irini, Kea: An Examination of Technology and Organization in a Bronze Age Community of Practice', *AJA* 124: 381–416.

Aberson, M., M. Biella, M. Wullschleger, and M. Di Fazio (eds.) (2014), *Entre archéologie et histoire: dialogues sur divers peoples de l'Italie préromaine.* Bern.

Acconcia, V. and G. Bartoloni (2007), 'La casa del re', *Materiali per Populonia* 6: 11–29.

Acconcia, V. and F. Cambi (2009), 'Lo scavo della spiaggia di Baratti a Populonia', in F. Cambi, F. Cavari, and C. Mascione (eds.), *Materiali da costruzione e produzione del ferro: studi sull'economia populoniese fra periodo etrusco e romanizzazione.* 171–80. Bari.

Acconcia, V. and M. Milletti (2009), 'Pratiche metallurgiche e circolazione di saperi all'origine di Populonia', in F. Cambi, F. Cavari, and C. Mascione (eds.), *Materiali da costruzione e produzione del ferro: studi sull'economia populoniese fra periodo etrusco e romanizzazione.* 141–7. Bari.

Acconcia, V. and V. Nizzo (2009), 'Indagini nell'area sud-orientale dell'acropoli: periodi medio e tardo-repubblicano', *Materiali per Populonia* 8: 61–92.

Achilli, A., A. Olivieri, M. Pala, E. Metspalu, S. Fornarino, A. Battaglia, M. Accetturo, I. Kutuev, E. Khusnutdinova, E. Pennarun, N. Cerutti, C. Di Gaetano, F. Crobu, D. Palli, G. Matullo, A.S. Santachiara-Benerecetti, L. Cavalli-Sforza, O. Semino, R. Villems, H.-J. Bandelt, A. Piazza, and A. Torroni (2007), 'Mitochondrial DNA Variation of Modern Tuscans Supports the Near Eastern Origin of Etruscans', *American Journal of Human Genetics* 80: 759–68.

Adams, J. (2003), *Bilingualism and the Latin Language*. Cambridge.
Adams, W.Y. and E.W. Adams (1991), *Archaeological Typology and Practical Reality: A Dialectical Approach to Artifact Classification and Sorting*. Cambridge.
Adinolfi, R. (1987), 'La *facis* protostorica e precoloniale di Pozzuoli e nuovi studi sulla fondazione di Dicearchia', *Puteoli. Studi di storia antica* 11: 93–105.
Agolli, E. (2014), *The Shaping of Social Complexity, Networks and Cultural Transmissions: Pottery from the Bronze and Iron Age Communities of Southern Illyria and Northern Epirus (2500–500 B.C.)*. PhD Dissertation. University of California, Los Angeles.
Agolli, E., E. Ndreçka, B. Kaufman, H. Ma, S. Liu, and J. Wang (2020), 'A Comparison of Handmade and Wheel-made Pottery Technology form the Iron Age Layers of the Cave of Tren (Southeast Albania): Investigating Fabric Composition and Decorative Surfaces through X-Ray Fluorescence Spectroscopy', in I. Miloglav (ed.), *Recent Developments in Archeometry and Archaeological Methodology in South-Eastern Europe*. 82–102. Newcastle upon Tyne.
Agostiniani, L. (2013), 'The Language', in J. Turfa (ed.), *The Etruscan World*. 457–77. London.
Agostiniani, L. (2016), 'Sull' aequipondium di Caere', *SE* 78: 157–71.
Agusta-Boularot, S., S. Huber, and W. Van Andriga (eds.) (2017), *Quand naissent les dieux. Fondation des sanctuaires antiques: motivations, agents, lieux*. Rome.
Alderighi, L. (2015), 'Rotte commerciali nel distretto minerario tirrenico tra VI e V secolo a.C.', in *La Corsica e Populonia. Atti del XXVIII Convegno di studi etruschi ed italici: Bastia – Alria, Piombino – Populonia, 25–29 ottobre 2011*. 461–82. Rome.
Alderighi, L., M. Benvenuti, F. Cambi, L. Chiarantini, C.X.H. Chiesa, A. Corretti, A. Dini, M. Firmati, L. Pagliantini, C. Principe, L. Quaglia, and L. Zito (2013), 'Aithale. Ricerche e scavi all'Isola d'Elba. Produzione siderurgica e territorio insulare nell'antichità', *ASNP* 5(2): 169–226.
Alessandri, A. (2013), *Latium Vetus in the Bronze Age and Early Iron Age/Il Latium Vetus nell'età del Bronzo e nella prima età del Ferro*. Oxford.
Alföldi, A. (1965), *Early Rome and the Latins*. Ann Arbor.
Algazi, G. (2005), 'Diversity Rules: Peregrine Horden and Nicholas Purcell's *Corrupting Sea*', *Mediterranean History Review* 20: 227–45.
Alizadeh, A. (2008), 'Mobile Pastoralism in Late Prehistory', in H. Barnard and W. Wendrich (eds.), *The Archaeology of Mobility: Old World and New World Nomadism*. 91–5. Los Angeles.
Alizadeh, A. (2010), 'The Rise of the Highland Elamite State in Southwestern Iran: "Enclosed" or Enclosing Nomadism?', *Current Anthropology* 51: 353–83.
Allan, W. (2001), 'Euripides in Megale Hellas: Some Aspects of the Early Reception of Tragedy', *G&R* 48: 67–86.
Altschul, J.H., K.W. Kintigh, M. Aldenderfer, E. Alonzi, I. Armit, J.A. Barceló, C.S. Beekman, P. Bickle, D.W. Bird, S.E. Ingram, E. Isayev, A.W. Kandel, R. Kiddey, H.T. Kienon-Kaboré, F. Niccolucci, C.S. Ragsdale, B.K. Scaffidi, and S.G. Ortman (2020), 'Opinion: To Understand How Migrations Affect Human Securities, Look to the Past', *Proceedings of the National Academy of Sciences* 117(34): 20342–5.
Anderson, B. (1972), 'The Idea of Power in Javanese Culture', in C. Holt (ed.), *Culture and Politics in Indonesia*. 1–69. Ithaca.
Anderson, B. (1983), *Imagined Communities: Reflections on the Origin and Spread of Nationalism*. London.

Andrade, T. (2010), 'A Chinese Farmer, Two African Boys, and a Warlord: Toward a Global Microhistory', *Journal of World History* 21: 573–91.

Andrea, Z. (1975), 'I contatti fra l'Albania del sud e l'Italia meridionale durante il primo ferro', in *Civiltà preistoriche e protostoriche della Daunia: atti del Colloquio Internazionale di Preistoria e Protostoria Della Daunia, Foggia, 24–29, aprile 1973*. 348–54. Florence.

Appadurai, A. (ed.) (1986), *The Social Life of Things: Commodities in Cultural Perspective*. Cambridge.

Aranguren, B., G. Giachi, and P. Pallecchi (2009), 'L'area siderurgica di Rondelli ed il contest produttivo etrusco nl Golfo di Follonica e al Puntone di Scarlino', in F. Cambi, F. Cavari, and C. Mascione (eds.), *Materiali da costruzione e produzione del ferro: studi sull'economia populoniese fra periodo etrusco e romanizzazione*. 159–62. Bari.

Arbeid, B. (2009), 'Urna cineraria fittile', in A. Romualdi (ed.), *Villa Corsini a Castello*. 217–20. Florence.

Armstrong, J. (2013), '"Bands of Brothers": Warfare and Fraternity in Early Rome', *JAH* 1: 53–69.

Armstrong, J. (2016a), *War and Society in Ancient Rome: From Warlords to Generals*. Cambridge.

Armstrong, J. (2016b), 'The Ties that Bind: Military Cohesion in Archaic Rome', in J. Armstrong (ed.), *Circum Mare: Themes in Ancient Warfare*. 101–19. Leiden.

Armstrong, J., J. Emmitt, and A. McAlister (forthcoming), 'Variations in Fe and Sn in Ancient Italian Bronze Armour and their Relationship to Production Techniques'.

Armstrong, J. and A. Rhodes-Schroder (eds.) (forthcoming), *Adoption, Adaption, and Innovation in Pre-Roman Italy: Paradigms for Cultural Change*. Turnhout.

Armstrong, J. and J. Richardson (2017), 'Authors, Archaeology, and Arguments: Evidence and Models for Early Roman Politics', *Antichthon* 51: 1–20.

Arnold, D.E. (1981), 'A Model for the Identification of Non-Local Ceramic Distribution: View from the Present', in H. Howard and E. Morris (eds.), *Production and Distribution: A Ceramic Viewpoint*. 31–44. Oxford.

Arnold, D.E. (1985), *Ceramic Theory and Cultural Process*. Cambridge.

Asheri, D. (1999), 'Processi di "decolonizzazione" in Magna Grecia: il caso di Poseidonia Lucana', in *La colonisation grecque en Méditerranée occidentale: actes de la rencontre scientifique en hommage à George Vallet*. 361–70. Rome-Naples.

Aslaksen, O. (2015), 'Travellers of the Bronze Age', *Archaeologia Austriaca* 99: 11–30.

Bachhuber, Ch. (2011), 'Negotiating Metal and the Metal Form in the Royal Tombs of Alacahöyük in North-Central Anatolia', in T. Wilkinson and S. Sherratt (eds.), *Interweaving Worlds: Systemic Interactions in Eurasia, 7th to 1st Millennia BC*. 158–74. Oxford.

Baglivo, B. (2013), 'Un ergasterion tarantino a Torre di Satriano: installazioni artigianali peril tetto dell'*anaktoron*', in M. Osanna and M. Vullo (eds.), *Segni del potere. Oggetti di lusso dal Mediterraneo nell'Appennino lucano di età arcaica*. 69–73. Venosa.

Bailo Modesti, G. and P. Gastaldi (eds.) (1999), *Prima di Pithecusa. I più antichi materiali greci del golfo di Salerno. Catalogo della mostra, 29 Aprile 1999, Pontecagnano Faiano, Museo Nazionale dell'Agro Picentino*. Naples.

Baitinger, H. (2018), 'La dedica di armi e armature nei santuari greci – una sintesi', in R. Graells i Fabregat and F. Longo (eds.), *Armi Votive in Magna Grecia*. 1–20. Mainz.

Bakhuizen, S.C. (1976), *Chalcis-in-Euboea, Iron and Chalcidians Abroad*. Leiden.
Balot, R.K. (2021), 'Epilogue: Identity, Politics, Power: From Classical Antiquity to the 21st Century', *Polis: The Journal for Ancient Greek and Roman Political Thought* 38: 127–33.
Barker, G. (1989), 'Archaeology of the Italian Shepherd', *Cambridge Classical Journal* 35: 1–19.
Barker, G., A. Grant, P. Beavitt, N. Christie, J. Giorgi, P. Hoare, T. Leggio, and M. Migliavacca (1991), 'Ancient and Modern Pastoralism in Central Italy. An Interdisciplinary Study in the Cicolano Mountains', *PBSR* 59: 15–88.
Barresi, L. (2016), *Distribution of Daunian Pottery in Croatia and Slovenia, its Influence along the Amber Route to Central Europe*. PhD Dissertation. Charles University, Prague.
Barresi, S. (2005), 'I vasi del Gruppo Intermedio e la prima fase della ceramografia italiota in ambito ionico: proposta di analisi e brevi considerazioni', in M. Denoyelle, F. Lippolis, M. Mazzei, and C. Pouzadoux (eds.), *La céramique apulienne. Bilan et perspectives. Actes de la table ronde de Naples, 2000*. 143–53. Naples.
Barresi, S. (2014), 'Sicilian Red-figure Vase-painting: The Beginning, the End', in S. Schierup and V. Sabetai (eds.), *The Regional Production of Red-Figure Pottery: Greece, Magna Grecia and Etruria*. 336–54. Copenhagen.
Barresi, S. (2018), 'Il Gruppo di Locri in Sicilia: proposte di analisi e riflessioni', in M. Denoyelle, C. Pouzadoux, and F. Silvestrelli (eds.), *Mobilità dei pittori e identità delle produzioni*. 39–61. Naples.
Barrett, J.C. (1987), 'Contextual Archaeology', *Antiquity* 61: 468–73.
Barrett, J.C. (2001), 'Agency, the Duality of Structure, and the Problem of the Archaeological Record', in I. Hodder (ed.), *Archaeological Theory Today*. 141–64. Cambridge.
Barth, F. (1961), *Nomads of South Persia: The Basseri Tribe of the Khamseh Confederacy*. Oslo.
Barth, F. (1969), *Ethnic Groups and Boundaries: The Social Organization of Culture Difference*. Oslo.
Bartoloni, G. (1989), *La cultura villanoviana: all'inizio della storia etrusca*. Rome.
Bartoloni, G. (2005), 'Populonia (Piombino, LI). The Necropolis of Piano and Poggio delle Granate', in P. Attema, A. Nijboer, and A. Zifferero (eds.), *Papers in Italian Archaeology VI: Communities and Settlements from the Neolithic to the Early Medieval Period*. 164–77. Oxford.
Bartoloni, G. (2015), 'Populonia e le isole del Tirreno centrale tra VIII e VII secolo a.C.', in *La Corsica e Populonia. Atti del XXVIII Convegno di studi etruschi ed italici: Bastia – Alria, Piombino – Populonia, 25–29 ottobre 201*. 337–54. Rome.
Bartoloni, G., F. Buranelli, V. D'Atri, and A. De Santis (1987), *Le urne a capanna rinvenute in Italia*. Florence.
Bartoloni, G., M. Milletti, and F. Pitzalis (2015), 'Populonia – Poggio del Telegrafo: l'ultima fase residenziale', *Materiali per Populonia* 11: 57–75.
Bartoloni, G. and M. Pandolfini (1972), 'OP 4–5 Veio (Isola Farnese). Continuazione degli scavi nella necropoli villanoviana in località Quattro Fontanili', *NSA* 26: 295–9.
Bass, B. (1998), 'Early Neolithic Offshore Accounts: Remote Islands, Maritime Exploitations, and the Trans-Adriatic Cultural Network', *JMA* 11: 165–91.
Batović, Š. (1975), 'Le relazioni tra la Daunia e la sponda orientale dell'Adriatico nell'età del Ferro', in *Civiltà preistoriche e protostoriche della Daunia: atti del*

Colloquio Internazionale di Preistoria e Protostoria Della Daunia, Foggia, 24–29, Aprile 1973. 340–7. Florence.

Baur, Ch. (2019), 'Tradition verpflichtet. Zur Chronologie und Entwicklung italischer Vollgriffschwerter', in S. Hye and U. Töchterle (eds.), *UPIKU:TAUKE Festschrift für Gerhard Tomedi zum 65. Geburtstag.* 12–80. Bonn.

Becker, H. (2002–2003 [2006]), 'The Etruscan *Castellum*: Fortified Settlements and Regional Autonomy in Etruria', *Etruscan Studies* 9: 85–95.

Becker, H. (2008), '*Urbs, Oppidum, Castellum, Vicus*: Settlement Differentiation and Landscape Nomenclature in Etruria', in G. Camporeale (ed.), *La città murata in Etruria: XXVth Convegno di Studi Etruschi ed Italici, Chianciano Terme, Sarteano, Chiusi, 30 marzo-3 aprile 2005: in memoria di Massimo Pallottino.* 71–8. Pisa.

Becker, H. (2010), 'The Written Word and Proprietary Inscriptions in Etruria', *Etruscan Studies* 13: 131–48.

Becker, H. (2013), 'Etruscan Political Systems and Law', in J. Turfa (ed.), *The Etruscan World.* 351–72. London.

Becker, H. (2017a), 'Economy in the Archaic and Classical Periods, 580–450 BCE', in A. Naso (ed.), *Etruscology.* 1013–29. Berlin.

Becker, H. (2017b), 'Economy in the Late Classical and Hellenistic Periods, 450–250 BCE', in A. Naso (ed.), *Etruscology.* 1129–40. Berlin.

Becker, H. (2020), 'Evidence for Etruscan Archives: Tracking the Epigraphic Habit in Tombs, the Sacred Sphere, and at Home', in R.D. Whitehouse (ed.), *Etruscan Literacy in Its Social Context.* 159–80. London.

Becker, M. (2015), 'Ancient Maya Markets: Architectural Grammar and Market Identifications', in E. King (ed.), *The Ancient Maya Marketplace: The Archaeology of Transient Space.* 90–110. Tuscon.

Bell, S. and P. Du Plessis (eds.) (2020), *Roman Law before the Twelve Tables: An Interdisciplinary Approach.* Edinburgh.

Benco, N.L. (1988), 'Morphological Standardization: An Approach to the Study of Craft Specialization', in C.C. Kolb and M. Kirkpatrick (eds.), *A Pot for All Reasons: Ceramic Ecology Revisited.* 57–72. Philadelphia.

Benelli, E. (2015), 'Un frammento di iscrizione lapidaria etrusca dall'acropoli di Populonia', in *La Corsica e Populonia. Atti del XXVIII Convegno di studi etruschi ed italici: Bastia – Alria, Piombino – Populonia, 25–29 ottobre 2011.* 329–35. Rome.

Bennett, J. (2010), *Vibrant Matter: A Political Ecology of Things.* Durham, NC.

Bentley, G. (1987), 'Ethnicity and Practice', *CSSH* 29: 24–55.

Ben-Yosef, E. (2016), 'Back to Solomon's Era: Results of the First Excavations at "Slaves" Hill (Site 34, Timna, Israel)', *BASOR* 376: 169–98.

Berg, I. (2004), 'The Meanings of Standardisation: Conical Cups in the Late Bronze Age Aegean', *Antiquity* 78: 74–85.

Berger, D., J. Soles, A. Giumlia-Mair, G. Brügmann, G. Galili, N. Lockhoff, and E. Pernicka (2019), 'Isotope Systematics and Chemical Composition of Tin Ingots from Mochlos (Crete) and Other Late Bronze Age Sites in the Eastern Mediterranean Sea: An Ultimate Key to Tin Provenance?', *PLoS ONE* 14(6): e0218326.

Berkin, J. (2003), *The Orientalizing Bucchero from the Lower Building at Poggio Civitate (Murlo).* Philadelphia.

Bernard, S. (2014), 'Ballast, Mining, and Stone Cargoes in the *Lex Portorii Asiae*', *ZPE* 191: 182–4.

Bernard, S. (2017), 'The Status and Mobility of Coroplasts and Building Workers in the Epigraphy of Central Italy, 300–50 BC', in P. Lulof, I. Manzini, and C. Rescigno (eds.), *Deliciae Fictiles V: Networks and Workshops. Architectural Terracottas and Decorative Roof Systems in Italy and Beyond.* 499–507. Oxford.

Berrendonner, C. (2009), 'La surveillance des poids et mesures par les autorités romaines: l'apport de la documentation épigraphique latine', *Cahiers Du Centre Gustave Glotz* 20: 351–70.

Bertinetti, M. (1985), 'Iscrizioni su materiali ponderali', in R. Bussi and V. Vandelli (eds.), *Misurare la terra; centuriazione e coloni nel mondo romano. Città, agricoltura, commercio. Materiali da Roma e dal suburbio.* 208–10. Modena.

Bežkovič, A.S. (1969), 'Nomadenwirtschaft und Lebensweise der Kirgisen (19. bis Anfang des 20. Jahrhunderts)', in L. Földes (ed.), *Viehwirtschaft und Hirtenkultur*, 94–111. Budapest.

Bhabha, H. (1994), *The Location of Culture.* London.

Biagi, F. and M. Milletti (2017), 'Nuovi dati sulla necropolis dell'età del Ferro di Poggio e Piano delle Granate a Populonia (LI)', *Archeologia Classica* 68: 375–408.

Bianco Peroni, V. (1970), *Le spade nell'Italia continentale.* München.

Biella, M.C. (2019), 'Gods of Value: Preliminary Remarks on Religion and Economy in Pre-Roman Italy', in C. Moser and C. Smith (eds.), *Transformations of Value: Lived Religion and the Economy. Religion in the Roman Empire 5.1.* 23–45. Tübingen.

Biella, M.C., R. Cascino, A.F. Ferrandes, and M. Revello Lami (eds.) (2018), *Gli artigiani e la città. Officine e aree produttive tra VIII e II sec. a.C. nell'Italia central tirrenica.* Rome.

Bietti Sestieri, A.M. (1992), *The Iron Age Community of Osteria dell'Osa: A Study of Socio-Political Development in Central Tyrrhenian Italy.* Cambridge.

Bietti Sestieri, A.M. and A. De Santis (2003), 'Il processo formativo della cultura laziale', in *Le comunità della preistoria italiana. Studi e ricerche sul neolitico e le età dei metalli. In memoria di Luigi Bernabò Brea. Atti della XXXV Riunione Scientifica IIPP (Lipari 2000).* 745–63. Florence.

Bietti Sestieri, A.M. and E. MacNamara (eds.) (2007), *Prehistoric Metal Artefacts from Italy (3500–720 B.C.E.) in the British Museum.* London.

Bird, J. (1958), 'Billingsgate: A Central Metropolitan Market', *The Geographical Journal* 124(4): 464–75.

Bishop, M. and J. Coulston (2006), *Roman Military Equipment: From the Punic Wars to the Fall of Rome.* 2nd ed. Oxford.

Blackman, M.J., G.J. Stein, and P.B. Vandiver (1993), 'The Standardization Hypothesis and Ceramic Mass Production: Technological, Compositional and Metric Indexes of Craft Specialization at Tell Leilan, Syria', *American Antiquity* 58: 60–80.

Blake, E. (2008), 'The Mycenaeans in Italy: A Minimalist Position', *PBSR* 76: 1–34.

Blake, E. (2013), 'Social Networks, Path Dependence, and the Rise of Ethnic Groups in Pre-Roman Italy', in C. Knappett (ed.), *Network Analysis in Archaeology: New Approaches to Regional Interaction.* 203–21. Oxford.

Blake, E. (2014), *Social Networks and Regional Identity in Bronze Age Italy.* Cambridge.

Blanton, R.E. and L.F. Fargher (2010), 'Evaluating Causal Factors in Market Development in Premodern States: A Comparative Study, with Critical Comments on the History of Ideas about Markets', in C.P. Garraty and B.L. Stark (eds.), *Archaeological Approaches to Market Exchange in Ancient Societies.* 207–26. Boulder.

Boardman, J. (1964), *The Greeks Overseas.* London.

Boccuccia, P., P. Desogus, F. Fratini, S.T. Levi, and E. Pecchioni (1995), 'Manufacturing Techniques, Raw Materials and Provenance of Italo-Mycenaean, Protogeometric and Early Geometric of Southern Italy and Daunian Middle Geometric Pottery at Coppa Nevigata (Foggia Province, Italy), XIII–VIII Century B.C.', in B. Fabbri (ed.), *European Ceramic Society, Fourth Conference. Riccione (Italy) October 2–6 1995*. 77–88. Faenza.

Bodinaku, N. (1990), 'Rreth origjinës dhe bartësve të qeramikës së pikturuar mat të kohës së vonë të bronzit dhe të asaj të hekurit/Sur l'origine et les porteurs de la céramique peinte mate de l'âge du Bronze recent et du Fer', *Iliria* 20: 65–95.

Boegehold, A.L. (1983), 'A New Attic Black Figure Potter', *AJA* 87: 89–90.

Bökönyi, S., E. Gal, and L. Bartosiewicz (2010), *The Chora of Metaponto 2: Archaeozoology at Pantanello and Five Other Sites*. Austin.

Boldizzoni, M. (2007), *The Poverty of Clio: Resurrecting Economic History*. Princeton.

Bonamici, M. (2015), 'Ricerche nel quartiere industrial di Populonia', in *La Corsica e Populonia. Atti del XXVIII Convegno di studi etruschi ed italici: Bastia – Alria, Piombino – Populonia, 25–29 ottobre 2011*. 409–57. Rome.

Bonfante, G. and L. Bonfante (2002), *The Etruscan Language: an Introduction*, revised edition. Manchester.

Bonfante, L. (1994), 'Scheda n. 26: *originis incertae*', in M. Cristofani (ed.), *Rivista di epigrafia etrusca. SE* 59: 269–70.

Bondioli, L., R. Corruccini, and R. Macchiarelli (1986), 'Familial Segregation in the Iron Age Community of Alfedena, Abruzzo, Italy, Based on Osteodental Trait Analysis', *American Journal of Physical Anthropology* 71: 393–400.

Bonghi Jovino, M. (1990), 'Artigiani e botteghe nell'Italia preromana. Appunti e riflessioni per un sistema dianalisi', in M. Bonghi Jovino (ed.), *Artigiani e botteghe nell'Italia preromana: Studi sulla coroplastica di area etrusco-laziale-campana*. 19–59. Rome.

Borges, J. (2000), 'The Analytical Language of John Wilkins', in E. Weiberger (ed.) and E. Allen (trans.), *Borges: Selected Non-Fictions*. 229–32. London.

Borgna, E. and P. Càssola Guida (2005), 'Some Observations on the Nature and Modes of Exchange between Italy and the Aegean in the Late Mycenaean Period', in R. Laffineur and E. Greco (eds.), *Emporia. Aegeans in the Central and Eastern Mediterranean: Proceedings of the 10th International Aegean Conference, Italian School of Archaeology, Athens, 14–18 April 2004*. 497–505. Liège and Austin.

Borgna, E. and S.T. Levi (2015), 'The Italo-Mycenaean Connection: Some Considerations on the Technological Transfer in the Field of Pottery Production', in W. Gauss, G. Klebinder-Gauss, and C. von Rüden (eds.), *The Transmission of Technical Knowledge in the Production of Ancient Mediterranean Pottery; Proceedings of the International Conference at the Austrian Archaeological Institute at Athens, 23rd–25th November 2012*. 115–38. Vienna.

Botchkovar, E.V., C.R. Tittle, and O. Antonaccio (2009), 'General Strain Theory: Additional Evidence Using Cross-cultural Data', *Criminology: An Interdisciplinary Journal* 47: 131–76.

Bottini, A. (1979), 'Una nuova necropoli nel melfese e alcuni problemi del periodo arcaico nel mondo indigeno', *Annali Archeologia e Storia Antica* 1: 77–94.

Bottini, A. (1980), 'L'area Melfese', in *Atti del ventesimo convegno di studi sulla Magna Grecia. Taranto 12–17 ottobre 1980*. 342–7. Taranto.

Bottini, A. (1981), 'Ruvo del Monte (Potenza) – Necropoli in contrada S. Antonio: scavi 1977', *NSA* 35: 183–288.

Bottini, A. (1985), 'Uno straniero e la sua sepoltura: la tomba 505 di Lavello', *Dialoghi di Archeologia* 3(3): 59–68.
Bottini, A. (1988), *Antike Helme. Sammlung Lipperheide und andere Bestände des Antikenmuseums Berlin*. Mainz.
Bottini, A. (1990), 'Il candelabro etrusco di Ruvo del Monte', *BA* 59: 1–14.
Bottini, A. (2011), 'Argento e ambra: il corredo della tomba 60 di Serra Del Cedro', *Siris* 11: 5–14.
Bottini, A. (2013), 'Eroi armati. Gli strumenti della guerra', in M. Osanna and M. Vullo (eds.), *Segni del potere. Oggetti di lusso dal Mediterraneo nell'Appennino lucano di età arcaica*. 145–58. Venosa.
Bottini, A., R. Graells i Fabregat, and M. Vullo (2019), *Metaponto. Tombe arcaiche della necropoli nord-occidentale*. Venosa.
Bottini, A. and E. Setari (2003), *La necropoli italica di Braida di Vaglio in Basilicata. Materiale dallo scavo del 1994 con una appendice di Mario Torelli e Luciano Agostiniani*. Rome.
Bottini, A. and M. Tagliente (1986), 'Forentum ritrovato', *Bollettino storico della Basilicata* 2: 65–76.
Bouma, J. (1996), *Religio Votiva: The Archaeology of Latial Votive Religion: The 5th–3rd C. BC Votive Deposit South West of the Main Temple at 'Satricum' Borgo Le Ferriere vol. I*. Groningen.
Bourdieu, P. (1977), *Outline of a Theory of Practice*. Cambridge.
Bourdieu, P. (1980), *The Logic of Practice*. Stanford.
Bourdin, S. (2012), *Les peuples de l'Italie preromaine: identites, territoires et relations inter-ethniques en Italie centrale et septentrionale*. Rome.
Bowes, K. (ed.) (2021), *The Roman Peasant Project 2009–2014: Excavating the Roman Rural Poor. Volume 1*. Philadelphia.
Bowser, B.J. and J.Q. Patton (2008), 'Learning and Transmission of Pottery Style: Women's Life Histories and Communities of Practice in the Ecuadorian Amazon', in M.T. Stark, B.J. Bowser, and L. Horne (eds.), *Cultural Transmission and Material Culture: Breaking Down Boundaries*. 105–29. Tucson.
Bradley, G. (1997), 'Iguvines, Umbrians and Romans: Ethnic Identity in Central Italy', in T. Cornell and K. Lomas (eds.), *Gender and Ethnicity in Ancient Italy*. 53–67. London.
Bradley, G. (2000a), *Ancient Umbria: State, Culture, and Identity in Central Italy from the Iron Age to the Augustan Era*. Oxford.
Bradley, G. (2000b), 'Tribes, States and Cities in Central Italy', in E. Herring and K. Lomas (eds.), *The Emergence of State Identities in Italy in the First Millennium BC*. 109–29. London.
Bradley, G. (2005), 'Aspects of the Cult of Hercules in Central Italy', in H. Bowden and L. Rawlings (eds.), *Herakles and Hercules: Exploring a Graeco-Roman Divinity*. 129–51. Swansea.
Bradley, G. (2020), *Early Rome to 290 BC: The Beginnings of the City and the Rise of the Republic*. Edinburgh.
Bradley, G., E. Isayev, and C. Riva, (eds.) (2007), *Ancient Italy: Regions Without Boundaries*. Exeter.
Brandherm, D. (2011), 'Bronzezeitliche Kamm- und Hörnerhelme – Überlegungen zu Ursprung, Verbreitung und symbolischem Gehalt', in U.L. Dietz and A. Jockenhövel (eds.), *Bronzen im Spannungsfeld zwischen praktischer Nutzung und symbolischer Bedeutung. Beiträge zum internationalen Kolloquium am 9. und 10. Oktober 2008 in Münster*. 39–54. Stuttgart.

Brandherm, D. and B. Sicherl (2001), 'Überlegungen zur Schwertproduktion der späten Urnenfelderzeit. Bemerkungen zur Herstellung späturnenfelderzeitlicher Vollgriffschwerter anhand zweier Beispiele von nördlich und südlich der Alpen', *Archäologisches Korrespondenzblatt* 31: 223–41.

Braudel, F. (1972), *The Mediterranean and the Mediterranean World in the Age of Philip II*. London.

Braudel, F. (1981–4), *Civilization and Capitalism, 15th – 18th Century*. New York.

Breglia, L. (1965), 'I precedenti della moneta vera e propria nel bacino del Mediterraneo', in *Atti del Congresso Internazionale di Numismatica (Roma 11–16 settembre 1961) I*. 5–17. Rome.

Bresson, A. (2000), *La cité marchande*. Paris.

Brigger, E. (2007), *La céramique fine du Premier Age du Fer d'I Fani (Lecce/Italie): contribution à l'étude des systèmes culturels indigènes du Protogéométrique Sud-italien au Géométrique Moyen et Récent I salentins*. PhD Dissertation. University of Geneva.

Briquel, D. (2003), 'Le Fanum Voltumnae: remarques sur le culte fédéral des cités étrusques', in A. Motte and C. Ternes (eds.), *Dieux, fêtes, sacré dans la Grèce et la Rome antiques*. 133–59. Turnhout.

Brock, A. (2016), 'Envisioning Rome's Prehistoric River Harbor: An Interim Report from the Forum Boarium', *Etruscan Studies* 19: 1–22.

Bromley, R.J. (1964), 'The Organization of Quito's Urban Markets: Towards a Reinterpretation of Periodic Central Places', *Transactions of the Institute of British Geographers* 62: 45–70.

Bromley, R.J., C.M. Good, and R. Symanski (1975), 'The Rationale of Periodic Markets', *Annals of the Association of American Geographers* 65: 530–7.

Broodbank, C. (2013), *The Making of the Middle Sea: A History of the Mediterranean from the Beginning to the Emergence of the Classical World*. London.

Brown, B. (2001), 'Thing Theory', *Critical Inquiry* 28: 1–22.

Brown, H. (2011), *A Study of Lead Ingot Cargoes from Ancient Mediterranean Shipwrecks*. MA Thesis. Texas A&M University.

Brubaker, R. (2004), *Ethnicity Without Groups*. Cambridge, MA.

Brughmans, T. (2010), 'Connecting the Dots: Towards Archaeological Network Analysis', *OJA* 29: 277–303.

Bruni, S. (2004), 'Presenze greche a Pisa', *AnnMusFaina* 11: 227–69.

Bruscella, A. (2009), 'La necropoli arcaica di loc. Toppo S. Antonio a Baragiano: un nuovo caso di studio', in M. Osanna and M. Scalici (eds.), *Lo spazio della memoria. Necropoli e rituali funerari nella Magna Grecia indigena, Atti della Tavola rotonda (Matera 11 dicembre 2009)*. Bari. = *Siris* 10: 21–35.

Bruscella, A. and S. Pagliuca (2013), 'Baragiano. Le tombe 35, 37 e 57', in M. Osanna and M. Vullo (eds.), *Segni del potere. Oggetti di lusso dal Mediterraneo nell'Appennino lucano di età arcaica*. 272–303. Venosa.

Bundrick, S. (2019), *Athens, Etruria, and the Many Lives of Greek Figured Pottery*. Madison.

Burns, M. (2003), 'The Homogenisation of Military Equipment under the Roman Republic', *Romanization? Digressus Supplement* 1: 160–76.

Busana, M.S., M. Bon, I. Cerato, S. Garavello, A.R. Ghiotto, M. Migliavacca, S. Nardi, D. Pizzeghello, and S. Zampieri (2012), 'Agricoltura e allevamento nell'agro orientale di *Altinum*: il caso di Ca'Tron', in M.S. Busana and P. Basso (eds.), *La lana nella Cisalpina romana: Economia e società. Studi in onore di Stefania Pesavento Mattioli*. 127–70. Padua.

Buxeda i Garrigós, J., R.E. Jones, B. Kilikoglou, S.T. Levi, Y. Maniatis, J. Mitchell, L. Vagnetti, K. Wardle, and A. Andreou (2003), 'Technology Transfer at the Periphery of the Mycenaean World: The Cases of Mycenaean Pottery Found in Central Macedonia (Greece) and the Plain of Sybaris (Italy)', *Archaeometry* 45: 263–84.

Caccioli, D. (2009), *The Villanovan, Etruscan, and Hellenistic Collections in the Detroit Institute of Arts*. Leiden.

Calandra, E. (2008), 'La Ceramica Sovraddipinta Apula e la Ceramica di Gnathia. Osservazioni e Spunti di Riflessione. Un'Ipotesi per Ruvo', *Annali della Facoltà di Letters e Filosofia dell'Università degli Studi di Milano* 16: 3–32.

Cambi, F. (2002), 'I confini del territorio di Populonia: stato della questione', *Materiali per Populonia* 1: 9–27.

Cambi, F., F. Cavari, and C. Mascione (eds.) (2009), *Materiali da costruzione e produzione del ferro: studi sull'economia populoniese fra periodo etrusco e romanizzazione*. Bari.

Camerieri, P. and T. Mattioli (2014), 'Obscura Itinera: A GIS-based Approach to Understand the Pre-Roman and Roman Transhumance Pathways in Umbria and Sabina Regions (Central Italy)', in G. Earl, T. Sly, A. Chrysanthi, P. Murrieta-Fores, C. Papadopulos, I. Romanowska, and D. Wheatley (eds.), *Archaeology in the Digital Era, Proceedings of the 40th Annual Conference of Computer Application and Quantitative Methods in Archaeology (CAA) Southampton, March 29, 2012*. 332–9. Amsterdam.

Camilli, A. (2016), 'La lavorazione del ferro a Populonia: considerazioni topografiche e cronologiche', *Res Antiquae* 13: 1–22.

Camilli, A. (2018), 'Populonia tra necropoli e scorie; appunti topografici sulla conca di Baratti', *Rassegna di Archeologia* 26: 87–132.

Campbell, B.C. and L. Barone (2012), 'Evolutionary Basis of Human Migration', in M.H. Crawford and B.C. Campbell (eds.), *Causes and Consequences of Human Migration*. 45–64. Cambridge.

Camporeale, G. (ed.) (1985), *L'Etruria mineraria*. Milan.

Cangiani, M. and C. Thomasberger (eds.) (2018), *Karl Polanyi: Economy and Society. Selected Writings*. Cambridge.

Canosa, M.G. (2007), *Una tomba principesca da Timmari*. Rome.

Canosa, M.G. (2014), 'Jazzo Fornasiello nel contesto del corridoio bradanico apulo lucano', in M. Castoldi (eds.), *Un Abitato Peuceta. Scavi a Jazzo Fornasiello (Gravina in Puglia -Bari) Prime indagini*. 11–20. Bari.

Cap, B. (2015), 'How to Know It When We See It: Marketplace Identification at the Classic Maya Site of Buenavista del Cayo, Belize', in E. King (ed.), *The Ancient Maya Marketplace. The Archaeology of Transient Space*. 111–37. Tucson.

Capdeville, G. (1999), 'Voltumna ed altri culti del territorio volsiniese', *Annali della Fondazione per il Museo 'Claudio Faina'* 6: 109–15.

Capozzi, R., A.C. Montanaro, and M. Campanale (2012), 'Tombe Aristocratiche Dall' Acropoli di Monte Sannace. Indagini sulle Strutture, sui Contesti e sulle Decorazioni Dipinte', *Taras* 32: 55–92

Cappuccini, L. (2007), 'I kyathoi etruschi di Santa Teresa di Gavorrano e il ceramista dei *paithina*', *RM* 113: 217–40.

Cardete, M.C. (2019), 'Long and Short-Distance Transhumance in Ancient Greece: The Case of Arkadia', *OJA* 38: 105–21.

Carollo, G. and M. Osanna (2009), 'Organizzazione territoriale e produzioni ceramiche specializzate in area nord-lucana: Torre di Satriano e Ripacandida', in M. Bettelli, C. De Faveri, and M. Osanna (eds.), *Prima delle colonie. Organizzazione territoriale e produzioni ceramiche specializzate in Basilicata e in Calabria settentrionale ionica nella prima età del ferro. Atti delle Giornate di Studio, Matera, 20–21 Novembre 2007*. 383–419. Venosa.

Carpenter, T.H. (2003), 'The Native Market for Red-figure Vases in Apulia', *MAAR* 48: 1–24.

Carpenter, T.H. (2009), 'Prolegomenon to the Study of Apulian Red-Figure Pottery', *AJA* 113: 27–38.

Carrer, F. (2015), 'Herding Strategies, Dairy Economy and Seasonal Sites in the Southern Alps: Ethnoarchaeological Inferences and Archaeological Implications', *JMA* 28: 3–22.

Carrer, F. (2016), 'The "Invisible" Shepherd and the "Visible" Dairyman: Ethnoarchaeology of Alpine Pastoral Sites in the Val di Fiemme (Eastern Italian Alps)', in J. Collis, M. Pearce, and F. Nicolis (eds.), *Summer Farms: Seasonal Exploitation of the Uplands from Prehistory to the Present*. 97–107. Sheffield.

Carrier, E.H. (1932), *Water and Grass: A Study in the Pastoral Economy of Southern Europe*. London.

Carroll, M. (2020), 'Invisible Foreigners at Rome? Identities in Dress Behaviour in the Imperial Capital', in S. de Blaauw, E. Enss, and P. Linscheid (eds.), *Contextus. Festschrift für Sabine Schrenk*. 169–88. Münster.

Carter, J.C. (2006), *Discovering the Greek Countryside at Metaponto*. Ann Arbor.

Carter, J.C. (2011a), 'Golden Harvests: The Expansion of the Mid-6th Century BC', in J.C. Carter and A. Prieto (eds.), *The Chora of Metaponto 3. Archaeological Survey – Bradano to Basento*. 677–726. Austin.

Carter, J.C. (2011b), 'The Refounding of Metaponto', in J.C. Carter and A. Prieto (eds.), *The Chora of Metaponto 3. Archaeological Survey – Bradano to Basento*. 809–68. Austin.

Catalli, F. (1988), 'Moneta straniera in Etruria', in T. Hackens (ed.), *Navies and Commerce of the Greeks, the Carthaginians and the Etruscans in the Tyrrhenian Sea: Proceedings of the European Symposium Held at Tavello, January 1987*. 465–93. Strasbourg.

Catalli, F. (1990), *Monete etrusche*. Rome.

Catalli, F. (2001), 'Coins', in M. Torelli (ed.), *The Etruscans*. 89–95. Venice.

Catalli, F. (2009), 'Problemi di cronologia numismatica: aes rude e aes signatum', in V. Jolivet (ed.), *Suburbium II: il suburbio di Roma dalla fine dell'età monarchica alla nascita del sistema delle ville (V-II secolo a.C.)*. 289–92. Rome.

Catalli, F. (2017), 'Coins and Mints', in A. Naso (ed.), *Etruscology*. 463–72. Berlin.

Cattani, M. (1988), 'Aes rude', in R.C. de Marinis (ed.), *Gli Etruschi a nord del Po, I*. 204–210. Mantua.

Cattani, M. (1996), 'Il sistema ponderale di Marzabotto', *Annali dell'Istituto italiano di numismatica* 42: 21–79.

Cattani, M. (2001), 'I pesi in pietra in Etruria padana', in C. Corti and N. Giordani (eds.), *Pondera: pesi e misure nell'antichità*. 89–94. Campogalliano.

Cavazzutti, C., R. Skeates, A. Millard, G. Nowell, J. Peterkin, M.B. Brea, A. Cardarelli, and L. Salzani (2019), 'Flows of People in Villages and Large Centres in Bronze Age Italy through Strontium and Oxygen Isotopes', *PLoS ONE* 14(1): 1–43.

Ceccarelli, L. (2012), 'Ethnicity and the Identity of the Latins. The Evidence from Sanctuaries between the Sixth and the Fourth Centuries BC', in G. Cifani and S. Stoddart (eds.), *Landscape, Ethnicity and Identity in the Archaic Mediterranean Area*. 108–19. Oxford.

Cedrini, M., A. Ambrosino, R. Marchionatti, and A. Caillé (2019), 'Mauss's the Gift, or the Necessity of an Institutional Perspective in Economics', *Journal of Institutional Economics* 16: 687–701.
Centauro, G.A. (2020), 'La Strada etrusca del Ferro, la "via direttissima" da Pisa a Spina', *Bollettino dell'Accademia degli Euteleti della Città di San Miniato* 87: 181–213.
Champion, C. (2017), *The Peace of the Gods: Elite Religious Practices in the Middle Roman Republic*. Princeton.
Chang, C. (2000), 'The Material Culture and Settlement History of Agro-Pastoralism in the Koinotis of Dhidhima: An Ethnoarchaeological Perspective', in S. Buck Sutton (ed.), *Contingent Countryside: Settlement, Economy, and Land Use in the Southern Argolid Since 1700*. 125–40. Stanford.
Chang, C. (2008), 'Mobility and Sedentism of the Iron Age Agropastoralists of Southeast Kazakhstan', in H. Barnard and W. Wendrich (eds.), *The Archaeology of Mobility: Old World and New World Nomadism*. 329–42. Los Angeles.
Chang, C. and H. Koster (1986), 'Beyond Bones: Toward an Archaeology of Pastoralism', *Advances in Archaeological Method and Theory* 9: 97–148.
Chayanov, A.V. (1966), *The Theory of Peasant Economy*. Illinois.
Chelotti, M., R. Gaeta, V. Morizio, and M. Silvestrini (1985), *Le epigrafi romane di Canosa. Vol. 1*. Bari.
Cherici, A. (2012), '"Asylum aperit": considerazioni sul *Fanum Voltumnae* e sui santuari emporici tra religione, commercio e politica', in G.M. della Fina (ed.), *Il Fanum Voltumnae e i santuari comunitari dell'Italia antica*. 293–326. Rome.
Cherry, J. (1988), 'Pastoralism and the Role of Animals in the Pre-and Protohistoric Economies of the Aegean', in C. Whittaker (ed.), *Pastoral Economies in Classical Antiquity*. 6–34. Cambridge.
Chiarantini, L., M. Benvenuti, P. Costagliola, M.E. Fedi, S. Guideri, and S. Romualdi (2009), 'Copper Production at Baratti (Populonia, Southern Tuscany) in the Early Etruscan Period (9th–8th Century BC)', *JAS* 36: 1626–36.
Childe, V.G. (1930), *The Bronze Age*. Cambridge.
Chilton, E.S. (ed.) (1999), *Material Meanings: Critical Approaches to the Interpretation of Material Culture*. Salt Lake City.
Choleva, M. (2012), 'The First Wheel-Made Pottery at Lerna: Wheel-Thrown or Wheel-Fashioned?', *Hesperia* 81: 343–81.
Choleva, M. (2019), 'Craft Behaviours during a Period of Transformations. The Introduction and Adoption of the Potter's Wheel in Central Greece during Early Bronze Age', in I. Caloi and C. Langohr (eds.), *Technology in Crisis: Technological Changes in Ceramic Production during Periods of Trouble*. 45–74. Louvain.
Christie, N., P. Beavitt, J.G. Santonja, V.G. Senís, and J. Segui (2007), 'Peopling the Recent Past in the Serra de L'Altmirant: Shepherds and Farmers at the Margins', *International Journal of Historical Archaeology* 11: 304–21.
Ciampoltrini, G. (1994–5), 'Note per l'epigrafia di Populonia romana', *RassArch* 12: 591–604.
Ciampoltrini, G. (2003), 'Appunti per l'epigrafia dei porti dell'Etruria centrosettentrionale nella prima e media età imperiale', *Materiali per Populonia* 2: 317–25.
Ciampoltrini, G. (2018), 'Fonteblanda/Portus Telamonis. A "Trading Post" for Wine and Metals on the Central-Northern Tyrrhenian Coast in the 6th Century BC', in E. Gailledrat, M. Dietler, and R. Plana-Mallart (eds.), *The Emporion in the Ancient Western Mediterrannean: Trade and Colonial Encounters from the Archaic to the Hellenistic Period*. 143–54. Montpellier.

Ciampoltrini, G. and M. Zecchini (2007), 'La via Etruscan in locailtà "Al Frizzone" di Capannori: i saggi del 2004', in G. Ciampoltrini and M. Zecchini (eds.), *Gli etruschi della piana di Lucca: la via del Frizzone e il sistema di insediamenti tra 8. e 5. secolo a.C.* 121–52. Lucca.

Ciancio, A. (1989), 'Peucezia preromana. L'organizzazione del territorio e le strutture del popolamento', in A. Ciancio (ed.), *Archeologia e territorio. L'area peuceta. Atti del seminario di studi Gioia del Colle, Museo archeologico nazionale 12–14 novembre 1987*. 47–67. Gioia del Colle.

Ciancio, A. (1996), 'Lo Stile Lucano', in E. Lippolis (ed.), *Arte e artigianato in Magna Grecia*. 355–96. Naples.

Ciancio, A. (1997), *Silbíon: una città tra greci e indigeni: la documentazione archeologica dal territorio di Gravina in Puglia dall'ottavo al quinto secolo a.C.* Bari.

Ciancio, A. (2005), *I fili della meraviglia. L'abbigliamento di Greci e Apuli tra funzionalità e comunicazione*. Bari.

Ciancio, A. (2008), 'Necropoli e aree urbane. L'uso 'apulo' di seppellire intra ed extra muros nella Peucezia nel periodo tra VI e III sec. a.C.', in G. Bartoloni and M.G. Benedettini (eds.), *Sepolti tra i vivi. Evidenza ed interpretazione di contesti funerari in abitato. Atti del Convegno Internazionale, Roma, 26–29 aprile 2006*. 895–918. Rome.

Ciancio, A. (2010a), 'Ruoli e Società: il costume funerario tra VI e IV secolo a. C.', in L. Todisco (ed.), *La Puglia centrale dall'età del bronzo all'alto medioevo. Archeologia e storia. Atti del convegno di studi (Bari, 15–16 giugno 2009)*. 225–38. Rome.

Ciancio, A. (2010b), 'La Peucezia nel sistema del commercio arcaico', in L. Todisco (ed.), *La Puglia centrale dall'età del bronzo all'alto medioevo. Archeologia e storia. Atti del convegno di studi (Bari, 15–16 giugno 2009)*. 291–7. Rome.

Ciancio, A. and V. L'Abbate (eds.) (2012), *Norba-Conversano: archeologia e storia della città e del territorio*. Bari.

Ciancio, A. and P. Palmentola (eds.) (2019), *Monte Sannace – Thuriae. Nuove ricerche e studi*. Bari.

Ciancio, A. and F. Radina (1983), 'Madonna delle Grazie (Rutigliano): campagna di scavo 1979', *Taras* 3: 7–61.

Ciancio, A. and A. Riccardi (2005), 'I siti della Peucezia', in A. Ciancio (ed.), *I fili della meraviglia. L'abbigliamento di Greci e Apuli tra funzionalità e comunicazione*. 57–85. Bari.

Cifani, G. (2012), 'Approaching Ethnicity and Landscapes in Pre-Roman Italy: The Middle Tiber Valley', in G. Cifani and S. Stoddart (eds.), *Landscape, Ethnicity and Identity in the Archaic Mediterranean Area*. 144–62. Oxford.

Cifani, G. (2016), 'L'economia di Roma nella prima età repubblicana (V-IV secolo a.C.): alcune osservazioni', in M. Aberson, M. Biella, M. Di Fazio, P. Sanchez, and M. Wullschleger (eds.), *L'Italia centrale e la creazione di una koiné culturale? I percorsi della 'romanizzazione'. Atti del convegno, Roma 2014*. 151–81. Bern.

Cifani, G. (2021), *The Origins of the Roman rconomy: From the Iron Age to the Early Republic in Mediterranean Perspective*. New York.

Cifani, G. and S. Stoddart (eds.) (2012), *Landscape, Ethnicity and Identity in the Archaic Mediterranean Area*. Oxford.

Cipriani, M. (2000), 'Italici a Poseidonia nella seconda metà del V sec. a.C. Nuove ricerche nella necropoli del Gaudoo', in E. Greco and F. Longo (eds.), *Paestum. Scavi, studi, ricerche. Bilancio di un decennio (1988–1998)*. 197–212. Paestum.

Cipriani, M. and F. Longo (eds.) (1996), *I Greci in Occidente: Poseidonia e i Lucani*. Naples.

Ciriello, R., E. Setari, and A. Bottini (1991), 'Lavello (Potenza). Località Casinetto. Una tomba emergente. Nota preliminare', *BA* 11: 201–3.

Clackson, J., P. James, K. McDonald, L. Tagliapietra, and N. Zair (eds.) (2020), *Migration, Mobility and Language Contact in and Around the Ancient Mediterranean*. Cambridge.

Coarelli, F. (1975), 'Nota Complementare: *Lucus Feroniae*', *Studi Classici e Orientali* 24: 164–5.

Coarelli, F. (1987), *I santuari del Lazio in età Repubblicana*. Rome.

Cocchiaro, A. (ed.) (2002), *Egnazia: le tombe a camera*. Bari.

Cocchi Ercolani, E. (1975), 'Repertorio dei ritrovamenti di pane di rame. Contributo allo studio delle fasi premonetali in Italia', *Rivista Italiana di Numismatica* 23: 7–47.

Coghlan, H.H. (1975), *Notes on the Prehistoric Metallurgy of Copper and Bronze in the Old World, Pitt Rivers Museum, University of Oxford*. 2nd ed. Oxford.

Cohen, S. and M. Naglak (2020), 'Infant Burials as Mediators of House Identity at Iron Age Gabii', in M. Mogetta (ed.), *Élite Burial Practices and Processes of Urbanization at Gabii: The Non-adult Tombs from Area D of the Gabii Project Excavations*. 141–56. Portsmouth, RI.

Colivicchi, F. (2004), 'L'altro vino. Vino, cultura e identità nella Puglia e Basilicata anelleniche', *Siris* 5: 23–68.

Colivicchi, F. (2006), 'Kantharoi attici per il vino degli Apuli', in F. Giudice and R. Panvini (eds.), *Il greco, il barbaro e la ceramica attica. Immaginario del diverso, processi di scambio e autorappresentazione degli indigeni. Atti del Convegno Internazionale di Studi, 14–19 maggio 2001*. 117–30. Rome.

Colivicchi, F. (2014), '"Native" Vase Shapes in South Italian Red-Figure Pottery', in T.H. Carpenter, K.M. Lynch, and E.G.D. Robinson (eds.), *The Italic People of Ancient Apulia: New Evidence from Pottery for Workshops, Markets, and Customs*. 213–42. Cambridge.

Collis, J., M. Pearce, and F. Nicolis (eds.) (2016), *Summer Farms: Seasonal Exploitation of the Uplands from Prehistory to the Present*. Sheffield.

Colonna, G. (1985), *Santuari d'Etruria: (Arezzo, 19 maggio 20 ott. 1985; catalogo)*. Milan.

Colonna, G. (1988), 'Il lessico istituzionale etrusco e la formazione della città, specialmente in Emilia Romagna', in *La Formazione della città preromana in Emilia Romagna: atti del convego di studi, Bologna-Marzabotto, 7–8 dicembre 1985*. 15–36. Bologna.

Colonna, G. (2003), 'Osservazioni sulla tomba Tarquiniese della Nave', in A. Minetti (ed.), *pittura etrusca: problemi e prospettive*. 63–77. Siena.

Colonna, G. (2010), 'A proposito del primo tratatto romano-cartaginese (e della donazione pyrgense ad Astarte)', in G.M. Della Fina (ed.), *La grande Roma dei Tarquini. Atti del XVII convegno Internazional di studi sulla storie e l'archeologia dell'Etruria*. 275–303. Rome.

Congès, G. and M. Leguilloux (2012), 'La gestion des troupeaux transhumants dans la Crau d'Arles (Bouches-du-Rhone, France) à l'époque romaine données archéologiques et archéozoologiques', in M.S. Busana and P. Basso (eds.), *La lana nella Cisalpina romana: Economia e società. Studi in onore di Stefania Pesavento Mattioli*. 311–22. Padua.

Conrad, S. (2017), *What is Global History?* Princeton.

Cooley, A.E. (2013), *The Cambridge Manual of Latin Epigraphy*. Cambridge.

Cooley, A.E. and M.G.L. Cooley (2013), *Pompeii and Herculaneum: A Sourcebook*. London.
Corbier, M. (1983), 'Fiscus and Patrimonium: The Saepinum Inscription and Transhumance in the Abruzzi', *JRS* 73: 126–31.
Corbier, M. (1991), 'Constructing Kinship in Rome: Marriage, Divorce, Filiation and Adoption', in D. Kertzer and R. Saller (eds.), *The Family in Italy from Antiquity to the Present*. 127–44. New Haven.
Cornell, T.J. (1995), *The Beginnings of Rome: Italy and Rome from the Bronze Age to the Punic Wars (c. 1000–264 BCE)*. New York.
Cornell, T.J. (1997), 'Ethnicity as a Factor in Early Roman History', in T. Cornell and K. Lomas (eds.), *Gender and Ethnicity in Ancient Italy*. 9–21. London.
Corrente, M. (2005), 'Produzione e circolazione della ceramica a figure rosse a Canosa e nel territorio: i dati delle recenti scoperte', in M. Denoyelle, E. Lippolis, M. Mazzei, and C. Pouzadoux (eds.), *La céramique apulienne. Bilan et perspectives. Actes de la table ronde de Naples, 2000*. 59–76. Naples.
Corretti, A. (2009), 'Siderurgia in ambito elbano e populoniese: un contributo delle fonti letterarie', in F. Cambi, F. Cavari, and C. Mascione (eds.), *Materiali da costruzione e produzione del ferro: studi sull'economia populoniese fra periodo etrusco e romanizzazione*. 133–40. Bari.
Corretti, A. (2017), 'The Mines on the Island of Elba', in A. Naso (ed.), *Etruscology*. 445–62. Berlin.
Corretti, A. and M. Benvenuti (2001), 'The Beginning of Iron Metallurgy in Tuscany, with Special Reference to "Etruria Mineraria"', *Mediterranean Archaeology* 14: 127–45.
Corretti, A., L. Chiarantini, M. Benvenuti, and F. Cambi (2014), 'The Aithale Project: Men, Earth and Sea in the Tuscan Archipelago (Italy) in Antiquity. Perspectives, Aims and First Results', in B. Cech and T. Rehren (eds.), *Early Iron in Europe*. 181–96. Montagnac.
Corti, C. (2001), 'Pesi e contrappesi', in C. Corti, N. Giordani, and D. Neri (eds.), *Pondera, pesi e misure nell'antichità*. 191–212. Campogalliano.
Costello, E. and E. Svensson (2018), *Historical Archaeologies of Transhumance Across Europe*. New York.
Costin, C.L. and M.B. Hagstrum (1995), 'Standardization, Labor Investment, Skill, and the Organization of Ceramic Production in Late Prehispanic Highland Peru', *American Antiquity* 60: 619–39.
Cracolici, E. (2003), *I sostegni di fornace dal kerameikos di Metaponto*. Bari.
Craddock, P.T. (1984), 'The Metallurgy and Composition of Etruscan Bronze', *SE* 52: 211–71.
Craddock, P.T. (2000), 'From Hearth to Furnace: Evidences for the Earliest Metal Smelting Technologies in the Eastern Mediterranean', *Paléorient* 26: 151–65.
Craddock, P.T. and N.D. Meeks (1987), 'Iron in Ancient Copper', *Archaeometry* 29: 187–204.
Crawford, M.H. (ed.) (1996), *Roman Statutes*. 2 vols. London.
Cribb, R. (1991), *Nomads in Archaeology*. Cambridge.
Cristofani, M. (1969), 'Review of H. Hencken, *Tarquinia, Villanovans and Early Etruscans*', *Archeologia Classica* 21: 116–9.
Cristofani, M. (1975), 'Il "dono" nell Etruria arcaica', *Parola del passato* 30: 132–52.
Cristofani, M. (1986), 'Economia e societa', in G.P. Carratelli (ed.), *Rasenna. Storia e civilta degli Etruschi*. 79–156. Milan.

Cristofani, M. (1996), 'Due testi dell'Italia preromana. 1. Per regna Maricae. 2. Aequipondium etruscum', *Quaderni di Archeologia Etrusco-Italica* 25: 1–54.
Cucini, C. (1992), 'Due antichi impianti siderurgici presso Follonica (Grosseto, Toscana)', in E. Herring and R. Whitehouse (eds.), *Papers of the 4th Conference of Italian Archaeology: New Developments in Italian Archaeology*. 23–30. London.
Cucini, C. (2013), 'La lavorazione dei metalli a Genova dal V al I secolo a.C.', *Notizie Archeologiche Bergomensi* 21: 81–117.
Cunliffe, B. (2003), *The Extraordinary Voyage of Pytheas the Greek: The Man Who Discovered Britain*. London.
Curti, F. (2000), 'Le esportazioni della bottega del Pittore di Meleagro nel Mediterraneo Occidentale', in B. Sabattini (ed.), *La céramique attique du IVe siècle en Méditerranée occidentale (Arles, 1995)*. 25–34. Naples.
Cutler, J., B. Dimova, and M. Gleba (2020), 'Tools for Textiles: Textile Production at the Etruscan Settlement of Poggio Civitate, Murlo, in the Seventh and Sixth Centuries BC', *PBSR* 88: 1–30.
D'Accunto, M. (2018), 'Cumae in Campania in the Seventh Century BC', in X. Charalambidou and C. Morgan (eds.), *Interpreting the Seventh Century BC: Tradition and Innovation*. 293–329. Oxford.
D'Agostino, B. (2014), 'The Archaeological Background of the Analysed Pendent Semicircle Skyphoi from Pontecagnano', in M. Kerschner and I. Lemos (eds.), *Archaeometric Analyses of Euboean and Euboean Related Pottery: New Results and Their Interpretations. Proceedings of the Round Table Conference held at the Austrian Archaeological Institute in Athens, 15 and 16 April 2011*. 181–90. Vienna.
D'Agostino, B. and S. De Natale (1996), 'L'età del Ferro in Campania', in A.M. Bietti Sestieri and V. Kruta (eds.), *The Iron Age in Europe, Proceedings XIII International Congress UISPP (Forlì 1996)*. 107–12. Forlì.
Damato, A. (ed.) (2001), *Un luogo della Peucezia. Le scoperte archeologiche in contrada Bigetti*. Palo del Colle.
D'Andria, F. (1975), 'Scavi nella zona del Kerameikos (1973)', in D. Adamesteanu, D. Mertens, and F. D'Andria (eds.), *Metaponto I*. 355–452. Rome.
D'Andria, F. (1977), 'Cavallino (Lecce): ceramica ed elementi architettonici arcaici', *Mélanges de l'Ecole française de Rome. Antiquité* 89: 525–62.
D'Andria, F. (1979), 'Salento arcaico: la nuova documentazione archeologica', in *Salento Arcaico. Atti colloquio Int. Lecce 1979*. 15–28. Galatina.
D'Andria, F. (1984), 'Documenti del commercio arcaico tra Ionio e Adriatico', in *Magna Grecia, Epiro e Macedonia, Actes XXIV CSMG*. 321–77. Taranto.
D'Andria, F. (1988), 'Messapi e Peuceti', in *Italia, omnium terrarum alumna. La civiltà dei Veneti, Reti, Liguri, Celti, Piceni, Umbri, Latini, Campani e Iapigi*. 653–708. Milano.
D'Andria, F. (1997), 'Detectives a Metaponto', *Archeo* 13: 34–9.
D'Andria, F. (ed.) (2005), *Cavallino. Pietre, case e città della Messapia antica*. Ceglie Messapica.
D'Andria, F. and G. Semeraro (2000), 'Le ceramiche greco-orientali in Italia meridionale. Appunti sulla distribuzione', in *Magna Grecia e Oriente mediterraneo prima dell'età ellenistica. Atti del trentanovesimo convegno di studi sulla Magna Grecia, Taranto 1–5 ottobre 1999*. 457–501. Taranto.
D'Angiolillo, A. and V. Gasner (2017), 'Fornaci per ceramica, per laterizi e per la produzione del ferro a Velia', *FOLD&R* 376: 1–13.

D'Aversa, A. (1994), *Dizionario della lingua Etrusca*. Brescia.
Davies, B. (2005), 'Communities of Practice: Legitimacy Not Choice', *Journal of Sociolinguistics* 9: 557–81.
Davis, J. (2014), *Medieval Market Morality: Life, Law and Ethics in the English Marketplace, 1200–1500*. Cambridge.
Dawkins, R. (1976), *The Selfish Gene*. Oxford.
de Grummond, N. (1997), 'Poggio Civitate: A Turning Point', *Etruscan Studies* 4: 23–40.
de Grummond, N. (2004), 'For the Mother and for the Daughter: Some Thoughts on Dedications from Etruria and Praeneste', *Hesperia Supplements* 33: 351–70.
de Grummond, N. (2016), 'Ritual and Religion. Life at the Sanctuaries', in N. de Grummond and L. Pieraccini (eds.), *Caere*. 149–61. Austin.
de Grummond, N., P. Rowe, R. Marrinan, and G. Doran (1994), 'Excavations at Cetamura del Chianti, 1987–1991', *Etruscan Studies* 1(1): 6.
De Haas, T. (2011), *Fields, Farms and Colonists: Intensive Field Survey and Early Roman Colonization in the Pontine Region, Central Italy*. Groningen.
De Juliis, E.M. (1980), 'L'attivita archeologica in Puglia', in *L'epos greco in occidente: atti del Diciannovesimo Convegno di studi sulla Magna Grecia: Taranto, 7–12 ottobre 1979*. 425–42. Taranto.
De Juliis, E.M. (1981), 'Rutigliano (Bari. Scavi e Scoperte)', *SE* 49: 468–9.
De Juliis, E.M. (1995), *La ceramica geometrica della Peucezia*. Rome.
De Juliis, E.M. (2002), *La ceramica sovraddipinta apula*. Bari.
De Juliis, E.M. (ed.) (2007), *Rutigliano I. La necropoli di contrada Purgatorio Scavo 1978, Catalogo del Museo Nazionale di Taranto II.2*. Taranto.
De Juliis, E.M. (2010), 'La Peucezia: Caratteri Generali', in L. Todisco (ed.), *La Puglia centrale dall'età del bronzo all'alto medioevo. Archeologia e storia. Atti del convegno di studi (Bari, 15–16 giugno 2009)*. 151–68. Rome.
De Juliis, E.M., F. Galeandro, and P. Palmentola (2006), *La ceramica geometrica della Messapia*. Bari.
Delanda, M. (2006), *A New Philosophy of Society: Assemblage Theory and Social Complexity*. London.
Delanda, M. (2016), *Assemblage Theory*. Edinburgh.
de Ligt, L. (1993), *Fairs and Markets in the Roman Empire: Economic and Social Aspects of Periodic Trade in a Pre-industrial Society*. Leiden.
de Ligt, L. and P.W. de Neeve (1988), 'Ancient Periodic Markets: Festivals and Fairs', *Athenaeum* 66: 391–416.
Della Corte, M. (1965), *Case ed abitanti di Pompei*. Naples.
Della Fina, G.M. (ed.) (2013), *Mobilità geografica e mercenariato nell'Italia preromana. Atti del XX convegno internazionale di studi sulla storia e l'archeologia dell'Etruria*. Rome.
Del Monte, R. (2019), 'Il Popolamento Antico nel Territorio Di Monte Sannace', in A. Ciancio and P. Palmentola (eds.), *Monte Sannace – Thuriae. Nuove ricerche e studi*. 37–77. Bari.
Delpino, F. (2005), 'Dinamiche sociali e innovazioni rituali a Tarquinia villanoviana: le tombe I e II del sepolcreto villanoviano', in *Dinamiche di sviluppo delle città nell'Etruria meridionale, Atti XXIII Convegno di Studi Etruschi e Italici (Roma, Cerveteri, Tarquinia, Montalto di Castro, Viterbo 2001)*. 343–58. Pisa-Rome.
De Marinis, R.C. (1999), 'Il confine occidentale del mondo protoveneto/paleoveneto dal Bronzo finale alle invasioni galliche del 388 a.C.', in *Protostoria e Storia del*

<<Venetorum Angulus>>, *Atti XX Convegno di Studi Etruschi e Italici (Portogruaro-Quarto d'Altino-Este-Adria 1996)*. 511–64. Pisa.

Demetriou, D. (2012), *Negotiating Identity in the Ancient Mediterranean: The Archaic and Classical Greek Multiethnic Emporia*. Cambridge.

Dench, E. (1995), *From Barbarians to New Men: Greek, Roman, and Modern Perceptions of Peoples of the Central Apennines*. Oxford.

Dench, E. (2005), *Romulus' Asylum: Roman Identities from the Age of Alexander to the Age of Hadrian*. Oxford.

Denoyelle, M. (1993), 'Sur la personnalité du Peintre d'Arnò. Un point de jonction entre Grande-Grèce et Etrurie', *Revue Archéologique*: 53–70.

Denoyelle, M. (1996), 'Le peintre d'Analatos: essai de synthèse et perspectives nouvelles', *Antike Kunst* 39: 71–87.

Denoyelle, M. (1997), 'Attic or Non-Attic? The Case of the Pisticci Painter', in J. Oakley, W. Coulsen, and O. Palagia (eds.), *Athenian Potters and Painters: The Conference Proceedings*. 395–405. Oxford.

Denoyelle, M. and M. Iozzo (2009), *La céramique grecque d'Italie méridionale et de Sicile: productions coloniales et apparentées du VIIIe au IIIe siècle av. J.-C*. Paris.

Denoyelle, M., C. Pouzadoux, and F. Silvestrelli (2018), 'Presentazione', in M. Denoyelle, C. Pouzadoux, and F. Silvestrelli (eds.), *Mobilità dei pittori e identità delle produzioni*. 5–14. Naples.

Denoyelle, M. and F. Silvestrelli (2019), 'La construction des ateliers à figures rouges métapontins et lucaniens. Le cas du Peintre des Choéphores', in O. de Cazanove, A. Duplouy, and V. Capozzoli (eds.), *La Lucanie entre deux mers: archéologie et patrimoine. Actes du Colloque international, Paris, 5–7 Novembre 2015*. 807–20. Naples.

Denti, M. (2018), 'Archilochos Did Not Sail Alone to the Bountiful Shores of Siris: Parian and Naxian Potters in Southern Italy in the 7th Century BC', in D. Katsonopoulou (ed.), *Paros and Its Colonies. Fourth International Conference on the Archaeology of Paros and the Cyclades, Paros 11–14 June 2015*. 39–62. Athens.

Denti, M. and C. Bellamy (eds.) (2016), *La céramique dans les contextes archéologiques "mixtes". Autour de la Méditerranée antique*. Rennes.

Denti, M. and M. Villette (2013), 'Ceramisti greci dell'Egeo in un atelier indigeno d'Occidente. Scavi e ricerche sullo spazio artigianale dell'Incoronata nella valle del Basento (VIII-VII secolo a.C.)', *BA* 17: 1–36.

De Polignac, F. (1995), *Cults, Territory, and the Origins of the Greek City-state*. Chicago.

D'Ercole, M.C. (2017), 'Economy and Trade', in A. Naso (ed.), *Etruscology*. 143–63. Berlin.

De Santis, A. (2005), 'Da capi guerrieri a principi: la strutturazione del potere politico nell'Etruria proto urbana', in *Dinamiche di sviluppo delle città nell'Etruria meridionale, Atti XXIII Convegno di Studi Etruschi e Italici (Roma, Cerveteri, Tarquinia, Montalto di Castro, Viterbo 2001)*. 615–31. Pisa-Rome.

De Santis, A. (2011), *Politica e leader nel Lazio ai tempi di Enea*. Rome.

De Santis, A., G. Mieli, C. Rosa, R. Matteucci, A. Celant, C. Minniti, P. Catalano, F. De Angelis, S. Di Giannantonio, C. Giardino, and P. Giannini (2010), 'Le fasi di occupazione nell'area centrale di Roma in età protostorica: nuovi dati dagli scavi nel Foro di Cesare', *Scienze dell'Antichità* 16: 259–84.

Descœudres, J.-P. and E. Robinson (1993), *La 'chiusa' alla Masseria del Fano: un sito messapico arcaico presso Salve in Provincia di Lecce*. Lecce.

Desiderio, A.M. (2018), 'Fenomeni di mobilità a Pontecagnano in età Orientalizzante: i dati dalle necropoli', in A. Cipriani, A. Pontradolfo, and A.C. Scafuro (eds.), *Dialoghi sull'archeologia della Magna Grecia e del Mediterraneo. Atti del II Convegno Internazionale di Studi, Paestum, 28–30 giugno 2017*. 453–62. Paestum.

De Siena, A. (1993a), 'Corredo tombale. Da Metaponto, loc. Pizzica d'Onofrio, tomba 18', in A. Bottini (ed.), *Armi. Gli strumenti della guerra in Lucania*. 181–6. Bari.

De Siena, A. (1993b), 'Corredo tombale. Da Metaponto, necropoli occidentale, loc. Crucinia, tomba 17', in A. Bottini (ed.), *Armi. Gli strumenti della guerra in Lucania*. 123–33. Bari.

Di Bisceglie, A. (2015 [2016]), 'L'evoluzione del rituale funerario nella Lucania settentrionale dall'età arcaica al IV secolo: tra persistenze e innovazioni', *Taras. Rivista di Archeologia* 35: 65–88.

Dietler, M. (2010), *Archaeologies of Colonialism: Consumption, Entanglement and Violence in Ancient Mediterranean France*. Berkeley.

Dietler, M. and B. Hayden (eds.) (2001), *Feasts: Archaeological and Ethnographic Perspectives on Food, Politics, and Power*. Washington, DC.

Dietler, M. and I. Herbich (1998), 'Habitus, Techniques, Style: An Integrated Approach to the Social Understanding of Material Culture and Boundaries', in M.T. Stark (ed.), *The Archaeology of Social Boundaries*. 232–62. Washington, DC.

Dietrich, O. (2012), 'Travelling or Not? Tracing Individual Mobility Patterns of Late Bronze Age Metalworkers in the Carpathian Basin', *Satu Mare – Studii şi Comunicări. Seria Archeologie* 28: 211–29.

Di Fazio, M. (2012), 'The Role of an Italic Goddess in the Process of Integration of Cultures in Republican Italy', in S. Roselaar (ed.), *Processes of Integration and Identity Formation in the Roman Republic*. 337–54. Leiden.

Di Fazio, M. (2020), *I Volsci: un popolo 'liquido' nel Lazio antico*. Rome.

Di Fazio, M. and S. Paltineri (eds.) (2019), *La società gentilizia nell'Italia antica tra realtà e mito storiografico*. Bari.

Diffendale, D., P. Brocato, N. Terrenato, and A. Brock (2016), 'Sant'Omobono: An Interim *Status Quaestionis*', *JRA* 29: 7–42.

Di Lieto, M. (2008), 'Per una carta archeologica del territorio di Baragiano', in A. Russo and H. Di Giuseppe (eds.), *Felicitas Temporum. Dalla terra alle genti: la Basilicata settentrionale tra archeologia e storia*. 39–43. Potenza.

Dolfini, A. (2019), 'From the Neolithic to the Bronze Age in Central Italy: Settlement, Burial, and Social Change at the Dawn of Metal Production', *Journal of Archaeological Research* 28: 503–56.

Dolfini, A., I. Angelini, and G. Artioli (2020), 'Copper to Tuscany – Coals to Newcastle? The Dynamics of Metalwork Exchange in Early Italy', *PLoS ONE* 15: e0227259.

Donnellan, L. and V. Nizzo (2016), 'Conceptualising Early Greek Colonisation. Introduction to the Volume', in L. Donnellan, V. Nizzo, and G.J. Burgers (eds.), *Conceptualising Early Colonisation: Contextualising Early Colonisation Vol. 2*. 9–20. Brussels and Rome.

Doonan, R.C.P. and D. Dungworth (2013), 'Experimental Archaeometallurgy in Perspective', in D. Dungworth and R.C.P. Doonan (eds.), *Accidental and Experimental Archaeometallurgy*. 1–10. London.

Dornan, J. (2002), 'Agency and Archaeology: Past, Present, and Future Directions', *Journal of Archaeological Method and Theory* 9: 303–29.

Duday, H. (2009), *The Archaeology of the Dead: Lectures in Archaeothanatology*. Oxford.
Duplouy, A. (2006), *Le prestige des élites. Recherches sur les modes de reconnaissance sociale en Grèce entre les Xeet Ve siècles avant J.-C.* Paris.
Dyson-Hudson, R. and N. Dyson-Hudson (1980), 'Nomadic Pastoralism', *Annual Review of Anthropology* 9: 15–61.
Earle, T. and K. Kristiansen (2010), *Organizing Bronze Age Societies*. Cambridge.
Echeverría, F. (2011), 'Weapons, Technological Determinism, and Ancient Warfare', in G. Fagan and M. Trundle (eds.), *New Perspectives on Ancient Warfare*. 21–56. Leiden.
Edlund-Berry, I.E.M. (1992), 'Etruscans at Work and Play: Evidence for an Etruscan Calendar', in H. Froning, T. Hölscher, and H. Mielsch (eds.), *Kotinos: Festschrift für Erika Simon*. 330–8. Mainz.
Edlund-Berry, I.E.M. (2006), 'Ritual Space and Boundaries in Etruscan Religion', in N. de Grummond and E. Simon (eds.), *The Religion of the Etruscans*. 116–31. Austin.
Eerkens, J.W. and R.L. Bettinger (2001), 'Techniques for Assessing Standardization in Artifact Assemblages: Can We Scale Material Variability?', *American Antiquity* 66: 493–504.
Egg, M. (1996), *Das Hallstattzeitliche Fürstengrab von Strettweg bei Judenburg in der Obersteiermark*. Mainz.
Egg, M. (2017), 'War and Weaponry', in A. Naso (ed.), *Etruscology*. 165–77. Berlin.
Egg, M. and G. Tomedi (2002), 'Ein Bronzehelm aus dem Mittelbronzezeitlichen Depotfund vom Piller, Gemeinde Fliess, in Nordtirol', *Archäologisches Korrespondenzblatt* 32: 543–60.
Elder, O. (2020), 'Population, Migration and Language in the City of Rome', in J. Clackson, P. James, K. McDonald, L. Tagliapietra, and N. Zair (eds.), *Migration, Mobility and Language Contact in and around the Ancient Mediterranean*. 268–95. Cambridge.
Elia, D. (2018), 'Il Gruppo di Locri in Calabria meridionale: sviluppo di una tradizione siceliota', in M. Denoyelle, C. Pouzadoux, and F. Silvestrelli (eds.), *Mobilità dei pittori e identità delle produzioni*. 75–93. Naples.
Ellingsen, D., L. Møller, and J. Aaseth (2015), 'Copper', in G.F. Nordberg, B.A. Fowler, and M. Nordberg (eds.), *Handbook on the Toxicology of Metals*. 765–86. London.
Ellis, S.J.R. (2018), *The Roman Retail Revolution: The Socio-economic World of the Taberna*. Oxford.
Emberling, G. (1997), 'Ethnicity in Complex Societies: Archaeological Perspectives', *Journal of Archaeological Research* 5(4): 295–344.
Emery, M., R. Stark, T. Murchie, S. Elford, H. Schwarcz, and T. Prowse (2018), 'Mapping the Origins of Imperial Roman Works (1st–4th century CE) at Vagnari, Southern Italy, using 87Sr/86Sr and δ18O Variability', *American Journal of Physical Anthropology* 166: 837–50.
Emiliozzi, A. (2017), 'Vehicles and Roads', in A. Naso (ed.), *Etruscology*. 407–24. Boston.
Eramo, G., I.M. Muntoni, S. Gallo, and A. De Siena (2018), 'Approaching the Early Greek Colonization in Southern Italy: Ceramic Local Production and Imports in the Siritis Area (Basilicata)', *Journal of Archaeological Science: Reports* 21: 995–1008.

Erb-Satullo, N.L. (2019), 'The Innovation and Adoption of Iron in the Ancient Near East', *Journal of Archaeological Research* 27: 557–607.
Eriksen, T. (1993), *Ethnicity and Nationalism: Anthropological Perspectives*. London.
Esposito, A. and J. Zurbach (2014), 'Technological Standardization and Cultural Contact: Some Methodological Considerations and Two Case Studies', in A. Kotsonas (ed.), *Understanding Standardization and Variation in Mediterranean Ceramics, Mid 2nd to Late 1st Millennium BC*. 39–47. Leuven.
Farney, G. (2007), *Ethnic Identity and Aristocratic Competition in Republican Rome*. Cambridge.
Farney, G. (2008), 'The Mamilii, Mercury and the Limites. Aristocratic Genealogy and Political Conflict in Republican Rome', *Athenaeum* 96: 251–60.
Farney, G. (2014), 'Romans and Italians', in J. McInerney (ed.), *A Companion to Ethnicity in the Ancient Mediterranean*. 437–54. Chichester.
Farney, G. and G. Bradley (eds.) (2018), *The Peoples of Ancient Italy*. Berlin.
Feeney, D. (2016), *Beyond Greek: The Beginnings of Latin Literature*. Cambridge, MA.
Fernández-Götz, M. (2020), 'Urbanisation and Deurbanisation in the European Iron Age: Definitions, Debates, and Cycles', in L. Zamboni, M. Fernández-Götz, and C. Metzner-Nebelsick (eds.), *Crossing the Alps: Early Urbanism between Northern Italy and Central Europe (900–400 BC)*. 27–42. Leiden.
Fernández-Götz, M., H. Wendling, and K. Winger (eds.) (2014), *Paths to Complexity: Centralisation and Urbanisation in Iron Age Europe*. Oxford.
Finley, M. (1972), *The World of Odysseus, revised edition*. London.
Finley, M. (1973), *The Ancient Economy*. Berkeley.
Fioriello, C. (2002), 'Le vie di comunicazione in Peucezia: il comparto Ruvo-Bitonto', *AnnBari* 45: 75–136.
Fioriello, C. (2017), *Poediculorum Oppida: spazi urbani della Puglia centrale in età romana*. Oxford.
Fiorini, L. and M. Torelli (2007), 'La fusione, Afrodite e l'emporion', *FACTA* 1: 75–106.
Fiorini, L. and M. Torelli (2010), 'Quarant'anni di ricerche a Gravisca', in L.B. van der Meer (ed.), *Material Aspects of Etruscan Religion, Proceedings Colloquium Leiden, May 29 and 30 2008*. 29–49. Leuven.
Firmati, M. (2017), 'Attività metallurgica nella fortificazione ellenistica di Ghiaccio Forte (Scansano, GR) (fine IV-inizi III sec. a.C.)', *Scienze dell'Antichità* 23: 299–304.
Fisher, N. and H. van Wees (eds.) (2015), *Aristocracy in Antiquity: Redefining Greek and Roman Elites*. Cardiff.
Fishman, J. and O. Garcia (eds.) (2010), *Handbook of Language and Ethnic Identity*. Vol. 1. Oxford.
Flache, A. (2018), 'Between Monoculture and Cultural Polarization: Agent-based Models of the Interplay of Social Influence and Cultural Diversity', *Journal of Archaeological Method and Theory* 25: 996–1023.
Florenzano, A., and A.M. Mercuri (2013), 'Dal polline nei sedimenti alla ricostruzione del paesaggio e dell'economia di Torre di Satriano', in M. Osanna and M. Vullo (eds.), *Segni del potere. Oggetti di lusso dal Mediterraneo nell'Appennino lucano di età arcaica*. 163–8. Venosa.
Földes, L. (1961), 'Esztena und Esztena-Genossenschaft bei den Szeklern', in L. Földes (ed.), *Viehzucht und Hirtenleben in Ostmitteleuropa. Ethnographische Studien*. 283–328. Budapest.

Fontannaz, D. (2014), 'Production and Functions of Apulian Red-Figure Pottery in Taras: New Contexts and Problems of Interpretation', in T.H. Carpenter, K. Lynch, and E.G.D. Robinson (eds.), *The Italic People of Ancient Apulia: New Evidence from Pottery for Workshops, Markets, and Customs*. 71–95. Cambridge.

Forbes, R.J. (1966), 'Heat and Heating', in R.J. Forbes (ed.), *Studies in Ancient Technology, Vol. 6*, 1–103. Leiden.

Forenbaher, S. (ed.) (2009), *A Connecting Sea: Maritime Interaction in Adriatic Prehistory*. Oxford.

Forenbaher, S. (2018), *Special Place, Interesting Times: The Island of Palagruža and Transitional Periods in Adriatic Prehistory*. Oxford.

Fowler, W. (1899), *The Roman Festivals of the Period of the Republic*. London.

Fragnoli, P. (2021), 'Re-assessing the Notion(s) of Craft Standardization through Diversity Statistics: A Pilot Study on Late Chalcolithic Pottery from Arslantepe in Eastern Anatolia', *PloS ONE* 16(1): e0245660.

Frayn, J. (1984), *Sheep-rearing and the Wool Trade in Italy during the Roman Period*. Liverpool.

Frayn, J. (1993), *Markets and Fairs in Roman Italy*. Oxford.

Frieman, C.J., J. Brück, K. Reebay-Salisbury, S. Bergerbrant, S. Montòn Subìas, J. Sofaer, Ch.J. Knüsel, H. Vandkilde, M. Giles, and P. Treherne (2017), 'Ageing Well: Treherne's "Warrior's Beauty" Two Decades Later', *EJA* 20: 36–73.

Frier, B. and D. Kehoe (2007), 'Law and Economic Institutions', in W. Scheidel, I. Morris, and R. Saller (eds.), *The Cambridge Economic History of the Greco-Roman World*. 113–43. Cambridge.

Fugazzola Delpino, M.A. and E. Pellegrini (2009–2010), 'Due ripostigli dell'Italia centrale tirrenica: Santa Marinella e Goluzzo. Produzione e circolazione dei metalli in Italia centrale tra la fine dell'età del Bronzo e gli inizi dell'età del Ferro', *Bullettino di Paletnologia Italiana* 98: 25–172.

Fulminante, F. (2012), 'Ethnicity, Identity and State Formation in the Latin Landscape. Problems and Approaches', in G. Cifani and S. Stoddart (eds.), *Landscape, Ethnicity and Identity in the Archaic Mediterranean Area*. 89–107. Oxford.

Fulminante, F. (2014), *The Urbanization of Rome and Latium From the Bronze Age to the Archaic Era*. Cambridge.

Gabba, E. (1975), 'Mercati e Fiere nell'Italia romana', *SCO* 24: 141–63.

Gábor Tarbay, J. (2018), '"Looted Warriors" from Eastern Europe', *Dissertationes Archaeologicae* 3(6): 313–59.

Galeandro, F. (2005), *Egnazia tra Peucezia e Messapia: il contributo della ceramica geometrica*. Bari.

Galeandro, F. (2010), 'Occupazione ed articolazione del territorio tra il VI e IV secolo a.C.', in L. Todisco (ed.), *La Puglia centrale dall'età del bronzo all'alto medioevo. Archeologia e storia. Atti del convegno di studi (Bari, 15–16 giugno 2009)*. 195–206. Rome.

Galili, E., N. Gale, and B. Rosen (2013), 'A Late Bronze Age Shipwreck with a Metal Cargo from Hishuley Carmel, Israel', *IJNA* 42: 2–23.

Gallagher, C. and S. Greenblatt (2000), *Practicing New Historicism*. Chicago.

Gallo, S. (2019), 'Peucezi e Greci, fra Tradizione, Interazione e Ibridismo. La Documentazione Archeologica a Monte Sannace tra VIII e VII Sec. a.C.', in A. Ciancio and P. Palmentola (eds.), *Monte Sannace – Thuriae. Nuove ricerche e studi*. 165–81. Bari.

Gardner, C. (2018), *Metalworking Crucibles in Roman Britain*. PhD Dissertation. University College London.

Gargano, M.P. (2001), 'Catalogo', in A. Damato (ed.), *Un luogo della Peucezia. Le scoperte archeologiche in contrada Bigetti*. 66–121. Palo del Colle.

Gargano, M.P. (2019), 'Le Tombe degli Scavi Scarfì 1957–1961', in A. Ciancio and P. Palmentola (eds.), *Monte Sannace – Thuriae. Nuove ricerche e studi*. 621–54. Bari.

Gargola, D. (2017), *The Shape of the Roman Order: The Republic and Its Spaces*. Chapel Hill.

Garraty, C.P. (2010), 'Investigating Market Exchange in Ancient Societies: A Theoretical Review', in C.P. Garraty and B.L. Stark (eds.), *Archaeological Approaches to Market Exchange in Ancient Societies*. 3–32. Boulder.

Gastaldi, P. (1998), *Pontecagnano II.4. La necropoli del Pagliarone. Annali del Dipartimento di Studi del Mondo Classico e del Mediterraneo Antico*. Naples.

Gell, A. (1998), *Art and Agency: An Anthropological Theory*. Oxford.

Genovesi, S. and C. Megale (2016), 'The Roman Settlement of Poggio del Molino: The Late Republican Fort and the Early Imperial Farm', *FOLD&R* 347: 1–15.

Georgakopoulou, M. (2016), 'Mobility and Early Bronze Age Southern Aegean Metal Production', in E. Kiriatzi and C. Knappett (eds.), *Human Mobility and Technological Transfer in the Prehistoric Mediterranean*. 46–67. Cambridge.

Ghobrial, J.-P. (2014), 'The Secret Life of Elias of Babylon and the Uses of Global Microhistory', *Past and Present* 222: 51–93.

Ghobrial, J.-P. (ed.) (2019a), *Global History and Microhistory*. *P&P* 242. Oxford.

Ghobrial, J.-P. (2019b), 'Introduction: Seeing the World Like a Microhistorian', *P&P* 242: 1–22.

Giammatteo, T. (2009), 'I risultati preliminari delle analisi archeometriche', in M. Osanna, L. Colalangelo, and G. Carollo (eds.), *Lo Spazio del Potere. La residenza ad abside, l'anaktoron, l'episcopio a Torre di Satriano. Atti del secondo convegno di studi su Torre di Satriano (Tito, 27–28 settembre 2008)*. 205–16. Venosa.

Giardino, C. (1995), *Il Mediterraneo Occidentale fra XIV e VIII secolo a.C. Cerchie minerarie e metallurgiche/The West Mediterranean between the 14th and 8th Centuries B.C. Mining and Metallurgical Spheres*. Oxford.

Giardino, C. and F. Lugl (2001), 'L'attività siderurgica nel Giardino Romano', *BullCom* 102: 321–2.

Giardino, L. (2005), '*Herakleia* e Metaponto: dalla *polis* italiota all'abitato protoimperiale', in *Tramonto della Magna Grecia. Atti del quarantaquattresimo convegno di studi sulla Magna Grecia, Taranto, 24–28 settembre 2004*. 387–432. Taranto.

Giddens, A. (1984), *The Constitution of Society: Outline of the Theory of Structuration*. Cambridge.

Gillis, C. (1990), 'Akrotiri and Its Neighbours to the South: Conical Cups Again', in D.A. Hardy, C. Doumas, J.A. Sakellarakis, and P.M. Warren (eds.), *Thera and the Aegean World III, I: Proceedings of the third International Congress, Santorini, Greece, 3–9 September, 1989*. 98–117. London.

Gilotta, F. (2014), 'Le classique et la commandite dans la céramique figurée étrusque au passage du v" au Iv" siède: quelques aspects de la question', in L. Ambrosini and V. Jolivet (eds.), *Les potiers d'Étrurie et leur monde: contacts, échanges, transferts. Hommages à Mario A. Del Chiaro*. 323–32. Paris.

Ginzburg, C. and C. Poni (1991), 'The Name and the Game: Unequal Exchange and the Historiographic Marketplace', in E. Muir and G. Ruggiero (eds.), *Microhistory and the Lost Peoples of Europe*. 1–10. Baltimore.

Giudice, F. (2002), 'La ceramica attica dell'Adriatico e la rotta di distribuzione verso gli empori padani', in M. Luni and L. Braccesi (eds.), *I Greci in Adriatico. Atti del Convegno Internazionale (Urbino, 21–24 ottobre 1999)*. 171–210. Rome.

Giudice, G. (2007), *Il tornio, la nave, le terre lontane: ceramografi attici in Magna Grecia nella seconda metà del V secolo a.C.: rotte e vie di distribuzione*. Rome.

Giuliani, L. (1995), *Tragik, Trauer und Trost. Bildvasen für eine Apulische Totenfeier*. Berlin.

Giuliano, A. (2006), 'Protoattici in Occidente', in B. Adembri (ed.), *Aeimnestos. Miscellanea di studi per Mauro Cristofani*. 64–72. Florence.

Gleba, M. (2009), 'Textile Tools in Ancient Italian Votive Contexts: Evidence of Dedication or Production?', in M. Gleba and H. Becker (eds.), *Votives, Places and Rituals in Etruscan Religion*. 69–84. Leiden.

Gleba, M. (2011), 'The "Distaff Side" of Early Iron Age Aristocratic Identity in Italy', in M. Gleba and H.W. Horsnæs (eds.), *Communicating Identity in Italic Iron Age Communities*. 26–32. Oxford.

Gleba, M., C. Heitz, H. Landenius Enegren, and F. Meo (2018), 'At the Crossroads of Textile Cultures: Textile Production and Use at the South Italian Archaic Site of Ripacandida', *JMA* 31: 27–51.

Gleba, M. and J. Pasztokai-Szeöke (2013), *Making Textiles in Pre-Roman and Roman Times: People, Places, Identities*. Oxford.

Glinister, F. (1997), 'What is a Sanctuary?', *Cahiers du Centre Gustave Glotz* 8: 61–80.

Goldman, I. (1975), *The Mouth of Heaven*. New York.

Good, C. (1975), 'Periodic Markets and Traveling Traders in Uganda', *Geographical Review* 65: 49–72.

Gori, G. (2014), 'Etruscan Sports and Festivals', in T. Scanlon (ed.), *Sport in the Greek and Roman Worlds. Vol. 2*. 190–7. Oxford.

Gori, I. (2007), 'La grande città etrusca "dimenticata"', *Corriere della Sera*. www.corriere.it/Primo_Piano/Cronache/2007/02_Febbraio/16/etruschi.shtml?refresh_ce-cp. [Accessed 20/6/2020].

Gori, M. and T. Krapf (2015), 'The Bronze and Iron Age Pottery from Sovjan', *Iliria* 39: 91–135.

Gosden, C. (2004), *Archaeology and Colonialism: Cultural Contact from 5000 BC to the Present*. Cambridge.

Gosner, L. and J. Hayne (eds.) (forthcoming), *Local Experiences of Connectivity and Mobility in the Ancient West-Central Mediterranean*. Sheffield.

Gosselain, O.P. (1998), 'Social and Technical Identity in a Clay Crystal Ball', in M. Stark (ed.), *The Archaeology of Social Boundaries*. 78–106. Washington, DC.

Gosselain, O.P. (2000), 'Materializing Identities: An African Perspective', *Journal of Archaeological Method and Theory* 7: 187–217.

Gosselain, O.P. (2016a), 'Commentary: On Fluxes, Connections and their Archaeological Manifestations', in E. Kiriatzi and C. Knappett (eds.), *Human Mobility and Technological Transfer in the Prehistoric Mediterranean*. 193–205. New York.

Gosselain, O.P. (2016b), 'The World Is Like a Beanstalk: Historicizing Potting Practice and Social Relations in the Niger River Area', in A.P. Roddick and A.B. Stahl (eds.), *Knowledge in Motion: Constellations of Learning across Time and Place*. 36–66. Tuscon.

Gosselain, O.P. (2018), 'Pottery Chaînes Opératoires as Historical Documents', in T. Spear (ed.), *The Oxford Encyclopedia of African Historiography: Methods and Sources*. 1–41. Oxford.

Govi, E. (ed.) (2017), *La città etrusca e il sacro. Santuari e istituzioni politiche. Atti del Convegno, Bologna 21–23 gennaio 2016*. Bologna.
Graeber, D. (2011), *Debt: The First 5,000 Years*. New York.
Graham, S. (2009), 'The Space Between: The Geography of Social Networks in the Tiber Valley', in F. Coarelli and H. Patterson (eds.), *Mercator Placidissimus: The Tiber Valley in Antiquity: New Research in the Upper and Middle River Valley*. 671–86. Rome.
Granovetter, M. (1985), 'Economic Action and Social Structure: The Problem of Embeddedness', *American Journal of Sociology* 91: 481–510.
Greco, G. (1980), 'Le fasi cronologiche dell'abitato di Serra di Vaglio', in E. Lattanzi (ed.), *Attività archeologica in Basilicata, 1964–1977: Scritti in onore di Dinu Adamesteanu*. 367–404. Matera.
Green, J.R. (1976), 'An Addition to the Volcani Group', *AJA* 80: 188–9.
Gregorovius, F. (1978), *Wanderjahre in Italien*. Munich.
Greiner, C. (2003), *Die Peuketia: Kultur und Kulturkontakte in Mittelapulien vom 8. bis 5. Jh. v. Chr.* Remshalden.
Grelle, F. (1989), 'L'ordinamento territoriale della Peucezia e le forme della romanizzazione', in A. Ciancio (ed.), *Archeologia e territorio. L'area peuceta. Atti del seminario di studi Gioia del Colle, Museo archeologico nazionale 12–14 novembre 1987*. 111–6. Gioia del Colle.
Gros, P. (1995), 'Hercule à Glanum: Sanctuaires de transhumance et développement "urbain"', *Gallia* 52: 311–31.
Gruen, E. (2011), *Rethinking the Other in Antiquity*. Princeton.
Gruen, E. (2020), *Ethnicity in the Ancient World – Did It Matter?* Berlin.
Gualtieri, M. (2012), '"Late Apulian" Red-figure Vases in Context: A Case Study', in S. Schierup and B. Bundgaard Rasmussen (eds.), *Red-Figure Pottery in Its Ancient Setting. Acts of the International Colloquium Held at the National Museum of Denmark in Copenhagen, November 5–6, 2009*. 60–8. Aarhus.
Guarducci, M. (1967), *Epigrafia Greca*. Rome.
Guggisberg, M. (2017), 'Polyphem und der Käse: Anmerkungen zum Krater des Aristonothos von Cerveteri', in L. Cappuccini, C. Leypold, and M. Mohr (eds.), *Fragmenta Mediterranea. Contatti, tradizioni e innovazioni in Grecia, Magna Grecia, Etruria e Roma. Studi in onore di Christoph Reusser*. 91–103. Florence.
Guglielmino, R. (2012), 'Il bitume di Roca. Breve nota su una sostanza negletta negli studi di protostoria italiana', *ASNP* 4: 99–114, 200.
Haack, M.-L. (2014), 'Enquête sur l'économie du sanctuaire étrusque de Gravisca', in D. Frère and L. Hugot (eds.), *Étrusques, Les plus heureux des hommes*. 199–209. Rennes.
Haack, M.-L. (2017), 'Ritual and Cults, 580–450 BCE', in A. Naso (ed.), *Etruscology*. 1001–12. Berlin.
Hales, S. and T. Hodos (2010), *Material Culture and Social Identities in the Ancient World*. Cambridge.
Hall, E. (1989), *Inventing the Barbarian: Greek Self-definition through Tragedy*. Oxford.
Hall, J. (1997), *Ethnic Identity in Greek Antiquity*. Cambridge.
Hall, J. (2002), *Hellenicity: Between Ethnicity and Culture*. Chicago.
Halstead, P. (1996), 'Pastoralism or Household Herding? Problems of Scale and Specialization in Early Greek Animal Husbandry', *World Archaeology* 28: 20–42.
Halstead, P. (2006), 'Sheep in the Garden: The Integration of Crop and Livestock Husbandry in Early Farming Regimes of Greece and Southern Europe', in

D. Serjeantson and D. Field (eds.), *Animals in the Neolithic of Britain and Europe*. 42–55. Oxford.

Hansen, S. (2010), 'Communication and Exchange between the Northern Caucasus and Central Europe in the Fourth Millennium BC', in S. Hansen, A. Hauptmann, I. Motzenbäcker, and E. Pernicka (eds.), *Von Majkop bis Trialeti. Gewinnung und Verbreitung von Metallen und Obsidian in Kaukasien im 4.-2. Jt. v. Chr*. 297–316. Bonn.

Harris, J. (2007), 'Fanum Voltumnae: Is the Mystery Resolved?', *Current World Archaeology* 26: 23–6.

Harris, W.V. (1971), *Rome in Etruria and Umbria*. Oxford.

Harris, W.V. (ed.) (2005), *Rethinking the Mediterranean*. Oxford.

Hartmann, N. (1985), 'The Use of Iron in 9th and 8th Century Etruria', in C. Malone and S. Stoddart (eds.), *Papers of Italian Archaeology IV*. 285–94. Oxford.

Hassig, R. (1982), 'Periodic Markets in Pre-Columbian Mexico', *American Antiquity* 47: 346–55.

Hauptmann, A., R. Maddin, and M. Prange (2002), 'On the Structure and Composition of Copper and Tin Ingots Excavated from the Shipwreck of Uluburun', *BASO* 328: 1–30.

Heitz, C. (2015a), 'Ripacandida: An Indigenous Graveyard and the Greek Periphery', *Accordia Research Papers* 14: 103–21.

Heitz, C. (2015b), 'Mobile Pastoralists in Archaic Southern Italy? The Use of Social and Material Evidence for the Detection of an Ancient Economy', *Ethnographisch-Archäologische Zeitschrift* 56: 135–62.

Heitz, C. (2016), 'Von „ganzen Häusern" zu großen Männern? Beobachtungen zu Veränderungen in der Struktur süditalischer Gemeinschaften in archaischer Zeit am Beispiel der Nekropole von Ripacandida/Basilicata (Süditalien)', *BABESCH* 91: 43–67.

Heitz, C. (2020), 'Pastorale Wirtschaft im Apenningebiet. Von historischer Zeit bis in die Vorgeschichte', in M. Kasper, R. Rollinger, A. Rudigier, and K. Ruffing (eds.), *Wirtschaften in den Bergen. Von Bergleuten, Hirten, Bauern, Künstlern, Händlern und Unternehmern*. 251–67. Vienna.

Heitz, C. (2021), *Gesellschaft und Wirtschaft im archaischen Süditalien. Ein Modell zu Identität und Hexis, ausgehend von Ripacandida und weiteren binnenländischen Gemeinschaften*. Wiesbaden.

Helm, M. (2020), 'Poor Man's War – Rich Man's Fight: Military Integration in Republican Rome', in J. Armstrong and M. Fronda (eds.), *Romans at War: Soldiers, Citizens, and Society in the Roman Republic*. 99–115. New York.

Helms, M. (1988), *Ulysses' Sail: An Ethnographic Odyssey of Power, Knowledge, and Geographical Distance*. Princeton.

Helms, M. (1993), *Craft and the Kingly Ideal: Art, Trade, and Power*. Austin.

Hencken, H. (1968), *Tarquinia, Villanovans and Early Etruscans*. Cambridge, MA.

Hencken, H. (1971), *The Earliest European Helmets*. Harvard.

Henneberg, R.J. (1998), *Dental Health and Affiliations of Inhabitants of the Ancient Greek Colony of Metaponto, Italy (6th–3rd Century BC)*. PhD Dissertation. University of the Witwatersrand, Johannesburg.

Herring, E. (1995), 'Emblems of Identity. An Examination of the Use of Matt-painted Pottery in the Native Tombs of the Salento Peninsula in the 5th and 4th Centuries BC', in N. Christie (ed.), *Settlement and Economy, 1500 BC- AD 1500*. 135–42. Oxford.

Herring, E. (1998), *Explaining Change in the Matt-Painted Pottery of Southern Italy: Cultural and Social Explanations for Ceramic Development from the 11th to the 4th Centuries B.C.* Oxford.

Herring, E. (2009), '"To See Oursels as Others See Us!" The Construction of Native Identities in Southern Italy', in E. Herring and K. Lomas (eds.), *The Emergence of State Identities in Italy in the First Millennium BC.* 45–77. London.

Herring, E. (2017), '"You'll Get a Belt from Your Da": Military Prowess, Status and Masculinity and the Evidence of the Bronze Belts from South Italy', in E. Herring and E. O'Donoghue (eds.), *Papers in Italian Archaeology VII. The Archaeology of Death.* 22–30. Oxford.

Herring, E. (2020), 'Emblems of Identity Revisited: Gender and the Messapian Trozzella', *AWE* 19: 247–55.

Herring, E., R. Whitehouse, and J. Wilkins (eds.) (1992), *Papers of the Fourth Conferences of Italian Archaeology: New Developments in Italian Archaeology.* London.

Hilditch, J. (2008), *Reconstructing Technical Choice, Social Practice and Networks of Exchange in the Middle Bronze Age of the Cyclades: The Ceramic Perspective.* PhD Dissertation. University of Exeter.

Hilditch, J. (2014), 'Analyzing Technological Standardization: Revisiting the Minoan Conical Cup', in A. Kotsonas (ed.), *Understanding Standardization and Variation in Mediterranean Ceramics, Mid 2nd to Late 1st Millennium BC.* 25–37. Leuven.

Hirth, K.G. (1996), 'Political Economy and Archaeology: Perspectives on Exchange and Production', *Journal of Archaeological Research* 4: 203–39.

Hirth, K.G. (2010), 'Finding the Mark in the Marketplace: The Organization, Development, and Archaeological Identification of Market Systems', in C.P. Garraty and B.L. Stark (eds.), *Archaeological Approaches to Market Exchange in Ancient Societies.* 227–47. Boulder.

Hirth, K.G. (2016), *The Aztec Economic World: Merchants and Markets in Ancient Mesoamerica.* New York.

Hitchcock, L., R. Laffineur, and J. Crowley (eds.) (2008), *Dais: The Aegean Feast: Proceedings of the 12th International Aegean Conference/12e Rencontre Égéenne Internationale, University of Melbourne, Centre for Classics and Archaeology, 25–29 March 2008.* Liège.

Hodder, I. (1979), 'Economic and Social Stress and Material Culture Patterning', *American Antiquity* 44: 446–54.

Hodder, I. (2012), *Entangled: An Archaeology of the Relationships between Humans and Things.* London.

Hodder, I. and C. Orton (1976), *Spatial Analysis in Archaeology.* Cambridge.

Hodges, R. (1988), *Primitive and Peasant Markets.* Oxford.

Hodos, T. (2008), *Local Responses to the Colonization in the Iron Age Mediterranean.* New York.

Hoffmann-Lange, U. (2007), 'Methods of Elite Research', in R. Dalton and H. Klingermann (eds.), *The Oxford Handbook of Political Behavior.* 910–28. Oxford.

Holleran, C. (2012), *Shopping in Ancient Rome: The Retail Trade in the Late Republic and the Principate.* Oxford.

Holleran, C. (2018), 'The Retail Trade', in A. Claridge and C. Holleran (eds.), *A Companion to the City of Rome.* 459–71. Somerset.

Honeychurch, W. (2014), 'Alternative Complexities: The Archaeology of Pastoral Nomadic States', *Journal of Archaeological Research* 22: 277–326.

Horden, P. and N. Purcell (2000), *The Corrupting Sea: A Study of Mediterranean History*. Oxford.
Horden, P. and N. Purcell (2005), 'Four Years of Corruption: A Response to the Critics', in W.V. Harris (ed.), *Rethinking the Mediterranean*. 348–76. Oxford.
Horne, L. (1982), 'Fuel for the Metal Worker', *Expedition Magazine* 25: 6–13.
Humphreys, S. (2004), *The Strangeness of Gods: Historical Perspectives on the Interpretation of Athenian Religion*. Oxford.
Humphreys, S. (2018), *Kinship in Ancient Athens: An Anthropological Analysis*. Oxford.
Hunt, L. (2014), *Writing History in the Global Era*. New York.
Hunt, P. (2018), *Ancient Greek and Roman Slavery*. Malden, MA.
Hurwit, J.M. (2015), *Artists and Signatures in Ancient Greece*. Cambridge.
Hütteroth, W.-D. (1959), *Bergnomaden und Yaylabauern im mittleren kurdischen Taurus*. Marburg.
Hütteroth, W.-D. (1982), *Türkei*. Darmstadt.
Iacono, F. (2018), *The Archaeology of Late Bronze Age Interaction and Mobility at the Gates of Europe: People, Things and Networks around the Southern Adriatic Sea*. London.
Iaia, C. (1999a), *Simbolismo funerario e ideologia alle origini di una civiltà urbana. Forme rituali nelle sepolture 'villanoviane' a Tarquinia e Vulci, e nel loro entroterra*. Florence.
Iaia, C. (1999b), 'Le Arcatelle di Tarquinia: dati e ipotesi sull'organizzazione planimetrica della necropoli protostorica', *Bollettino della Società Tarquiniense di Arte e Storia* 28: 5–21.
Iaia, C. (2005), *Produzioni toreutiche della prima età del ferro in Italia centro-settentrionale. Stili decorativi, circolazione, significato*. Pisa-Rome.
Iaia, C. (2007a), 'Elements of Female Jewellery in Iron Age Latium and South Etruria: Identity and Cultural Communication in a Boundary Zone', in M. Blečić, M. Črešnar, B. Hänsel, A. Hellmuth, E. Kaiser, and C. Metzner-Nebelsick (eds.), *Scripta Praehistorica in Honorem Biba Teržan*. 519–31. Ljubliana.
Iaia, C. (2007b) 'Identità e comunicazione nell'abbigliamento femminile dell'area circumadriatica fra IX e VII secolo a.C', in P. Von Eles (ed.), *Le ore e i giorni delle donne: Dalla quotidianità alla sacralità tra VIII e VII secolo a.C.* 25–36. Verucchio.
Iaia, C. (2013a), 'Metalwork, Rituals and the Making of Élite Identity in Central Italy at the Bronze Age-Iron Age Transition', in E. Alberti and S. Sabatini (eds.), *Exchange Networks and Local Transformations: Interactions and Local Changes in Europe and the Mediterranean between Bronze and Iron Age*. 102–16. Oxford.
Iaia, C. (2013b), 'Warrior Identity and the Materialization of Power in Early Iron Age Etruria', *Accordia Research Papers* 12: 71–95.
Iaia, C. (2015), 'Smiths and Smithing in Bronze Age "Terramare"', in R. Kelm (ed.), *Archaeology and Crafts: Experiences and Experiments on Traditional Skills and Handicrafts in Archaeological Open-Air Museums in Europe; Proceedings of the VI. OpenArch-Conference in Albersdorf, Germany, 23–27 September 2013*. 78–93. Husum.
Iaia, C. (2017), 'Handicraft (10th cent. – 730 BCE)', in A. Naso (ed.), *Etruscology*. 730–57. Berlin.
Iaia, C. (2019), '3.1. La tomba di guerriero Monterozzi 3 della necropoli delle Arcatelle', in A. Cardarelli and A. Naso (eds.), *Etruschi maestri artigiani. Nuove prospettive da Cerveteri e Tarquinia*. 143–6. Naples.

Iaia, C. and M. Pacciarelli (2012), 'La cremazione in area medio-tirrenica fra Bronzo finale e Primo ferro', in C. Rovira Hortalà, F.J. Lòpez Cachero, and F. Mazière (eds.), *Les necropòlis d'incineraciò entre l'Ebre i el Tìber (segles IX-VI a.C.): metodologia, pràctiques funeràries i societat*. 341–55. Barcelona.
Ingold, T. (1993), 'The Temporality of the Landscape', *World Archaeology* 25: 152–74.
Ingold, T. (2011), *Being Alive: Essays on Movement, Knowledge and Description*. London.
Ingold, T. (2015), *The Life of Lines*. London.
Iozzo, M. (1994), *Ceramica 'calcidese'. Nuovi documenti e problemi riproposti. Atti e Memorie della Società Magna Grecia, terza serie, II (1993)*. Rome.
Isayev, E. (2009), 'Unintentionally Being Lucanian: Dynamics Beyond Hybridity', in S. Hales and T. Hodos (eds.), *Material Culture and Social Identities in the Ancient World*. 201–26. Cambridge.
Isayev, E. (2017), *Migration, Mobility and Place in Ancient Italy*. Cambridge.
Isayev, E. (2020), 'Elusive Migrants of Ancient Italy', in J. Clackson, P. James, K. McDonald, L. Tagliapietra, and N. Zair (eds.), *Migration, Mobility and Language Contact in and Around the Ancient Mediterranean*. 53–74. Cambridge.
Isayev, E. and S. Müller Wille (2022), 'Hospitality and Knowledge: Linnaeus's hosts on his Laplandic Journey (1732)', in A. Mack and T. Kitlinski (eds.), *Hospitality. Special Issue of Social Research* 89.1.
Jacobs, J. (1972), *The Economy of Cities*. London.
Jaspers, K. (1953), *The Origin and Goal of History*. London.
Jeffra, C.D. (2015), 'Experimental Approaches to Archaeological Ceramics: Unifying Disparate Methodologies with the *Chaîne Opératoire*', *Archaeological and Anthropological Sciences* 7: 141–9.
Jenkins, R. (1997), *Rethinking Ethnicity: Arguments and Explorations*. London.
Jennings, J. (2010), *Globalizations and the Ancient World*. Cambridge.
Jew, D., R. Osborne, and M. Scott (eds.) (2016), *M. I. Finley: An Ancient Historian and His Impact*. Cambridge.
Joas, H. and R. Bellah (eds.) (2012), *The Axial Age and Its Consequences*. Harvard.
Jockenhövel, A. (1974), 'Eine Bronzeamphore des 8. Jahrunderts v. Chr. von Gevelinghausen, Kr. Meschede (Sauerland)', *Germania* 52: 16–54.
Jones, R., S.T. Levi, M. Bettelli, and L. Vagnetti (2014), *Italo-Mycenaean Pottery: The Archaeological and Archaeometric Dimensions*. Rome.
Jones, S. (1997), *The Archaeology of Ethnicity: Constructing Identities in the Past and Present*. London.
Jorge Dias, A. (1969), 'Das Hirtenwesen in Portugal', in L. Földes (ed.), *Viehwirtschaft und Hirtenkultur. Ethnographische Studien*. 790–814. Budapest.
Kaster, R.A. (2011), *Macrobius. Saturnalia, Volume I: Books 1–2*. Cambridge, MA.
Keegan, J. (1993), *A History of Warfare*. London.
Kenrick, P.M. (1993), 'Italian Terra Sigillata: A Sophisticated Roman Industry', *OJA* 12: 235–42.
Killgrove, K. and J. Montgomery (2016), 'All Roads Lead to Rome: Exploring Human Migration to the Eternal City through Biochemistry of Skeletons from Two Imperial-era Cemeteries (1st–3rd c AD)', *PLoS ONE* 11(2): 1–30.
Kindstedt, P. (2012), *Cheese and Culture: A History of Cheese and Its Place in Western Civilization*. White River Junction.
Kindt, J. (2013), *Rethinking Greek Religion*. Cambridge.

Kiriatzi, E. and C. Knappett (eds.) (2016), *Human Mobility and Technological Transfer in the Prehistoric Mediterranean*. New York.

Kleijwegt, M. (2002), 'Cum vicensimariis magnam mantissam habet (Petronius Satyricon 65.10)', *AJP* 123: 275–86.

Knapp, A.B. and P. van Dommelen (2010), 'Material Connections: Mobility, Materiality and Mediterranean Identities', in P. van Dommelen, R. Alexander, and A.B. Knapp (eds.), *Material Connections in the Ancient Mediterranean: Mobility, Materiality, and Identity*. 1–18. New York.

Knappett, C. (2005), *Thinking Through Material Culture: An Interdisciplinary Perspective*. Philadelphia.

Knappett, C. (2011), *An Archaeology of Interaction: Network Perspectives on Material Culture and Society*. Oxford.

Knappett, C. (2013), *Network Analysis in Archaeology: New Approaches to Regional Interaction*. Oxford.

Knappett, C. and S. Van der Leeuw (2014), 'A Developmental Approach to Ancient Innovation: The Potter's Wheel in the Bronze Age East Mediterranean', *Pragmatics & Cognition* 22: 64–92.

Kohler, C. and A. Naso (1991), 'Appunti sulla funzione di alari e spiedi nelle società arcaiche dell'Italia centro-meridionale', in E. Herring, R. Whitehouse, and J. Wilkins (eds.), *Papers of the Fourth Conference of Italian Archaeology, Vol. 2*. 41–63. London.

Kok, R.A.E. (2009), 'Un nucleo di tombe della necropoli di Melfi-Pisciolo. Riflessioni sulla rappresentazione dell'identità nello spazio funerario', in M. Osanna and M. Scalici (eds.), *Lo spazio della memoria. Necropoli e rituali funerari nella Magna Grecia indigena, Atti della Tavola rotunda (Matera 11 dicembre)*. 65–80. Matera.

Kopczyńska-Jaworska, B. (1961), 'Das Hirtenwesen in den polnischen Karpaten', in L. Földes (ed.), *Viehzucht und Hirtenleben in Ostmitteleuropa. Ethnographische Studien*. 389–438. Budapest.

Kopytoff, I. (1986), 'The Cultural Biography of Things: Commoditization as a Process', in A. Appadurai (ed.), *The Social Life of Things: Commodities in Social Perspective*. 64–94. Cambridge.

Korkuti, M. (1985), 'Marrëdhëniet midis dy brigjeve të Adriatikut në epokën e bronzit dhe të hekurit/I rapporti fra le due coste dell'adriatico meridionale nell'epoca del bronzo e del ferro', *Iliria* 15: 93–109.

Koster, H. (2000), 'Neighbors and Pastures: Reciprocity and Access to Pasture', in S. Sutton and K. Adams (eds.), *Contingent Countryside: Settlement, Economy, and Land Use in the Southern Argolid since 1700*. 241–61. Stanford.

Kotsonas, A. (2014), 'Standardization, Variation, and the Study of Ceramics in the Mediterranean and Beyond', in A. Kotsonas (ed.), *Understanding Standardization and Variation in Mediterranean Ceramics, Mid 2nd to Late 1st Millennium BC*. 7–23. Leuven.

Kuijpers, M. (2013), 'The Sound of Fire, Taste of Copper, Feel of Bronze, and Colours of the Cast: Sensory Aspects of Metalworking Technology', in M.L.S. Sørensen and K. Rebay-Salisbury (eds.), *Embodied Knowledge: Perspectives on Belief and Technology*. 137–50. Oxford.

Kuijpers, M. (2018a), *An Archaeology of Skill: Metalworking Skill and Material Specialization in Early Bronze Age Central Europe*. London and New York.

Kuijpers, M. (2018b), 'The Bronze Age, a World of Specialists? Metalworking from the Perspective of Skill and Material Specialization', *EJA* 21: 550–71.

Kunz, L. (1969), 'Die traditionelle Milch- und Käsewirtschaft in Mittel- und Westmähren', in L. Földes (ed.), *Viehwirtschaft und Hirtenkultur. Ethnographische Studien.* 706–34. Budapest.

Kurti, R. (2012), 'Qelibari gjatë periudhës së Bronzit të Vonë dhe të Hekurit në Shqipëri/Amber during Late Bronze Age and Iron Age in Albania', *Iliria* 36: 73–108.

Kurti, R. (2020), 'Common Trends and Regional Particularities in the Western Balkan Iron Age: The Female Belt Adornment in the 7th–6th Centuries BCE Northern Albania', in M. Gavranović, D. Heilmann, A. Kapuran, and M. Verčík (eds.), *Spheres of Interaction Contacts and Relationships between the Balkans and Adjacent Regions in the Late Bronze/Iron Age (13th – 5th Centuries BCE). Proceedings of the Conference Held at the Institute of Archaeology, Belgrade 15–17 September, 2017.* 217–52. Rahden.

Kvamme, K.L., M.T. Stark, and W.A. Longacre (1996), 'Alternative Procedures for Assessing Standardization in Ceramic Assemblages', *American Antiquity* 61: 116–26.

Lambrugo, C. (2014), 'Funus Acerbum. Sepolture Infantili in Abitato a Jazzo Fornasiello (Gravina di Puglia)', in M. Castoldi (ed.), *Un Abitato Peuceta. Scavi a Jazzo Fornasiello (Gravina in Puglia -Bari) Prime indagini.* 59–74. Bari.

Lambrugo, C. (2018), 'Peuceti artigiani. Spunti di riflessione da Jazzo Fornasiello (Gravina in Puglia, Bari)', in F. Giacobello (ed.), *Savoir-faire antichi e moderni. Pittori e officine ceramiche nell'Apulia di V e IV secolo a.C.* 55–70. Milan.

Langslow, D. (2012), 'Integration, Identity, and Language Shift: Strengths and Weaknesses of the "Linguistic" Evidence', in S. Roselaar (ed.), *Processes of Integration and Identity Formation in the Roman Republic.* 289–309. Leiden.

Lanza Catti, E. (2011), 'Diversificazione funzionale dei manufatti ceramici in rapporto al contesto: il caso della ceramica "di Gnathia" nella Peucezia preromana', in *Tra Protostoria e Storia. Studi in Onore di Loredana Capuis.* 265–79. Rome.

Latour, B. (1996), 'Where Are the Missing Masses? The Sociology of a Few Mundane Artifacts', in W. Bijker and J. Law (eds.), *Shaping Technology/Building Society: Studies in Sociotechnical Change.* 225–58. Cambridge, MA.

Latour, B. (2005), *Reassembling the Social – An Introduction to Actor-Network-Theory.* Oxford.

Lave, J. and E. Wenger (1991), *Situated Learning: Legitimate Peripheral Participation.* Cambridge.

Lechtman, H. (1977), 'Style in Technology- Some Early Thoughts', in H. Lechtman and R. Merrill (eds.), *Material Culture: Styles, Organization and Dynamics of Technology.* 3–20. St. Paul.

Lefebvre, H. (1974/1991), *The Production of Space.* Malden, MA.

Lehoërff, A. (2007), *L'artisanat du bronze en Italie centrale, 1200–725 avant notre ère; le métal des dépôts volontaires.* Rome.

Lemonnier, P. (1986), 'The Study of Material Culture Today: Towards an Anthropology of Technical Systems', *Journal of Anthropological Archaeology* 5: 47–86.

Lemos, I. (2002), *The Protogeometric Aegean: The Archaeology of the Late Eleventh and Tenth Centuries BC.* Oxford.

Levy, T., A. Levy, D.R. Sthapathy, D. Sr. Sthapathy, and D. Sw. Sthapathy (2007), *Masters of Fire – Hereditary Bronze Casters of South India.* Bochum.

Lewis, D. (2017), 'Notes on Slave Names, Ethnicity, and Identity in Classical and Hellenistic Greece', in M. Nowak, A. Łatjar, and J. Urbanik (eds.), *Tell Me Who You Are: Labelling Status in the Graeco-Roman World.* 169–99. Truskaw.

Lewthwaite, J. (1981), 'Plains Tails from the Hills: Transhumance in Mediterranean Archaeology', in A. Sheridan and G. Bailey (eds.), *Economic Archaeology: Towards an Integration of Ecological and Social Approaches.* 57–66. Oxford.
Lippert, A. (ed.) (2011), *Die zweischaligen ostalpinen Kammhelme und verwandte Helmformen der späten Bronze- und frühen Eisenzeit.* Salzburg.
Lippolis, E. (2007), 'Ceramica a figure rosse apula (tarda)', in E.M. De Juliis (ed.), *Rutigliano I, La necropoli di contrada Purgatorio. Scavo 1978. Catalogo del Museo Nazionale Archeologico di Taranto, volume II.2.* 431–61. Taranto.
Lippolis, E. (2018), 'La mobilità del ceramografo dalla formazione alla produzione. Problemi generali e un caso di studio: il pittore di Dario e il suo ambiente artigianale', *Archeologia Classica* 69: 73–111.
Lippolis, E. and M. Mazzei (2005), 'La ceramica apula a figure rosse: aspetti e problemi', in M. Denoyelle, E. Lippolis, M. Mazzei, and C. Pouzadoux (eds.), *La céramique apulienne. Bilan et perspectives. Actes de la table ronde de Naples, 2000.* 11–18. Naples.
Lomas, K. (2002), 'The Polis in Italy: Ethnicity, Colonization, and Citizenship in the Western Mediterranean', in R. Brock and S. Hodgkinson (eds.), *Alternatives to Athens: Varieties of Political Organization and Community in Ancient Greece.* 167–85. Oxford.
Lomas, K. (2012), 'Space, Boundaries and the Representation of Identity in the Ancient Veneto c. 600–400 BC', in G. Cifani and S. Stoddart (eds.), *Landscape, Ethnicity and Identity in the Archaic Mediterranean Area.* 187–206. Oxford.
Lombardi, N. (1999), 'Struttura e quotidianità dell'attività pastorale', in E. Petrocelli (ed.), *La civiltà della transumanza. Storia, cultura e valorizzazione dei tratturi e del mondo pastorale in Abruzzo, Molise, Puglia, Campania e Basilicata.* 19–42. Isernia.
Lombardo, M. (1994a), 'La necropoli arcaica di Tor Pisana a Brindisi. Evidenze e problemi interpretativi', in C. Marangio and A. Nitti (eds.), *Scritti di antichità in memoria di Benita Sciarra Bardaro.* 171–7. Fasano.
Lombardo, M. (1994b), 'Tombe, necropoli e riti funerari in "Messapia": evidenze e problemi', *Studi di Antichità* 7: 25–45.
Lombardo, M. (2014), 'Iapygians: The Indigenous Populations of Ancient Puglia in the Fifth and Fourth Centuries B.C.E.', in T.H. Carpenter, K. Lynch, and E.G.D. Robinson (eds.), *The Italic People of Ancient Apulia: New Evidence from Pottery for Workshops, Markets, and Customs.* 36–68. Cambridge.
Long, L., L.-F. Gantès, and M. Rival (2006), 'L'épave Grand Ribaud F. Un chargement de produits étrusques du début du Ve siècle avant J.-C.', in S. Gori and M.C. Bettini (eds.), *Gli Etruschi da Genova ad Ampurias: atti del XXIV convegno di studi etruschi ed italici, Marseille – Lattes, 26 settembre – 1 ottobre 2002.* 455–95. Pisa.
Longacre, W.A. (1999), 'Standardization and Specialization: What's the Link?', in J.M. Skibo and G. Feinman (eds.), *Pottery and People: A Dynamic Interaction.* 44–58. Salt Lake City.
Lo Porto, F.G. (1973), *Civilta indigena e penetrazione greca nella Lucania orientale.* Rome.
Lo Porto, F.G. (1976), 'L'attività archeologica in Puglia', in *La Magna Grecia in età Romana. Atti del quindicesimo Convegno di studi sulla Magna Grecia. Taranto, ottobre 1975.* 635–45. Naples.
Lo Porto, F.G. (1977), 'Recenti scoperte archeologiche in Puglia', in *Locri Epizefirii: atti del sedicesimo Convegno di studi sulla Magna Grecia, Taranto, 3–8 ottobre 1976.* 725–45. Naples.

Lo Porto, F.G. (1988–1989), 'Metaponto (Matera) – Rinvenimenti nella città antica e nel suo retroterra ellenizzato', *NSA* 8(42–4): 299–441.
Lo Porto, F.G. (2004), *Il deposito prelaconico di Borgo Nuovo a Taranto*. Rome.
Lo Porto, F.G. and F. Ranaldi (1990), 'Le "lastre dei cavalieri" di Serra di Vaglio', *Monumenti Antichi. Serie Miscellanea* III(6): 291–317.
Lo Schiavo, F. (2012), 'Interconnessioni fra Mediterraneo e Atlantico nell'età del bronzo: il punto di vista della Sardegna', *Cuadernos de Arqueología Mediterránea* 21: 107–34.
Lo Schiavo, F., P. Falchi, and M. Milletti (2013), 'Sardegna ed Etruria tirrenica: identità in formazione: ripostigli e scambi della fase di transizione fra la fine del Bronzo Finale e la prima età del Ferro', in S. Bruni and G.C. Cianferoni (eds.), *Δόσις δ'ολίγη τε φίλη τε. Studi in onore di Antonella Romualdi*. 371–416. Florence.
Lo Schiavo, F. and M. Milletti (2011), 'Una rilettura del ripostiglio di Falda della Guardiola, Populonia (LI)', *Archaeological Classica* 62: 309–55.
Lucchese, C. (2010), 'L'importazione della Ceramica Attica', in L. Todisco (ed.), *La Puglia centrale dall'età del bronzo all'alto medioevo. Archeologia e storia. Atti del convegno di studi (Bari, 15–16 giugno 2009)*. 299–306. Rome.
Lucentini, N. (2009), 'La collezione civica di Ascoli Piceno: i cinturoni pancera a losanga e gancio', in G. De Marinis and G. Paci (eds.), *Omaggio a Nereo Alfieri. Contributi all'Archeologia Marchigiana, Atti del Convegno di Studi (Loreto 9–11 maggio 2005)*. 305–44. Tivoli.
Lucy, S. (2005), 'Ethnic and Cultural Identities', in M. Díaz-Andreu, S. Lucy, S. Babić, and D. Edwards (eds.), *The Archaeology of Identity: Approaches to Gender, Age, Status, Ethnicity and Religion*. 86–109. London.
Lyons, P. and J.J. Clark (2012), 'A Community of Practice in Diaspora: The Rise and Demise of Roosevelt Red Ware', in L.S. Cordell and J. Habicht-Mauche (eds.), *Potters and Communiteis of Practice: Glaze Paint and Polychrome Pottery in the American Southwest, A. D. 1250–1700*. 19–33. Tuscon.
Lytra, V. (2016), 'Language and Ethnic Identity', in S. Preece (ed.), *The Routledge Handbook of Language and Identity*. 131–45. London.
MacDonald, B.R. (1981), 'The Emigration of Potters from Athens in the Late Fifth Century B. C. and Its Effect on the Attic Pottery Industry', *AJA* 85: 159–68.
MacDonald, B.R. (1982), 'The Import of Attic Pottery to Corinth and the Question of Trade during the Peloponnesian War', *JHS* 102: 113–23.
Mackil, E. (2017), 'Property Claims and State Formation in the Archaic Greek World', in C. Ando and S. Richardson (eds.), *Ancient States and Infrastructural Power: Europe, Asia, and America*. 63–90. Philadelphia.
MacMullen, R. (1970), 'Market-Days in the Roman Empire', *Phoenix* 24: 333–41.
Maggiani, A. (1972), 'Scheda n. 13', in M. Cristofani (ed.), *Rivista di epigrafia etrusca. SE* 40: 408–9.
Maggiani, A. (1992), 'Le iscrizioni di età tardo classica ed ellenistica', in A. Romualdi (ed.), *Populonia in età ellenistica: i materiali dalle necropoli; atti del seminario, Firenze 30 giugno 1986*. 179–92. Florence.
Maggiani, A. (2001a), 'Pesi e bilance in Etruria', in C. Corti and N. Giordani (eds.), *Pondera. Pesi e misure nell'antichità*. 67–73. Campogalliano.
Maggiani, A. (2001b), 'Dagli archivi dei Cusu. Considerazioni sulla tavola bronzea di Cortona', *Rivista di Archeologia* 25: 94–114.
Maggiani, A. (2002), 'La libbra etrusca. Sistemi ponderali e monetazione', *SE* 65–68: 163–99.

Maggiani, A. (2004), 'I Greci nell'Etruria più settontrionale', *AnnMuseoFaina* 11: 149–80.
Maggiani, A. (2006), 'Rotte e tappe nel Tirreno settontrionale', in S. Gori and M.C. Bettini, (eds.), *Gli Etruschi da Genova ad Ampurias: atti del XXIV convegno di studi etruschi ed italici, Marseille – Lattes, 26 settembre – 1 ottobre 2002*). 435–53. Pisa.
Maggiani, A. (2007), 'Auvele Feluskes: della stele di Vetulonia e di altre dell'Etruria settentrionale', *Rivista di Archeologia* 31: 67–75.
Maggiani, A. (2009), 'La libbra etrusca. Addenda', *SE* 73: 135–48.
Maggiani, A. (2012), 'Ancora sui sistemi ponderali in Etruria: pesi di pietra dal territorio fiesolano', *MEFRA* 124: 393–405.
Maggiani, A. (2017), 'Weights and Balances', in A. Naso (ed.), *Etruscology*. 473–83. Berlin.
Maggiani, A. and M.A. Rizzo (2001), 'L'area sacra in località S. Antonio', in A.M. Moretti Sgubini (ed.), *Veio, Cerveteri, Vulci: città d'Etruria a confronto*. 143–5. Rome.
Maggiani, A. and M.A. Rizzo (2005), 'Cerveteri. Le campagne di scavo in loc. Vigna Parrocchiale e S. Antonio', in *Dinamiche di sviluppo delle città nell'Etruria meridionale. Veio, Caere, Tarquinia, Vulci. Atti del XXIII convegno di Studi Etruschi ed Italici, 1–6 ottobre 2001*. 175–83. Rome.
Magnani, S. (2003), *Geografia storica del mondo antico*. Bologna.
Magno, M. (1999), 'Le battaglie per la censuazione e l'uso agroindustriale del Tavoliere di Puglia', in E. Petrocelli (ed.), *La civiltà della transumanza. Storia, cultura e valorizzazione die tratturi e del mondo pastorale in Abruzzo, Molise, Puglia, Campania e Basilicata*. 43–53. Isernia.
Malkin, I. (1994), *Myth and Territory in the Spartan Mediterranean*. Cambridge.
Malkin, I. (1998), *The Returns of Odysseus: Colonisation and Ethnicity*. Berkeley.
Malkin, I. (2004), 'Postcolonial Concepts and Ancient Greek Colonization', *Modern Language Quarterly* 65: 341–64.
Malkin, I. (2011), *A Small Greek World: Networks in the Ancient Mediterranean*. Oxford.
Malkin, I. (2014), 'Between Collective and Ethnic Identities: A Conclusion', in C. Müller and A.-E. Veïsse (eds.), *Identité ethnique et culture matérielle dans le monde grec*. 283–92. Besançon.
Manfredi-Selvaggi, F. (1999), 'Il paesaggio storico nell'ambiente della transumanza', in E. Petrocelli (ed.), *La civiltà della transumanza. Storia, cultura e valorizzazione dei tratturi e del mondo pastorale in Abruzzo, Molise, Puglia, Campania e Basilicata*. 211–20. Isernia.
Manning, J. (2018), *The Open Sea: The Economic Life of the Ancient Mediterranean World from the Iron Age to the Rise of Rome*. Princeton.
Mannino, K. (1997), 'Le importazioni attiche in Puglia nel V sec. a.C.', *Ostraka* 6: 389–99.
Mannino, K. (2004), 'I Vasi Attici di Età Classica nella Puglia Anellenica: Osservazioni sui Contesti di Rinvenimento', in M. Luni and L. Braccesi (eds.), *I Greci in Adriatico. Atti del Convegno Internazionale (Urbino, 21–24 ottobre 1999)*. 333–55. Rome.
Mannino, K. (2006), *Vasi attici nei contesti della Messapia, 480–350 a.C.* Bari.
Maran, J. and P.W. Stockhammer (eds.) (2012), *Materiality and Social Practice: Transformative Capacities of Intercultural Encounters*. Oxford.
Maras, D. (2015), '*Populonia ex insula Corsica*. Ancora sulla fondazione di Populonia', in *La Corsica e Populonia. Atti del XXVIII Convegno di studi etruschi ed italici: Bastia – Alria, Piombino – Populonia, 25–29 ottobre 2011*. 47–60. Rome.

Maras, R. (2017), 'Religion', in A. Naso (ed.), *Etruscology*. 277–316. Berlin.
Marchi, D. and S.M. Borgognini Tarli (2002), 'The Skeletal Biology of Two Italian Peninsular Magna Graecia Necropoles, Timmari and Montescaglioso', *HOMO – Journal of Comparative Human Biology* 53: 59–78.
Marin, M.M. (1981), 'Problemi topografici dell'antica citta di Ruvo', in *Atti del VI Convegno dei Comuni Messapici, Peuceti e Dauni*. 121–267. Bari.
Marino, J. (1988), *Pastoral Economics in the Kingdom of Naples*. Baltimore.
Marinow, W. (1961), 'Die Schaftzucht der nomadisierenden Karakatschanen in Bulgarien', in L. Földes (ed.), *Viehzucht und Hirtenleben in Ostmitteleuropa. Ethnographische Studien*. 147–96. Budapest.
Marsden, P. (2005), 'Recent Developments in Network Measurement', in P. Carrington, J. Scott, and S. Wasserman (eds.), *Models and Methods in Social Network Analysis*. Cambridge.
Mascaro, I. and F. Cuteri (1995), *Colline Metallifere. Inventario del patrimonio minerario e mineralogico in Toscana. Aspetti naturalistici e storico-geografici*. Florence.
Mascaro, I., S. Guideri, and M. Benvenuti (1991), *Inventario del patrimonio minerario e mineralogico in Toscana. Aspetti naturalistici e storico-geografici*. Florence.
Mason, R. (2014), 'Weapon Wednesday: The Nugent Marathon Corinthian Helmet', *Royal Ontario Museum: Collections and Research*. www.rom.on.ca/en/collections-research/blog/staff/Robert%20Mason [Accessed 4/9/2020].
Massa-Pairault, F.-H. (2016), 'Autour su "*Fanum Voltumnae*": Réflexions, Hypothèses et Propositions pour un débat', *RA* 61: 107–54.
Massey, D. (2005), *For Space*. London.
Mattingly, D. (2009), 'Cultural Crossovers: Global and Local Identities in the Classical World', in S. Hales and T. Hodos (eds.), *Material Culture and Social Identities in the Ancient World*. 283–96. Cambridge.
Mauss, M. (2016), *The Gift* (trans. J. Guyer). Chicago.
Mazzei, M. (1996), 'Lo stile apulo tardo', in E. Lippolis (ed.), *I Greci in Occidente. Arte e artigianato in Magna Grecia*. 403–6. Naples.
McCormick, M., G. Huang, G. Zambotti, and J. Lavash (2013), 'Roman Road Network (version 2008)', in *DARMC Scholarly Data Series, Data Contribution Series #2013-5*. Cambridge, MA. https://doi.org/10.7910/DVN/TI0KAU
McDonald, K. (2019), 'Education and Literacy in Ancient Italy: Evidence from the Dedications to the Goddess Reitia', *JRS* 109: 131–59.
McDonald, K. and J. Clackson (2020), 'The Language of Mobile Craftsmen in the Western Mediterranean', in J. Clackson, P. James, K. McDonald, L. Tagliapietra, and N. Zair (eds.), *Migration, Mobility and Language Contact in and Around the Ancient Mediterranean*. 75–97. Cambridge.
McPhee, I.D. (2015), 'A Red-figure Bell-Krater in Dundee: A Campanian Vase-Painter of the Late 5th Century?', *NumAntClass* 44: 33–49.
McPhee, I.D. (2018), 'The Auckland Cup, the Chequer Painter and the Spinelli Painter', in M. Bernabò Brea, M. Cultraro, M. Gras, C. Martinelli, C. Pouzadoux, and U. Spigo (eds.), *A Madeleine Cavalier*. 295–303. Naples.
Meeks, N.D. (1986), 'Tin-rich Surfaces on Bronze – Some Experimental and Archaeological Considerations', *Archaeomtery* 28: 133–62.
Merkel, J.F. (1982), *Reconstruction of Bronze Age Copper Smelting Experiments Based on the Archaeological Evidence from Timna, Israel*. PhD Dissertation. University College London.

Merkel, J.F. (1983), 'Summary of Experimental Results for Late Bronze Age Copper Smelting and Refining', *MASCAJ* 2: 173–6.
Merkel, J.F. (1985), 'Ore Benefication during the Late Bronze Age/Early Iron Age at Timna, Israel', *MASCAJ* 3: 164–70.
Mertens, D. (2006), *Städte und Bauten der Westgriechen. Von der Kolonisationszeit bis zur Krise um 400 vor Christus*. Munich.
Mertens, J. (ed.) (1995), *Herdonia. Scoperta di una città*. Bari.
Mertens-Horn, M. (1992), 'Die archaischen Baufriese aus Metapont', *RM* 99: 1–122.
Michels, A.K. (1967), *The Roman Calendar of the Roman Republic*. Princeton.
Michetti, L.M. (2016), 'Ports: Trade, Cultural Connections, Sanctuaries, and Emporia', in N. de Grummond and L. Pieraccini (eds.), *Caere*. 73–86. Austin.
Michetti, L.M. (2017), 'Harbors', in A. Naso (ed.), *Etruscology*. 391–405. Berlin.
Mientjes, A.C. (2004), 'Modern Pastoral Landscapes on the Island of Sardinia (Italy). Recent Pastoral Practices in Local versus Macro-economic and Macro-political Contexts', *Archaeological Dialogues* 10: 161–90.
Mientjes, A.C. (2010), 'Pastoral Communities in the Sardinian Highlands (Italy): A View on Social Mobility', *Ethnos* 75: 148–70.
Migliavacca, M., F. Saggioro, and U. Sauro (2013), 'Ethnoarchaeology of Pastoralism: Fieldwork in the Highlands of the Lessini Plateau (Verona, Italy)', in F. Lugli, A. Stoppiello, and S. Biagetti (eds.), *Ethnoarchaeology: Current Research and Field Methods. Conference Proceedings, Rome 13th-14th May 2010*. 217–23. Oxford.
Mitro, R. and F. Notarangelo (2016), *Melfi. Le necropoli di Pisciolo e Chiuchiari*. Venosa.
Moatti, C. (2013), 'Immigration and Cosmopolitanization', in P. Erdkamp (ed.), *The Cambridge Companion to Ancient Rome*. 77–92. Cambridge.
Mödlinger, M. (2014), 'Bronze Age Bell Helmets: New Aspects on Typology, Chronology and Manufacture', *Prähistorische Zeitschrift* 88: 152–79.
Mödlinger, M. (2017), *Protecting the Body in War and Combat: Metal Body Armour in Bronze Age Europe*. Vienna.
Mödlinger, M. (2018), 'Body Armour in the European Bronze Age', in A. Dolfini, R. Crellin, C. Horn, and M. Uckelmann (eds.), *Prehistoric Warfare and Violence: Quantitative and Qualitative Approaches*. 177–98. New York.
Mödlinger, M. and Z. El Morr (2013), 'European Bronze Age Sheet Metal Objects: 3,000 Years of High-Level Bronze Manufacture', *JOM* 66: 171–7.
Mödlinger, M., R. de Oro Calderon, and R. Haubner (2019), 'Arsenic Loss during Metallurgical Processing of Arsenical Bronze', *Archaeological and Anthropological Sciences* 11(1): 33–40.
Mödlinger, M. and Ch. Tsirogiannis (2020), 'Recent Cases of Unprovenanced Armour in the Antiquities Market and Its Clients', *Archäologisches Korrespondenzblatt* 50: 323–37.
Moesta, H. (1983), *Erze und Metalle, Ihre Kulturgeschichte im Experiment*. Berlin.
Molloy, B. and M. Mödlinger (2020), 'The Organisation and Practice of Metal Smithing in Later Bronze Age Europe', *Journal of World Prehistory* 33: 169–232.
Montanaro, A.C. (2006), *Gli Ori di Ruvo di Puglia tra Greci ed Etruschi*. Bari.
Montanaro, A.C. (2007), *Ruvo di Puglia e il suo territorio: le necropoli: i corredi funerari tra la documentazione del XIX secolo e gli scavi moderni*. Rome.
Montanaro, A.C. (2010), 'Presenze allogene in Peucezia', in L. Todisco (ed.), *La Puglia centrale dall'età del bronzo all'alto medioevo. Archeologia e storia. Atti del convegno di studi (Bari, 15–16 giugno 2009)*. 185–94. Rome.

Montanaro, A.C. (2012), *Ambre figurate. Amuleti e ornamenti dalla Puglia preromana*. Rome.

Montanaro, A.C. (2015), 'Le ambre figurate in Italia meridionale tra VIII e V sec. a.C. Note sui centri di produzione e sulle botteghe', *Taras* 35: 35–64.

Moorey, P.R.S. (2001), 'The Mobility of Artisans and Opportunities for Technology Transfer between Western Asia and Egypt in the Late Bronze Age', in A.J. Shortland (ed.), *The Social Context of Technological Change: Egypt and the Near East, 1650–1150 BC*. 1–14. Oxford.

Morandi, M. (1999), 'Il paesaggio geografico, le emergenze architettoniche a i luoghi abitati', in E. Petrocelli (ed.), *La civiltà della transumanza. Storia, cultura e valorizzazione dei tratturi e del mondo pastorale in Abruzzo, Molise, Puglia, Campania e Basilicata*. 193–210. Isernia.

Moretti, M. (1960), 'Tarquinia – La tomba della nave', *BA* 14: 346–52.

Moretti Sgubini, A.M. (2006), '*Lucus Feroniae*: recenti scoperte', *RPAA* 78: 111–38.

Morris, I. (1989), 'Circulation, Deposition, and the Formation of the Greek Iron Age', *Man* 24: 502–19.

Morris, I. (2003), 'Mediterraneanization', *Mediterranean Historical Review* 18: 30–55.

Morris, I. (2007), 'Early Iron Age Greece', in W. Scheidel, I. Morris, and R. Saller (eds.), *The Cambridge Economic History of the Graeco-Roman World*. 211–41. Cambridge.

Morris, S.P. (2006), 'Illyrica Pix: The Exploitation of Bitumen in Ancient Albania', in L. Bejko and R. Hodges (eds.), *New Directions in Albanian Archaeology: Studies Presented to Muzafer Korkuti*. 94–106. Tirana.

Morris, S.P. (2014), 'Bitumen at Lofkënd: Deposits, Sherds, and Containers', in L. Bejko, S.P. Morris, J.K. Papadopoulos, and L.A. Schepartz (eds.), *The Excavation of the Prehistoric Burial Tumulus at Lofkënd, Albania*. 476–82. Los Angeles.

Mouritsen, H. (1998), *Italian Unification: A Study in Ancient and Modern Historiography*. London.

Muhly, J. and V. Kassianidou (2012), 'Parallels and Diversities in the Production, Trade and Use of Copper and Iron in Crete and Cyprus from the Bronze Age to the Iron Age', in A. Whitley, G. Cadogan, M. Iacovou, and K. Kopaka (eds.), *Parallel Lives: Ancient Island Societies in Crete and Cyprus*. 119–40. London.

Muhly, J., R. Maddin, T. Stech, and E. Özgen (1985), 'Iron in Anatolia and the Nature of the Hittite Iron Industry', *AS* 35: 67–84.

Müller, N.S., V. Kilikoglou, and P.M. Day (2015), 'Home-Made Recipes: Tradition and Innovation in Bronze Age Cooking Pots from Akrotiri, Thera', in M. Spataro and A. Villing (eds.), *Ceramics, Cuisine and Culture: The Archaeology and Science of Kitchen Pottery in the Ancient Mediterranean World*. 37–48. Oxford.

Murray, O. (1990), 'Cities of Reason', in O. Murray and S. Price (eds.), *The Greek City from Homer to Alexander*. 1–25. Oxford.

Murray, O. (1991), 'History and Reason in the Ancient City', *PBSR* 59: 1–13.

Murray, S. (2017), *The Collapse of the Mycenaean Economy: Imports, Trade, and Institutions 1300–700 BCE*. Cambridge.

Murray, S. (2020), 'Big Data and Greek Archaeology: Potential, Hazards, and a Case Study from Early Greece', in C. Cooper (ed.), *New Approaches to Ancient Material Culture in the Greek & Roman World: 21st-Century Methods and Classical Antiquity*. 63–78. Leiden.

Nafissi, M. (2005), *Ancient Athens and Modern Ideology: Value, Theory and Evidence in Historical Sciences. Max Weber, Karl Polanyi and Moses Finley*. London.

Naglak, M. and N. Terrenato (2019), 'A House Society in Iron Age Latium? Kinship and State Formation in the Context of New Discoveries at Gabii', in M. Di Fazio and S. Paltineri (eds.), *La società gentilizia nell'Italia antica tra realtà e mito storiografico*. 3–21. Bari.
Naso, A. (2006), 'Anathemata etruschi nel Mediterraneo orientale', *Annali del Museo Faina* 13: 351–416.
Naso, A. (2014), 'Pendent Semicircle Skyphoi from Central and Southern Italy in the Light of the Archaeometric Results', in M. Kerschner and I. Lemos (eds.), *Archaeometric Analyses of Euboean and Euboean Related Pottery. New Results and Their Interpretations. Proceedings of the Round Table Conference Held at the Austrian Archaeological Institute in Athens, 15 and 16 April 2011*. 169–79. Vienna.
Naso, A. (2020), 'Frauen der Früheisenzeit. Weibliche Tracht und etnische Identität auf der italischen Halbinsel am Beispiel der Cinturoni', *Mitteilungen des Deutschen Archäologischen Instituts Römische Abteilung* 126: 13–37.
Neeft, C.W. (2018), 'Itinerant Craftsmen: Two Corinthians in Taranto', *Mediterranea* 15: 47–58.
Negrini, C., M. Mazzoli, and G. Di Lorenzo (2018), 'The Helmets of Verucchio: Production and Significance', *Etruscan and Italic Studies* 21: 78–97.
Neil, S. (2012), 'Identity Construction and Boundaries: Hellenistic Perugia', in S. Roselaar (ed.), *Processes of Integration and Identity Formation in the Roman Republic*. 51–70. Leiden.
Neipert, M. (2006), *Der Wanderhandwerker*. Rahden.
Nenci, G. (1976), 'Il βαρβαρος πολεμος fra Taranto e gli Iapigi e gli αναθηματα tarentini a Delfi', *ASNP* 6: 719–38.
Nerantzis, N. (2012), 'Shaping Bronze by Heat and Hammer: An Experimental Reproduction of Minoan Copper Alloy Forming Techniques', *Mediterranean Archaeology and Archaeometry* 12: 237–47.
Nerantzis, N. (2015), 'Experimental Simulation Study of Prehistoric Bronze Working: Testing the Effects of Work-hardening on Replicated Alloys', in A. Hauptmann and D. Modarressi-Tehrani (eds.), *Archaeometallurgy in Europe III*. 329–35. Bochum.
Nielsen, E.O. (1984), 'Lotus Chain Plaques', in M.G. Marzi Costagli and L. Tamagno Perna (eds.), *Studi di antichità in onore di Guglielmo Maetzke*. 397–9. Rome.
Nielsen, E.O. (1995), 'Aspetti della produzione artigianale a Poggio Civitate', in E. Formigli (ed.), *Preziosi in oro, avorio, osso e corno: arte e tecniche degli artigiani etruschi: atti del seminario di studi ed esperimenti*. 19–26. Siena.
Nijboer, A.J. (1998), *From Household Production to Workshops. Archaeological Evidence for Economic Transformations, Pre-Monetary Exchange and Urbanization in Central Italy from 800 to 400 B.C.E.* PhD Dissertation. University of Groningen.
Nijboer, A.J. (2004), 'Characteristics of Emerging Towns in Central Italy, 900/800 to 400 BC', in P. Attema (ed.), *Centralization, Early Urbanization in First Millennium BC Italy and Greece, Part 1: Italy*. 137–56. Leuven.
Nijboer, A.J. (2017), 'Economy, 730–580 BCE', in A. Naso (ed.), *Etruscology*. 901–20. Berlin.
Nijboer, A.J. (2018), 'Across Cultures: The Introduction of Iron in the Western Mediterranean, 10th and 9th centuries BC', in M. Bentz and T. Helms (eds.), *Craft Production Systems in Cross-cultural Perspective*. 61–81. Bonn.
Nørgaard, H. (2014), 'Are Valued Craftsmen as Important as Prestige Goods: Ideas about Itinerant Craftsmanship in the Nordic Bronze Age', in S. Reiter, H. Nørgaard, Z. Kölcze, and C. Rassmann (eds.), *Ideas about Itinerant Craftsmanship in the Nordic Bronze Age*. 37–52. Højbjerg.

Nørgaard, H. (2018), *Bronze Age Metalwork: Techniques and Traditions in the Nordic Bronze Age 1500–1100 BC*. Oxford.
Norman, C. (2013), *The Iron Age Stelae of Daunia (Italy)*. PhD Dissertation. University of Sydney.
North, D.C. (1991), 'Institutions', *Journal of Economic Perspectives* 5: 97–112.
North, D., J. Wallis, and B. Weingast (2009), 'Violence and the Rise of Open-Access Orders', *Journal of Democracy* 20: 55–68.
Nowak, C. (2016), *Bestattungsrituale in Unteritalien vom 5. bis 4. Jh. v. Chr. Überlegungen zur sogenannten Samnitisierung Kampaniens*. Wiesbaden.
Nowlin, J. (forthcoming), 'At the Margins of "Orientalization": Funerary Ritual and Local Practice in Apennine Central Italy', in L. Gosner and J. Hayne (eds.), *Local Experiences of Connectivity and Mobility in the Ancient West-Central Mediterranean*. Sheffield.
Oberweiler, C., P. Lera, R. Kurti, G. Touchais, O.C. Aslaksen, C. Blein, G. Elezi, M. Gori, T. Krapf, Y. Maniatis, and S. Wagner (2020), 'Mission archéologique franco-albanaise du bassinde Korçë', *Bulletin archéologique des Écoles françaises à l'étranger: Balkans*: 1–59.
Osanna, M. (2009), 'Le terrecotte architettoniche dell'anaktoron di Torre di Satriano: il fregio e la sfinge', in M. Osanna, L. Colangelo, and G. Carollo (eds.), *Lo spazio del potere. La residenza ad abside, l'anaktoron, l'episcopio a Torre di Satriano. Atti del secondo convegno di studi su Torre di Satriano, Tito, 27–28 settembre 2008*. 157–75. Venosa.
Osanna, M. (2010), 'Torre di Sariano et Braida di Vaglio. Des palais indigènes à la périphérie du monde de la polis greque archaïque', *Les Dossiers d'Archéologie* 339: 26–33.
Osanna, M. (2013a), 'Un palazzo come un tempio: l'anaktoron di Torre di Satriano', in M. Osanna and M. Vullo (eds.), *Segni del potere. Oggetti di lusso dal Mediterraneo nell'Appennino lucano di età arcaica*. 45–68. Venosa.
Osanna, M. (2013b), 'L'Entroterra Lucano tra Bradano e Sinni nel III secolo a.C.', in *La Magna Grecia da Pirro ad Annibale Atti del cinquantaduesimo Convegno di Studi sulla Magna Grecia. Taranto Settembre 2012*. 621–57. Bari.
Osanna, M. (2015), 'Seats of Power and Power of Consumption in the Hinterland of the Ionian Coast of Southern Italy during the Archaic Age', in E. Kistler, B. Öhlinger, M. Mohr, and M. Hoernes (eds.), *Sanctuaries and the Power of Consumption. Networking and the Formation of Elites in the Archaic Western Mediterranean World. Proceedings of the International Conference in Innsbruck, 20th-23rd March 2012*. 435–57. Wiesbaden.
Osanna, M. and V. Capozzoli (eds.) (2012), *Lo spazio del potere II. Nuove ricerche nell'area dell'anaktoron di Torre di Satriano. Atti del terzo e quarto convegno di studi su Torre di Satriano. Tito, 16–17 ottobre 2009; 29–30 Settembre 2010*. Venosa.
Osanna, M., L. Colangelo, and G. Carollo (eds.) (2009), *Lo spazio del potere. La residenza ad abside, l'anaktoron, l'episcopio a Torre di Satriano. Atti del secondo convegno di studi su Torre di Satriano, Tito, 27–28 Settembre 2008*. Venosa.
Osborne, R. (2018), *The Transformation of Athens: Painted Pottery and the Creation of Classical Greece*. Princeton.
Overbeck, M. (2018), *Die Gießformen in West- und Süddeutschland (Saarland, Rheinland-Pfalz, Hessen, Baden-Württemberg, Bayern)*. Stuttgart.
Pacciarelli, M. (2001), *Dal villaggio alla città. La svolta proto-urbana del 1000 a.C. nell'Italia tirrenica*. Florence.

Pacciarelli, M. (2017a), 'The Transition from Village Communities to Protourban Societies', in A. Naso (ed.), *Etruscology*. 561–80. Berlin.
Pacciarelli, M. (2017b), 'Society 10th cent. – 730 BCE', in A. Naso (ed.), *Etruscology*. 759–77. Berlin.
Pace, A. (2014), 'Jazzo Fornasiello e le Dinamiche Culturali dell'Area Bradanica. L'Indicatore della Coppetta Monoansata', in M. Castoldi (eds.), *Un Abitato Peuceta. Scavi a Jazzo Fornasiello (Gravina in Puglia -Bari) Prime indagini*. 75–106. Bari.
Paddock, J. (1993), *The Bronze Italian Helmet: The Development of the Cassis from the Last Quarter of the Sixth Century B. C. to the Third Quarter of the First Century A.D*. PhD Dissertation. University College London.
Padilla Peralta, D. (2020), *Divine Institutions: Religions and Community in the Middle Roman Republic*. Princeton.
Pagès, G., S. Leroy, and C. Sanchez (2020), 'Non-metallurgical Iron Ore Trade in the Roman Mediterranean: An Initial Synthesis of Provenance and Use in the Case of Imperial *Colonia Narbo Martius* (Narbonne, Aude, France)', *Archaeological and Anthropological Sciences* 12: 140.
Pagès, G., L. Long, P. Fluzin, and P. Dillmann (2008), 'Réseaux de production et standards de commercialisation du fer antique en Méditerranée: les demi-produits des épaves romaines des Saintes-Maries-de-la-Mer (Bouches-du-Rhône)', *RAN* 41: 261–83.
Pagliantini, L. (2019), *Aithale: L'isola d'Elba. Territorio, Paessaggi, Risorse*. Bari.
Pallottino, M. (1984), *Storia della prima Italia*. Milan.
Papadimitriou, G. (2001), 'Simulation Study of Ancient Bronzes. Their Mechanical and Metalworking Properties', in Y. Bassiakos, E. Aloupi, and G. Fakorelis (eds.), *Archaeometry Issues in Greek Prehistory and Antiquity*. 587–608. Athens.
Papadopoulos, J.K. (1996), 'Innovations, Imitations and Ceramic Style: Modes of Production and Modes of Dissemination', in R. Laffineur and P.P. Betancourt (eds.), *TEXNH. Craftsmen, Craftswomen and Craftsmanship in the Aegean Bronze Age*. 449–62. Liège.
Papadopoulos, J.K. (2001), 'Magna Achaea. Akhaian Late Geometric and Archaic Pottery in South Italy and Sicily', *Hesperia* 70: 373–460.
Papadopoulos, J.K. (2009), 'The Relocation of Potters and the Dissemination of Style: Athens, Corinth, Ambrakia, and the Agrinion Group', in J.H. Oakley and O. Palagia (eds.), *Athenian Potters and Painters Volume II*. 232–40. Oxford.
Parise, N. (1985), 'La prima monetazione etrusca. Fondamenti metrologici e funzioni', in M. Cristofani (ed.), *Commercio Etrusco Arcaico. Atti dell'Incontro di studio. 5–7 dicembre 1983*. 257–61. Rome.
Pasquinucci, M. (1979), 'La Transumanza nell'Italia Romana', in E. Gabba and M. Pasquinucci (eds.), *Strutture agrarie e allevamento transumante nell'Italian Romana (III-I sec. A. C.)*. 75–184. Pisa.
Pearce, M. (2016), 'Hard Cheese: Upland Pastoralism in the Italian Bronze and Iron Ages', in J. Collis, M. Pearce, and F. Nicolis (eds.), *Summer Farms: Seasonal Exploitation of the Uplands from Prehistory to the Present*. 47–56. Sheffield.
Peeples, M. (2018), *Connected Communities: Networks, Identity, and Social Change in the Ancient Cibola World*. Tuscon.
Pelgrom, J. and T. Stek (2010), 'A Landscape Archaeological Perspective on the Functioning of a Rural Cult Place in Samnium: Field Surveys Around the Sanctuary of S. Giovanni in Galdo (Molise)', *Journal of Ancient Topography* 20: 41–102.

Pellegrino, C., C. Rizzo, and T. Grimaldi (2017), 'Dall'Irpinia alla costa tirrenica: fenomeni di mobilità e integrazione in Campania tra VIII e VII secolo a.C.', in V. Franciosi, A. Visconti, A. Avagliano, and V. Saldutti (eds.), *Appellati nomine lupi. Giornata internazionale di Studi sull'Hirpinia e gli Hirpini. Napoli, 28 febbraio 2014.* 207–73. Naples.

Pennetta, A., D. Fico, G. Eramo, I. Muntoni, and G. Benedetto (2020), 'Extending the Inter-Adriatic Trade of Bitumen beyond the Fifth Millennium BCE', *Organic Geochemistry* 142: 1–8.

Perkins, P. (2000), 'Urbanisation, Settlement, Burial and People in the Albegna Valley', in E. Herring and K. Lomas (eds.), *The Emergence of State Identities in Italy.* 91–108. London.

Perkins, P. (2009), 'DNA and Etruscan Identity', in P. Perkins and J. Swaddling (eds.), *Etruscan by Definition: Papers in Honour of Sybille Haynes.* 95–111. London.

Perkins, P. (2010), 'The Cultural and Political Landscape of the Ager Caletranus, North-West of Vulci', in P. Fontaine (ed.), *L'Etrurie et l'ombrie avant Rome: Cité et Territoire.* 103–21. Brussels.

Perkins, P. (2012), 'Production and Commercialization of Etruscan Wine in the Albegna Valley', in A. Ciacci, P. Rendini, and A. Zifferero (eds.), *Archeologia della Vite e del Vino in Toscana e nel Lazio. Dalle Tecniche dell'Indagine Archeologica alle Prospettive della Biologia Molecolare.* 413–26. Borgo San Lorenzo.

Perkins, P. (2017), 'DNA and Etruscan Identity', in A. Naso (ed.), *Etruscology.* 109–19. Berlin.

Perkins, P. and L. Walker (1990), 'Survey of an Etruscan City at Doganella, in the Albegna Valley', *PBSR* 58: 1–143.

Pernicka, E. (1998), 'Die Ausbreitung der Zinnbronze im 3. Jahrtausend', in B. Hänsel (ed.), *Mensch und Umwelt in der Bronzezeit Europas.* 135–47. Kiel.

Peruzzi, B. (2014), 'The (D)evolution of Grave Good Assemblages in Peucetia in the 3rd Century', in A. Small (ed.), *Beyond Vagnari, New Themes in the Study of Roman South Italy.* 33–9. Bari.

Petrarulo, G. (2012), 'New Considerations Regarding the Seascape Fresco in the Tomb of the Ship (Tomba della Nave) at Tarquinia', *Etruscan Studies* 15: 115–45.

Petta, V. and A.R. Russo (2017), 'Mobilità e integrazione a Pontecagnano tra V e IV secolo a.C.', in A. Pontradolfo and A.C. Scafuro (eds.), *Dialoghi sull'archeologia della Magna Grecia e del Mediterraneo. Atti del I Convegno Internazionale di Studi, Paestum, 7–9 settembre 2016.* 815–26. Paestum.

Pevnick, S. and E. Agolli (2015), 'The Pottery from the Tombs and Tumulus Fill', in L. Bejko, S.P. Morris, J.K. Papadopoulos, and L.A. Schepartz (eds.), *The Excavation of the Prehistoric Burial Tumulus at Lofkënd, Albania.* 227–324. Los Angeles.

Pickles, S. and E. Peltenburg (1998), 'Metallurgy and Society and the Bronze/Iron Transition in the East Mediterranean and the Near East', in V. Kassianidou and G. Papasavvas (eds.), *Eastern Mediterranean Metallurgy and Metalwork in the Second Millennium BC. A Conference in Honour of James D. Muhly. Nicosia 10th–11th October 2009.* 94–106. Oxford.

Piketty, T. (2014), *Capital in the Twenty-First Century.* Cambridge.

Pitts, M. (2019), *The Roman Object Revolution: Objectscapes and Intra-cultural Connectivity in Northwest Europe.* Amsterdam.

Pitts, M. and M.J. Versluys (eds.) (2014), *Globalisation and the Roman World: World History, Connectivity, and Material Culture.* Cambridge.

Poehler, E., J. van Roeggen, and B. Crowther (2019), 'The Iron Streets of Pompeii', *AJA* 123: 237–62.
Poggesi, G., L. Donati, E. Bocci, G. Millemaci, L. Pagnini, and P. Pallecchi (2005), 'Prato-Gonfienti: un nuovo centro etrusco sulla via per Marzabotto', in G. Sassatelli and E. Govi (eds.), *Culti, Forma urbana e artiginato a Marzabotto. Nuove prospettive di ricera. Atti del Convegno di studi. Bologna. S. Giovanni in Monte 3–4 Giugno 2003*. 267–300. Bologna.
Poggesi, G., L. Donati, E. Bocci, G. Millemaci, L. Pagnini, and P. Pallecchi (2010), 'Poggesi-Gonfienti: un insediamento tardo-arcaico fra Arno e Bisenzio', in M. Bentz and C. Reusser (eds.), *Etruskisch-italische und römisch-republikanische Häuser*. 123–33. Wiesbaden.
Polanyi, K. (1944), *The Great Transformation*. New York.
Porter, A. (2012), *Mobile Pastoralism and the Formation of Near Eastern Civilizations: Weaving Together Society*. Cambridge.
Potts, C. (2015), *Religious Architecture in Latium and Etruria, c. 900–500 BC*. Oxford.
Pouzadoux, C. (2013), *Éloge d'un prince daunien: Mythes et images en Italie méridionale au IVe siècle av. J.-C*. Rome.
Pouzadoux, C. (2017), 'Productions et mobilités artisanales. L'exemple de la céramique à figures rouges italiote', in *Ibridazione ed integrazione in Magna Grecia: forme modelli dinamiche. Atti del cinquantaquattresimo convegno di studi sulla Magna Grecia, Taranto 2014*. 189–208. Taranto.
Primas, M. (2008), *Bronzezeit zwischen Elbe und Po. Strukturwandel in Zentraleuropa 2200–800 v. Chr*. Bonn.
Prowse, T., H. Schwarcz, P. Garnsey, M. Knyf, R. Macchiarelli, and L. Bondioli (2007), 'Isotopic Evidence for Age-related Immigration to Imperial Rome', *American Journal of Physical Anthropology* 132: 510–9.
Pugliese Carratelli, G. (ed.) (1996), *The Western Greeks*. Venice.
Puglisi, S.M. (1959), *La Civiltà Appenninica: Origine delle Comunità Pastorali in Italia*. Florence.
Purcell, N. (2005), 'The Ancient Mediterranean: The View from the Customs House', in W.V. Harris (ed.), *Rethinking the Mediterranean*. 200–32. Oxford.
Quercia, A. (2015), 'The Production and Distribution of Early Greek-style Cooking Wares in Areas of Cultural Contact: The Case of Southern Italy and Sicily', in W. Gauß, G. Klebinder-Gauß, and C. von Rüden (eds.), *The Transmission of Technical Knowledge in the Production of Ancient Mediterranean Pottery. Proceedings of the International Conference at the Austrian Archaeological Institute at Athens. 23rd – 25th November 2012*. 311–32. Vienna.
Rastrelli, A. (1993), 'Scavi e scoperte di Chianciano Terme: l'edificio sacro di Fucoli', In *La civiltà di Chiusi e del suo territorio: Atti del XVII Convegno di Studi Etruschi ed Italici, Chianciano Terme, 28 maggio–1 giugno 1989*. 463–76. Florence.
Rathmann, H., B. Kyle, E. Nikita, L. Harvati, and G. Saltini Semerari (2019), 'Population History of Southern Italy during Greek Colonization Inferred from Dental Remains', *American Journal of Physical Anthropology* 170: 519–34.
Rathmann, H., G. Saltini Semerari, and K. Harvati (2017), 'Evidence for Migration Influx into the Ancient Greek Colony of Metaponto: A Population Genetics Approach Using Dental Nonmetric Traits', *International Journal of Osteoarchaeology* 27: 453–64.
Rebay-Salisbury, K. (2012), 'Inhumation and Cremation: How Burial Practices are Linked to Beliefs', in M.L. Stig Sørensen and K. Rebay-Salisbury (eds.), *Embodied Knowledge: Perspectives on Belief and Technology*. 15–26. Oxford.

Recchia, G., H. Tomas, and M. Gori (2018), 'The Cetina Phenomenon Across the Adriatic During the 2nd Half of the 3rd Millennium BC: New Data and Research Perspectives', in A. Gravina (ed.), *Atti del trentottesimo convegno nazionale sulla Preistoria, Protostoria, Storia della Daunia, San Severo, 18–19 novembre 2017*. 197–216. San Severo.

Rendeli, M. (1993), *Città aperta: Ambiente e paesaggio rurale organizzato nell'Etruria meridionale costiera durante l'età orientalizzante e arcaica*. Rome.

Renfrew, C. (1975), 'Trade as Action at a Distance: Questions of Integration and Communication', in J.A. Sabloff and C.C. Lamberg-Karlovsky (eds.), *Ancient Civilization and Trade*. 3–59. Albuquerque.

Riccardi, A. (ed.) (2003), *Gli antichi Peucezi a Bitonto: documenti ed immagini dalla necropoli di via Traiana: Catalogo del Museo archeologico della Fondazione De Palo Ungaro*. Bari.

Riccardi, A. (ed.) (2008), *Donne e guerrieri da Ruvo e Bitonto: le scoperte del III millennio*. Bari.

Rice, P.M. (2015), *Pottery Analysis, A Sourcebook*. 2nd ed. Chicago.

Ridgway, D. (1992), *The First Western Greeks*, Cambridge.

Riva, C. (2009), *The Urbanisation of Etruria: Funerary Practices and Social Change, 700–600 BC*. Cambridge.

Riva, C. (2010), 'Trading Settlements and the Materiality of Wine Consumption in the North Tyrrhenian Sea Region', in B. Knapp and P. van Dommelen (eds.), *Material Connections: Mobility, Materiality and Mediterranean Identities*. 210–32. New York.

Riva, C. (2020), 'Commodities, the Instability of the Gift, and the Codification of Cultural Encounters in Archaic Southern Etruria', in M. Gleba, B. Marin Aguilera, and B. Dimova (eds.), *Dressing Cities: Economies of Production and Urbanisation in Mediterranean Europe 1000–500 BCE*. Cambridge.

Riva, C. (2021), *A Short History of the Etruscans*. London.

Riva, C. and S. Stoddart (1996), 'Ritual Landscapes in Archaic Etruria', in J. Wilkins (eds.), *Approaches to the Study of Ritual: Italy and the Mediterranean*. 91–109. London.

Roberts, C., J. Woodbridge, A. Palmisano, A. Bevan, R. Fyfe, and S. Shennan (2019), 'Mediterranean Landscape Change during the Holocene: Synthesis, Comparison and Regional Trends in Population, Land Cover and Climate', *The Holocene* 29: 923–37.

Robinson, E.G.D. (1990), 'Workshops of Apulian Red-Figure outside of Taranto', in J.P. Descœudres (ed.), *Eumousia: Ceramic and Iconographic Studies in honour of Alexander Cambitoglou*. 179–93. Sydney.

Robinson, E.G.D. (1996), 'La ceramic sovraddipinta monocroma: vasi dei Gruppi Xenone del Cigno Rosso', in E. Lippolis (ed.), *Arte e artigianato in Magna Grecia*. 447–52. Naples.

Robinson, E.G.D. (2007), 'Appendix: Analyses d'argile', in E. Brigger, *La céramique fine du Premier Age du Fer d'I Fani (Lecce/Italie): Contribution à l'étude des systèmes culturels indigènes du Protogéométrique Sud-italien au Géométrique Moyen et Récent I salentins*. 643–60. PhD Dissertation. University of Geneva.

Robinson, E.G.D. (2011), 'Identity in the Tomb of the Diver at Paestum', in M. Gleba and H. Horsnæs (eds.), *Communicating Identity in Italic Iron Age Communities*. 50–72. Oxford.

Robinson, E.G.D. (2014a), 'Greek Theatre in Non-Greek Apulia', in E. Csapo, H.R. Goette, J.R. Green, and P. Wilson (eds.), *The Greek Theatre in the Fourth Century BC*. 319–32. Berlin.

Robinson, E.G.D. (2014b), 'New PIXE-PIGME Analyses for South Italian Pottery', *Mediterranean Archaeology* 26: 15–41.
Roddick, A.P. (2016), 'Scalar Relations: A Juxtaposition of Craft Learning in the Lake Titicaca Basin', in A.P. Roddick and A.B. Stahl (eds.), *Knowledge in Motion: Constellations of Learning Across Time and Place*. 126–54. Tuscon.
Roddick, A.P. and A.B. Stahl (2016), 'Introduction: Knowledge in Motion', in A.P. Roddick and A.B. Stahl (eds.), *Knowledge in Motion: Constellations of Learning across Time and Place*. 3–35. Tuscon.
Rogan, T. (2017), *The Moral Economists: R. H. Tawney, Karl Polanyi, E. P. Thompson, and the Critique of Capitalism*. Cambridge.
Romanelli, P. (1948), 'Tarquinia. Scavi e ricerche nell'area della città', *NSA* 8(2): 193–270.
Romualdi, A. (1993), 'La *polis* nel periodo arcaico e l'attivita di lavorazione del ferro', in F. Fedeli, A. Galiberti, and A. Romualdi (eds.), *Populonia e il suo territorio. Profilo storico archeologico*. 102–17. Florence.
Roscino, C. (2019), 'Vasi dell'Officina del Pittore dell'Ilioupersis a Ruvo di Puglia', in F. Giacobello (ed.), *Savoir-faire antichi e moderni. Pittori e officine ceramiche nella Puglia di V e IV secolo a.C. Atti della giornata di studi Vicenza, Gallerie d'Italia-Palazzo Leoni Montanari, 28 Marzo 2015*. 88–113. Milan.
Roselaar, S. (ed.) (2012), *Processes of Integration and Identity Formation in the Roman Republic*. Leiden.
Roselaar, S. (2019), *Italy's Economic Revolution: Integration and Economy in Republican Italy*. Oxford.
Roux, V. (1994), 'La technique du tournage: définition et reconnaissance par les macrotraces', in D. Binder and J. Courtin (eds.), *Terre cuite et société. La céramique, document technique, économique, culturel*. 45–58. Juan-les-Pins.
Roux, V. (2003a), 'Ceramic Standardization and Intensity of Production: Quantifying Degrees of Specialization', *American Antiquity* 68: 768–82.
Roux, V. (2003b), 'A Dynamic Systems Framework for Studying Technological Change: Application to the Emergence of the Potter's Wheel in the Southern Levant', *Journal of Archaeological Method and Theory* 10: 1–30.
Roux, V. (2011), 'Anthropological Interpretation of Ceramic Assemblages: Foundations and Implementations of Technological Analysis', in S. Scarcella (ed.), *Archaeological Ceramics: A Review of Current Research*. 80–8. Oxford.
Roux, V. (2015), 'Ceramic Manufacture: The Chaîne Opératoire Approach', in A. Hunt (ed.), *The Oxford Handbook of Archaeological Ceramic Analysis*. Oxford.
Roux, V. (2016), *Ceramics and Society: A Technological Approach to Archaeological Assemblages*. New York.
Rowlands, M.J. (1971), 'Archaeological Interpretation of Prehistoric Metalworking', *World Archaeology* 3: 210–24.
Rozelle, S., J. Huang, and V. Benziger (2003), 'Continuity and Change in China's Rural Periodic Markets', *The China Journal* 49: 89–115.
Rubini, M. (1996), 'Biological Homogeneity and Familial Segregation in the Iron Age Population of Alfedena (Abruzzo, Italy), based on Cranial Discrete Traits Analysis', *International Journal of Osteoarchaeology* 6: 454–62.
Rubini, M., E. Bonafede, S. Mogliazza, and L. Moreschini (1997), 'Etruscan Biology: The Tarquinian Population, Seventh to Second Century BC (Southern Etruria, Italy)', *International Journal of Osteoarchaeology* 7: 202–11.
Rubini, M., S. Mogliazza, and R. Corruccini (2007), 'Biological Divergence and Equality during the First Millennium BC in Human Populations of Central Italy', *American Journal of Human Biology* 19: 119–31.

Ruby, P. (1993), 'Types et fonctions dans les typologies céramiques archéologiques. Quelques problèmes et quelques propositions', *AION* 15: 289–320.

Rucco, G. and G. Tagliamonte (2007), 'Stenio Pupidio, ceramografo campano', *Oebalus. Studi sulla Campania nell'antichità* 2: 135–51.

Rudenko, S.I. (1969), 'Studien über das Nomadentum', in L. Földes (ed.), *Viehwirtschaft und Hirtenkultur. Ethnographische Studien*. 15–32. Budapest.

Rüpke, J. (2019), *Peace and War in Rome: A Religious Construction of Warfare*. Stuttgart.

Rüpke, J. (2020), *Urban Religion: A Historical Approach to Urban Growth and Religious Change*. Berlin.

Russell, A. (2010), 'Foreign Materials, Islander Mobility and Elite Identity in Late Bronze Age Sardinia', in P. van Dommelen and A. Knapp (eds.), *Material Connections in the Ancient Mediterranean: Mobility, Materiality and Identity*. 106–26. London.

Russo, A. (2008a), 'Baragiano. L'archeologia del centro indigeno', in A. Russo and H. Di Giuseppe (eds.), *Felicitas Temporum. Dalla terra alle genti: la Basilicata settentrionale tra archeologia e storia*. 31–8. Potenza.

Russo, A. (2008b), 'Gli oggetti di Lusso', in A. Russo and H. Di Giuseppe (eds.), *Felicitas Temporum. Dalla terra alle genti: la Basilicata settentrionale tra archeologia e storia*. 46–88. Potenza.

Russo, A. and H. Di Giuseppe (eds.) (2008), *Felicitas Temporum. Dalla terra alle genti: la Basilicata settentrionale tra archeologia e storia*. Potenza.

Russo Tagliente, A. (1992), *Edilizia domestica in Apulia e Lucania. Ellenizzazione e società nella tipologia abitativa indigena tra VIII e III secolo A. D.* Galatina.

Sahlins, M. (1976), *The Use and Abuse of Biology: An Anthropological Critique of Sociobiology*. Ann Arbor.

Salzani, L. (1989), 'Fratta Polesine, Frattesina', *Quaderni di Archeologia del Veneto* 5: 66–8.

Salzani, L. (2000), 'Fratta Polesine. Il ripostiglio di bronzi n. 2 da Frattesina', *Quaderni di Archeologia del Veneto* 16: 38–46.

Salzman, P.C. (2004), *Pastoralists: Equality, Hierarchy, and the State*. Boulder.

Santillo Frizell, B. (1996), 'Per Itinera Callium. Report on a Pilot Project', *Opuscula Romana* 21: 57–81.

Santillo Frizell, B. (2009), *Arkadien – Mythos und Wirklichkeit*. Cologne.

Santostefano, A. (2018), 'Un nuovo *skyphos* del Gruppo di Locri dall'acropoli di Gela', in M. Denoyelle, C. Pouzadoux, and F. Silvestrelli (eds.), *Mobilità dei pittori e identità delle produzioni*. 63–73. Naples.

Sapiro, D. and B. Webler (2016), 'Fabrication of a Bronze Age Sword using Ancient Techniques', *JOM* 68: 3180–5.

Saredo Parodi, N. (2013), *Populonia: Inferno o paradiso? Il polo siderurgico di Populonia nell'antichità, un tentative di quantificazione*. Rome.

Sassatelli, G. (1981), 'Graffiti alfabetici e contrassegni nel villanoviano bolognese. Nuovi dati sulla diffusione dell'alfabeto in etruria padana', *Emilia Preromana* 9–10: 147–255.

Sassatelli, S. and E. Govi (2013), 'Etruria on the Po and the Adriatic', in J. Turfa (ed.), *The Etruscan World*. 281–300. London.

Scalici, M. (2009), 'Ruvo del Monte. La necropoli in loc. S. Antonio. Nuovi dati e prospettive di ricerca', in M. Osanna and M. Scalici (eds.), *Lo spazio della memoria. Necropoli e rituali funerari nella Magna Grecia indigena, Atti della Tavola rotonda (Matera 11 dicembre 2009)*. Bari. = *Siris* 10: 37–51.

Scalici, M. (2013), 'Torre di Satriano. Le tombe dell'*anaktoron*', in M. Osanna and M. Vullo (eds.), *Segni del potere. Oggetti di lusso dal Mediterraneo nell'Appennino lucano di età arcaica*. 236–44. Venosa.

Scarfì, B. (1961), 'Gioia del Colle. Scavi nella zona di Monte Sannace. Le tombe rinvenute nel 1957', *Monumenti Antichi dei Lincei* 45: 145–332.

Scheid, J. (2000), 'Pour une archéologie du rite', *Annales. Histoire, Sciences Sociales* 55: 615–22.

Scheid, J. (2012), 'Roman Animal Sacrifice and the System of Being', in C. Faraone and F. Naiden (eds.), *Greek and Roman Animal Sacrifice: Ancient Victims, Modern Observers*. 84–98. Cambridge.

Scheidel, W., I. Morris, and R. Saller (eds.) (2007), *The Cambridge Economic History of the Graeco-Roman World*. Cambridge.

Schierup, S. (2014), 'Patterns of Use in Early Metapontine Red-figure Pottery: Distribution, Shapes and Iconography', in S. Schierup and V. Sabetai (eds.), *The Regional Production of Red-figure Pottery: Greece, Magna Graecia and Etruria*. 191–215. Aarhus.

Schierup, S. and B. Bundgaard Rasmussen (eds.) (2012), *Red-figure Pottery in Its Ancient Setting: Acts of the International Colloquium Held at the National Museum of Denmark in Copenhagen, November 5–6, 2009*. Aarhus.

Schoenbrun, D. (2016), 'Pythons Worked: Constellating Communities of Practice with Conceptual Metaphor in Northern Lake Victoria, ca. A.D. 800 to 1200', in A.P. Roddick and A.B. Stahl (eds.), *Knowledge in Motion: Constellations of Learning Across Time and Place*. 216–46. Tucson.

Sciarrino, E. (2011), *Cato the Censor and the Beginnings of Latin Prose*. Columbus.

Scott, D. (1991), *Metallography and Microstructure of Ancient and Historic Metals*. Oxford.

Sebastiani, A. (2012), 'Spolverino (Albarese – GR): relazione alla II campagna di scavi archeologici', *FOLD&R* 271: 1–13.

Secord, J.A. (2004), 'Knowledge in Transit', *Isis* 95(4): 654–72.

Serino, M. (2019), *La bottega del Pittore di Himera e le altre officine protosiceliote. Stile, iconografia, contesti, cronologia*. Rome.

Serio, B. (2009), 'Lo scavo: struttura, articolazione degli spazi e fasi dell'edificio in proprietà Greco', in M. Osanna, L. Colangelo, and G. Carollo (eds.), *Lo spazio del potere. La residenza ad abside, l'anaktoron, l'episcopio a Torre di Satriano. Atti del secondo convegno di studi su Torre di Satriano, Tito, 27–28 Settembre 2008*. 117–25. Venosa.

Setari, E. (1999), 'Produzioni artigianali indigene. La 'fabbrica' di Ripacandida', *Siris* 1: 69–119.

Shaw, B.C. (1979), 'Rural Periodic Markets in Roman North Africa as Mechanisms of Social Integration and Control', in G. Dalton (ed.), *Research in Economic Anthropology: A Research Annual, Volume 2*. 91–117. Greenwich, CT.

Shaw, B.C. (1981), 'Rural Markets in North Africa and the Political Economy of the Roman Empire', *Antiquités Africaines* 17: 37–39.

Shaw, L. (2012), 'The Elusive Maya Marketplace: An Archaeological Consideration of the Evidence', *Journal of Archaeological Research* 20: 117–55.

Shennan, S. (1989), 'Introduction: Archaeological Approaches to Cultural Identity', in S. Shennan (ed.), *Archaeological Approaches to Cultural Identity*. 1–32. London.

Sherwin-White, A.A. (1973), *The Roman Citizenship*. Oxford.
Shipley, G. (2020), *Pseudo-Skylax's Periplous: the Circumnavigation of the Inhabited World: Text, Translation and Commentary*. Oxford.
Silvestrelli, F. (2018), 'Il repertorio morfologico delle ceramiche fini di Metaponto. Caratteristiche e trasformazioni nel V e nel IV secolo a.C.', in M. Denoyelle, C. Pouzadoux, and F. Silvestrelli (eds.), *Mobilità dei pittori e identità delle produzioni*. 133–58. Naples.
Simonjenko, I. (1961), 'Almenwirtschaftliche Schafzucht der ukrainischen Bevölkerung in den Waldkarpaten im 19. und zu Beginn des 20. Jahrhunderts' in L. Földes (ed.), *Viehzucht und Hirtenleben in Ostmitteleuropa. Ethnographische Studien*. 363–88. Budapest.
Skeates, R. (2017), 'Mobility and Place Making in Late Pleistocene and Early Holocene Italy', *JMA* 30: 167–88.
Skydsgaard, J. (1974), 'Transhumance in Ancient Italy', *ARID* 7: 7–36.
Small, A. (ed.) (1992), *An Iron Age and Roman Republican Settlement on Botromagno, Gravina di Puglia: Excavations of 1965–1974*. London.
Small, A. (2014a), 'Pots, People, and Places in Fourth-Century B.C.E. Apulia', in T.H. Carpenter, K.M. Lynch, and E.G.D. Robinson (eds.), *The Italic People of Ancient Apulia: New Evidence from Pottery for Workshops, Markets, and Customs*. 13–36. Cambridge.
Small, A. (2014b), 'Wool Production on the Saltus', in A. Small (ed.), *Beyond Vagnari, New Themes in the Study of Roman South Italy*. 57–9. Bari.
Smil, V. (2013), *Harvesting the Biosphere: What We Have Taken From Nature*. Cambridge, MA.
Smith, A.D. (1986), *The Ethnic Origins of Nations*. Oxford.
Smith, A.D. (1999), *Myths and Memories of the Nation*. Oxford.
Smith, C.A. (1974), 'Economics of Marketing Systems: Models from Economic Geography', in B. Siegel, A. Beals, and S. Tyler (eds.), *Annual Review of Anthropology, Volume 3*. 167–201. Palo Alto, CA.
Smith, C.A. (1976), *Regional Analysis*. New York.
Smith, C.J. (1996), *Early Rome and Latium: Economy and Society c. 1000–500 B.C.* Oxford.
Smith, C.J. (2005a), 'The Beginnings of Urbanization in Rome', in B. Cunliffe and R. Osborne (eds.), *Mediterranean Urbanization 800–600 BC*. 91–111. Oxford.
Smith, C.J. (2005b), 'Traders and Artisans in Archaic Central Italy', in H. Parkins and C.J. Smith (eds.), *Trade, Traders and the Ancient City*. 31–51. London.
Smith, C.J. (2006), *The Roman Clan: The Gens from Ancient Ideology to Modern Anthropology*. Cambridge.
Smith, C.J. (2007), 'The Hinterland of Rome: Latium and the Latins', in G. Bradley, E. Isayev, and C. Riva (eds.), *Ancient Italy, Regions Without Boundaries*. 161–78. Exeter.
Smith, C.J. (2019), 'Polis Religion, Lived Religion, Etruscan Religion. Thoughts on Recent Research', *Ocnus* 27: 85–106.
Smith, C.J. (2021), 'Craft and the Urban Community: Industriousness and Socioeconomic Development', in M. Gleba, B. Marín-Aguilera, and B. Dimova (eds.), *Making Cities: Economies of Production and Urbanisation in Mediterranean Europe 1000–500 BC*. 447–54 Cambridge.
Snodgrass, A. (1980), 'Iron and Early Metallurgy in the Mediterranean', in T.A. Wertime and J.D. Muhly (eds.), *The Coming of the Age of Iron*. 335–74. New Haven, CT.

Snodgrass, A. (1988), *Homer and the Artists: Text and Picture in Early Greek Art.* Cambridge.
Sprengel, U. (1971), *Die Wanderherdenwirtschaft im mittel- und südostitalienischen Raum.* Marburg.
Squatriti, P. (2002), 'Review Article: Mohammed, the Early Medieval Mediterranean, and Charlemagne', *Early Medieval Europe* 11: 263–79.
Stagno, A.M. (2019), 'Investigating Rural Change. Legal Access Rights and Changing Lifestyles in Rural Mountain Communities (Ligurian Apennines, Italy, 16th-21st Centuries)', *World Archaeology* 51: 311–27.
Stark, R., M. Emery, H. Schwarcz, A. Sperduti, L. Bondioli, O. Craig, and T. Prowse (2020), 'Imperial Roman Mobility and Migration at Velia (1st to 2nd c. CE) in Southern Italy', *JAS: Reports* 30: 102217.
Steininger, U. (1996), *Die archaische und frühklassische Großplastik Unteritaliens und ihr Verhältnis zum Mutterland.* Münster.
Stek, T. (2009), *Cult Places and Cultural Change in Republican Italy: A Contextual Approach to Religious Aspects of Rural Society after the Roman Conquest.* Amsterdam.
Stek, T. (2014), 'Roman Imperialism, Globalization, and Romanization in Early Roman Italy. Research Questions in Archaeology and Ancient History', *Archaeological Dialogues* 21: 30–40.
Stek, T. (2018a), 'Early Roman Colonization beyond the Romanizing Agro-town: Village Patterns of Settlement and Highland Exploitation in Central Italy', in B. Düring and T. Stek (eds.), *The Archaeology of Imperial Landscapes: A Comparative Study of Empires in the Ancient Near East and Mediterranean World.* 145–72. Cambridge.
Stek, T. (2018b), 'Exploring Non-urban Society in the Mediterranean: Hill-forts, Villages and Sanctuary Sites in Ancient Samnium, Italy', *Antiquity* 92(364): E5.
Štika, J. (1969), 'Salaschenwirtschaft in Ostmähren bis Mitte des 19. Jahrhunderts', in L. Földes (ed.), *Viehwirtschaft und Hirtenkultur: Ethnographische Studien.* 258–87. Budapest.
Stopponi, S. (2007), 'Notizie preliminari dallo scavo di Campo della Fiera', *Annali Della Fondazione per Il Museo 'Claudio Faina'* 14: 493–530.
Stopponi, S. (2011), 'Campo della Fiera at Orvieto: New Discoveries', in N. de Grummond and I. Edlund Berry (eds.), *The Archaeology of Sanctuaries and Ritual in Etruria.* 16–44. Portsmouth, RI.
Stopponi, S. (2013a), 'The Excavations at Campo della Fiera (Orvieto, TR)', in J. Turfa (ed.), *The World of the Etruscans.* 632–54. Philadelphia.
Stopponi, S. (2013b), 'La ricerca del *Fanum Voltumnae*. Gli scavi in località Campo della Fiera', in E. Pellegrini (ed.), *Da Orvieto a Bolsena: un percorso tra Etruschi e Romani.* 136–46. Pisa.
Strathern, A. (2019), *Unearthly Powers: Religious and Political Change in World History.* Cambridge.
Swaddling, J., P.T. Craddock, S. La Niece, and M. Hockey (2000), 'Breaking the Mould: The Overwrought Mirrors of Etruria', in D. Ridgway and E. Macnamara (eds.), *Ancient Italy in Its Mediterranean Setting, Studies in Honour of Ellen Macnamara.* 117–40. London.
Swedberg, R. (2005), 'Markets in Society', in N. Smelser and R. Swedberg (eds.), *The Handbook of Economic Sociology.* 233–53. Princeton.
Tacoma, L.E. (2016), 'Migrants Quarters at Rome?', in G. de Kleijn and S. Benoist (eds.), *Integration in Rome and the Roman World: Proceedings of the Tenth Workshop of the International Network Impact of Empire.* 127–46. Leiden.

Tagliamonte, G. (1994), *I Figli di Marte. Mobilità mercenari e mercenariato italici in Magna Grecia e Sicilia*. Rome.

Tarpini, R. (2001), 'Balance e stadere', in C. Corti, N. Giordani, and D. Neri (eds.), *Pondera, pesi e misure nell'antichità*. 179–90. Campogalliano.

Taylor, L.R. (1920), 'The Site of Lucus Feroniae', *JRS* 10: 29–36.

Taylor, M. (2020), 'Panoply and Identity in the Roman Republic', *PBSR* 88: 31–65.

Terpstra, T. (2019), *Trade in the Ancient Mediterranean: Private Order and Public Institutions*. Princeton.

Terrenato, N. (2019), *The Early Roman Expansion into Italy: Elite Negotiation and Family Agendas*. Cambridge.

Teržan, B., E. Borgna, and P. Turk (eds.) (2016), *Il ripostiglio della Grotta delle Mosche presso San Canziano del Carso – Depo iz Mušje jame pri Škocjanu na Krasu*. Ljubljana.

Thevenot, J.-P. (1991), *L'Age du Bronze en Bourgogne. Le dépôt de Blanot (Côte-d'Or)*. Dijon.

Thompson, J. (1989), *Transhumant Sheep-raising and the Rural Economy of Roman Italy, 200 BC-AD 200*. PhD Dissertation. University of Cambridge.

Todisco, L. (ed.) (2010), *La Puglia centrale dall'età del bronzo all'alto medioevo. Archeologia e storia. Atti del convegno di studi (Bari, 15–16 giugno 2009)*. Rome.

Todisco, L. (2012), 'Myth and Tragedy. Red-figure Pottery and Verbal Communication in Central and Northern Apulia in the Later Fourth Century BC', in K.G. Bosher (ed.), *Theater Outside Athens: Drama in Greek Sicily and South Italy*. 251–71. Cambridge.

Tofanelli, S., F. Brisighelli, P. Anagnostou, G.B.J. Busby, G. Ferri, M.G. Thomas, L. Taglioli, I. Rudan, T. Zemunik, C. Hayward, D. Bolnick, V. Romano, F. Cali, D. Luiselli, G.B. Shepherd, S. Tusa, A. Facella, and C. Capelli (2016), 'The Greeks in the West: Genetic Signatures of the Hellenic Colonisation in Southern Italy and Sicily', *European Journal of Human Genetics* 24: 429–36.

Tol, G. (forthcoming), 'The Archaic Countryside Revisited. A Ceramic Approach to the Study of Archaic Rural Infill in Latium Vetus', in J. Armstrong and A. Rhodes-Schroder (eds.), *Adoption, Adaption, and Innovation in Pre-Roman Italy: Paradigms for Cultural Change*. Turnhout.

Tolosa, M. (2017), *Epigrafía bilingüe del Occidente romano. El latín y las lenguas locales en las inscripciones bilingües y mixtas*. Zaragoza.

Tomas, H. (2017), 'Early Bronze Age Sailors of the Eastern Adriatic: The Cetina Culture and Its Impact', in M. Fotiadis, R. Laffineur, Y. Lolos, and A. Vlachopoulos (eds.), *Hesperos: The Aegean Seen from the West: Proceedings of the 16th International Aegean Conference, University of Ioannina, Department of History and Archaeology, Unit of Archaeology and Art History, 18–21 May 2016*. 215–22. Leuven.

Tooze, A. (2018), *Crashed: How a Decade of Financial Crises Changed the World*. London.

Torelli, M. (1986), 'Tarquinia and Its Emporion at Gravisca. A Case in Maritime Trade in the VIth century B.C.', in *Thracia Pontica, 3. Les Thraces et les colonies grecques, VII-V s. a.v. n. è., Troisième Symposium International Sozopol 1985*. 46–53. Sofia.

Torelli, N. (2003), 'L'iscrizione del lebete', in A. Bottini and E. Setari (eds.), *La Necropoli italica di Braida di Vaglio in Basilicata. Materiale dallo Scavo del 1994 con una Appendice di Mario Torelli e Luciano Agostiniani*. 113–8. Rome.

Torelli, M. (2004), 'Quali Greci a Gravisca?', *Annali della Fondazione per il Museo Claudio Faina* 11: 119–47.
Torelli, M. (2018), 'Storia del santuario di *Castrum Inui e dei suoi culti Inuus, Indiges, Aeneas*', in M. Torelli and E. Marroni (eds.), *Castrum Inui: Il Santuario di Inuus alla foce del Fosso dell'Incastro*. 481–509. Rome.
Toynbee, A. (1965), *Hannibal's Legacy: Rome and her Neighbours after Hannibal's Exit*. Oxford.
Treherne, P. (1995), 'The Warrior's Beauty: The Masculine Body and Self-identity in Bronze Age Europe', *JEurArch* 3: 105–44.
Treister, M. (2001), *Hammering Techniques in Greek and Roman Jewellery and Toreutics*. Leiden.
Trendall, A.D. (1983), *The Red-Figured Vases of Lucania, Campania and Sicily*. London.
Trendall, A.D. (1987), *The Red-Figured Vases of Paestum*. London.
Trendall, A.D. and A. Cambitoglou (1978–1984), *The Red-Figured Vases of Apulia. Volumes 1–2*. Oxford.
Trentacoste, A. (2020), 'Fodder for Change: Animals, Urbanisation, and Socio-Economic Transformation in Protohistoric Italy', *Theoretical Roman Archaeology Journal* 3: 1–17.
Trentacoste, A., E. Lightfoot, P. Le Roux, M. Buckley, S. Kansa, C. Esposito, and M. Gleba (2020), 'Heading for the Hills? A Multi-isotope Study of Sheep Management in First Millennium BC Italy', *Journal of Archaeological Science (Reports)* 29: 102036.
Trigger, B. (2006), *A History of Archaeological Thought*. Montreal.
Trivellato, F. (2011), 'Is There a Future for Italian Microhistory in the Age of Global History?', *California Italian Studies* 2(1).
Trucco, F. (2002), 'Strutture funerarie e uso dello spazio nella necropoli della prima età del ferro di Villa Bruschi Falgari a Tarquinia', in N. Negroni Catacchio (ed.), *Paesaggi d'acque, Atti del V Incontro di Studi Preistoria e Protostoria in Etruria, Vol. II*. 709–20. Milan.
Trucco, F., D. De Angelis, C. Iaia, and R. Vargiu (2005), 'Nuovi dati sul rituale funerario di Tarquinia nella prima età del ferro', in *Dinamiche di sviluppo delle città nell'Etruria meridionale, Atti XXIII Convegno di Studi Etruschi e Italici (Roma, Cerveteri, Tarquinia, Montalto di Castro, Viterbo 2001)*. 359–69. Pisa-Rome.
Tsetskhladze, G.R. (ed.) (2006), *Greek Colonisation: An Account of Greek Colonies and Other Settlements Overseas. Vol. 1*. Leiden.
Tsetskhladze, G.R. (ed.) (2008), *Greek Colonisation: An Account of Greek Colonies and Other Settlements Overseas. Vol. 2*. Leiden.
Tuck, A. (2014), 'Manufacturing at Poggio Civitate: Elite Consumption and Social Organization in the Etruscan Seventh Century', *Etruscan Studies* 17: 13–39.
Tuck, A. (2016), 'Poggio Civitate: Community Form in Inland Etruria', in A. Carpino and S. Bell (eds.), *A Companion to the Etruscans*. 105–16. Chichester.
Tuck, A. (2021), 'Resource and Ritual: Manufacturing and Production at Poggio Civitate', in M. Gleba, B. Marín-Aguilera, and B. Dimova (eds.), *Making Cities: Economies of Production and Urbanisation in Mediterranean Europe 1000–500 BC*. 147–160. Cambridge.
Turfa, J.M. (2006), 'The Etruscan Brontoscopic Calendar', in E. Simon and N. de Grummond (eds.), *The Religion of the Etruscans*. 173–90. Austin.
Turfa, J.M. (2012), *Divining the Etruscan World: The Brontoscopic Calendar and Religious Practice*. Cambridge.

Tylecote, R.F. (1987), *The Early History of Metallurgy in Europe*. London.
Tylecote, R.F. and P.F. Boydell (1978), 'Experiments on Copper Smelting Based on Early Furnaces Found at Tinna', in B. Rothenberg, R.F. Tylecote, and P.J. Boydell (eds.), *Chalcolithic Copper Smelting: Excavations and Experiments*. 27–48. London.
Uggeri, G. (1983), *La viabilità romana nel Salento*. Mesagne.
Uguzzoni, A. and F. Ghinatti (1968), *Le tavole greche di Eraclea. Pubblicazioni dell'Istituto di storia antica*, Vol. 7. Rome.
van der Meer, L.B. (2007), *Liber Linteus Zagrabiensis: The Linen Book of Zagreb: A Comment on the Longest Etruscan Text*. Leuven.
van der Meer, L.B. (2009), 'On the Enigmatic Deity Lur in the *Liber Linteus Zagrabiensis*', in M. Gleba and H. Becker (eds.), *Votives, Places and Rituals in Etruscan Religion*. 217–27. Leiden.
van der Meer, L.B. (2013), 'Campo della Fiera at Orvieto and *Fanum Voltumnae*: Identical Places?', *BABESCH* 88: 99–108.
van der Meer, L.B. (2014), 'The *Tabula Cortonensis* and Land Transactions', *Studi Etruschi* 76: 157–82.
van der Plicht, J. and A.J. Nijboer (2018), 'Around 1000 BC. Absolute Dates for the Final Bronze Age – Early Iron Age Transition in Italy: Wiggle-match 14C Dating of Two Tree-trunk Coffins from Celano', *Palaeohistoria* 59/60: 99–108.
Vandkilde, H. (2016), 'Bronzization: The Bronze Age as Pre-modern Globalization', *Prähistorische Zeitschrift* 91: 103–23.
van Dommelen, P. (2005), 'Urban Foundations? Colonial Settlement and Urbanization in the Western Mediterranean', *PBA* 126: 143–67.
van Dommelen, P. (2014), 'Moving On: Archaeological Perspectives on Mobility and Migration', *World Archaeology* 46: 477–83.
Van Oyen, A. (2016), 'Historicising Material Agency: From Relations to Relational Constellations', *Journal of Archaeological Method and Theory* 23: 354–78.
Van Wonterghem, F. (1999), 'Il culto di Ercole e la pastorizia nell'Italia centrale', in E. Petrocelli (ed.), *La civiltà della transumanza: storia, cultura e valorizzazione dei tratturi e delmondo pastorale in Abruzzo, Molise, Puglia, Campania e Basilicata*. 413–28. Isernia.
Vecchi, I. (2012), *Etruscan Coinage: A Corpus of the Struck Coinage of the Rasna*. Milan.
Veenman, F. (2002), *Reconstructing the Pasture: A Reconstruction of Pastoral Landuse in Italy in the First Millennium BC*. Amsterdam.
Ventresca Miller, A.R. and C.A. Makarewicz (eds.) (2018), *Isotopic Investigations of Pastoralism in Prehistory*. London.
Versluys, M. (2014), 'Understanding Objects in Motion. An Archaeological Dialogue on Romanization', *Archaeological Dialogues* 21: 1–20.
Viggiano, G. and H. van Wees (2013), 'The Arms, Armor, and Iconography of Early Greek Hoplite Warfare', in D. Kagan and G. Viggiano (eds.), *Men of Bronze: Hoplite Warfare in Ancient Greece*. 57–73. Princeton.
Vinson, S.P. (1972), 'Ancient Roads between Venosa and Gravina', *PBSR* 40: 58–90.
Volpe, G. (1990), *La Daunia nell'età della romanizzazione. Paesaggio agrario, produzione, scambi*. Bari.
von Eles, P. (ed.) (2002), *Guerriero e sacerdote. Autorità e comunità nell'età del ferro a Verucchio. La tomba del trono*. Florence.
von Hase, F.W. (1997), 'Présences ètrusques et italiques dans les sanctuaries grecs (VIII – VII siècle av. J.-C.)', in F. Gaultier and D. Briquel (eds.), *Les Etrusques, les*

plus religieux des hommes. État de la recherche sur la religion étrusque. 293–323. Paris.

von Merhart, G. (1940), 'Zu den ersten Metallhelmen Europas', *Berichte der Römisch-Germanischen Kommission* 30: 4–42.

Vos, A. (2018), *Mediterranean Migrants: Using Multiple Isotopic Analyses (87Sr/86Sr, δ18O and δ13C) to Identify Migration in the Settlements of Metaponto and Siris (Southern Italy) in the 6th–5th century BC*. MA Thesis. Leiden University.

Wagner-Hasel, B. (2000), *Der Stoff der Gaben. Kultur und Politik des Schenkens und Tauschens im archaischen Griechenland*. Frankfurt.

Wagner-Hasel, B. (2002), 'Kommunikationswege und die Entstehung überregionaler Heiligtümer: das Fallbeispiel Delphi', in E. Olshausen and H. Sonnabend (eds.), *Zu Wasser und zu Land. Verkehrswege in der antiken Welt*. 160–80. Stuttgart.

Walbank, F.W. (1957/1999), *A Historical Commentary on Polybius, Vol. I, Commentary on Books 1–6*. Oxford.

Waldbaum, J.C. (1980), 'The First Archaeological Appearance of Iron and the Transition to the Iron Age', in T.A. Wertime and J.D. Muhly (eds.), *The Coming of the Age of Iron*. 69–89. New Haven, CT.

Waldherr, G. (1999), 'Transhumanz', in H. Sonnabend (ed.), *Mensch und Landschaft in der Antike. Lexikon der Historischen Geographie*. 564–8. Stuttgart.

Waldherr, G. (2002), 'Das System der calles (Herdenwanderwege) im römischen Italien – Entstehung und infrastrukturelle Bedeutung', in E. Olshausen and H. Sonnabend (eds.), *Zu Wasser und zu Land. Verkehrswege in der antiken Welt. Stuttgarter Kolloquium zur historischen Geographie des Altertums 7, 1999*. 429–44. Stuttgart.

Wallace, R. (2008), *Zikh Rasna: A Manual of the Etruscan Language and Inscriptions*. Ann Arbor.

Warden, P.G. (1984), 'The Colline Metallifere: Prolegomena to the Study of Mineral Exploitation in Central Italy', in T. Hackens, N. Holloway, and R. Ross Holloway (eds.), *Crossroads of the Mediterranean: Papers Delivered at the International Conference on the Archaeology of Early Italy, Haffenreffer Museum, Brown University, 8–10 May 1981*. 349–64. Providence, RI.

Wenger, E. (1998), *Communities of Practice: Learning, Meaning, and Identity*. Cambridge.

Wengrow, D. (2011), 'Archival and Sacrificial Economies in Bronze Age Eurasia: An Interactionist Approach to the Hoarding of Metals', in T. Wilkinson and S. Sherratt (eds.), *Interweaving Worlds: Systemic Interactions in Eurasia, 7th to 1st millennia BC*. 135–44. Oxford.

Whitehouse, R. and J. Wilkins (1989), 'Greeks and Natives in South-east Italy: Approaches to the Archaeological Evidence', in T.C. Champion (ed.), *Centre and Periphery: Comparative Studies in Archaeology*. 102–26. London.

Whitehouse, R., J. Wilkins, and E. Herring (2000), *Botromagno: Excavation and Survey at Gravina in Puglia 1979–1985*. London.

Whittaker, C.R. (ed.) (1988), *Pastoral Economies in Classical Antiquity*. Cambridge.

Wiessner, P. (1983), 'Style and Social Information in Kalahari San Projectile Points', *American Antiquity* 49: 253–76.

Wiessner, P. (1990), 'Is There a Unity to Style?', in I. Hodder (ed.), *The Meanings of Things: Material Culture and Symbolic Expression*. 56–63. London.

Wilkins, J. (1992), 'Power and Idea Networks: Theoretical Notes on Urbanisation in the Early Mediterranean and Italy', in E. Herring, R. Whitehouse, and J. Wilkins

(eds.), *Papers of the Fourth Conference of Italian Archaeology, Vol. 1 The Archaeology of Power Part 1*. 221–30. London.
Winter, F. (2006), *Studies in Hellenistic Architecture*. Toronto.
Wiseman, T.P. (1974), 'Legendary Genealogies in Late-Republican Rome', *G&R* 21: 153–64.
Wobst, H.M. (1977), 'Stylistic Behavior and Information Exchange', in A. Reher (ed.), *Papers for the Director: Research Essays in Honor of James B. Griffen*. 317–42. Ann Arbor.
Woolf, G. (1998), *Becoming Roman: The Origins of Provincial Civilisation in Gaul*. Cambridge.
Woolf, G. (2014), 'Romanization 2.0 and Its Alternatives', *Archaeological Dialogues* 21: 45–50.
Woolf, G. (2017), 'Migration and the Metropolis: How Ancient Rome Stayed Great', *2017 Syme Lecture*. http://podcasts.ox.ac.uk/migration-and-metropolis-how-ancient-rome-stayed-great [Accessed 27/9/2021].
Woolf, G. (2020), *The Life and Death of Ancient Cities*. Oxford.
Wright, J.C. (ed.) (2004), *The Mycenaean Feast*. Princeton.
Yntema, D.G. (1982), 'Some Notes on Iapygian Pottery from the Otranto Excavations. A Preliminary Report', *Studi di Antichità* 3: 63–82.
Yntema, D.G. (1990), *The Matt-painted Pottery of Southern Italy: A General Survey of the Matt-painted Pottery Styles of Southern Italy during the Final Bronze Age and the Iron Age*. Galatina.
Yntema, D.G. (2011), 'Archaeology and the *Origo* Myths of the Greek *Apoikiai*', *Ancient West and East* 10: 243–66.
Yntema, D.G. (2013), *The Archaeology of South-East Italy in the First Millennium BC: Greek and Native Societies of Apulia and Lucania between the 10th and the 1st Century BC*. Amsterdam.
Yntema, D.G. (2014), *The Archaeology of South East Italy in the First Millennium B.C.* Amsterdam.
Yntema, D.G. (2016), 'Greek Groups in Southeast Italy during the Iron Age', in L. Donnellan, V. Nizzo, and G.J. Burgers (eds.), *Conceptualising Early Colonisation (Contextualising Early Colonisation Vol. 2)*. 209–23. Brussels and Rome.
Yoffee, N. and N. Terrenato (2015), 'Introduction: A History of the Study of Early Cities', in N. Yoffee (ed.), *The Cambridge World History*. 1–24. Cambridge.
Zaccagnini, C. (1983), 'Patterns of Mobility among Ancient Near Eastern Craftsmen', *JNES* 42: 245–64.
Zaccheo, L. (2006), *Pietra Fango Stramma. Tipologie abitative primitive dalla palude pontina alle barbagie*. Latina.
Zifferero, A. (1995), 'Economia, divinita e frontiera: sul ruolo di alcuni santuari di confine in Etruria meridionale', *Ostraka* 4: 333–50.
Zifferero, A. (2009), 'Attività minerarie e transferimento di saperi metallurgici nell'alto Tirreno: conoscenze attuali e prospettive di ricerca', in F. Cambi, F. Cavari, and C. Mascione (eds.), *Materiali da costruzione e produzione del ferro: studi sull'economia populoniese fra periodo etrusco e romanizzazione*. 149–56. Bari.
Zifferero, A. (2017), 'Mines and Metal Working', in A. Naso (ed.), *Etruscology*. 425–44. Berlin.
Zimmermann, T. (2007), 'Ein kupferzeitlicher Dolch im eisenzeitlichen Italien. Die notwendige Revision einer „sardischen" Stichwaffe aus dem Depotfund von San Francesco, Bologna', *ArchKorrblatt* 37: 51–6.

Zipf, G. (2006), 'Figural Representations from the Iron Age on the Apennine Peninsula Carriers, Motifs and Contexts of Images as seen on Bronze-Sheet Belt-Plates', in *Studi di protostoria in onore di Renato Peroni*. 674–9. Florence.

Zöbl, D. (1982), *Die Transhumanz (Wanderschafhaltung) der europäischen Mittelmeerländer im Mittelalter in historischer, geographischer und volkskundlicher Sicht*. Berlin.

Index

Adriatic Sea 99–101, 106–7, 109, 127–8, 153–4, 156–8, 160–2, 165–8, 171, 204, 218, 247, 249
aedile(s) 194, 196, 201–2
aes rude 71, 194–6, 200
agency 7, 17, 27, 31, 104, 109, 112, 241–2
ager: *Capenas* 149; *Faliscus* 149; *publicus* 207–8, 236
agriculture/agricultural 20, 40, 52, 154, 176, 205–6, 210, 222–3, 232–8; see also farms/farming; pastoralism; pastoralist(s)
Aithalia see Elba
Albania 100, 103–4, 106–9, 113–14, 117–18, 120, 125–6, 128
annealing 59, 62–5, 67, 69, 75, 78
anvil 53, 74, 115
Apennines 167, 171, 190, 207–8
Apulia 83, 86, 91, 94–5, 102, 106, 152–62, 165–9, 206–7, 210, 212, 215, 217
archaeothanatology 161
armour 36, 54–9, 62–5, 68–9, 72, 75–8, 80–1, 88, 131, 146–7
artisan(s) 15, 24, 27–8, 30, 36, 46–7, 57, 74, 77, 81, 83–4, 89–92, 94–8, 109, 111, 114, 128, 134, 140, 144–5, 150–1, 170, 191, 232, 247–9
askos/i 156, 161–2, 212, 215–16
assemblage (theory) 15, 29, 31
Athens 66, 76, 83, 91–3, 96–7, 159, 165, 201
Attica 47, 86

banquet 157, 159, 165, 209, 219–20; see also feast/feasting
Battle of Alalia 45
belt(s) 106, 130, 146–50, 159

bilingualism 84, 172, 230; see also multilingualism
blacksmith see smith
boundary 10, 30, 85, 149, 177, 184, 210, 232–3, 242; formation 26, 155, 165, 227; marker/object 112, 127
Bradano 156, 166, 168–9, 246
Braudel, F. 18, 29–30, 205, 233, 235–6
Brentesion/ Brindisi/ Brundisium 85, 88, 165
broker(age) 112, 121, 238, 249
bronze 37, 40, 43–5, 53–81, 97, 129, 131–7, 139–44, 146–8, 150, 159, 161, 164, 168, 181, 184–7, 192, 194–5, 197, 216–18, 221; alloy 42, 56, 58, 62, 64–9, 71, 75, 79; casting (metalwork technique) 53, 56, 59, 62–9, 72–3, 75, 78–80, 132, 134–5, 139, 143, 150; sheet bronze 56, 62–3, 68–9, 75, 78–9, 132, 134–5, 139, 146, 15; smelting 58–62, 66–72, 79–80, 250; working 38, 53–65, 67–71, 73–81, 139–40, 145, 149, 249, 250; see also *aes rude*; metal
Bronze Age 4, 6, 60, 66, 71–2, 74, 97, 108, 115, 124, 144, 165, 209, 229, 235; Early 62, 117; Final 43, 130–2, 139; Late 16–17, 54, 66, 72–3, 126, 131, 139, 143–5, 147, 150, 208; Middle 61, 75, 143
Broodbank, C. 5, 16, 54, 55, 107
bucchero 48, 181; see also pottery
burial(s) 43–4, 47–8, 51, 83, 87–9, 98, 106–7, 117, 129–37, 140, 143, 145–9, 152–4, 157–9, 162, 165, 212–14, 216–18, 221, 246; see also mortuary

Caere/Cerveteri 39–40, 48, 93, 132, 172, 175, 183–6, 192–8, 200–1, 247

calendar(s) 171, 176–8, 193, 197–9, 201–3, 250
calles *see* tratturo
Campania/Campanian 36–7, 40–2, 89, 91–5, 132, 140, 143, 168, 178, 217–18, 234, 245
Capena 149, 175, 203
Capua 95, 140, 168, 178, 197; *see also* Tabula Capuana
Carthage 86, 173
castellum/a 86, 180, 198
Cato (Elder) 51, 233, 236–7; *De Agricultura* 236–7
cauldron 164, 209, 218, 225; *see also* tripod
central Europe *see* Europe/European
ceramic(s) *see* pottery
ceramicist(s) *see* potter(s)
chaîne opératoire 8, 53, 56, 58–9, 62, 66, 69–70, 76, 79, 101, 112–13, 121, 126–7, 134, 250
charcoal 38, 42, 46, 56, 61, 67–8, 70, 80
Chianciano Terme 184–5, 192
Childe, V.G. 3, 24, 73, 81, 144
Chiusi 170, 175
clay 38, 67, 71, 90, 94–6, 112–14, 120–1, 123–4, 126, 143, 181
client/*cliens* 27, 74, 80
cohesion 226, 231–2, 242; battlefield 231
coin(s)/coinage 48, 184–5, 195–6, 199–200, 205, 240
colonisation (ancient) 36–7, 41, 49, 82, 85, 87, 90–1, 153, 159, 167, 189, 204, 223
colonisation (modern) *see* Europe/European
community 2–7, 9–15, 24–6, 28–30, 36, 39, 42, 50–2, 66, 70, 74, 79–80, 83, 85, 88–90, 99–100, 104, 108–13, 127, 132, 134, 137, 144–5, 152–4, 159, 165, 168–9, 196, 204, 208, 210–11, 214, 216, 220–5, 232, 236–9, 241, 242–3, 246–9, 251; formation 24–6, 30, 124, 134, 158, 161, 197, 226–30, 240, 242–3; institution(s) 24–5, 134, 161, 196, 198, 201, 221, 231, 239; of practice 58, 100–1, 105, 110–13, 121, 124, 126–7, 247, 250–1
connectivity 2, 4–6, 8–9, 11, 13–14, 16–17, 24, 33–5, 40, 42–4, 47, 51–2, 109, 127, 153, 189, 216, 227–33, 235, 237, 240–5, 247, 249–51
contract(s) 19, 208, 218, 222–3, 236, 245, 247, 249

copper 38, 42, 54, 58–62, 66–8, 70–1, 145, 209; *see also* bronze; metal
Corinth/Corinthian 62–4, 69, 90–1, 96, 98, 104, 159, 167, 205, 248
craft(s) 15, 27–30, 37, 42, 44, 72, 75, 80, 105, 112, 130, 137, 139, 144, 149–51, 182, 209, 249; specialisation 28, 47, 49, 58, 72, 75, 80, 97, 100, 113–16, 118, 143–5, 150–1, 205–6, 209–10, 221, 225
craftperson/craftpeople 8, 28, 43, 46–7, 56–8, 62–4, 66, 68, 71–7, 79–81, 91, 104–5, 107, 110–11, 127, 129, 138–40, 144–5, 150–1, 191, 203, 206, 220–1, 248–50
creole/creolising 5; *see also* hybrid/hybridity
crucible 62–3, 67–8, 73

Daunia/Daunian 153, 159, 212, 215
Dicearchia *see* Pozzuoli
Diodorus Siculus 35–8, 40–1, 66, 76–7
Dionysius I (Syracuse) 37, 66, 76–7, 80, 250
Dionysius of Halicarnassus 227, 240
distaff 210, 225, 246
diversity 1–2, 17, 34, 82–3, 86, 90, 97, 120, 124, 222, 238, 248
DNA 12, 17, 87, 238
drove road *see* tratturo

economy 15–16, 18–21, 24, 31–3, 35, 38, 42–3, 47, 50–1, 130, 146, 170, 180, 183, 202, 205–6, 208–9, 220–1, 223–4, 233, 237, 241; *see also* trade
egalitarian 145, 214, 222
Elba 33, 35–8, 41–7, 49–52, 58, 60, 182
elite(s) 5, 11, 15–16, 20, 22–8, 30, 43–52, 54–8, 70–1, 74–5, 79–81, 86, 89, 94, 96, 98, 100, 109, 132, 136, 144–5, 147, 150–1, 169, 174, 182, 194, 201–2, 208, 216–18, 221–2, 228–9, 233, 249–50
emporion/emporium 36, 41, 88, 171–3, 182, 197, 199, 200, 202–3, 239
Ennius, Quintus 230
environment 13, 17–18, 80, 100, 111, 114, 221, 224, 233–4, 241, 250
epigraphy 11, 40, 48, 50–2, 74, 83, 85–6, 89, 91, 96, 140, 198, 201, 207, 230; *see also* inscription(s)
ethnic/ethnicity 1–2, 4–5, 7, 9–11, 13, 83–4, 86, 88–9, 97, 105, 148–9, 154, 226–31, 233, 237–8, 240–2, 246–7

308 Index

ethnogenesis 4, 226
ethnography 27, 46, 68, 71–2, 108, 115, 144, 165, 209–10, 214, 220, 223, 233–4, 237, 241
Etruria 33, 37, 41–2, 45–9, 79, 93, 129, 131–2, 137, 140–1, 143, 146–7, 149–51, 159, 170–1, 173–4, 176–7, 182–5, 191–2, 197–201, 203, 245, 248–50; *Etruria mineraria* 33, 44, 58; northern 33, 35, 39–43, 45–52, 140, 179; southern 40, 45, 93, 130–2, 134, 140, 145, 148–9
Etruscan(s) 7, 16–17, 36–8, 40–5, 48–51, 57, 72, 83, 87–9, 91, 93, 129, 136, 139, 141, 143, 145–6, 149, 161, 168, 170–203, 217–18, 225, 238; *see also* inscription(s)
Europe/European 54, 62, 74, 131, 139, 144–5, 150, 205, 250; central 129, 132, 135, 137, 139–40, 142–3, 147, 150; colonialism (modern) 5–6
exchange 5, 13, 15–16, 18–20, 28, 30, 32, 34–6, 41–3, 47–8, 74, 81, 97, 106–9, 112, 127–9, 145, 157, 161, 170–1, 173–5, 178, 181–2, 184, 190, 194–8, 200, 202–4, 217–18, 222, 238, 242, 244, 247–50
export(s) 38, 44, 46, 48, 51, 84, 109, 173, 191, 250; *see also* import(s); trade

Fanum Voltumnae 173–6, 182, 197, 201, 203
farms/farming 10, 39, 75, 87, 171, 180, 187–8, 191, 222–3, 233, 235–7; farmer 170–1, 176, 179, 189, 199–200, 203, 206, 208, 222–3, 232, 234, 236–7, 245; *see also* agriculture/agricultural
feast/feasting 135, 155, 165, 176, 178, 218–20; *see also* banquet
Feriae Latinae 240, 251; *see also* Jupiter
festival(s) 57, 70, 171, 173–6, 182, 203, 228, 232, 238–40, 242–3, 250–1
Fonteblanda 39–40
Fossa Bradanica 165–8
frieze 218–20
furnace 35, 38, 41, 46, 56, 60–2, 67–8, 70, 73, 78–9

gender 129–30, 134, 145, 149, 162, 214, 222, 246, 249
genealogy 13, 26; mythic 239–40
genetic(s) 33, 85–7, 140
Gillos 85

Gonfienti 171, 182–3, 185, 190–1
grave goods 43, 45, 157, 159, 214, 217; *see also* burial(s); mortuary
Gravisca(e) 39, 172–3, 182, 198, 200, 239

habitus 9, 110–11, 127, 158
Hallstatt 139, 142–3, 150
hammer(s) 53, 67–8, 73, 75, 78–9; hammered/hammering 36, 46, 59, 61–5, 67–9, 72, 75, 78, 134–5, 138, 140, 143, 150
helmet(s) 54–5, 62–5, 69, 73, 77–8, 130, 132–44, 149–50; *see also* armour
Herakles/Hercules 90, 196–7, 239
heroes (mythic) 27, 138; heroic 205
Hernici 226, 240
Homer 25, 72, 146
Horden, P. 5, 16, 33–4, 55, 84
hospitality/*hospitium* 54, 56, 81, 247; *hospitales/hospitalis* 86, 247
household 46, 56, 74, 108–9, 115, 171, 205, 214, 238, 246; home 76, 108, 206, 237
hybrid/hybridity 2, 5–6, 54, 151, 159, 241, 247; hybridisation 140, 168; *see also* creole/creolising
Hydruntum *see* Otranto

identity/identities 1–5, 6–7, 9–10, 13–15, 20–1, 29, 54, 56, 83, 89, 99, 104, 109–10, 121, 127, 129–30, 134, 137, 146, 148–9, 153, 157, 158–9, 169, 189, 226, 227–32, 239–43, 247, 249, 251; civic 226, 228, 232
Illyria/Illyrians 107–8, 153
import(s) 11, 47–8, 54–5, 90–1, 97, 101, 107, 109, 120, 139–40, 150, 156–7, 159, 160, 165, 167–8, 172–3, 181, 200, 212, 214, 217, 219, 222; *see also* export(s); trade
inscription(s) 4, 48–50, 77, 85–6, 89–91, 95, 185, 190, 192–6, 207, 220, 230, 235, 236, 245; Etruscan 40, 49, 218 (*see also* Etruscan(s)); votive 90; *see also* epigraphy
iron 33–52, 60–1, 68, 71, 74–5, 114, 122, 161, 198, 200, 209, 220, 250; economy 35, 38, 51; ore 35, 37, 39, 41–2, 46–7, 60, 250; production 33, 36–7, 41–3, 45–6, 51–2; smelting 46, 49, 51, 61, 68, 70; technology 33; trade 33, 43, 48, 182; weapons 45–6,

51, 62; (*see also* weapon(s)); working 37–9, 44, 49, 53, 77, 80; *see also* metal
Iron Age 4, 17, 24, 31, 33–4, 52, 59–61, 105–8, 126, 132, 134, 150, 225, 250; Early 16–17, 26, 54, 56, 66, 117, 129–33, 135–8, 149–50
Isayev, E. 1–3, 6, 12, 15, 34, 56, 82–4, 86, 89, 204, 226, 231, 236–7, 247–8, 251
isotope analysis 5, 12, 86–7, 224
itinerant/itinerancy 14, 73, 90–1, 95–6, 98, 144, 165, 171, 173, 189
ivory 181

Jupiter 57, 240; Latiaris 240 (*see also Feriae Latinae*)

Kainua *see* Marzabotto
kiln(s) 56, 67–8, 73–4, 95, 167, 239
kin/kinship 31, 134, 165, 229, 231, 237–8

labour 42, 48, 56, 58, 60, 67–70, 81, 172, 220, 222–3, 236–8, 246, 248
Lampas 94
Latium 11, 40, 42–3, 45, 58, 131–2, 134, 207, 210, 245; Latium Vetus 131, 148–9
lex 201, 236; *Agraria* 207, 235; *Irnitana* 201; *Licinia-Sextia* 236
Liber Linteus (Zagreb mummy) 177–8, 193
Livy (Titus Livius) 54, 165, 170, 174–5, 201, 227, 231, 236, 239, 248
Locri 93; *see also* painters, Locri Group
longue durée 16, 205
loom(s) 30, 220; loom weight(s) 210, 212, 220; *see also* textile(s); weaving
Lucania/Lucanian 1, 87, 93, 161, 167, 207, 212, 215, 238, 251
Lucus Feroniae 175–6, 203, 238

Manning, J. 18–22
market(s) 12, 18–21, 28–31, 41, 46, 49–51, 65, 74–6, 99–104, 108–12, 167, 171–84, 189–203, 207, 210, 214–16, 222–4, 228, 235, 238–40, 246, 250; Mayan 198–9
marriage 108, 149, 214, 228, 238
Marzabotto 39, 171, 184, 189–92, 195
Mauss, M. 19
mercenary/mercenaries 76, 94
merchant(s) 7, 13, 15, 30, 36–7, 40, 50, 57, 96, 170–4, 175, 189, 197–9, 206, 232, 236; *see also* market(s); trade

Messapia/Messapian 85, 88, 91, 153
metal 33, 36–48, 50–2, 56, 58–81, 106–7, 129–51, 159, 162, 164, 173, 181, 188–91, 249; ore(s) 33, 35–42, 44, 46–8, 51, 58–62, 66–71, 250; *see also aes rude*; metal
Metaponto/Metapontum 85–9, 91–55, 156, 161, 167, 207, 217, 248
migrant(s) 85–8, 90–2, 97–8, 100, 204
migration 12, 85–97, 99–101, 104, 106–7, 109, 125, 206–8, 223, 245
mine(s) 37–8, 40–2, 40, 47, 49, 51, 59–60, 66–7, 69–72; mining 36–8, 48, 58–60, 67–70, 79, 209
mobility 12–13, 43, 74, 76, 80, 82–90, 94–8, 101, 106, 108, 120, 144–5, 150, 204–5, 208, 210, 223–4, 235–6, 239, 242, 244–5, 248–51
mortuary: context(s) 132, 146; deposition(s) 118, 130, 155, 162, 249 (*see also* grave goods); practice(s) 48, 50, 129, 132–4, 145–6, 153, 157, 165, 168; *see also* burial(s)
multilingualism 230; *see also* bilingualism
Murlo *see* Poggio Civitate
myth(s) 9, 25–7, 83, 98, 237, 239–40; origin/*origo* 9, 83, 201, 239–40, 248

network(s) 5–6, 9, 11–14, 17–18, 23, 30–1, 36–9, 41–2, 44, 47–8, 52, 54–8, 66–70, 80–1, 98, 107–9, 129, 140, 145, 149, 166–8, 170, 203, 208, 216–21, 228–31, 239–43, 246, 248, 250; network analysis 4, 9, 17, 29, 232
New Institutional Economics (NIE) 12, 15, 19–21, 23, 25, 31, 34, 202
nundinae 175–8, 182–3, 197–8, 202; *see also* market(s)

Oedipus 205
onomastic(s) 50, 85–6, 218, 230
ore(s) *see* metal
origin/*origo* myth(s) *see* myth(s)
Orvieto *see* Volsinii
Oscan 89, 94–5, 189, 230
Otranto/Hydruntum 100, 102, 104, 106–7, 113, 117–19, 124–5

Paestum *see* Poseidonia/Paestum
painters: Arnò 92–3; Chequer 91–3; Choephoroi 92, 94; Locri Group 92–3 (*see also* Locri); Lucera 95; Volcani 95

pastoralism 12, 205–10, 215, 222, 224–5, 233–6; transhumance 12, 14, 205–11, 214, 220–2, 233–6, 239, 245
pastoralist(s) 209–11, 214–16, 220, 222–3, 238, 245–6; *see also* shepherd(s)
pasture 205–8, 214, 222, 224, 233–6, 246
patron/patronage 27, 74, 145, 248–9
petrography 121
Peucetia/Peucetian 94, 152–69
Pian d'Alma 188–9
Pisa 37, 39, 45, 48, 50
Pithekoussai/Pithecussae 37, 41–2
Poggio Civitate 44, 181
Polanyi, K. 16, 18–19, 21
ponderarium/a 189, 196–9
Pontecagnano 43, 90, 132, 143
Populonia 36–52, 70, 184, 195, 200
Poseidonia/Paestum 89, 93–5, 98
postcolonial 3
potter(s) 14, 83, 90–3, 95–8, 99–102, 113
potter's wheel 90, 101, 111, 115, 121, 125–6
pottery 10, 12, 47–8, 54–5, 57, 83–5, 90–7, 99–109, 112–13, 115, 127, 132, 134, 137, 144, 151, 156, 158–9, 167, 169, 248; matt-painted 90, 99–104, 108–28, 155, 159–60, 163–5, 249; production 62, 67–8, 71, 74, 80, 107, 111–13, 120; sub-geometric 156, 159–60, 164–5, 167
Pozzuoli 36, 41
product(s): primary 235; secondary 222, 235
Purcell, N. 5, 16, 33–4, 55, 84
Pyrgi 25, 39–40, 172, 239
Pythagoras 85

raiding *see* war/warfare
recycle/recycling 56, 59, 66–71, 73, 79
Ripacandida 211–17, 222, 246
road(s) 165–8, 171, 174–5, 192, 235; *Via Appia* 165–6; *Via Traiana* 165, 167; *see also* network(s)
Rome 39–40, 49, 51, 54, 57, 77, 88, 95, 173, 176, 183–4, 193, 196–7, 201–2, 227, 230–2, 239–40, 247
Romulus 237
Rondelli 38–9, 187
Roselle 49
Ruvo 84, 94–6, 98, 157, 165, 167–8; Ruvo-Satriano ware 212, 214–15

Saepinum (inscription) 207, 235, 245
Salento 99–107, 113–14, 120–7
Samnium/Samnite 152, 207, 218, 226–7, 232
sanctuary 10, 24, 70, 82, 85–6, 141–2, 172–5, 182, 191–2, 197–9, 203, 218, 221–2, 228, 238–42, 250–1; *see also* shrine(s); temple(s)
San Mauro Forte 90
seasonal/seasonality 70, 205–9, 214, 216, 220–4, 234, 236–8, 245–6
sedentism 12, 210, 214, 221–3, 236–7, 246, 251
Servius Tullius 177
shepherd(s) 205–10, 214–15, 223–4, 233–8, 245; *see also* pastoralist(s)
shipwreck 60, 66, 85, 191; Grand Ribaud F 39–40; Uluburun 61
shop(s) 171, 182–3, 191, 197; *see also* market(s); merchant(s); workshop(s)
shrine(s) 57, 173–4; *see also* sanctuary; temple(s)
Sicily 37, 85, 87, 91–4
smelting *see* bronze; iron
smith 36, 39–41, 44–7, 50, 52, 73–4, 81, 136, 144–5, 150–1, 249; *see also* bronze; iron
societa gentilizia 43–4
spindle whorl 210, 212
standardisation 108, 113–20, 149, 194–6
statonica 206–7, 211, 217; *see also* pastoralism; pastoralist(s)
style 3, 7–8, 54–6, 68, 74–7, 91–6, 100–6, 109–12, 139, 145–50, 156, 169, 249–50
sword(s) 45, 62, 77, 130, 132, 136–9, 143, 149–50, 212; *see also* weapon(s)
Sybaris 84
symposion/symposium 165, 221
Syracuse/Syracusa 37, 45, 76, 91–3

Tabula: *Capuana* 178; *Cortonensis* 193
Taranto/Tarentum 83, 88, 98, 102–3, 117–19, 221
Tarquinia 37, 132–8, 140, 143, 172, 184, 197, 200, 238; Tomb of the Ship 172; *see also* mortuary
technology 5, 7, 11, 33, 36, 44, 46–7, 49, 51, 54, 56–8, 74, 82, 85, 90, 94–6, 98–9, 108–9, 120, 130, 135, 138–40, 145, 150–1, 162, 228, 244, 249, 251

temple(s) 24–6, 49, 51, 57, 76–7, 175, 192, 196–7, 239, 243, 250–1
textile(s) 71, 74, 80, 156, 181, 209, 212, 214–16, 235, 239; *see also* loom(s); weaving
theatre 84, 202
theory of practice 110
Thucydides 86
tin 36, 53, 62, 66–7, 70–1, 73; *see also* bronze; metal
Torre di Satriano 90, 98, 219–21
trade 5, 9, 11–14, 23, 27, 30, 34, 36, 40–4, 60, 66, 81, 83–4, 91, 97, 101, 107–8, 140, 145, 150, 152–3, 166–8, 170–5, 189, 191, 202, 222, 228, 233–4, 236–9, 241–2, 248–50; *see also* iron; wine
trader(s) *see* merchant(s)
transhumance *see* pastoralism
tratturo 166, 168, 206–7, 221, 224–5, 234–5
Trendall, D. 92–3, 95
tripod 124, 209, 225; *see also* cauldron

urban 10, 18, 22, 24, 26, 39, 49, 52, 58, 80–1, 83, 86, 130–2, 134, 136, 145, 151, 171, 177, 180, 182–3, 203, 225, 228–9, 232–3, 235, 239, 242, 247
urbanisation 17, 21–2, 25, 46, 83, 131, 145, 249

Veii 132–3, 146–7, 149, 174, 176, 201, 247
Verucchio 138, 140

Vetulonia 39, 43, 48, 186–9, 191
Villanovan(s) 43, 45, 129, 132, 135–6, 139–43, 145, 147
Volsci 226, 232, 240
Volsinii 174–5, 203, 239
Volterra 180, 184–5, 200
votive(s) 25, 90, 172, 174–5, 239–40, 251
Vulci 43, 79, 132, 138, 185, 217

war/warfare 43, 45, 51, 76–7, 83–4, 134–5, 149, 152, 229–31, 244; raiding 226, 230–1
warrior(s) 43, 45, 71–2, 76, 130, 132, 134, 137–8, 146, 150, 218
weapon(s) 44–6, 51, 62, 76, 88, 130–2, 136, 146, 159, 212, 218, 244, 250; *see also* sword(s)
weaving 210, 246; *see also* loom(s); textile(s)
weight(s) 48, 182–98, 201–3
wine 162–3, 165, 221, 234; trade 34, 40–2, 77, 173, 192, 249; *see also* trade
wood 46, 56, 61, 67, 132, 138, 175, 208–9
wool 71, 209–10, 235–6, 238
workshop(s) 37–8, 51, 58, 69, 72, 75–7, 79–80, 93, 95–6, 112, 115–16, 132, 136, 141–3, 146, 150, 167, 171, 181–2, 191, 215, 250

xenia 86

zilath 193, 201

Taylor & Francis eBooks

www.taylorfrancis.com

A single destination for eBooks from Taylor & Francis with increased functionality and an improved user experience to meet the needs of our customers.

90,000+ eBooks of award-winning academic content in Humanities, Social Science, Science, Technology, Engineering, and Medical written by a global network of editors and authors.

TAYLOR & FRANCIS EBOOKS OFFERS:

- A streamlined experience for our library customers
- A single point of discovery for all of our eBook content
- Improved search and discovery of content at both book and chapter level

REQUEST A FREE TRIAL
support@taylorfrancis.com